Konohana Kitan

1

Sakuya Amano

K O N O H A N A   K I T A N
C O N T E N T S

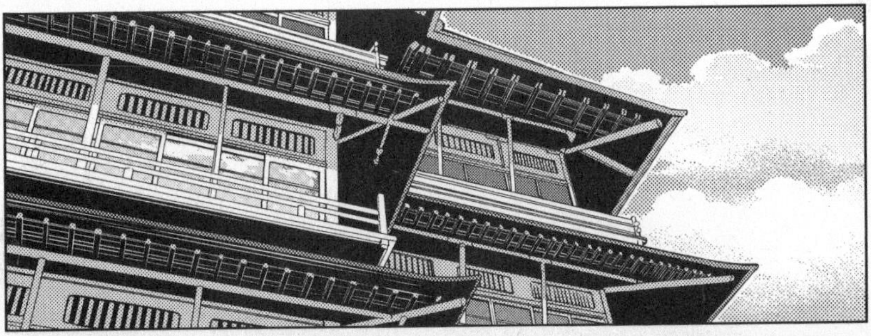

Konohana Kitan ~Introduction~

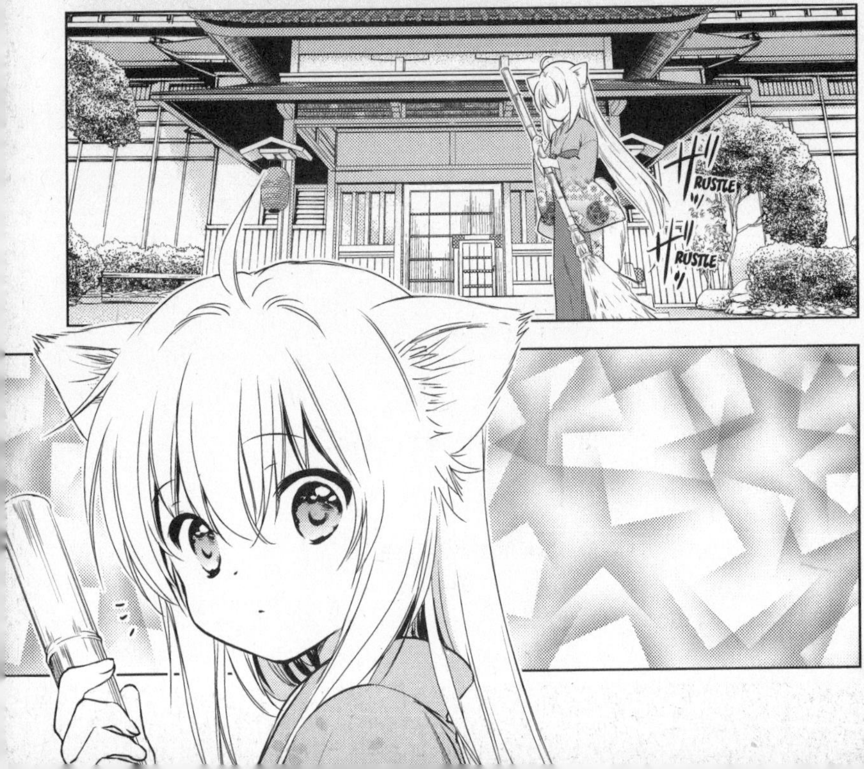
RUSTLE
RUSTLE

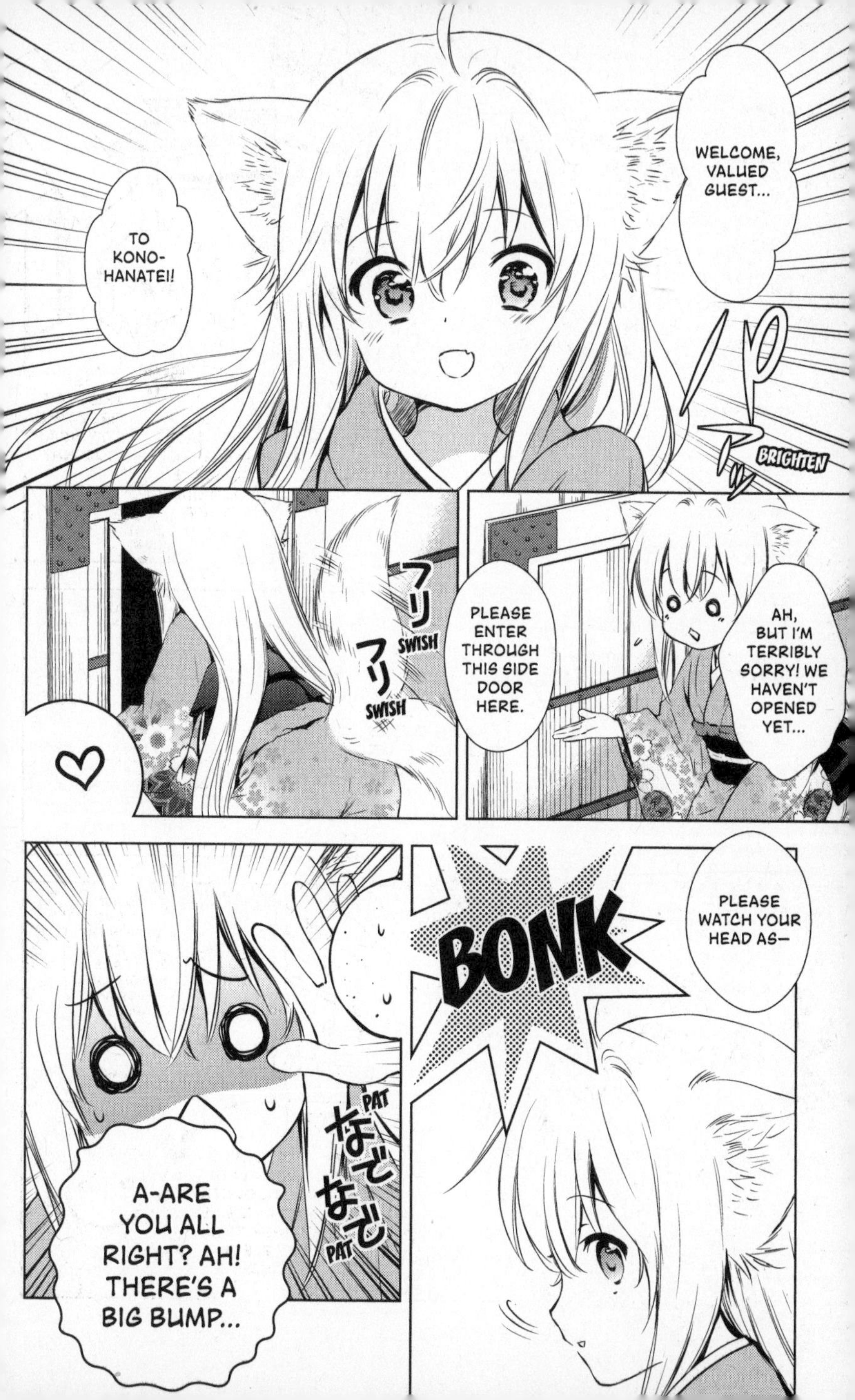
WELCOME, VALUED GUEST...
TO KONO-HANATEI!
BRIGHTEN
AH, BUT I'M TERRIBLY SORRY! WE HAVEN'T OPENED YET...
PLEASE ENTER THROUGH THIS SIDE DOOR HERE.
フリ SWISH
フリ SWISH
♡
PLEASE WATCH YOUR HEAD AS—
BONK
なで PAT
なで PAT
A-ARE YOU ALL RIGHT? AH! THERE'S A BIG BUMP...

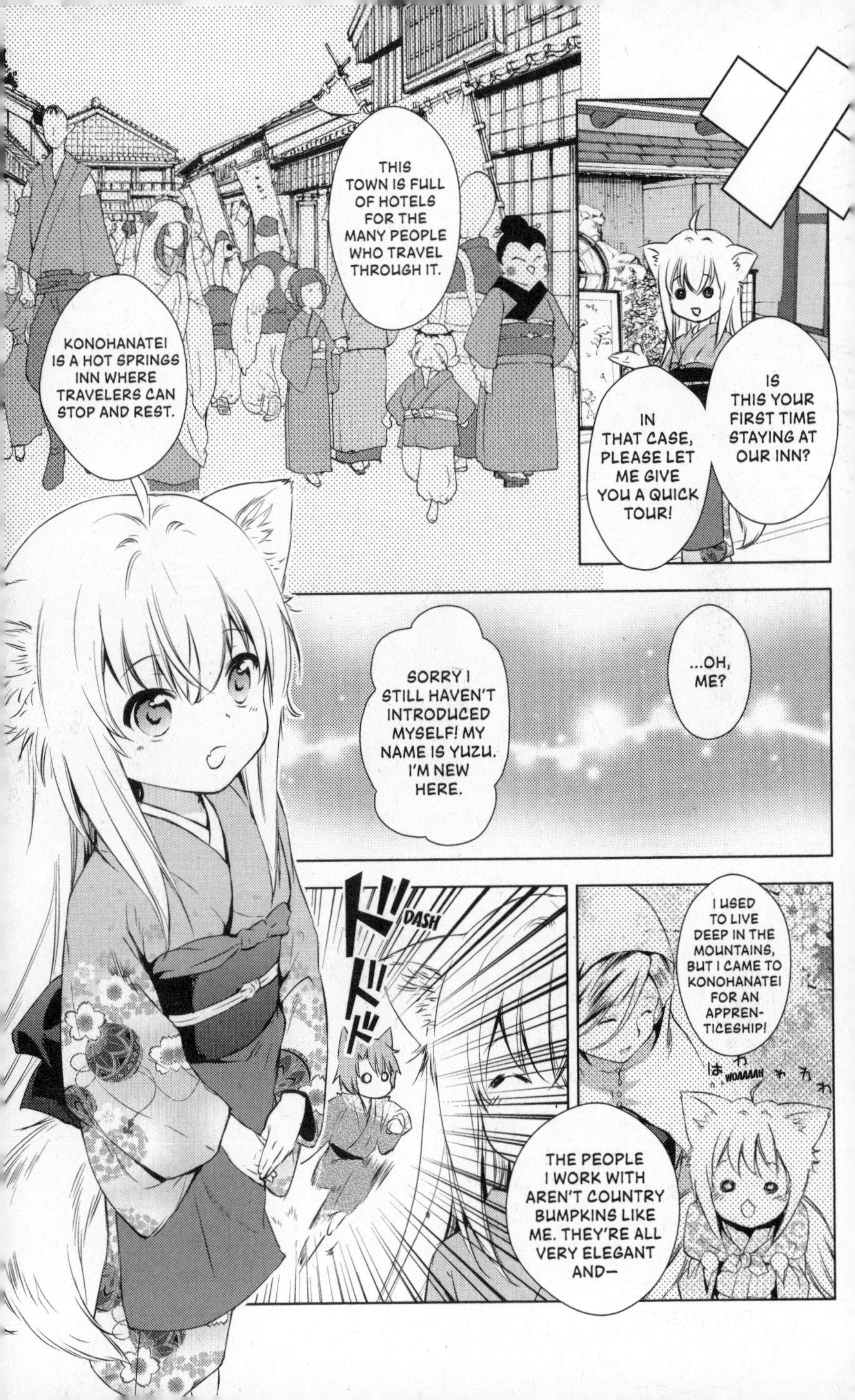
IS THIS YOUR FIRST TIME STAYING AT OUR INN?
IN THAT CASE, PLEASE LET ME GIVE YOU A QUICK TOUR!
THIS TOWN IS FULL OF HOTELS FOR THE MANY PEOPLE WHO TRAVEL THROUGH IT.
KONOHANATEI IS A HOT SPRINGS INN WHERE TRAVELERS CAN STOP AND REST.
...OH, ME?
SORRY I STILL HAVEN'T INTRODUCED MYSELF! MY NAME IS YUZU. I'M NEW HERE.
I USED TO LIVE DEEP IN THE MOUNTAINS, BUT I CAME TO KONOHANATEI FOR AN APPREN-TICESHIP!
WOAAAAH
THE PEOPLE I WORK WITH AREN'T COUNTRY BUMPKINS LIKE ME. THEY'RE ALL VERY ELEGANT AND—
DASH

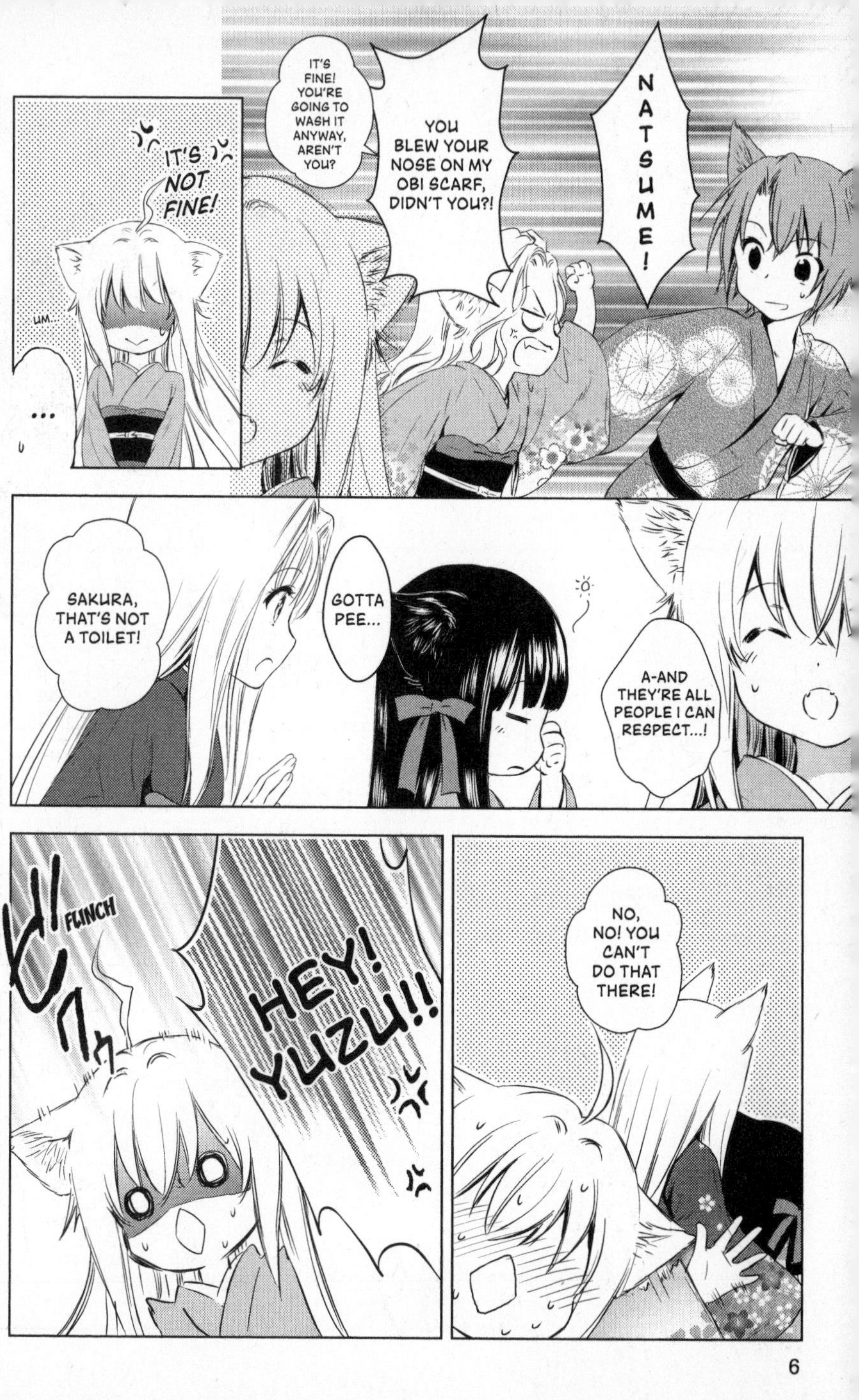
NATSUME!
YOU BLEW YOUR NOSE ON MY OBI SCARF, DIDN'T YOU?!
IT'S FINE! YOU'RE GOING TO WASH IT ANYWAY, AREN'T YOU?
IT'S NOT FINE!
UM...
...
A-AND THEY'RE ALL PEOPLE I CAN RESPECT...!
GOTTA PEE...
SAKURA, THAT'S NOT A TOILET!
NO, NO! YOU CAN'T DO THAT THERE!
HEY! YUZU!!
FLINCH

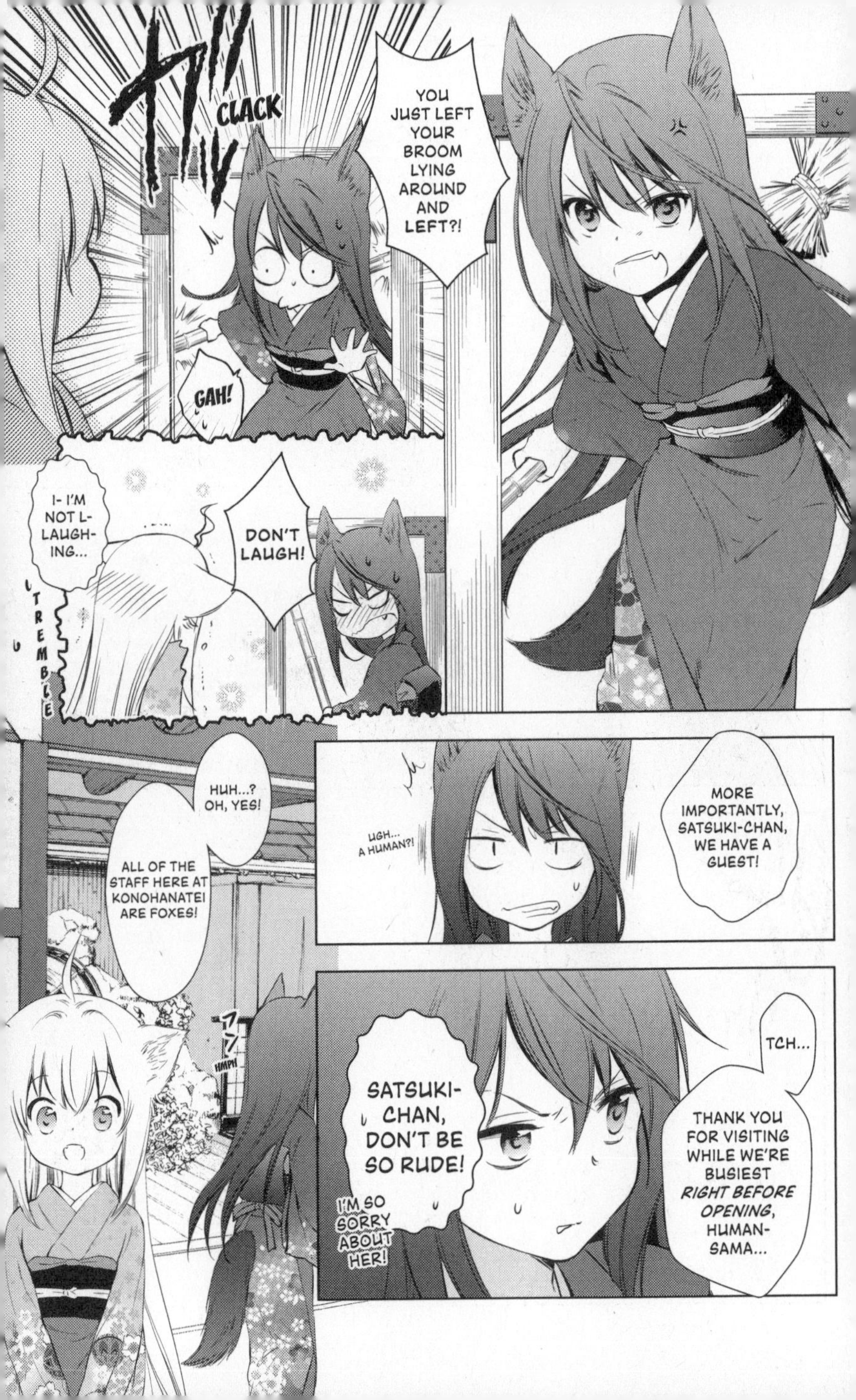
YOU JUST LEFT YOUR BROOM LYING AROUND AND LEFT?!
CLACK
GAH!
DON'T LAUGH!
I- I'M NOT L-LAUGHING...
TREMBLE
MORE IMPORTANTLY, SATSUKI-CHAN, WE HAVE A GUEST!
UGH... A HUMAN?!
HUH...? OH, YES!
ALL OF THE STAFF HERE AT KONOHANATEI ARE FOXES!
TCH...
THANK YOU FOR VISITING WHILE WE'RE BUSIEST *RIGHT BEFORE OPENING*, HUMAN-SAMA...
SATSUKI-CHAN, DON'T BE SO RUDE!
I'M SO SORRY ABOUT HER!
HMPH

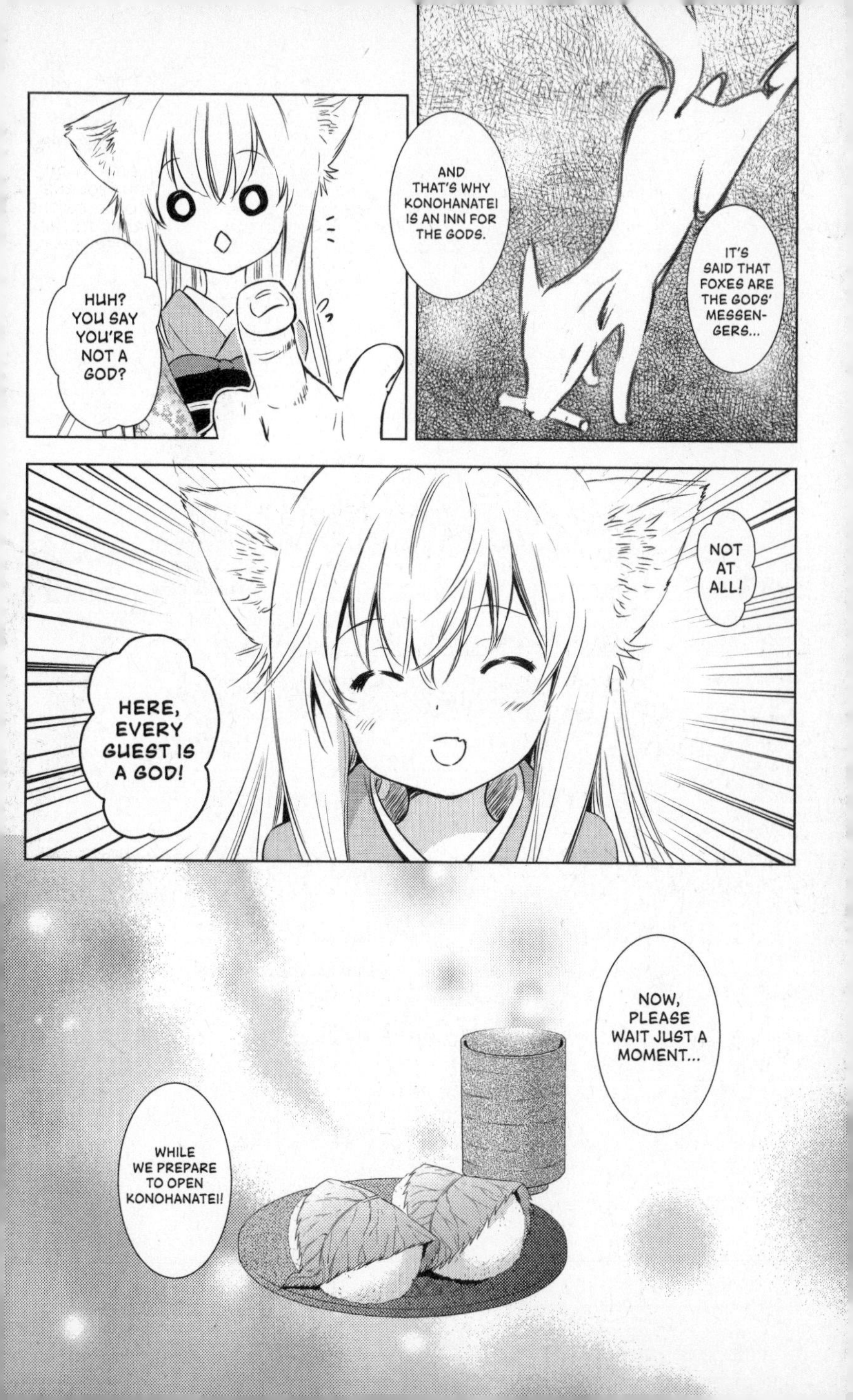
IT'S SAID THAT FOXES ARE THE GODS' MESSEN-GERS...
AND THAT'S WHY KONOHANATEI IS AN INN FOR THE GODS.
HUH? YOU SAY YOU'RE NOT A GOD?
NOT AT ALL!
HERE, EVERY GUEST IS A GOD!
NOW, PLEASE WAIT JUST A MOMENT...
WHILE WE PREPARE TO OPEN KONOHANATEI!

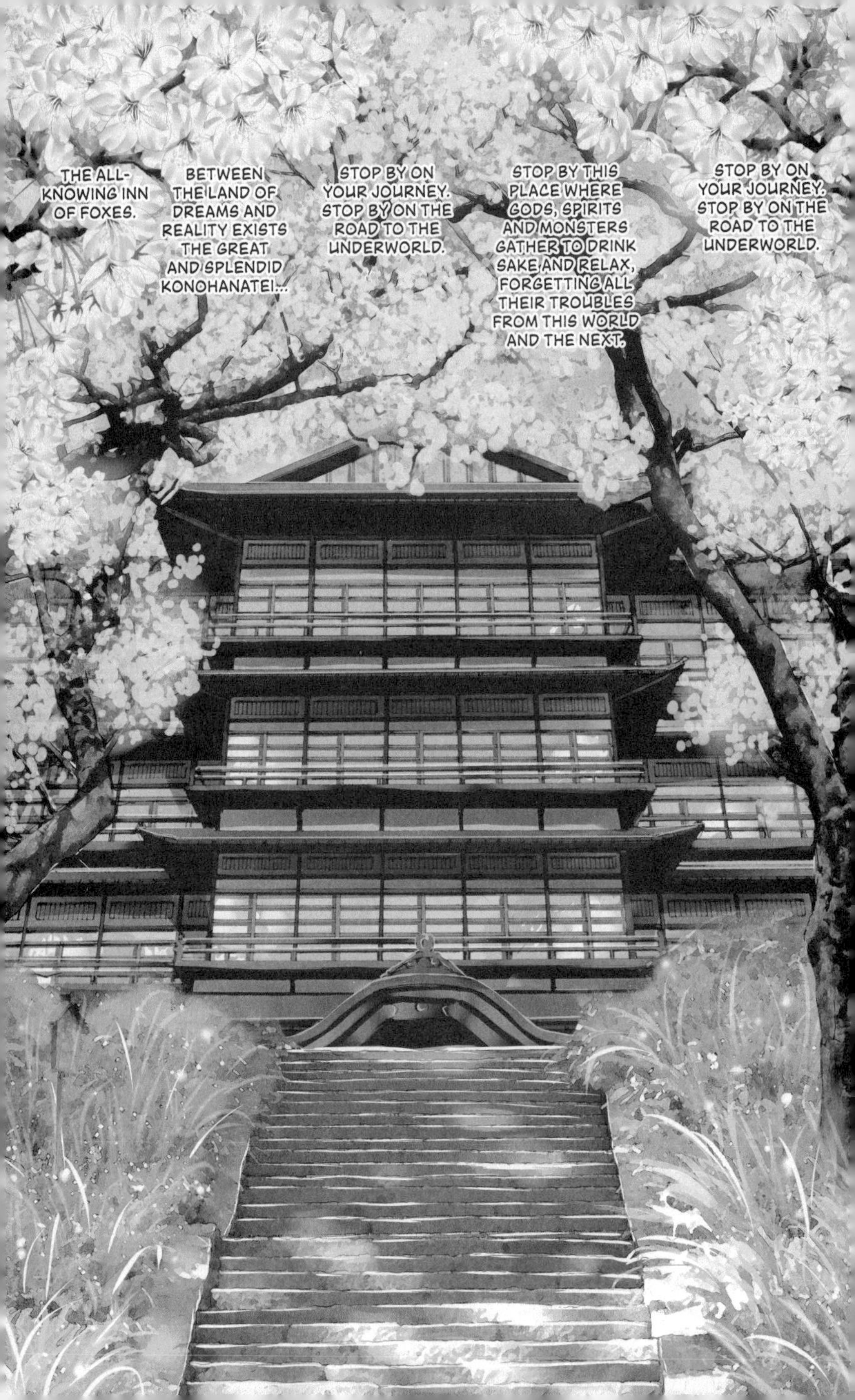
STOP BY ON YOUR JOURNEY. STOP BY ON THE ROAD TO THE UNDERWORLD.
STOP BY THIS PLACE WHERE GODS, SPIRITS AND MONSTERS GATHER TO DRINK SAKE AND RELAX, FORGETTING ALL THEIR TROUBLES FROM THIS WORLD AND THE NEXT.
STOP BY ON YOUR JOURNEY. STOP BY ON THE ROAD TO THE UNDERWORLD.
BETWEEN THE LAND OF DREAMS AND REALITY EXISTS THE GREAT AND SPLENDID KONOHANATEI...
THE ALL-KNOWING INN OF FOXES.

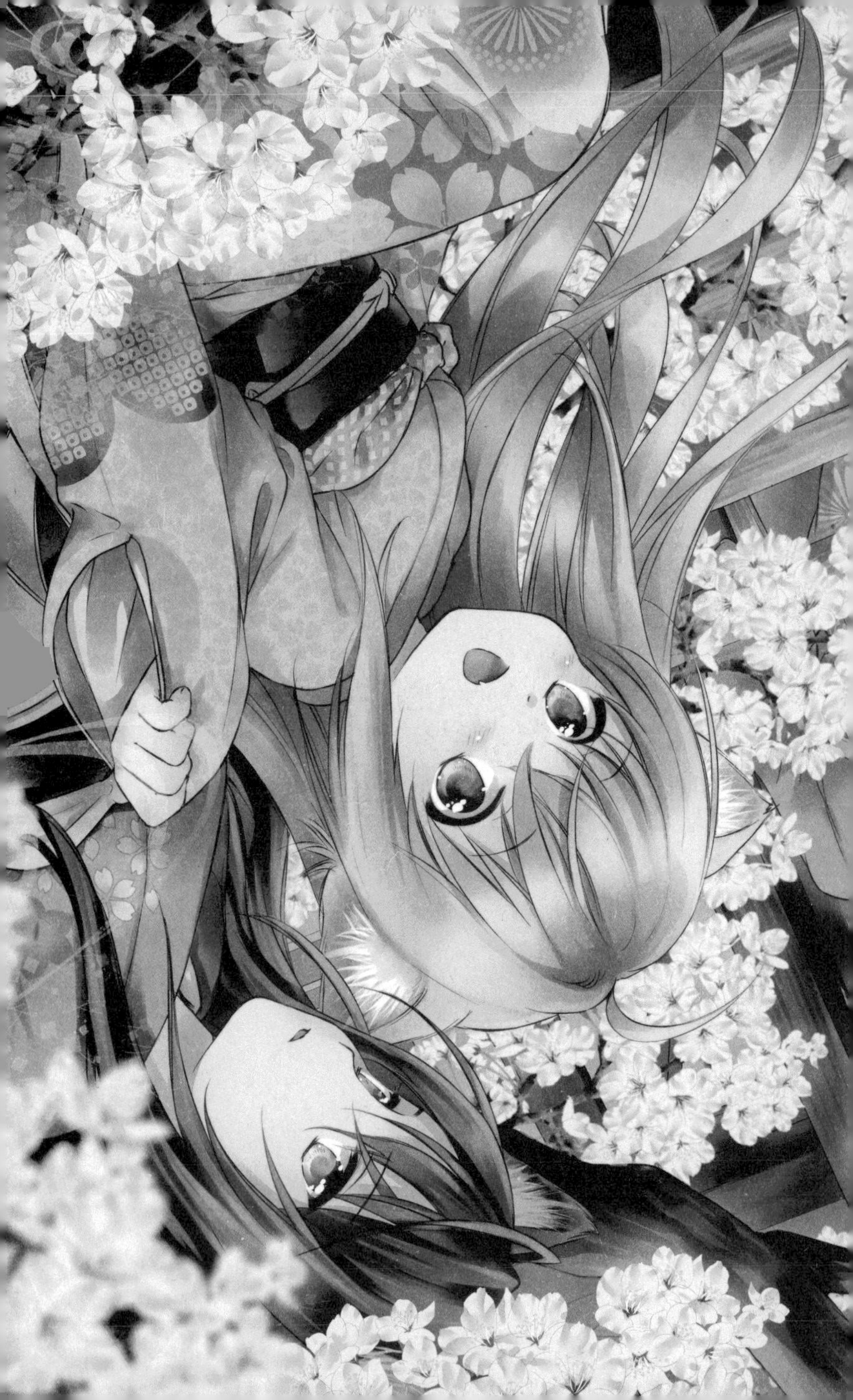

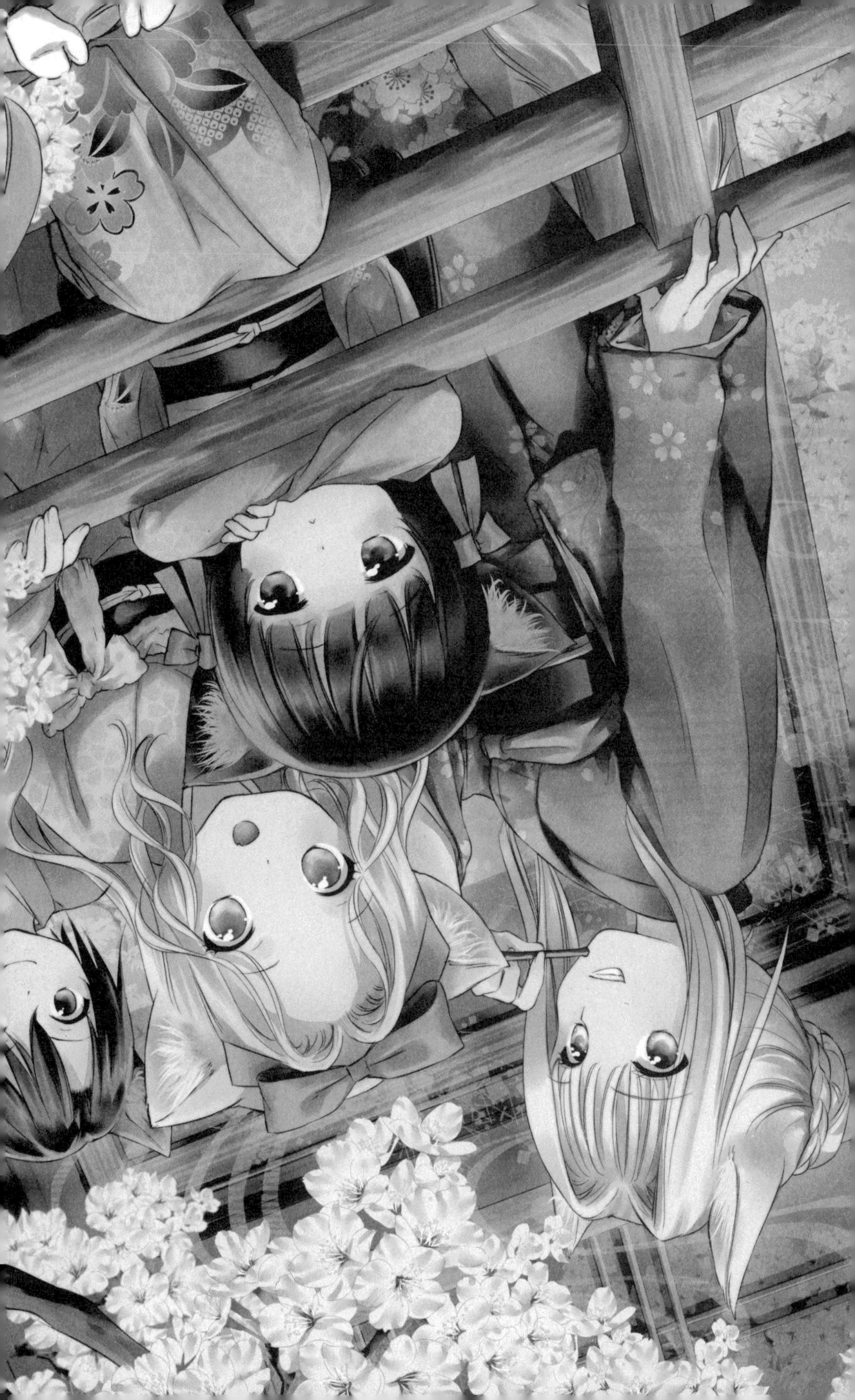

KONOHANA KITAN

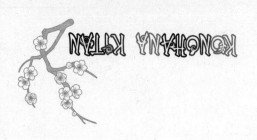

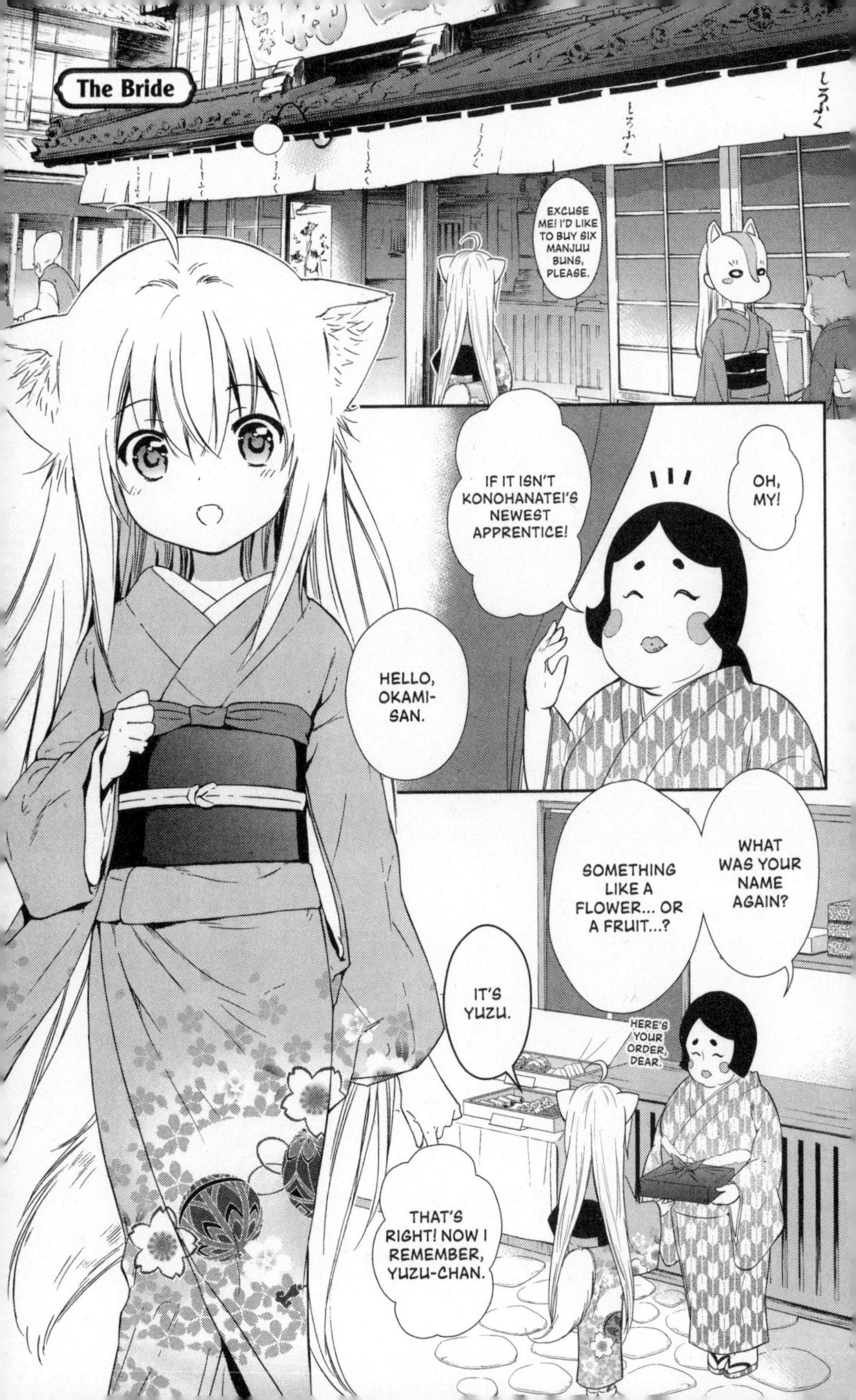
The Bride
EXCUSE ME! I'D LIKE TO BUY SIX MANJUU BUNS, PLEASE.
OH, MY!
IF IT ISN'T KONOHANATEI'S NEWEST APPRENTICE!
HELLO, OKAMI-SAN.
WHAT WAS YOUR NAME AGAIN?
SOMETHING LIKE A FLOWER... OR A FRUIT...?
IT'S YUZU.
HERE'S YOUR ORDER, DEAR.
THAT'S RIGHT! NOW I REMEMBER, YUZU-CHAN.

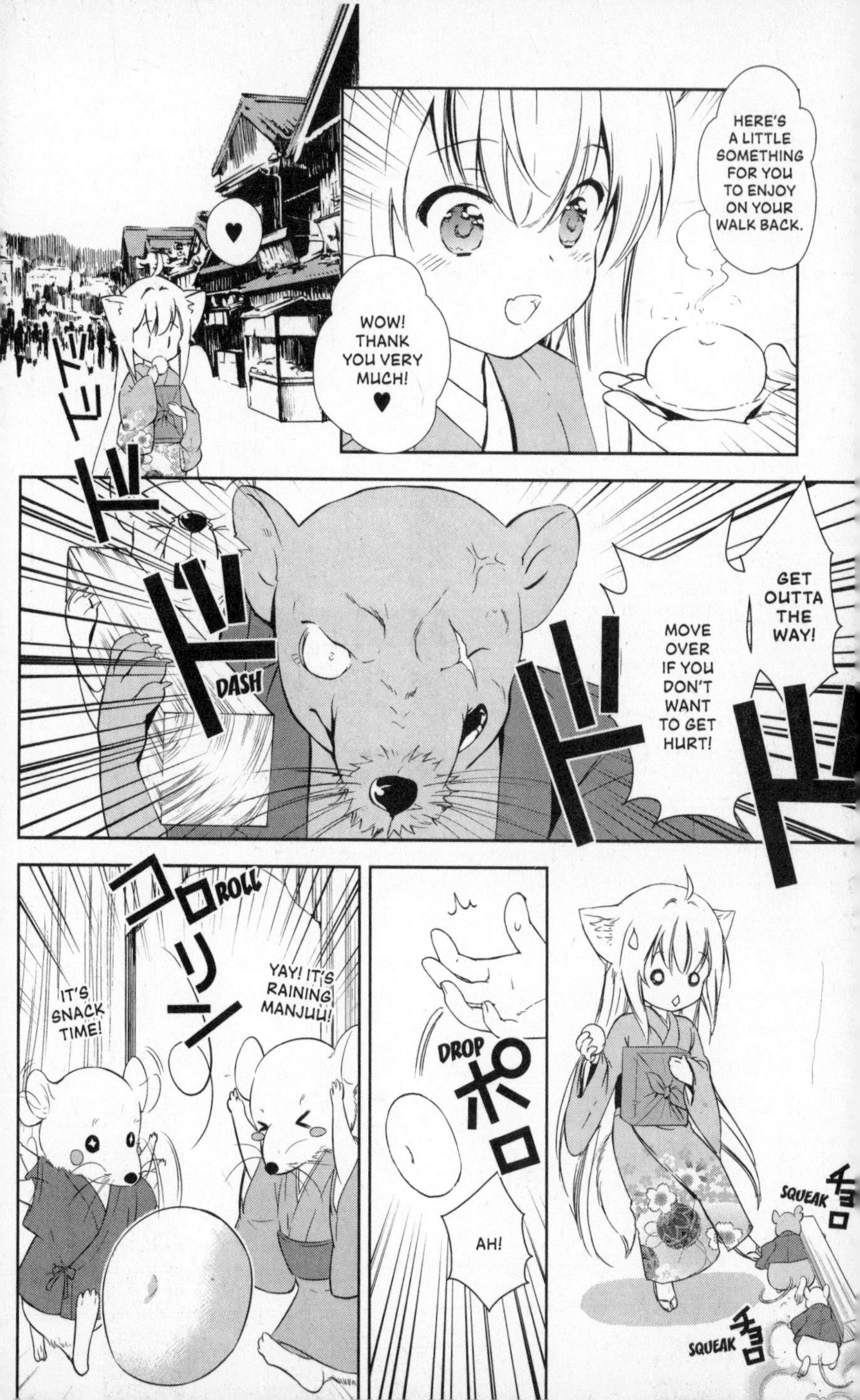
HERE'S A LITTLE SOMETHING FOR YOU TO ENJOY ON YOUR WALK BACK.
WOW! THANK YOU VERY MUCH! ♥
♥
GET OUTTA THE WAY!
MOVE OVER IF YOU DON'T WANT TO GET HURT!
DASH
SQUEAK
SQUEAK
DROP
AH!
ROLL
YAY! IT'S RAINING MANJUU!
IT'S SNACK TIME!

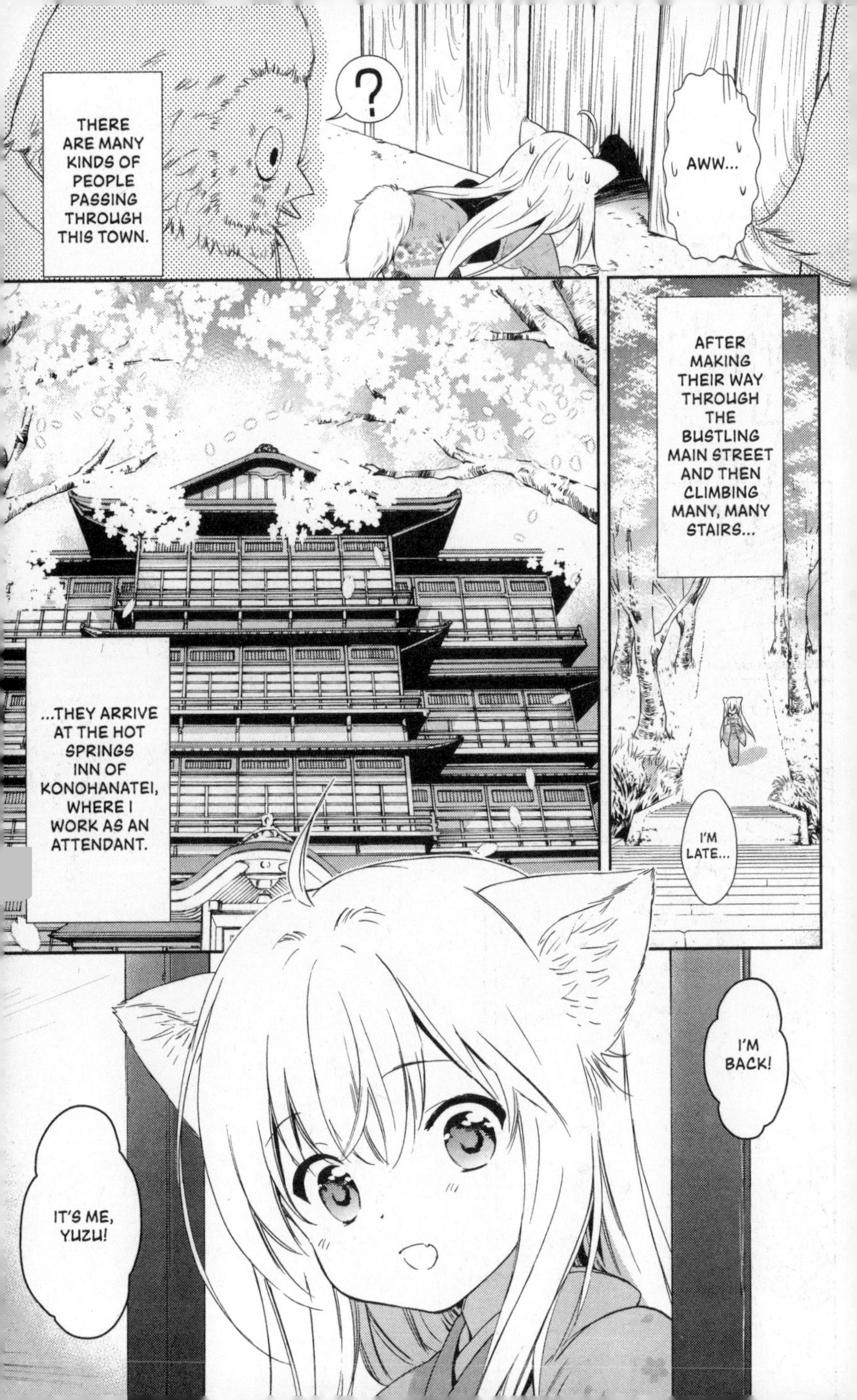
AWW...
?
THERE ARE MANY KINDS OF PEOPLE PASSING THROUGH THIS TOWN.
AFTER MAKING THEIR WAY THROUGH THE BUSTLING MAIN STREET AND THEN CLIMBING MANY, MANY STAIRS...
I'M LATE...
...THEY ARRIVE AT THE HOT SPRINGS INN OF KONOHANATEI, WHERE I WORK AS AN ATTENDANT.
I'M BACK!
IT'S ME, YUZU!

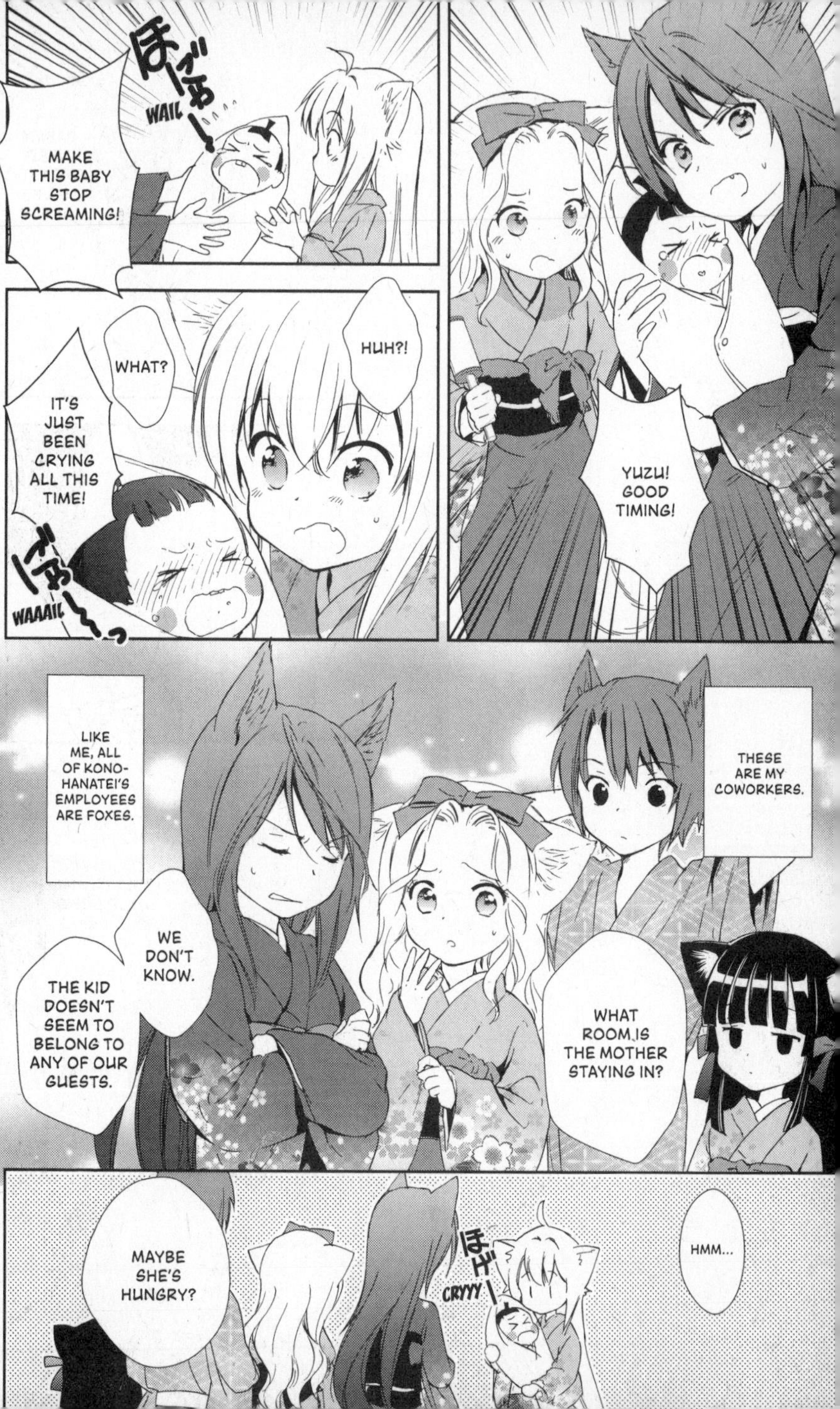
YUZU! GOOD TIMING!
WAIL
MAKE THIS BABY STOP SCREAMING!
HUH?!
WHAT?
IT'S JUST BEEN CRYING ALL THIS TIME!
WAAAIL
THESE ARE MY COWORKERS.
LIKE ME, ALL OF KONO-HANATEI'S EMPLOYEES ARE FOXES.
WHAT ROOM IS THE MOTHER STAYING IN?
WE DON'T KNOW.
THE KID DOESN'T SEEM TO BELONG TO ANY OF OUR GUESTS.
HMM...
CRYYY
MAYBE SHE'S HUNGRY?

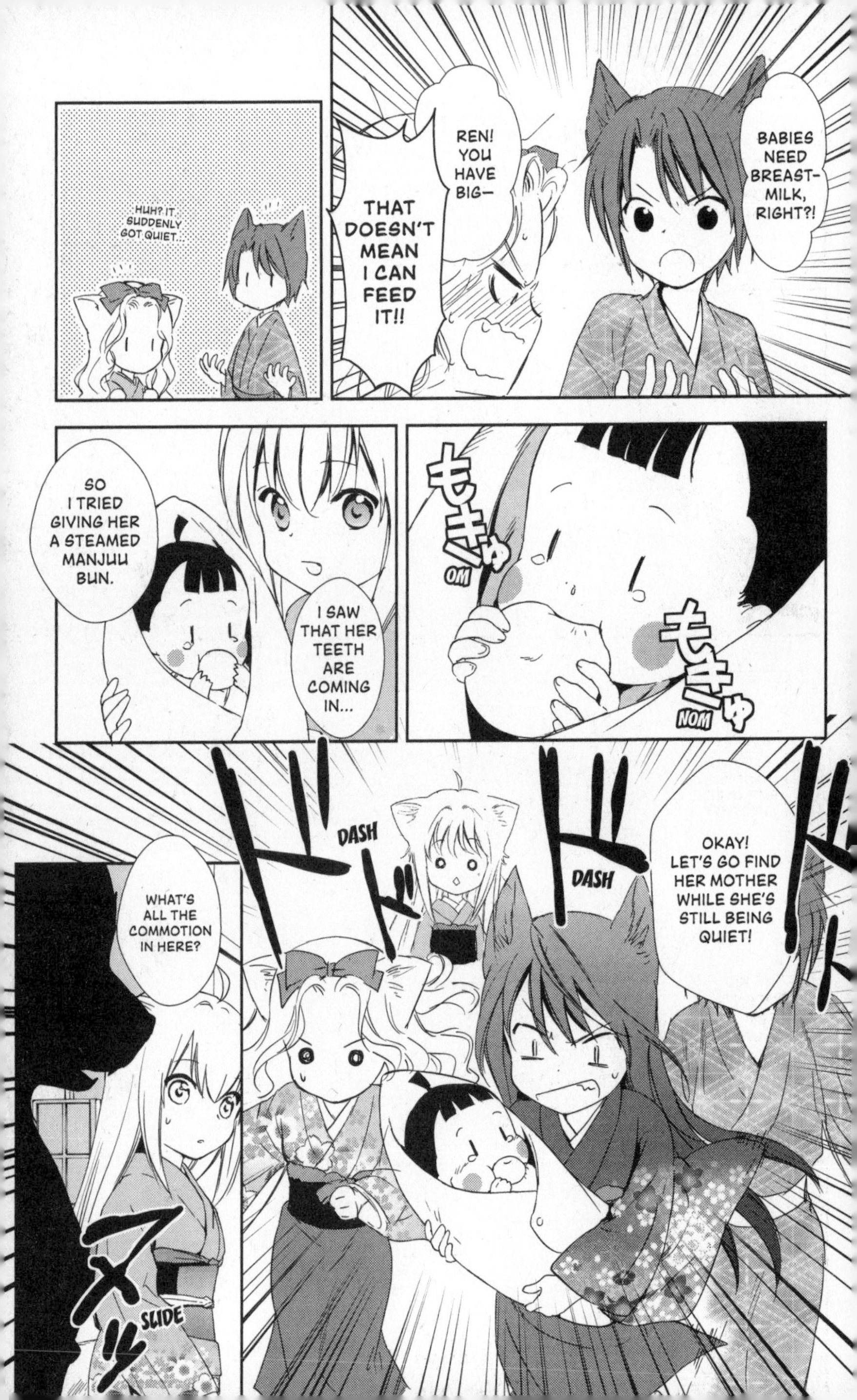
BABIES NEED BREAST-MILK, RIGHT?!
REN! YOU HAVE BIG—
THAT DOESN'T MEAN I CAN FEED IT!!
HUH? IT SUDDENLY GOT QUIET...
OM
NOM
SO I TRIED GIVING HER A STEAMED MANJUU BUN.
I SAW THAT HER TEETH ARE COMING IN...
OKAY! LET'S GO FIND HER MOTHER WHILE SHE'S STILL BEING QUIET!
DASH
DASH
WHAT'S ALL THE COMMOTION IN HERE?
SLIDE

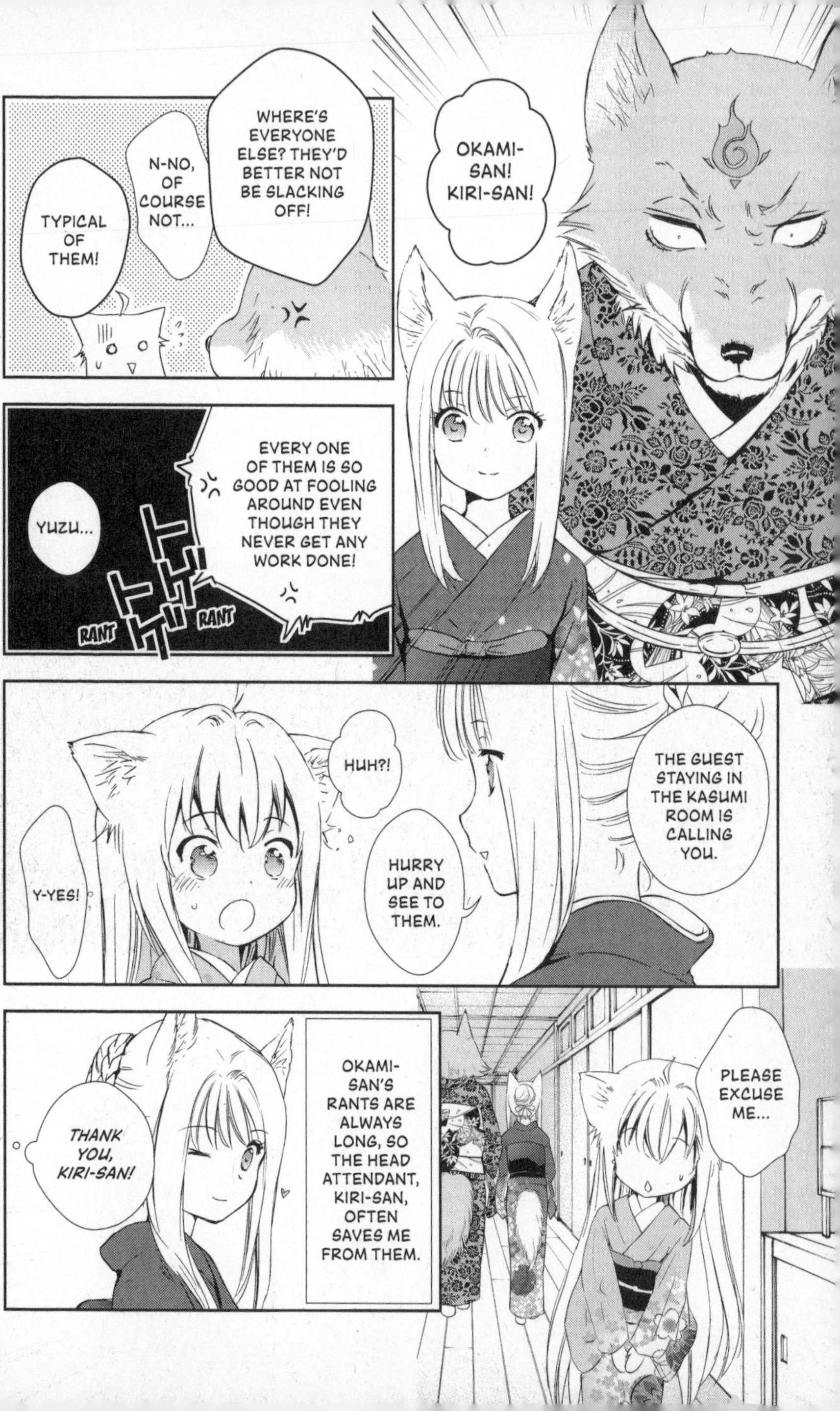
OKAMI-SAN! KIRI-SAN!
WHERE'S EVERYONE ELSE? THEY'D BETTER NOT BE SLACKING OFF!
N-NO, OF COURSE NOT...
TYPICAL OF THEM!
EVERY ONE OF THEM IS SO GOOD AT FOOLING AROUND EVEN THOUGH THEY NEVER GET ANY WORK DONE!
RANT
RANT
YUZU...
THE GUEST STAYING IN THE KASUMI ROOM IS CALLING YOU.
HUH?!
HURRY UP AND SEE TO THEM.
Y-YES!
PLEASE EXCUSE ME...
OKAMI-SAN'S RANTS ARE ALWAYS LONG, SO THE HEAD ATTENDANT, KIRI-SAN, OFTEN SAVES ME FROM THEM.
THANK YOU, KIRI-SAN!

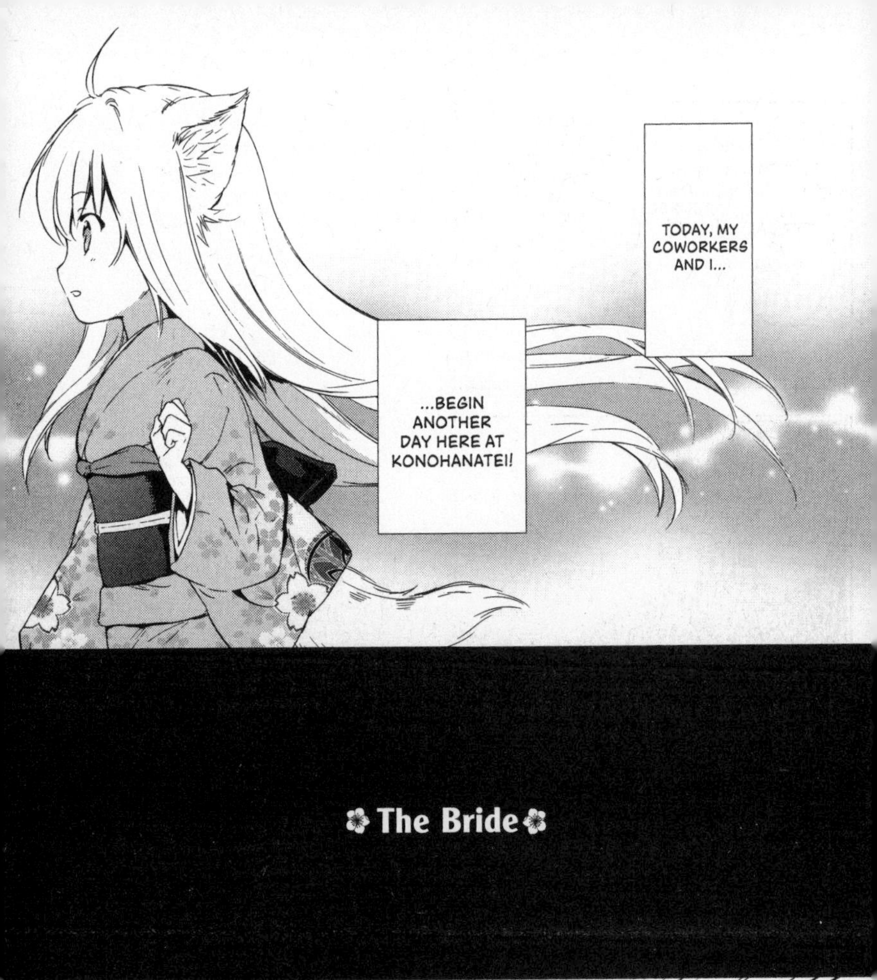
TODAY, MY COWORKERS AND I...
...BEGIN ANOTHER DAY HERE AT KONOHANATEI!

The Bride

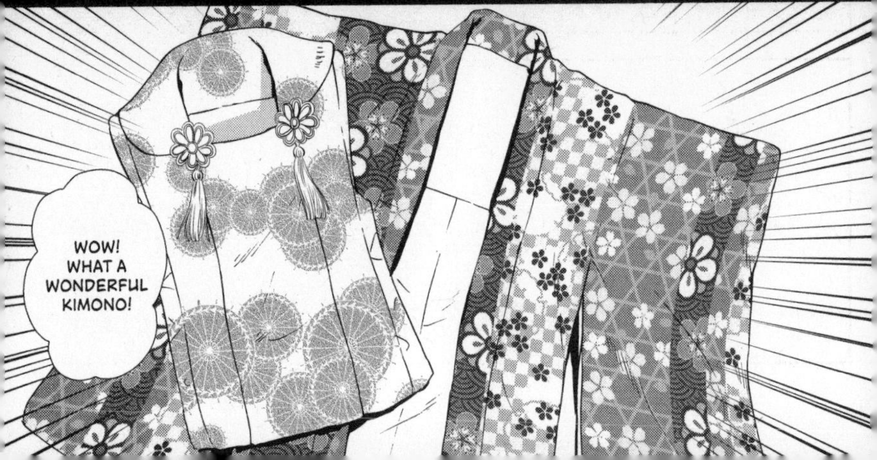
WOW! WHAT A WONDERFUL KIMONO!

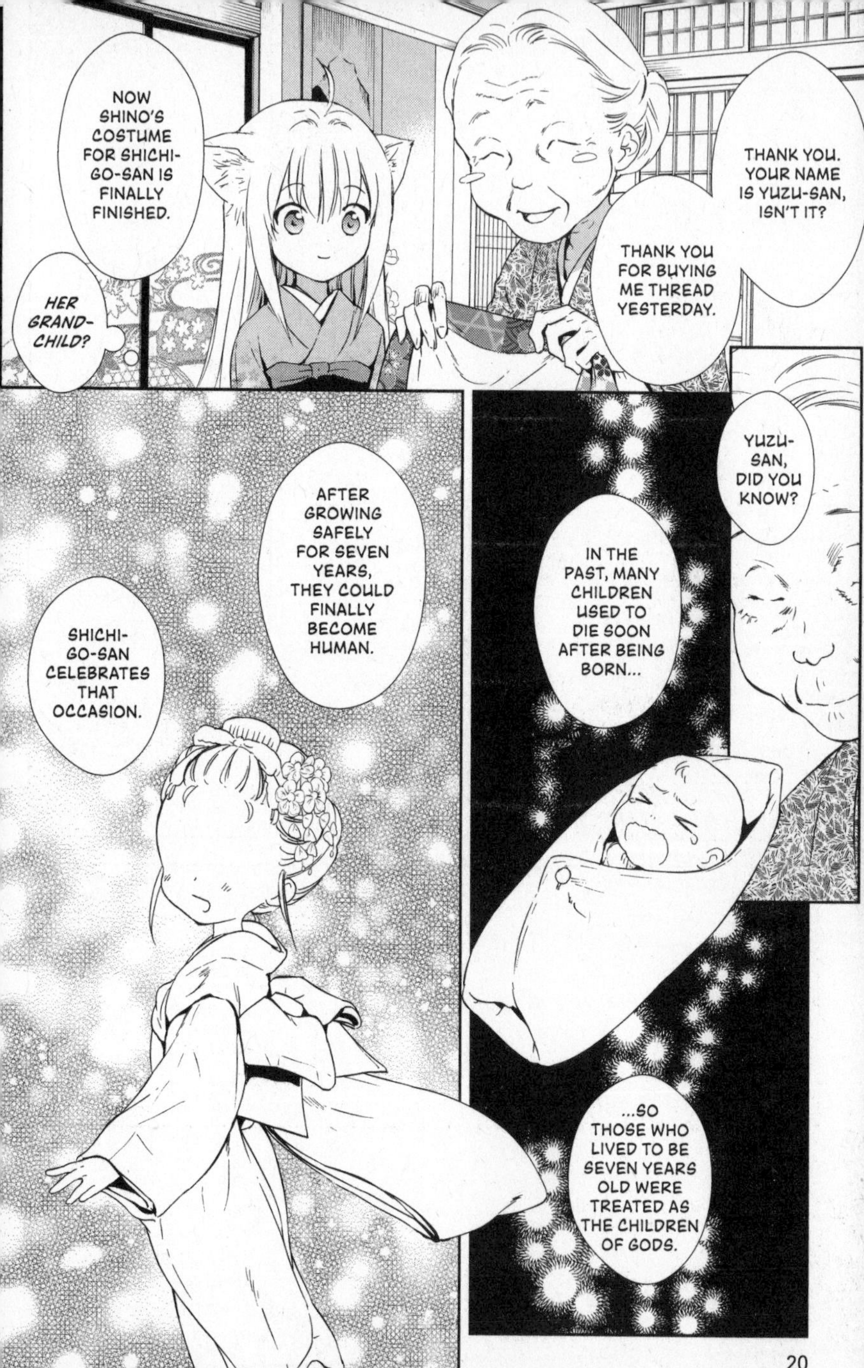
THANK YOU. YOUR NAME IS YUZU-SAN, ISN'T IT?
THANK YOU FOR BUYING ME THREAD YESTERDAY.
NOW SHINO'S COSTUME FOR SHICHI-GO-SAN IS FINALLY FINISHED.
HER GRAND-CHILD?
YUZU-SAN, DID YOU KNOW?
IN THE PAST, MANY CHILDREN USED TO DIE SOON AFTER BEING BORN...
...SO THOSE WHO LIVED TO BE SEVEN YEARS OLD WERE TREATED AS THE CHILDREN OF GODS.
AFTER GROWING SAFELY FOR SEVEN YEARS, THEY COULD FINALLY BECOME HUMAN.
SHICHI-GO-SAN CELEBRATES THAT OCCASION.

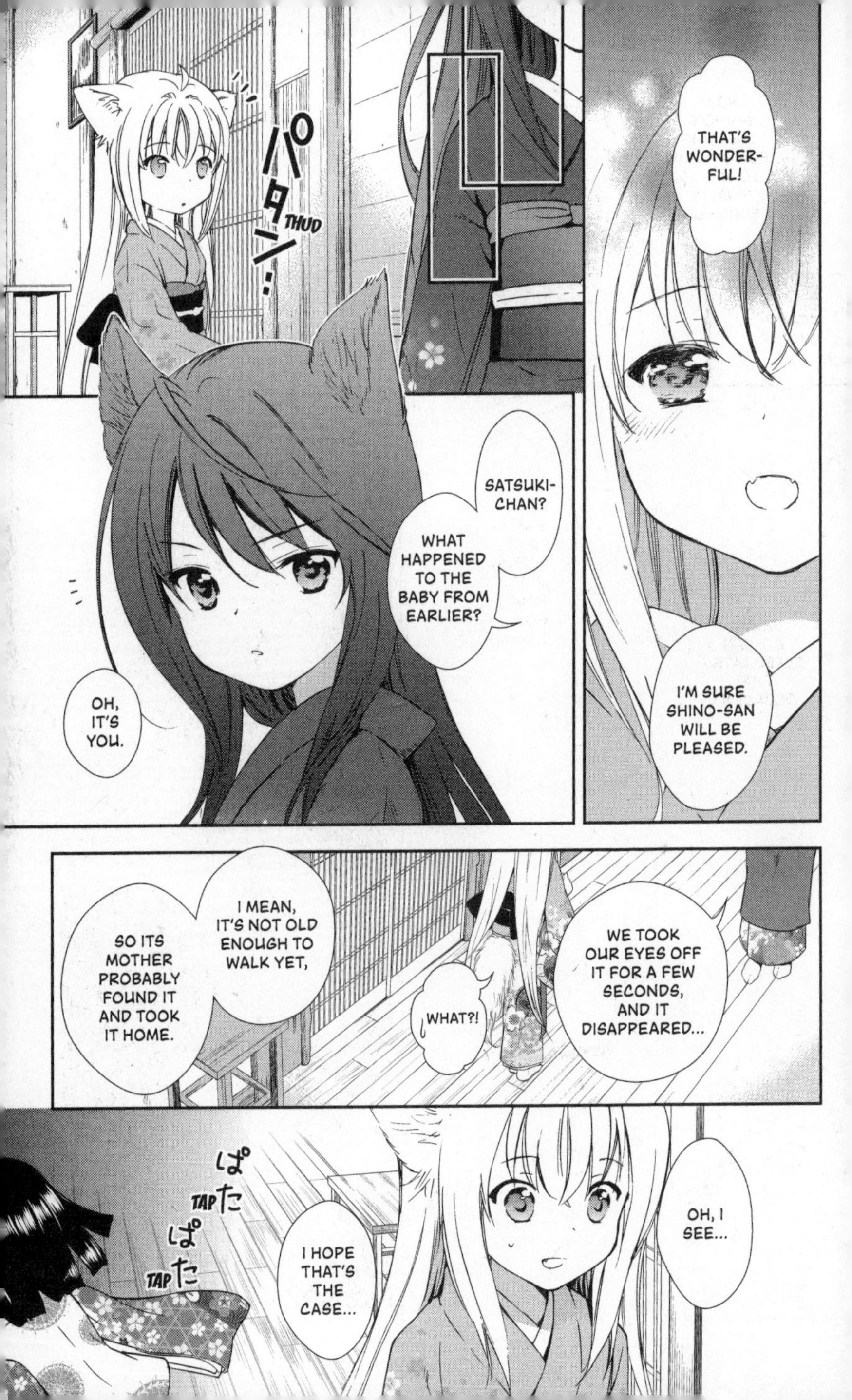
THAT'S WONDER-FUL!
I'M SURE SHINO-SAN WILL BE PLEASED.
パタン THUD
SATSUKI-CHAN?
WHAT HAPPENED TO THE BABY FROM EARLIER?
OH, IT'S YOU.
WE TOOK OUR EYES OFF IT FOR A FEW SECONDS, AND IT DISAPPEARED...
WHAT?!
I MEAN, IT'S NOT OLD ENOUGH TO WALK YET,
SO ITS MOTHER PROBABLY FOUND IT AND TOOK IT HOME.
OH, I SEE...
I HOPE THAT'S THE CASE...
ぱた TAP
ぱた TAP

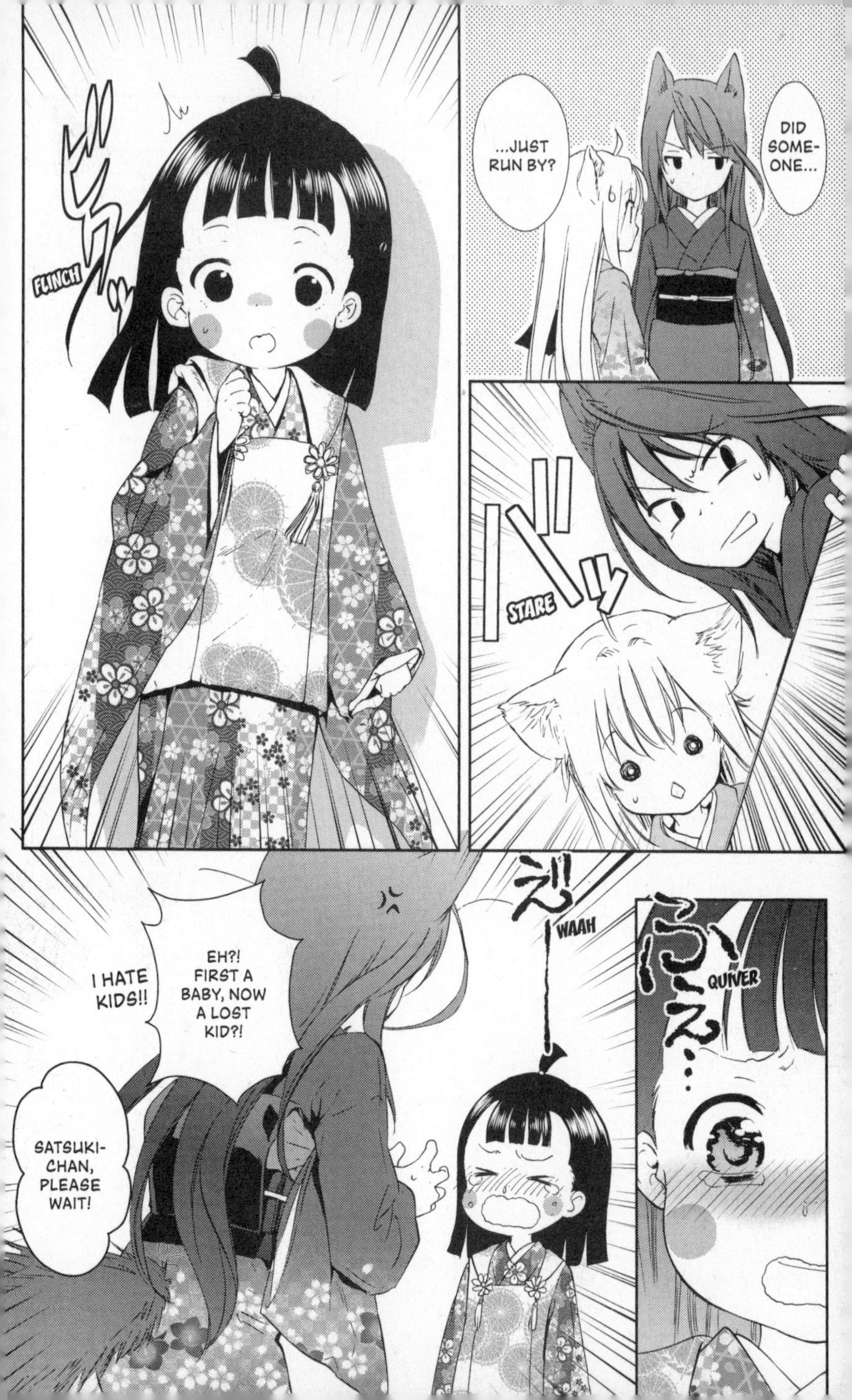
DID SOME-ONE...
...JUST RUN BY?
STARE
FLINCH
QUIVER
WAAH
EH?! FIRST A BABY, NOW A LOST KID?!
I HATE KIDS!!
SATSUKI-CHAN, PLEASE WAIT!

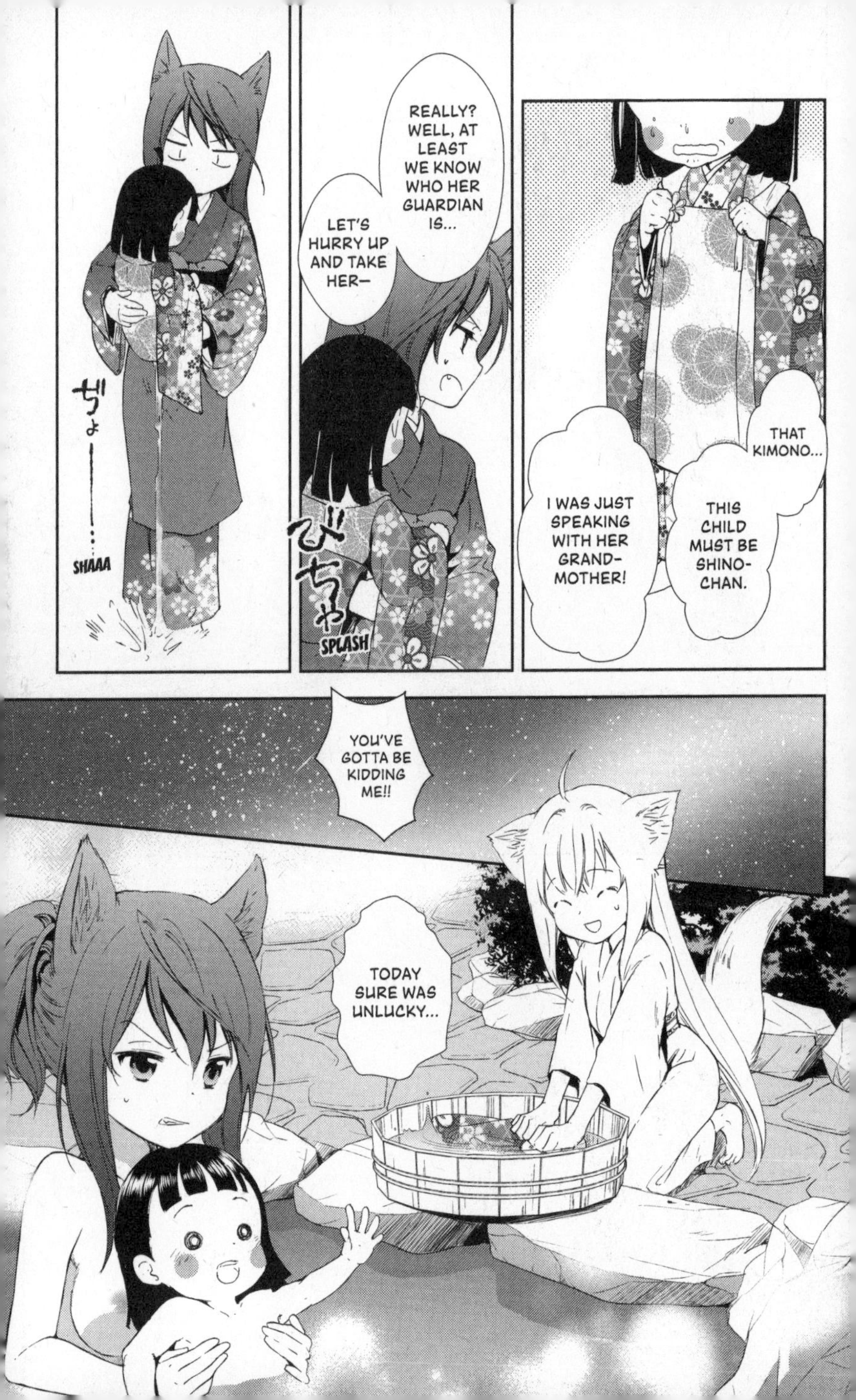
THAT KIMONO...
THIS CHILD MUST BE SHINO-CHAN.
I WAS JUST SPEAKING WITH HER GRAND-MOTHER!
REALLY? WELL, AT LEAST WE KNOW WHO HER GUARDIAN IS...
LET'S HURRY UP AND TAKE HER—
びちゃ
SPLASH
ぢょ————……
SHAAA
YOU'VE GOTTA BE KIDDING ME!!
TODAY SURE WAS UNLUCKY...

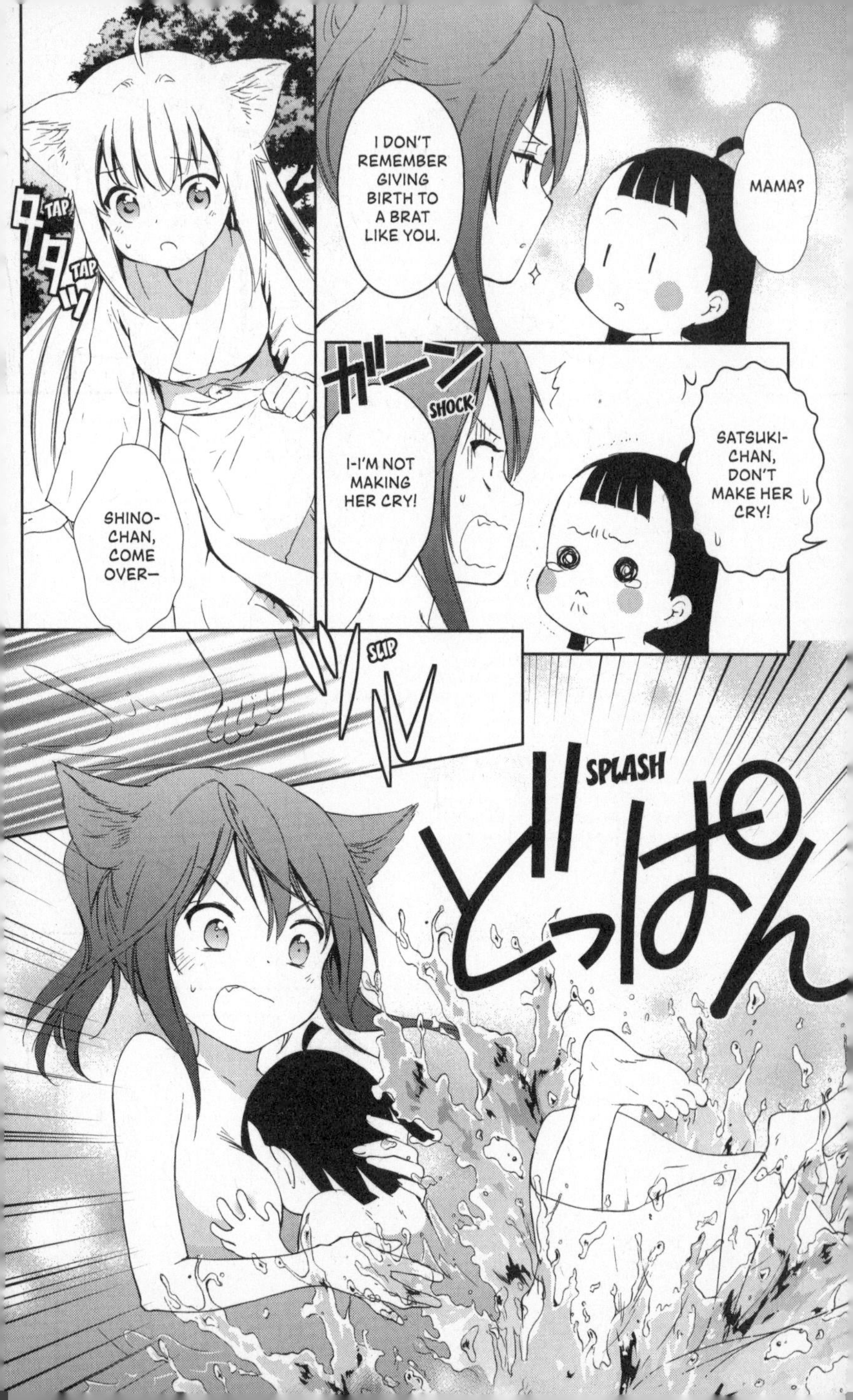
MAMA?
I DON'T REMEMBER GIVING BIRTH TO A BRAT LIKE YOU.
SATSUKI-CHAN, DON'T MAKE HER CRY!
ガーン
SHOCK
I-I'M NOT MAKING HER CRY!
タタッ
TAP TAP
SHINO-CHAN, COME OVER—
SLIP
どっぽん
SPLASH

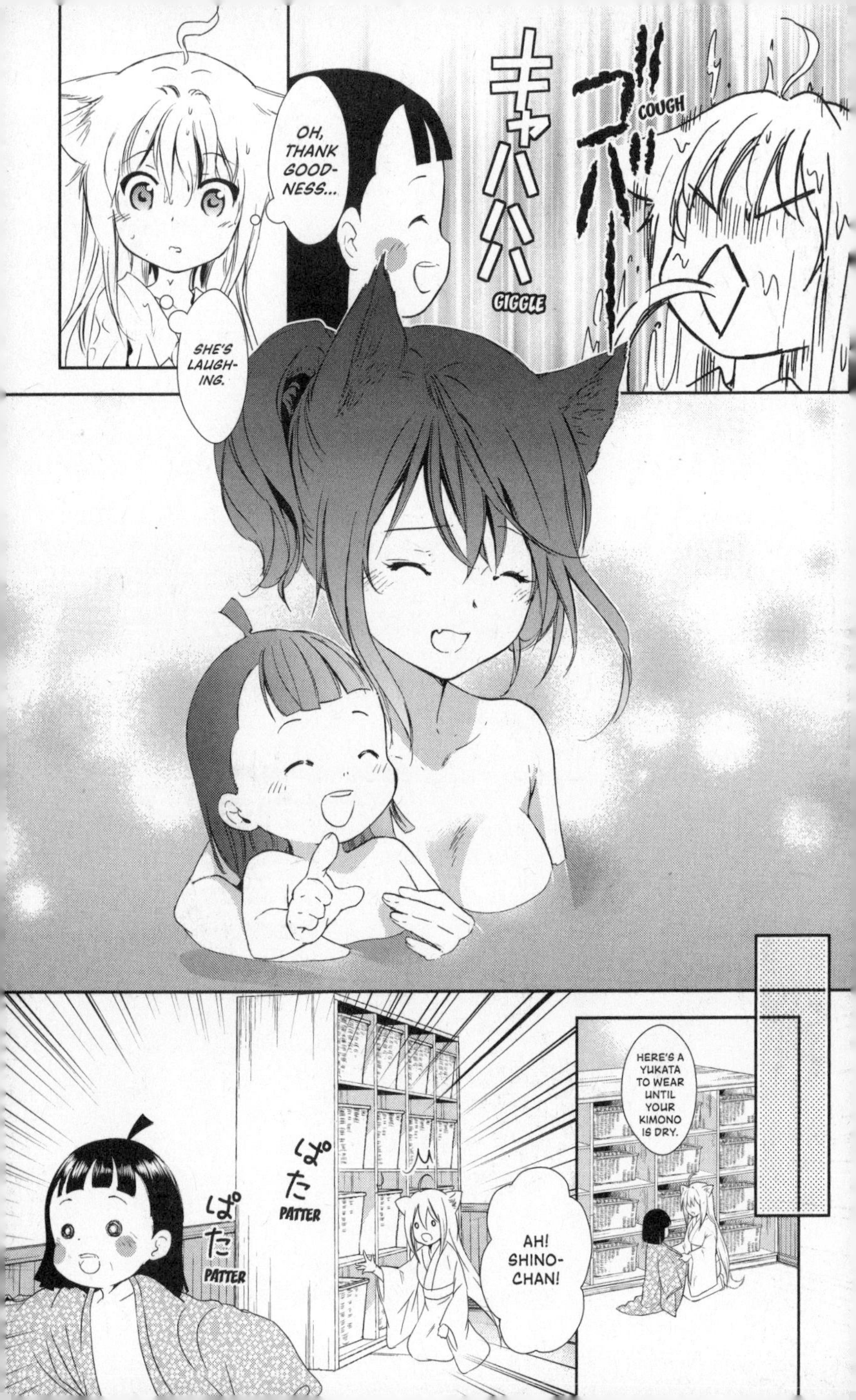
ゴバッ
COUGH
キャハハハ
GIGGLE
OH, THANK GOOD-NESS...
SHE'S LAUGH-ING.
HERE'S A YUKATA TO WEAR UNTIL YOUR KIMONO IS DRY.
AH! SHINO-CHAN!
ぱた
PATTER
ぱた
PATTER

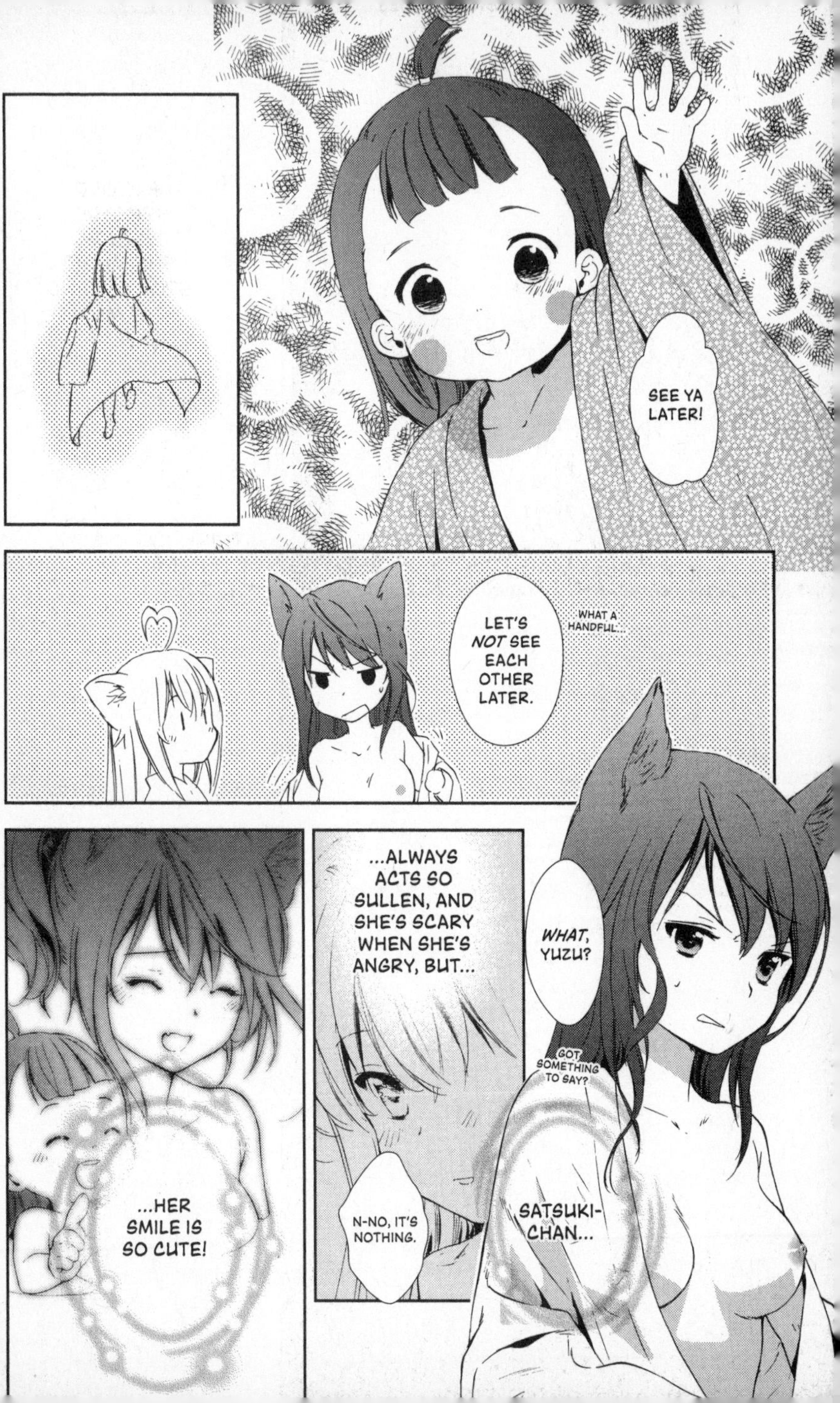
SEE YA LATER!
LET'S *NOT* SEE EACH OTHER LATER.
WHAT A HANDFUL...
SATSUKI-CHAN...
WHAT, YUZU?
GOT SOMETHING TO SAY?
N-NO, IT'S NOTHING.
...ALWAYS ACTS SO SULLEN, AND SHE'S SCARY WHEN SHE'S ANGRY, BUT...
...HER SMILE IS SO CUTE!

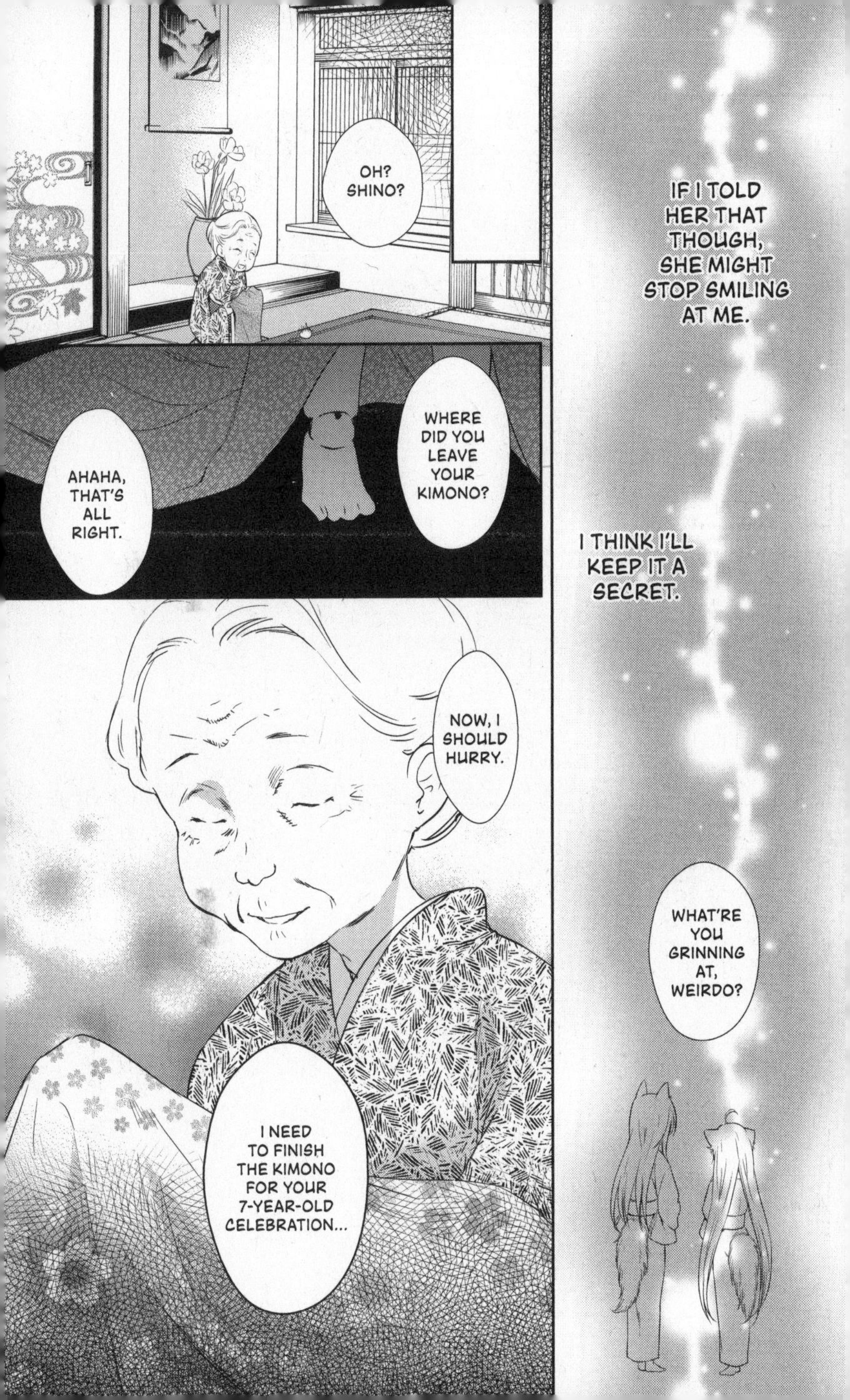
IF I TOLD HER THAT THOUGH, SHE MIGHT STOP SMILING AT ME.
I THINK I'LL KEEP IT A SECRET.
WHAT'RE YOU GRINNING AT, WEIRDO?
OH? SHINO?
WHERE DID YOU LEAVE YOUR KIMONO?
AHAHA, THAT'S ALL RIGHT.
NOW, I SHOULD HURRY.
I NEED TO FINISH THE KIMONO FOR YOUR 7-YEAR-OLD CELEBRATION...

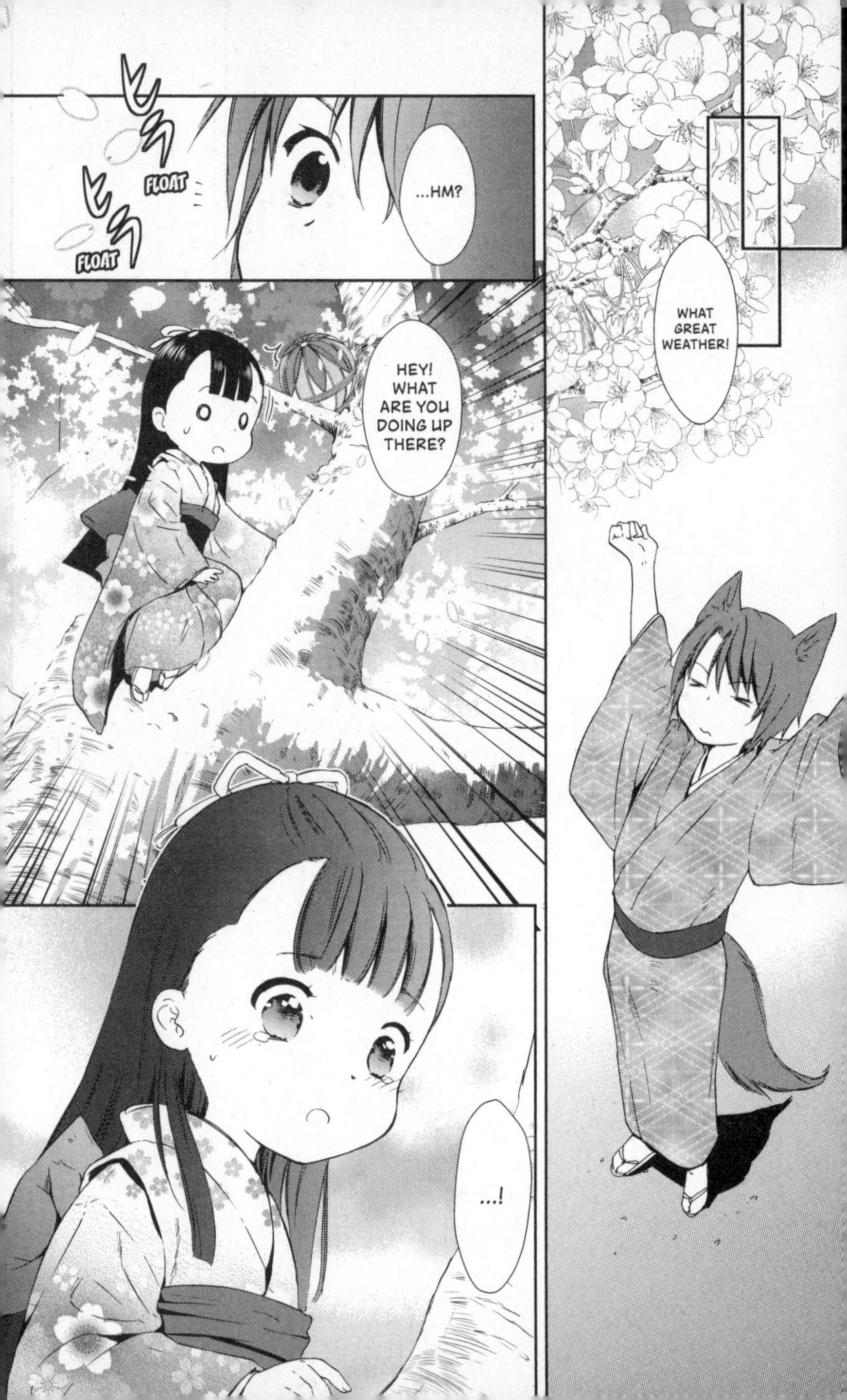
WHAT GREAT WEATHER!
FLOAT
FLOAT
...HM?
HEY! WHAT ARE YOU DOING UP THERE?
...!

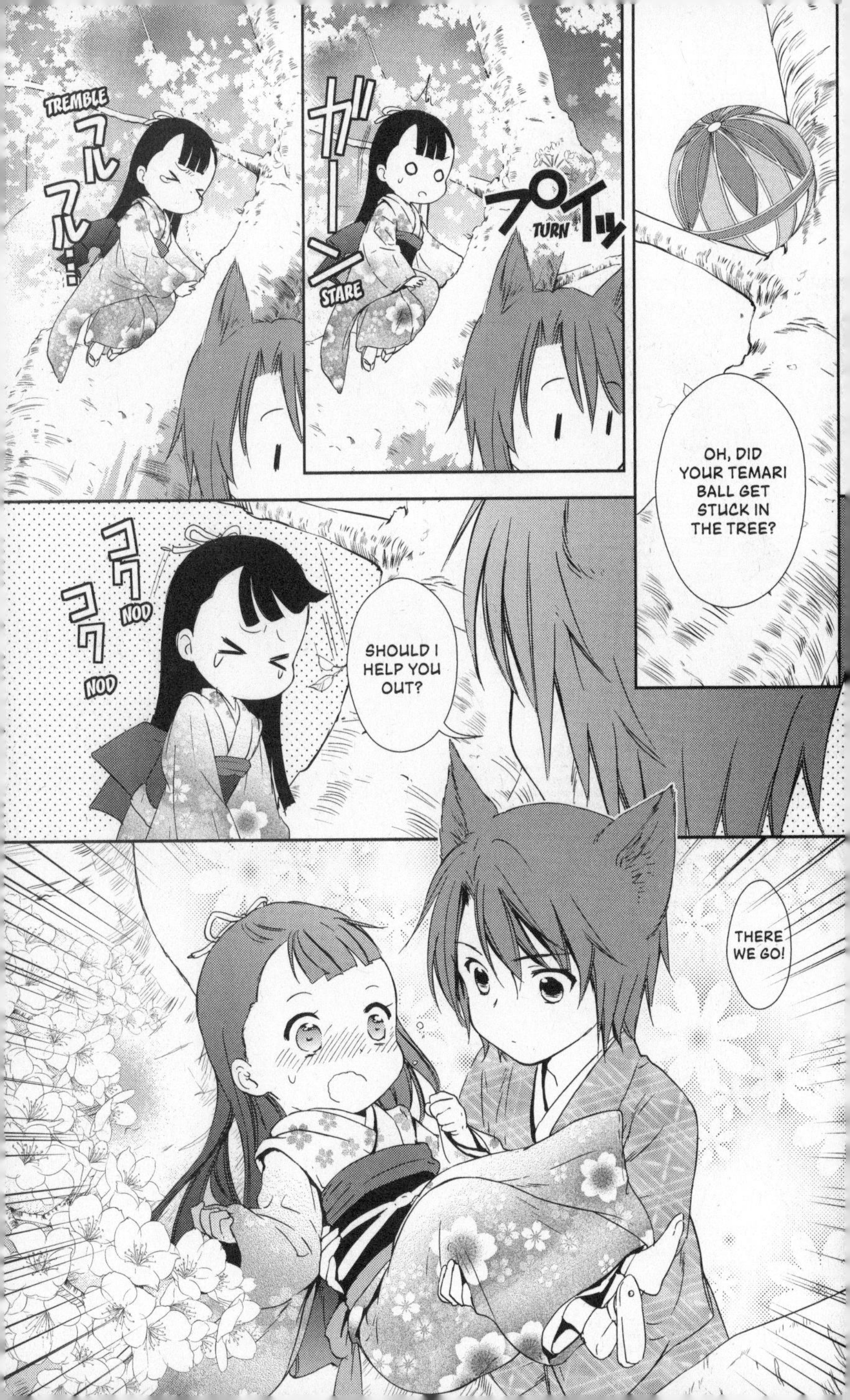
OH, DID YOUR TEMARI BALL GET STUCK IN THE TREE?
ガーン
STARE
プイッ
TURN
TREMBLE
フルフル…
SHOULD I HELP YOU OUT?
コクコク
NOD
NOD
THERE WE GO!

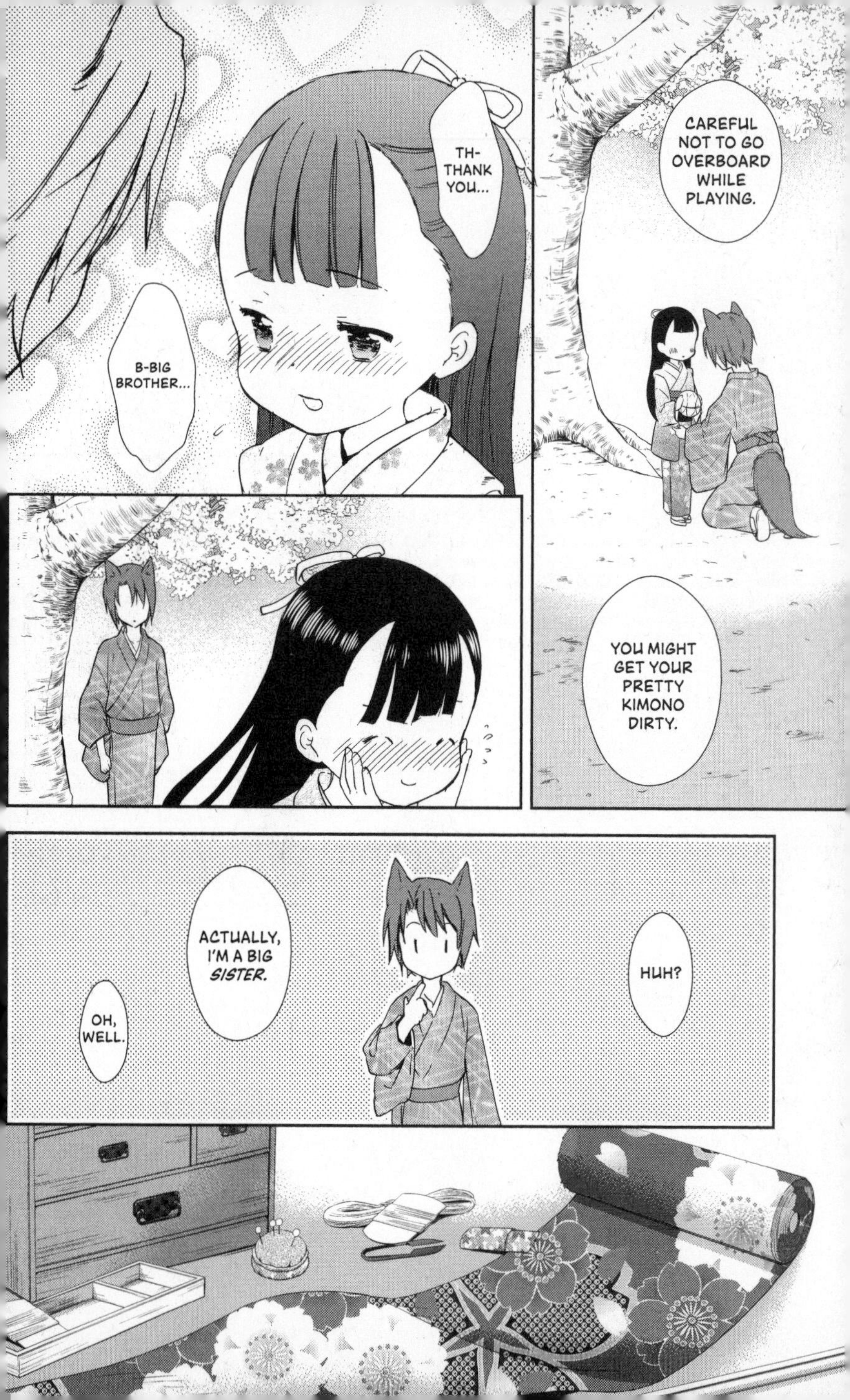
CAREFUL NOT TO GO OVERBOARD WHILE PLAYING.
YOU MIGHT GET YOUR PRETTY KIMONO DIRTY.
TH-THANK YOU...
B-BIG BROTHER...
HUH?
ACTUALLY, I'M A BIG *SISTER.*
OH, WELL.

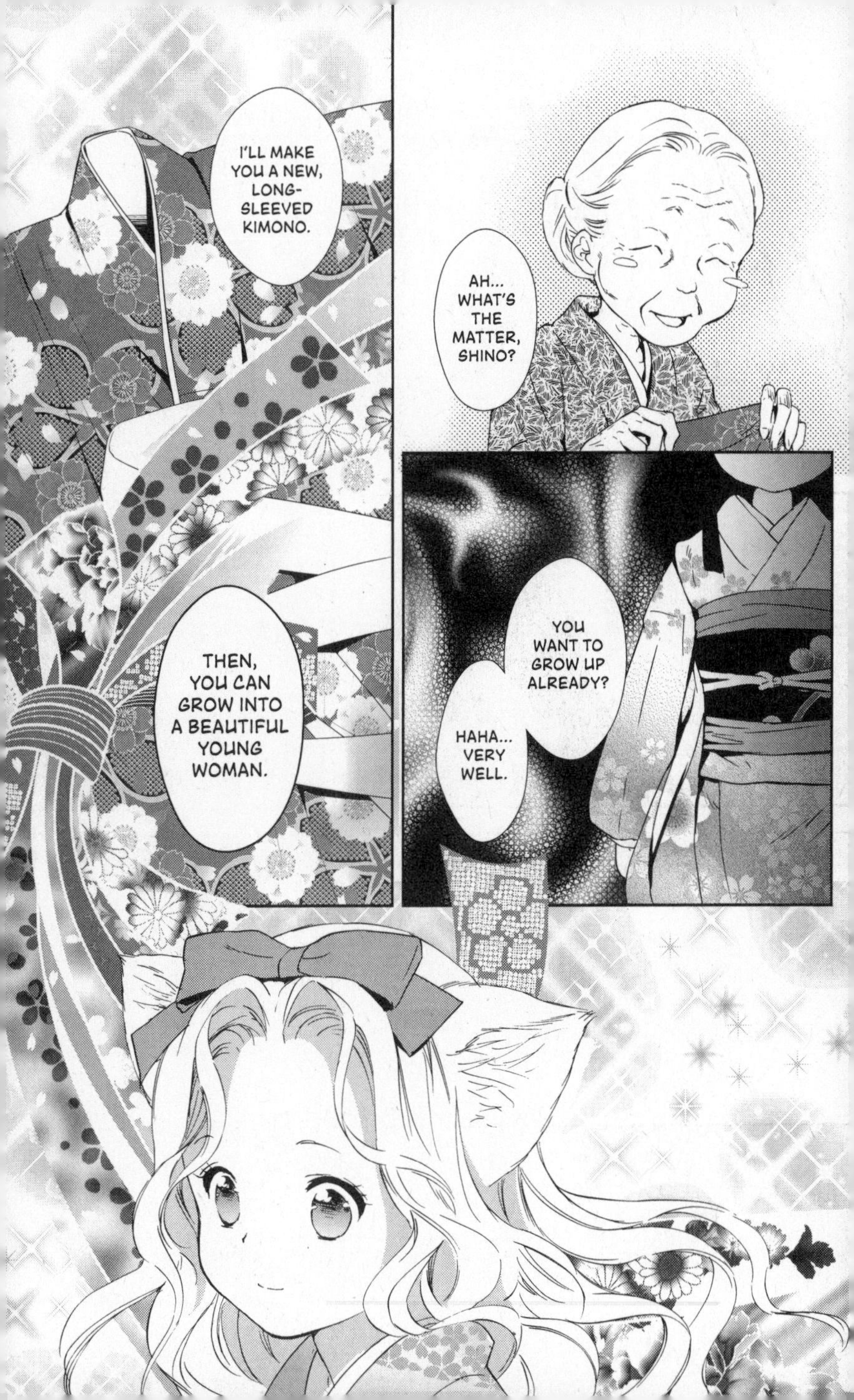
AH... WHAT'S THE MATTER, SHINO?
YOU WANT TO GROW UP ALREADY?
HAHA... VERY WELL.
I'LL MAKE YOU A NEW, LONG-SLEEVED KIMONO.
THEN, YOU CAN GROW INTO A BEAUTIFUL YOUNG WOMAN.

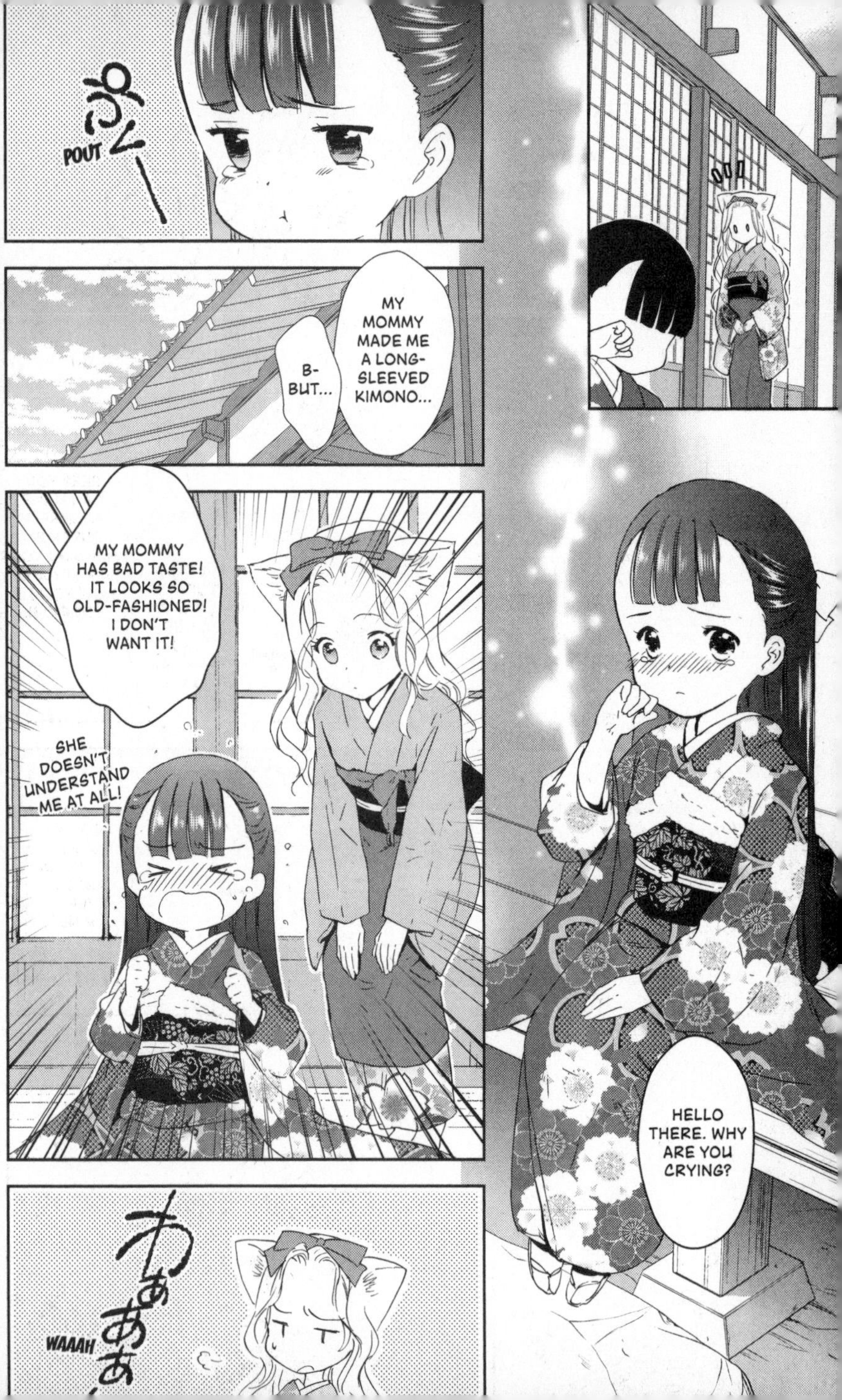
HELLO THERE. WHY ARE YOU CRYING?
ぷくー
POUT
MY MOMMY MADE ME A LONG-SLEEVED KIMONO...
B-BUT...
MY MOMMY HAS BAD TASTE! IT LOOKS SO OLD-FASHIONED! I DON'T WANT IT!
SHE DOESN'T UNDERSTAND ME AT ALL!
わあああ
WAAAH

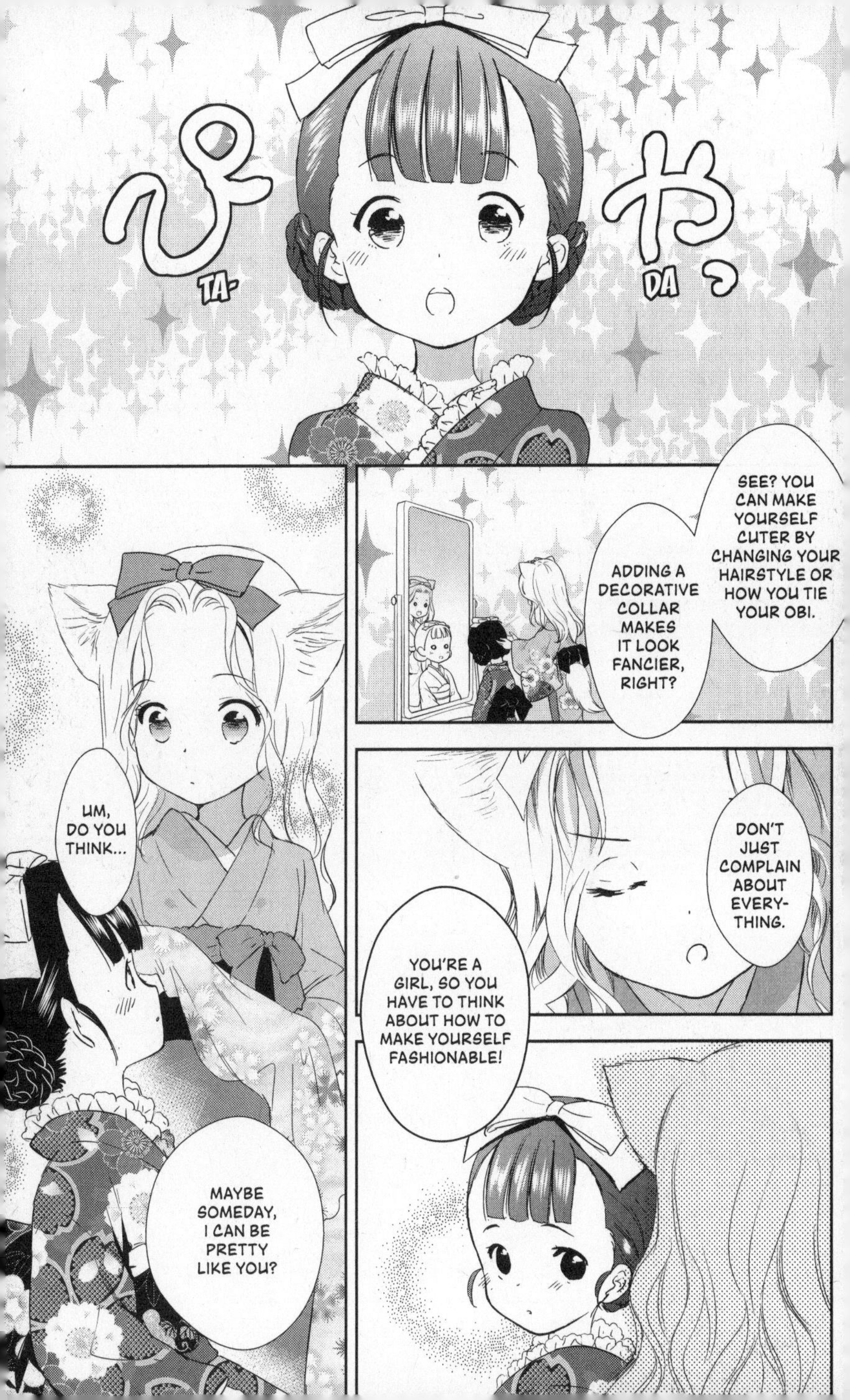
ぴやっ
TA-
DA
SEE? YOU CAN MAKE YOURSELF CUTER BY CHANGING YOUR HAIRSTYLE OR HOW YOU TIE YOUR OBI.
ADDING A DECORATIVE COLLAR MAKES IT LOOK FANCIER, RIGHT?
DON'T JUST COMPLAIN ABOUT EVERY-THING.
YOU'RE A GIRL, SO YOU HAVE TO THINK ABOUT HOW TO MAKE YOURSELF FASHIONABLE!
UM, DO YOU THINK...
MAYBE SOMEDAY, I CAN BE PRETTY LIKE YOU?

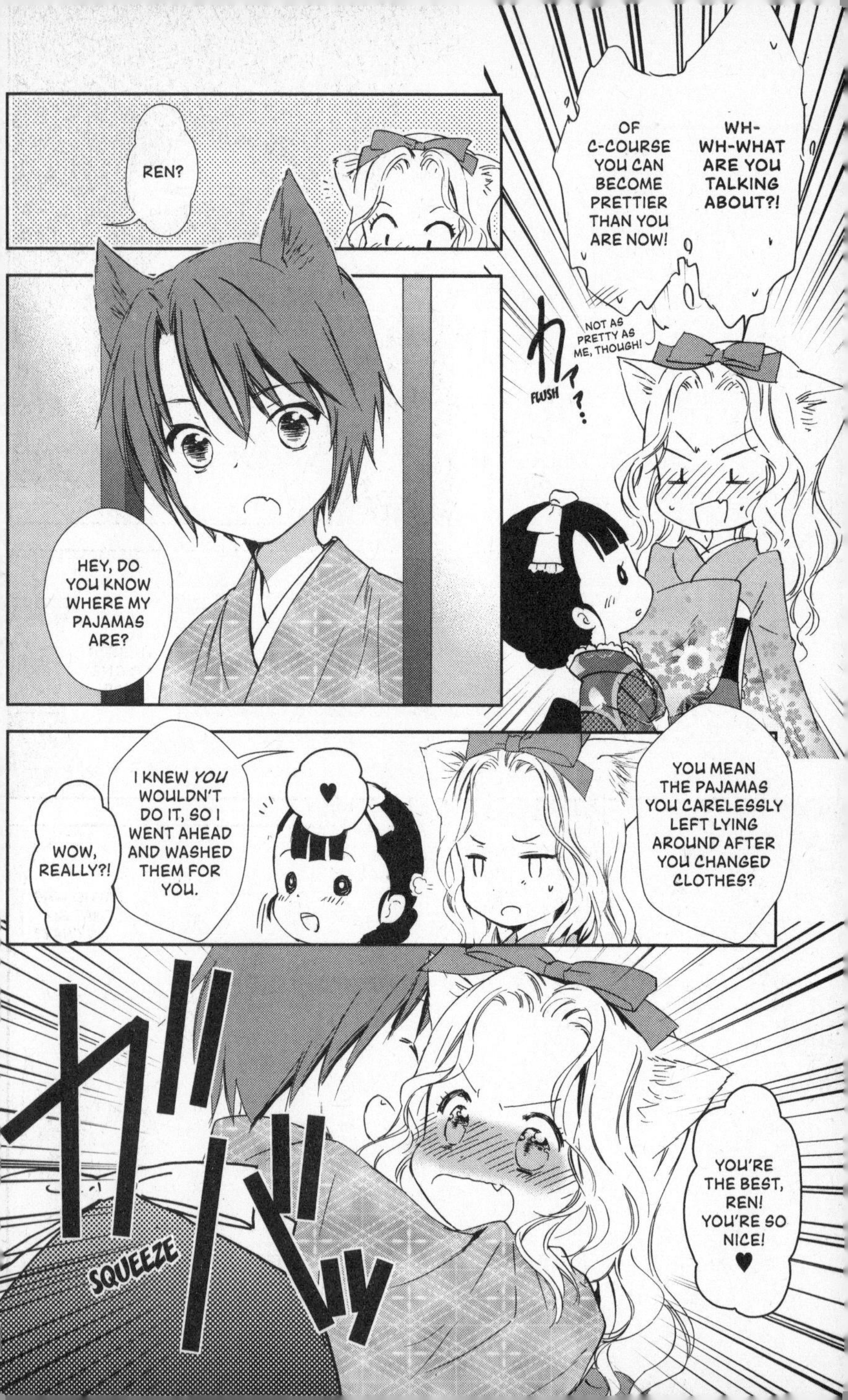
WH- WH-WHAT ARE YOU TALKING ABOUT?!
OF C-COURSE YOU CAN BECOME PRETTIER THAN YOU ARE NOW!
NOT AS PRETTY AS ME, THOUGH!
FLUSH
REN?
HEY, DO YOU KNOW WHERE MY PAJAMAS ARE?
YOU MEAN THE PAJAMAS YOU CARELESSLY LEFT LYING AROUND AFTER YOU CHANGED CLOTHES?
I KNEW *YOU* WOULDN'T DO IT, SO I WENT AHEAD AND WASHED THEM FOR YOU.
WOW, REALLY?!
YOU'RE THE BEST, REN! YOU'RE SO NICE! ♥
SQUEEZE

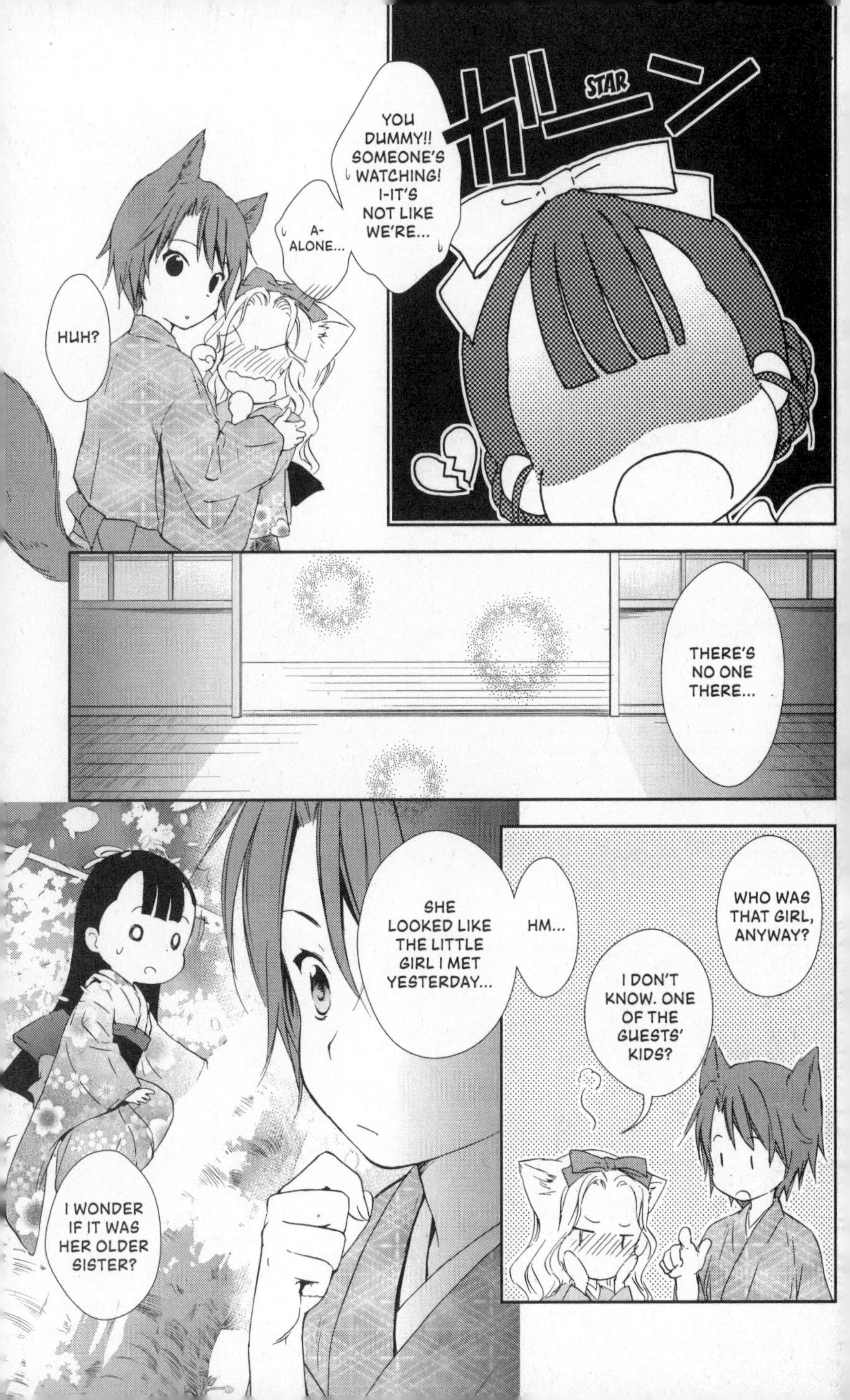
STAR
YOU DUMMY!! SOMEONE'S WATCHING! I-IT'S NOT LIKE WE'RE...
A-ALONE...
HUH?
THERE'S NO ONE THERE...
WHO WAS THAT GIRL, ANYWAY?
I DON'T KNOW. ONE OF THE GUESTS' KIDS?
HM...
SHE LOOKED LIKE THE LITTLE GIRL I MET YESTERDAY...
I WONDER IF IT WAS HER OLDER SISTER?

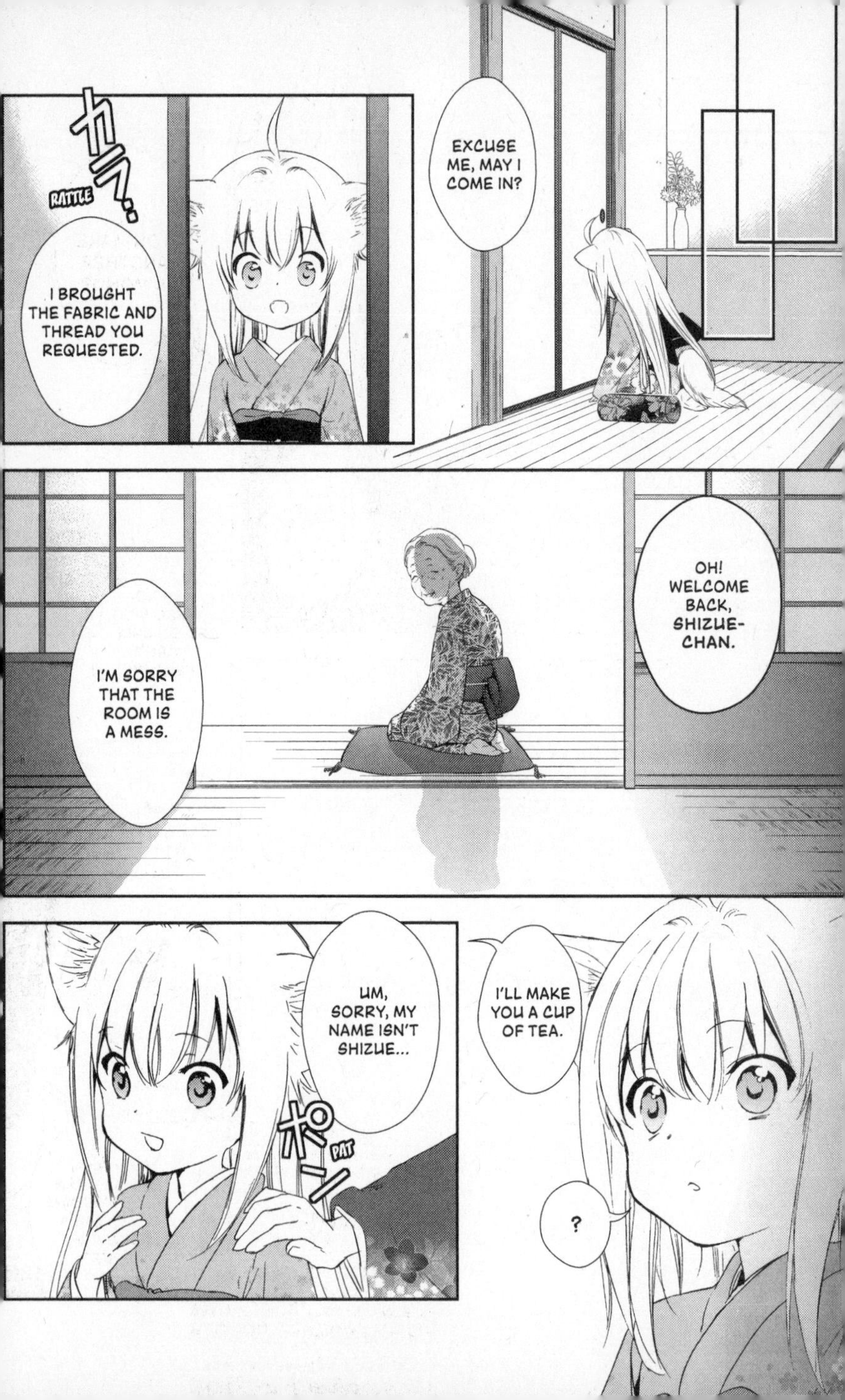
EXCUSE ME, MAY I COME IN?
RATTLE
I BROUGHT THE FABRIC AND THREAD YOU REQUESTED.
OH! WELCOME BACK, SHIZUE-CHAN.
I'M SORRY THAT THE ROOM IS A MESS.
I'LL MAKE YOU A CUP OF TEA.
?
UM, SORRY, MY NAME ISN'T SHIZUE...
PAT

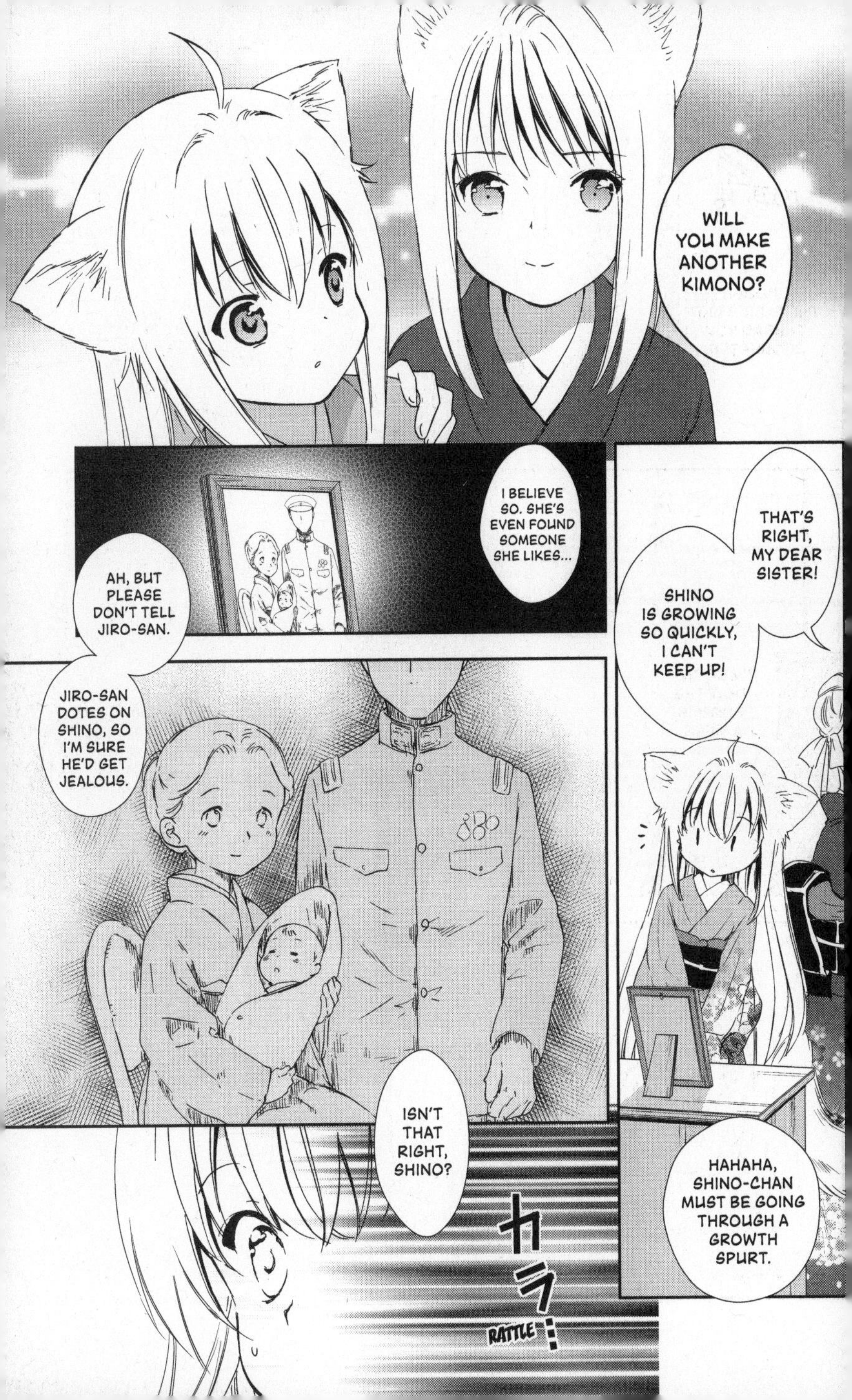
WILL YOU MAKE ANOTHER KIMONO?
THAT'S RIGHT, MY DEAR SISTER!
SHINO IS GROWING SO QUICKLY, I CAN'T KEEP UP!
HAHAHA, SHINO-CHAN MUST BE GOING THROUGH A GROWTH SPURT.
I BELIEVE SO. SHE'S EVEN FOUND SOMEONE SHE LIKES...
AH, BUT PLEASE DON'T TELL JIRO-SAN.
JIRO-SAN DOTES ON SHINO, SO I'M SURE HE'D GET JEALOUS.
ISN'T THAT RIGHT, SHINO?
カラ
RATTLE

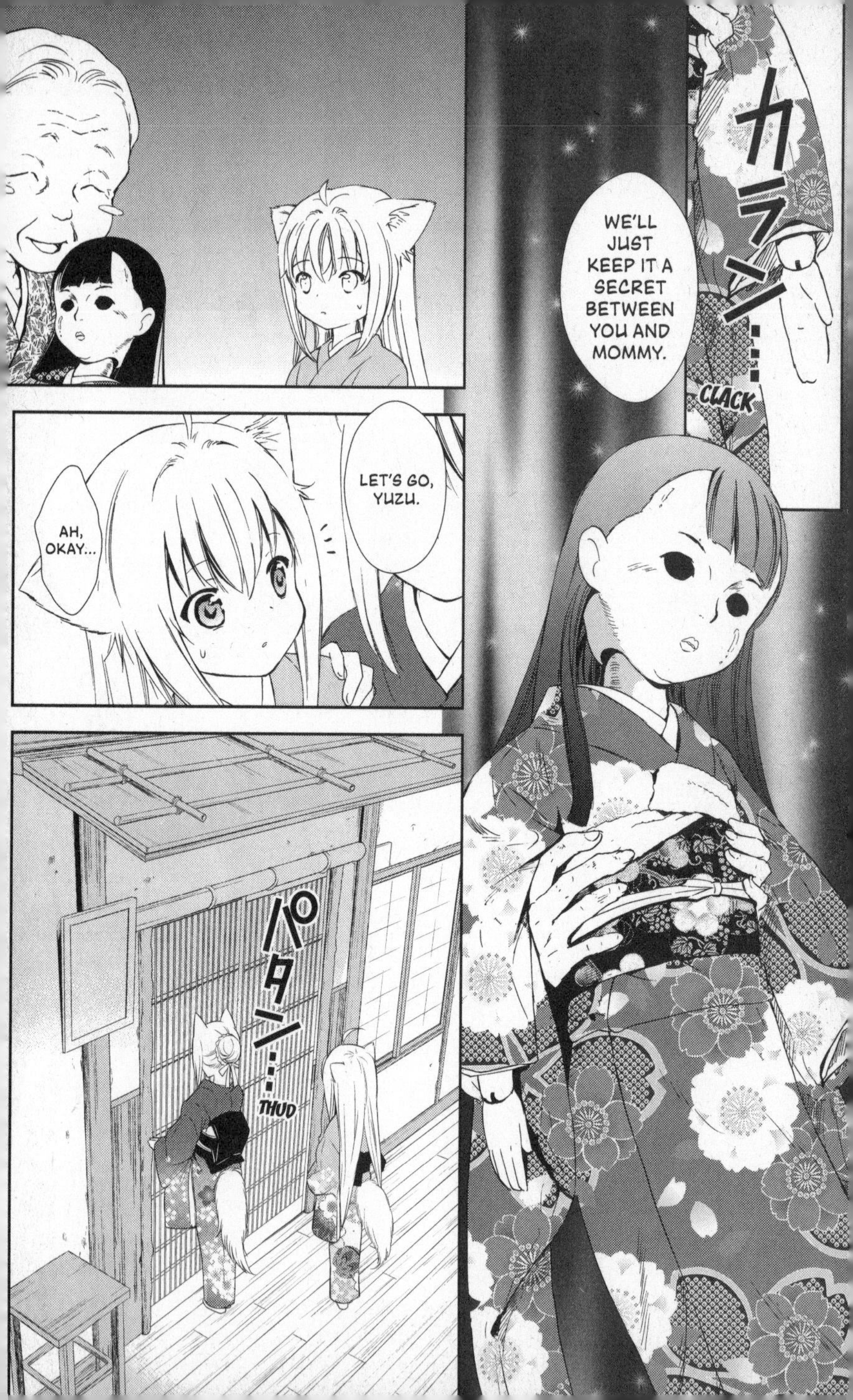
カラン…
CLACK
WE'LL JUST KEEP IT A SECRET BETWEEN YOU AND MOMMY.
LET'S GO, YUZU.
AH, OKAY...
パタン…
THUD

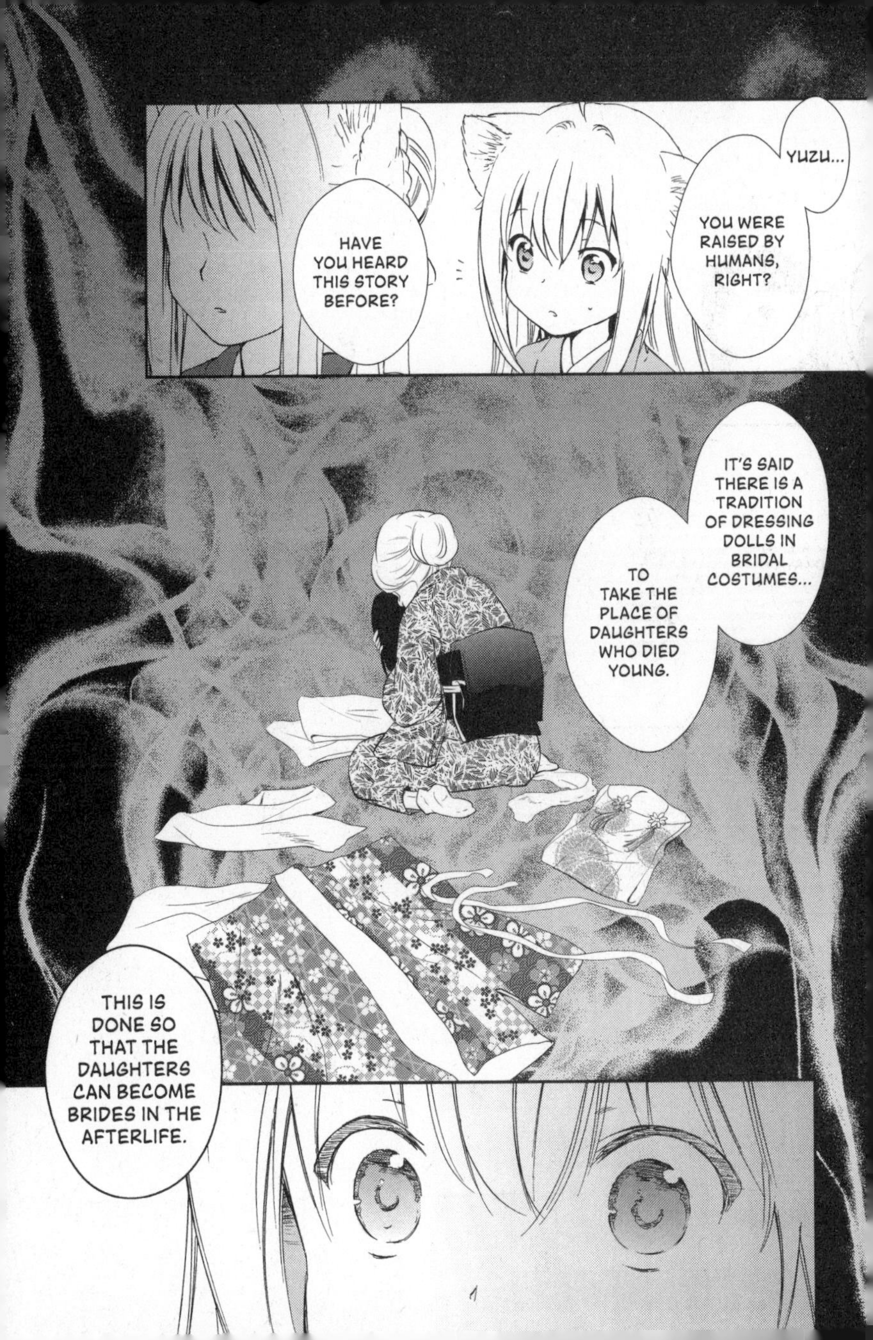
YUZU... YOU WERE RAISED BY HUMANS, RIGHT?
HAVE YOU HEARD THIS STORY BEFORE?
IT'S SAID THERE IS A TRADITION OF DRESSING DOLLS IN BRIDAL COSTUMES...
TO TAKE THE PLACE OF DAUGHTERS WHO DIED YOUNG.
THIS IS DONE SO THAT THE DAUGHTERS CAN BECOME BRIDES IN THE AFTERLIFE.

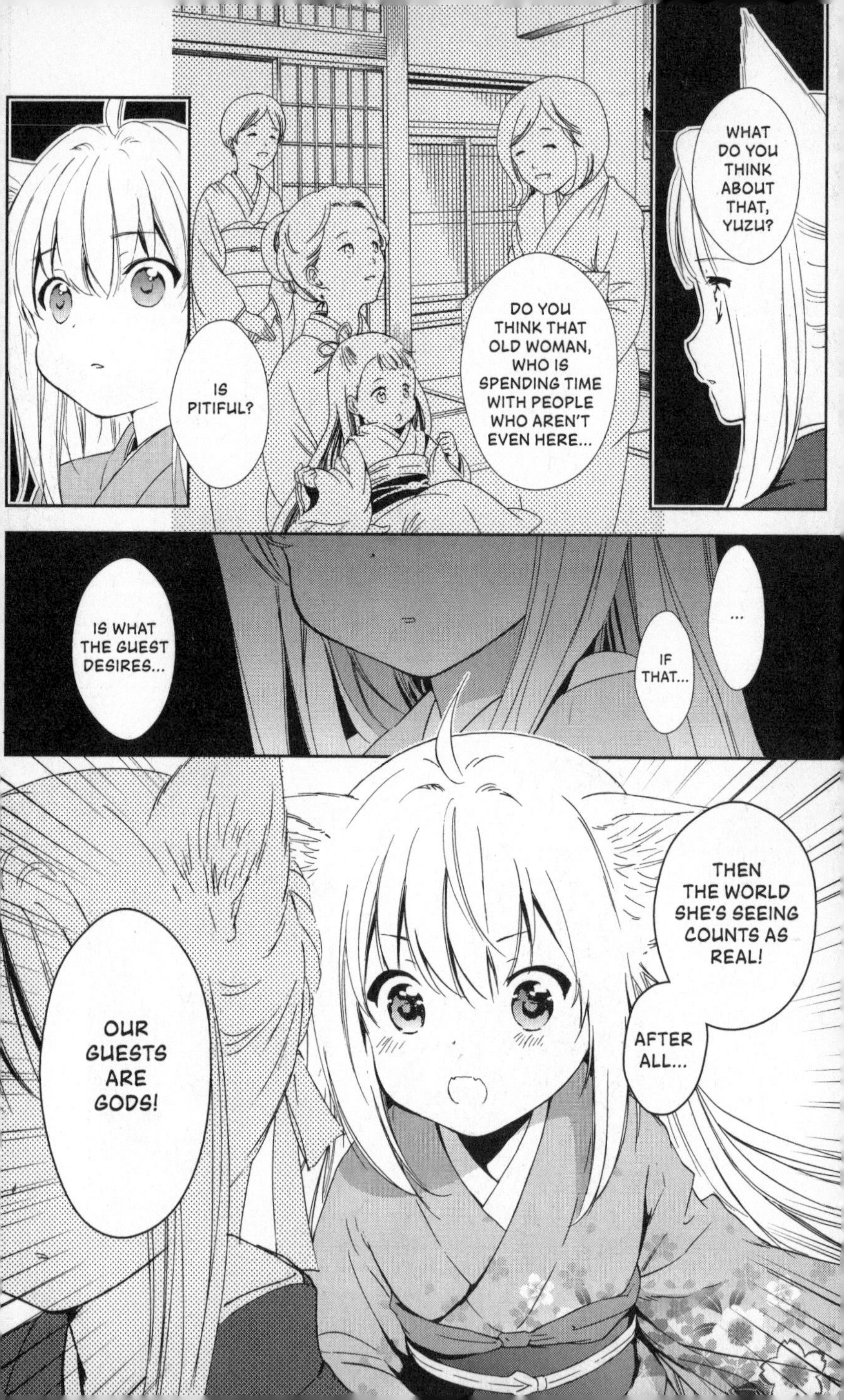
WHAT DO YOU THINK ABOUT THAT, YUZU?
DO YOU THINK THAT OLD WOMAN, WHO IS SPENDING TIME WITH PEOPLE WHO AREN'T EVEN HERE...
IS PITIFUL?
...
IF THAT...
IS WHAT THE GUEST DESIRES...
THEN THE WORLD SHE'S SEEING COUNTS AS REAL!
AFTER ALL...
OUR GUESTS ARE GODS!

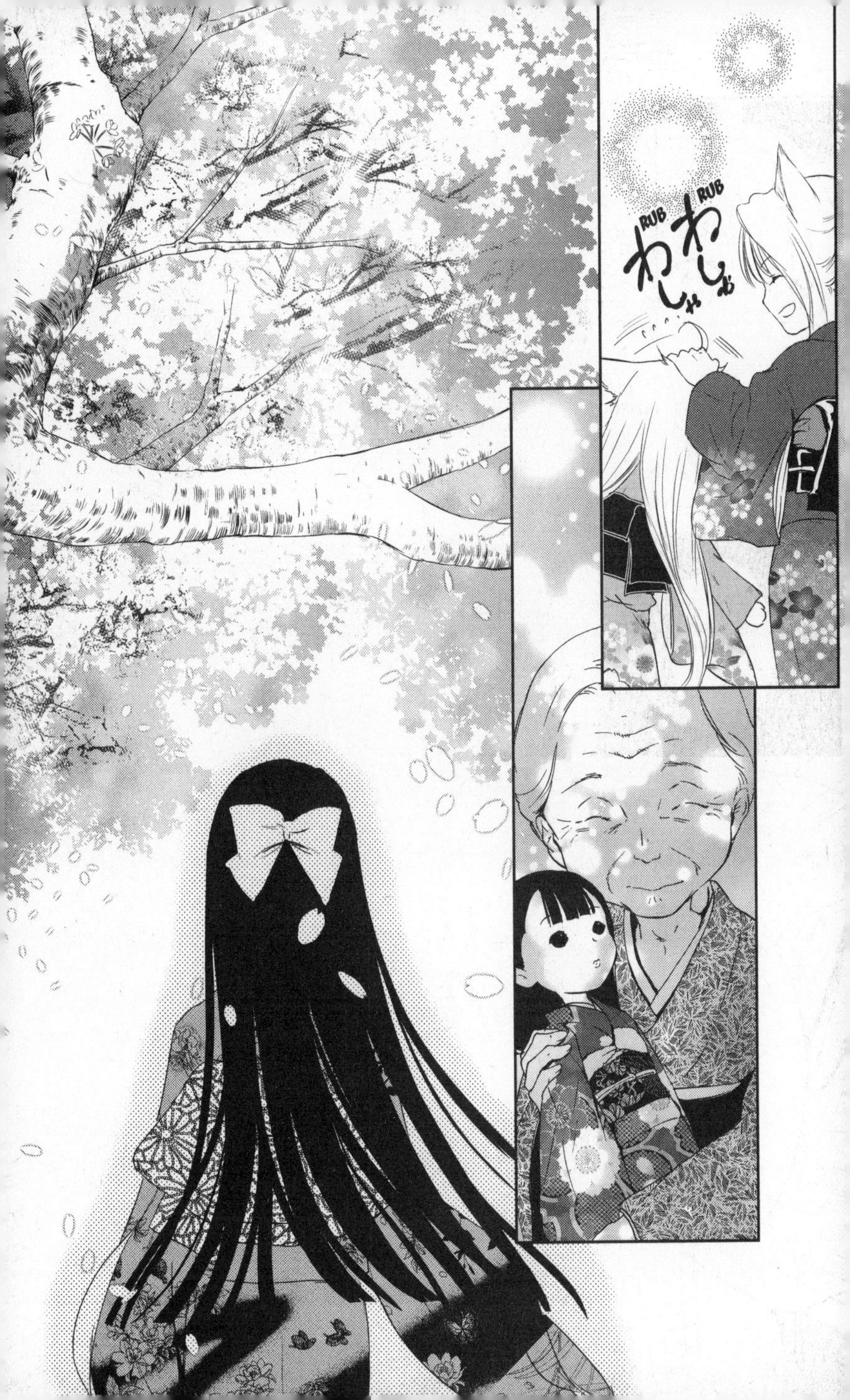
RUB RUB

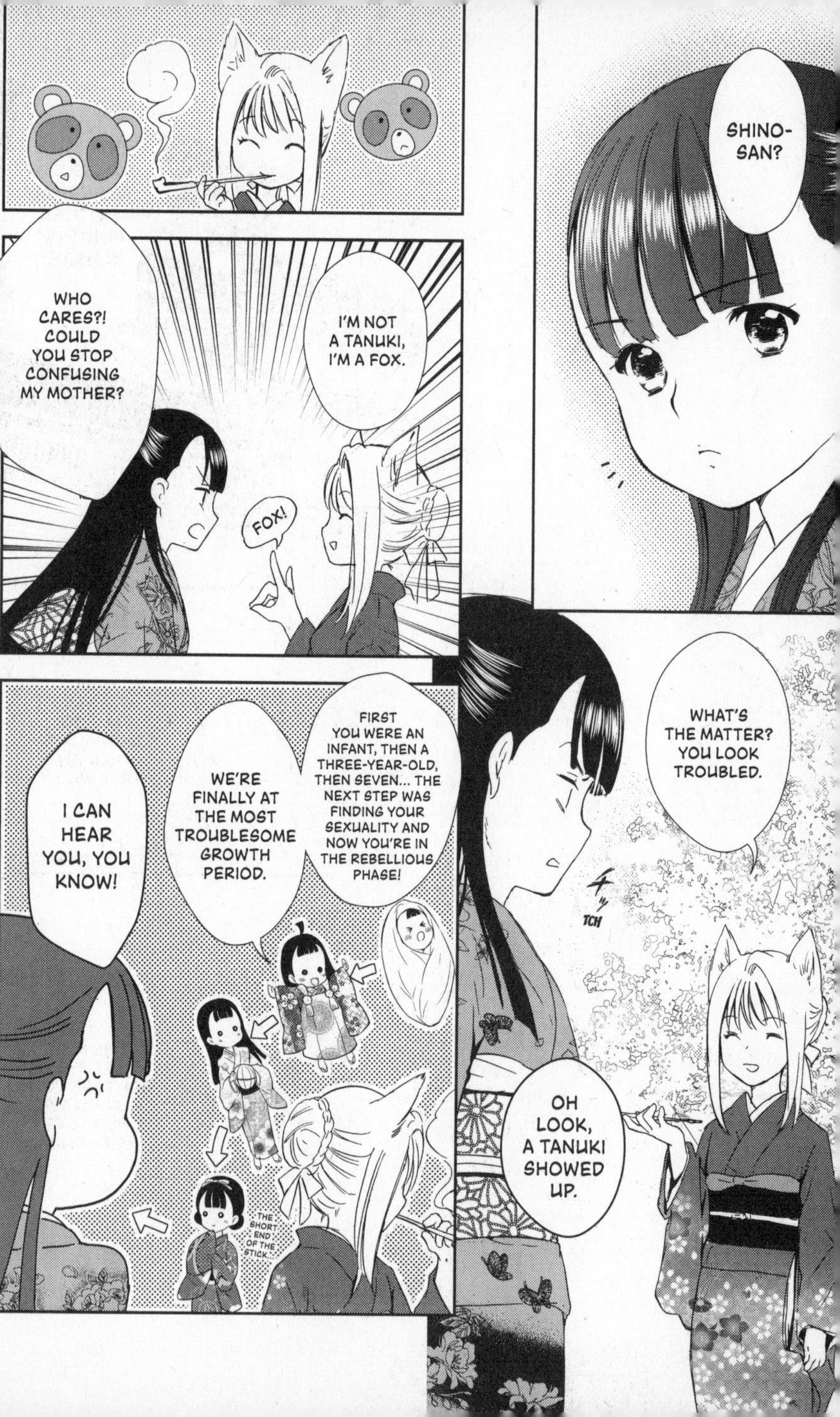
SHINO-SAN?
WHAT'S THE MATTER? YOU LOOK TROUBLED.
TCH
OH LOOK, A TANUKI SHOWED UP.
I'M NOT A TANUKI, I'M A FOX.
WHO CARES?! COULD YOU STOP CONFUSING MY MOTHER?
FOX!
FIRST YOU WERE AN INFANT, THEN A THREE-YEAR-OLD, THEN SEVEN... THE NEXT STEP WAS FINDING YOUR SEXUALITY AND NOW YOU'RE IN THE REBELLIOUS PHASE!
WE'RE FINALLY AT THE MOST TROUBLESOME GROWTH PERIOD.
I CAN HEAR YOU, YOU KNOW!
THE SHORT END OF THE STICK...

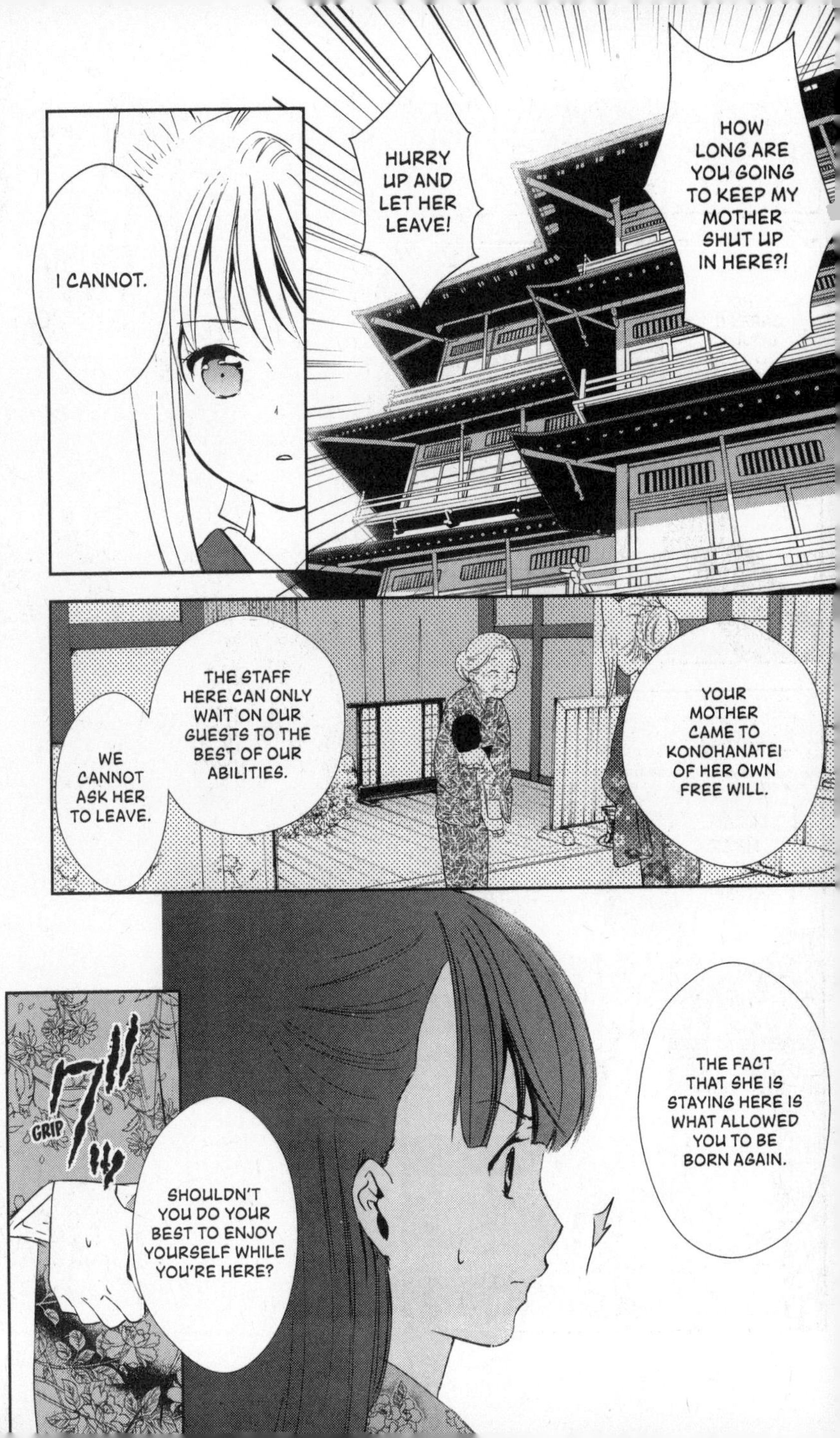
HOW LONG ARE YOU GOING TO KEEP MY MOTHER SHUT UP IN HERE?!
HURRY UP AND LET HER LEAVE!
I CANNOT.
YOUR MOTHER CAME TO KONOHANATEI OF HER OWN FREE WILL.
THE STAFF HERE CAN ONLY WAIT ON OUR GUESTS TO THE BEST OF OUR ABILITIES.
WE CANNOT ASK HER TO LEAVE.
THE FACT THAT SHE IS STAYING HERE IS WHAT ALLOWED YOU TO BE BORN AGAIN.
SHOULDN'T YOU DO YOUR BEST TO ENJOY YOURSELF WHILE YOU'RE HERE?
GRIP

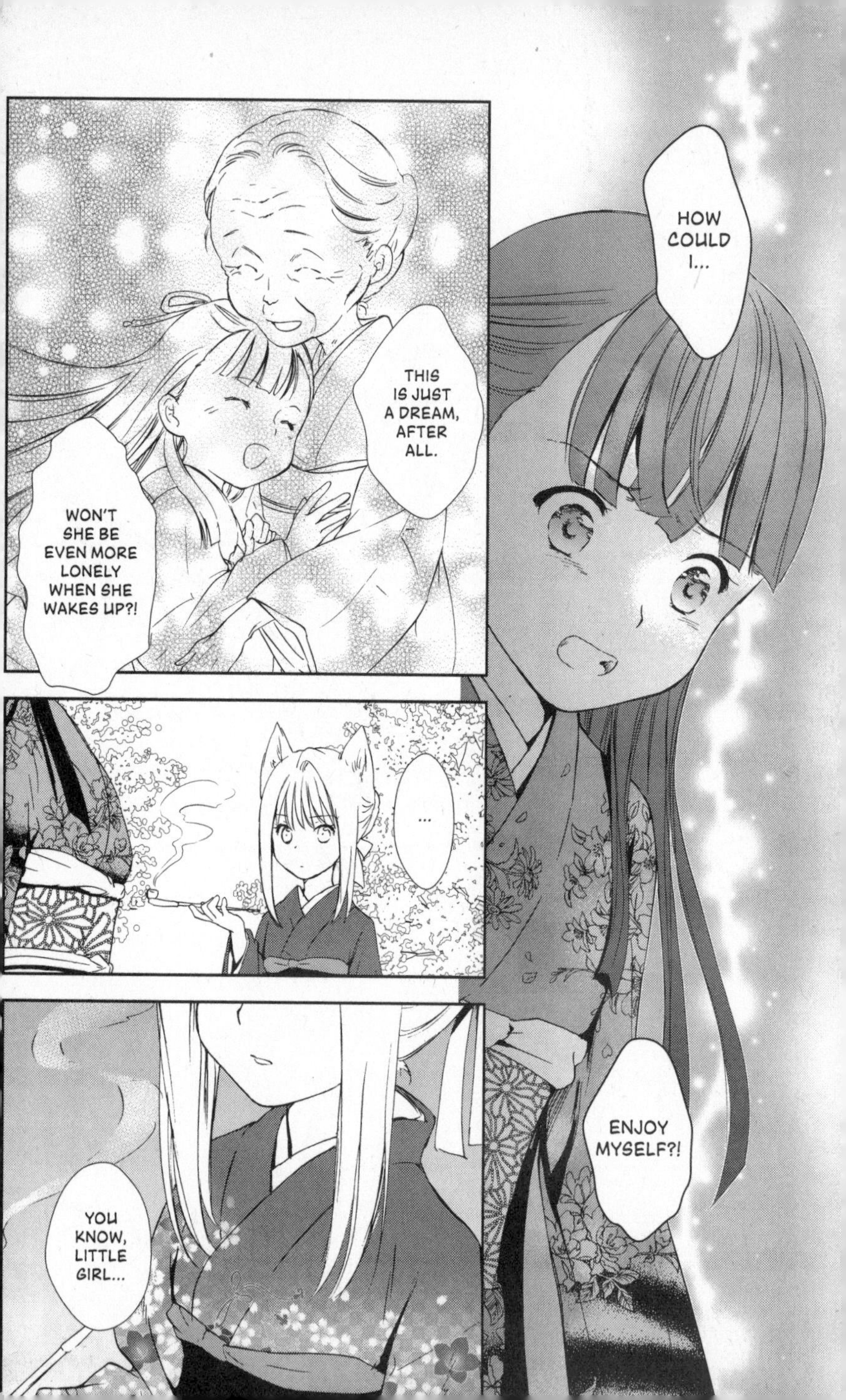
HOW COULD I...
ENJOY MYSELF?!
THIS IS JUST A DREAM, AFTER ALL.
WON'T SHE BE EVEN MORE LONELY WHEN SHE WAKES UP?!
...
YOU KNOW, LITTLE GIRL...

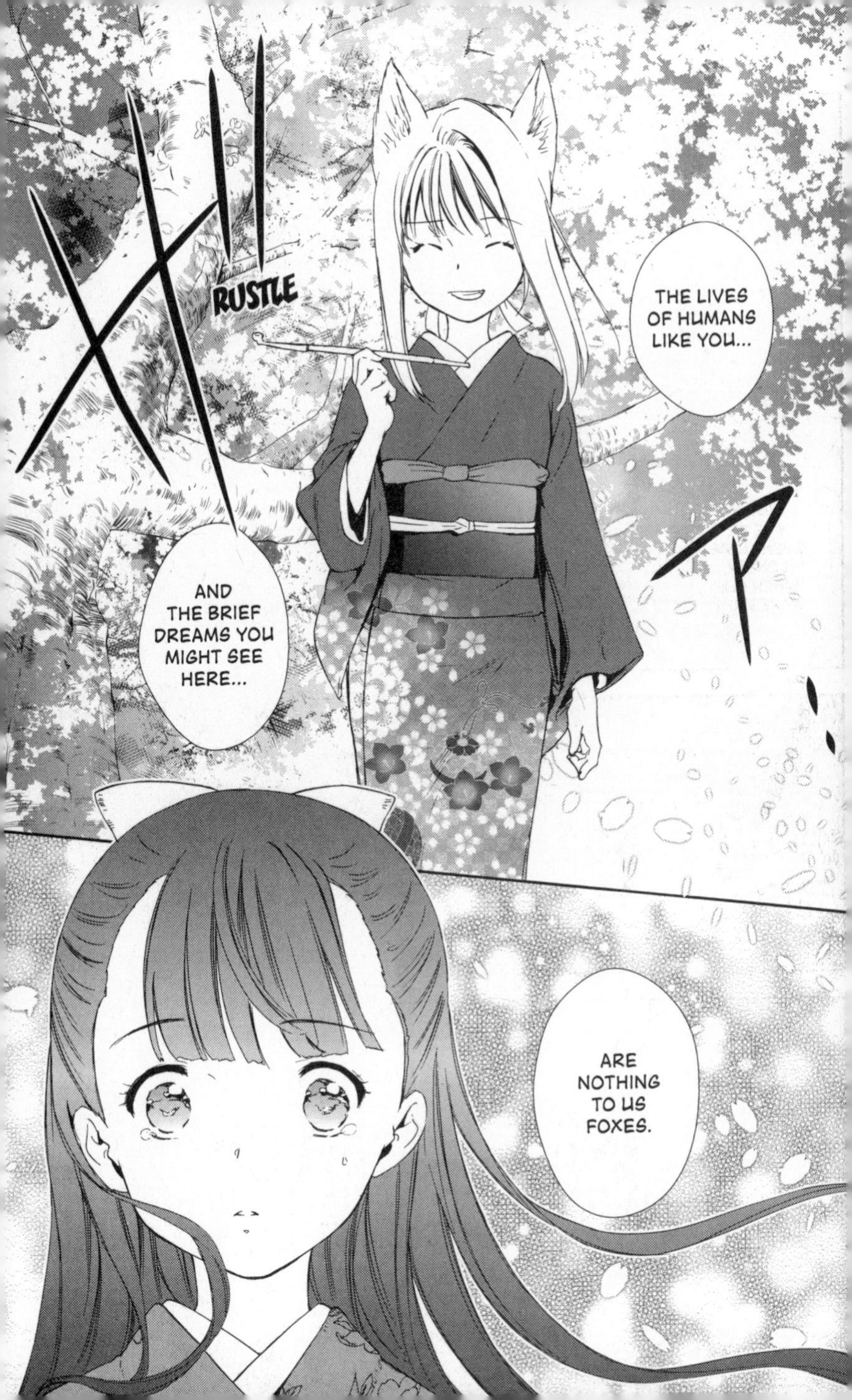
THE LIVES OF HUMANS LIKE YOU...
RUSTLE
AND THE BRIEF DREAMS YOU MIGHT SEE HERE...
ARE NOTHING TO US FOXES.

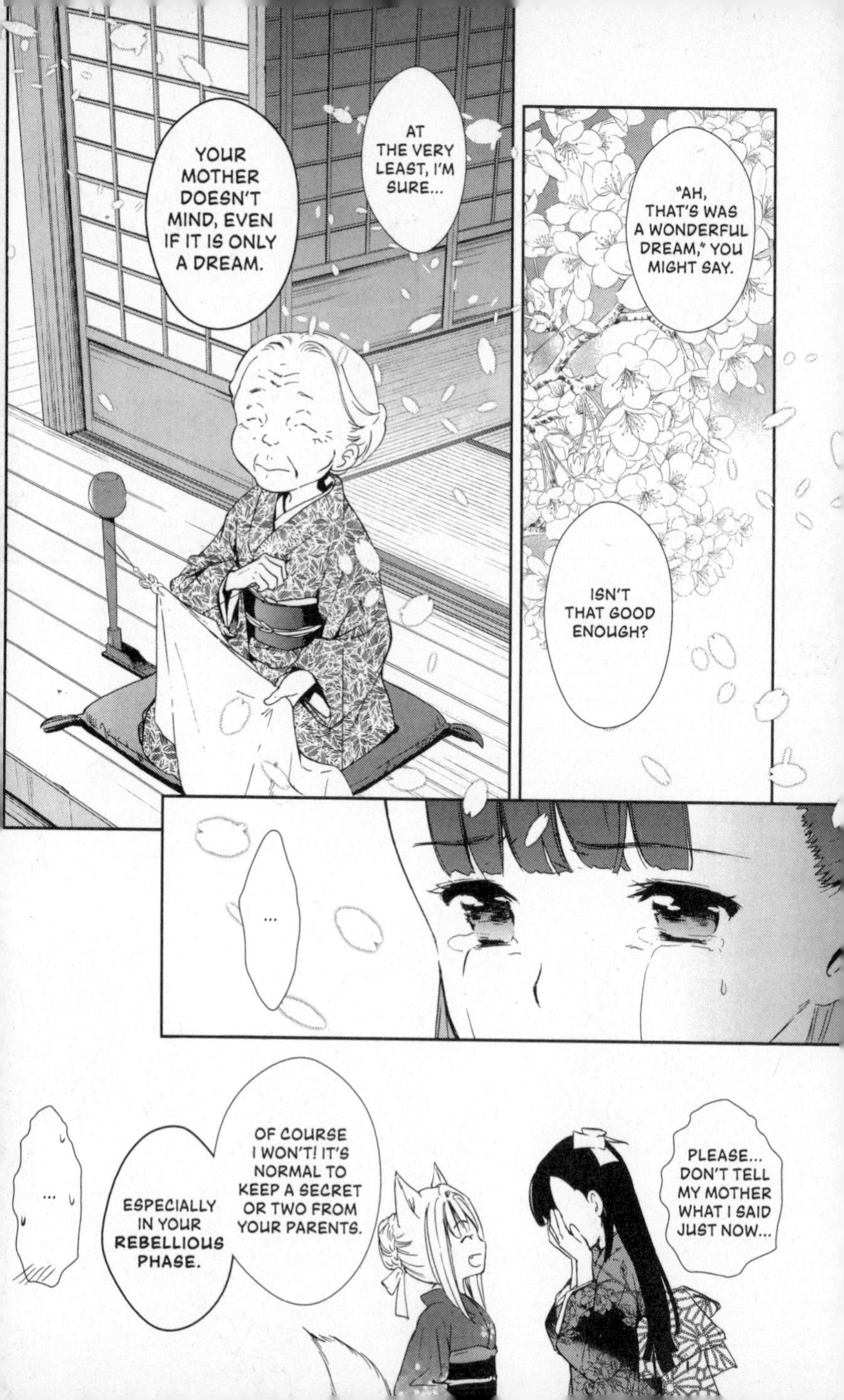
"AH, THAT'S WAS A WONDERFUL DREAM," YOU MIGHT SAY.
ISN'T THAT GOOD ENOUGH?
AT THE VERY LEAST, I'M SURE...
YOUR MOTHER DOESN'T MIND, EVEN IF IT IS ONLY A DREAM.
...
PLEASE... DON'T TELL MY MOTHER WHAT I SAID JUST NOW...
OF COURSE I WON'T! IT'S NORMAL TO KEEP A SECRET OR TWO FROM YOUR PARENTS.
ESPECIALLY IN YOUR REBELLIOUS PHASE.
...

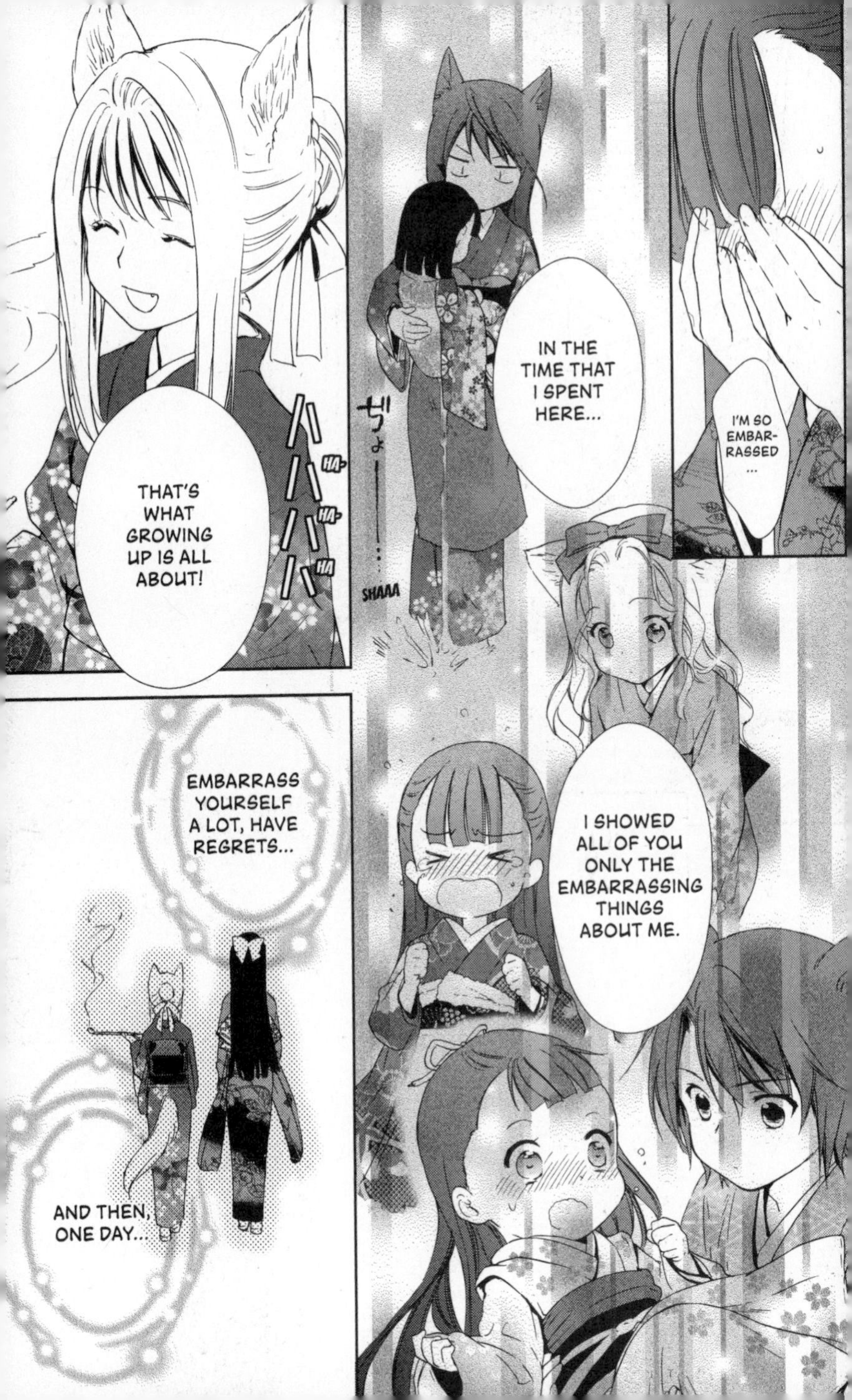
I'M SO EMBARRASSED...
IN THE TIME THAT I SPENT HERE...
SHAAA
I SHOWED ALL OF YOU ONLY THE EMBARRASSING THINGS ABOUT ME.
HA HA HA
THAT'S WHAT GROWING UP IS ALL ABOUT!
EMBARRASS YOURSELF A LOT, HAVE REGRETS...
AND THEN, ONE DAY...

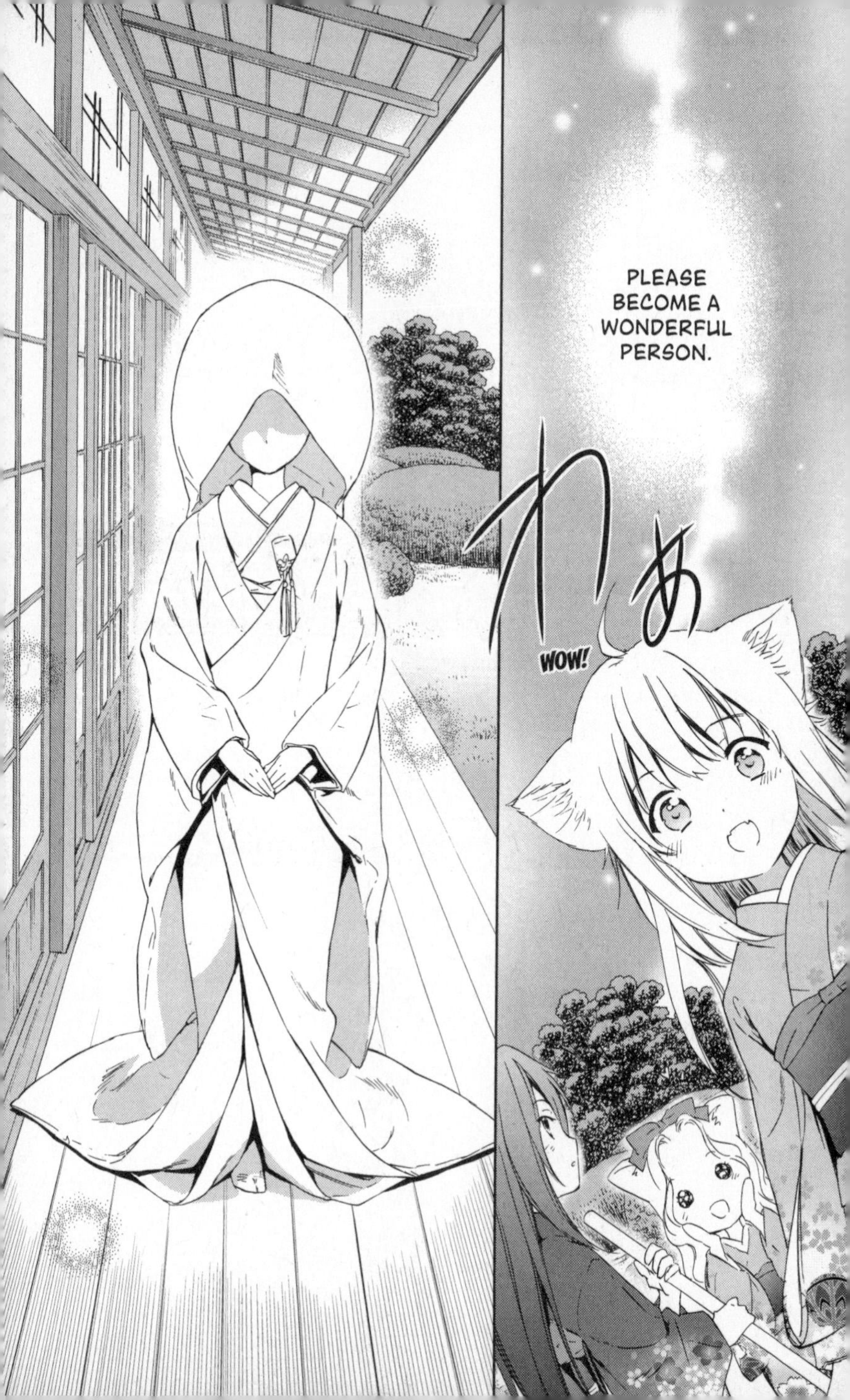
PLEASE BECOME A WONDERFUL PERSON.
わあ
WOW!

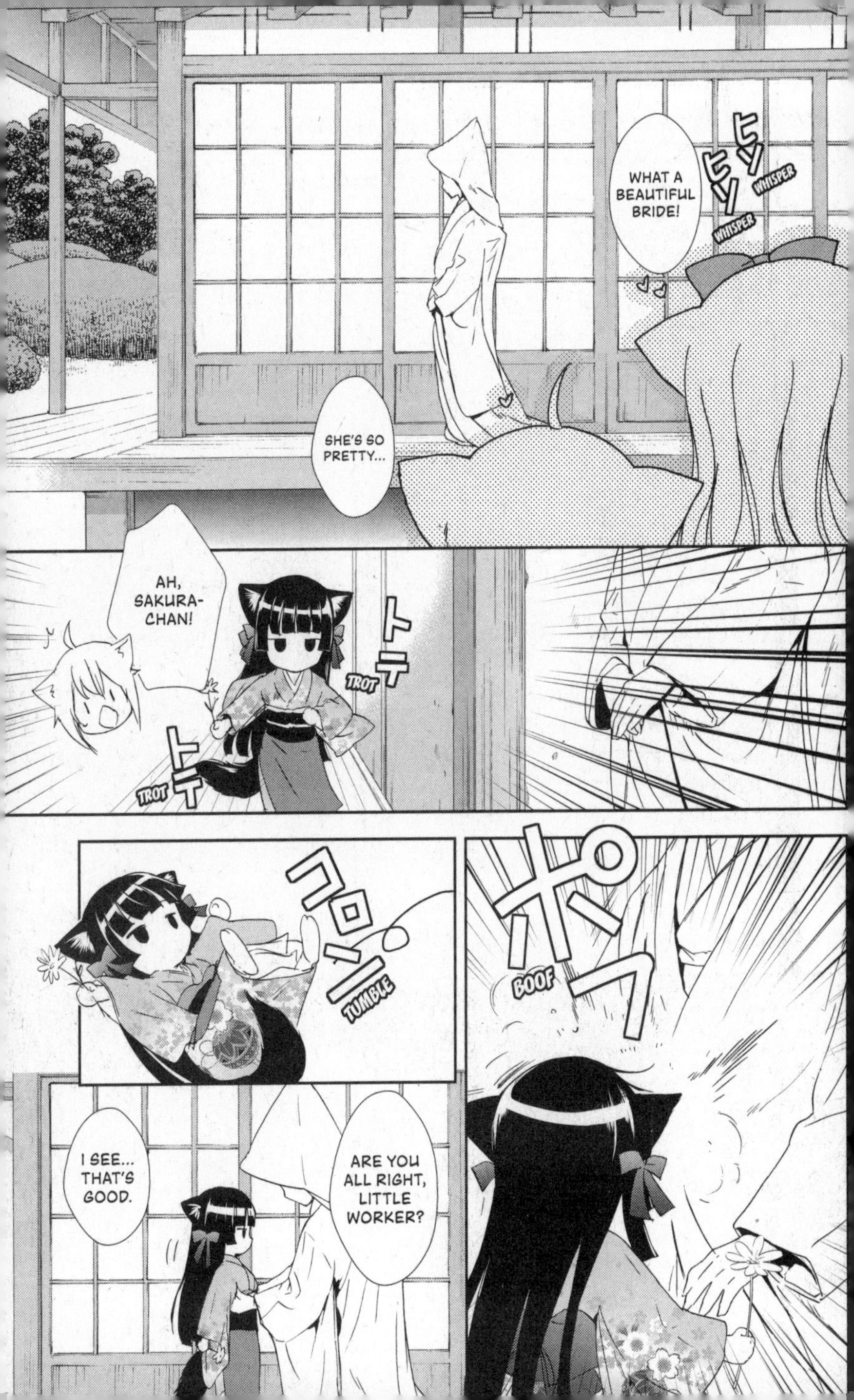
ヒソ
WHISPER
ヒソ
WHISPER
WHAT A BEAUTIFUL BRIDE!
SHE'S SO PRETTY...
AH, SAKURA-CHAN!
トテ
TROT
トテ
TROT
ポフ
BOOF
コロン
TUMBLE
ARE YOU ALL RIGHT, LITTLE WORKER?
I SEE... THAT'S GOOD.

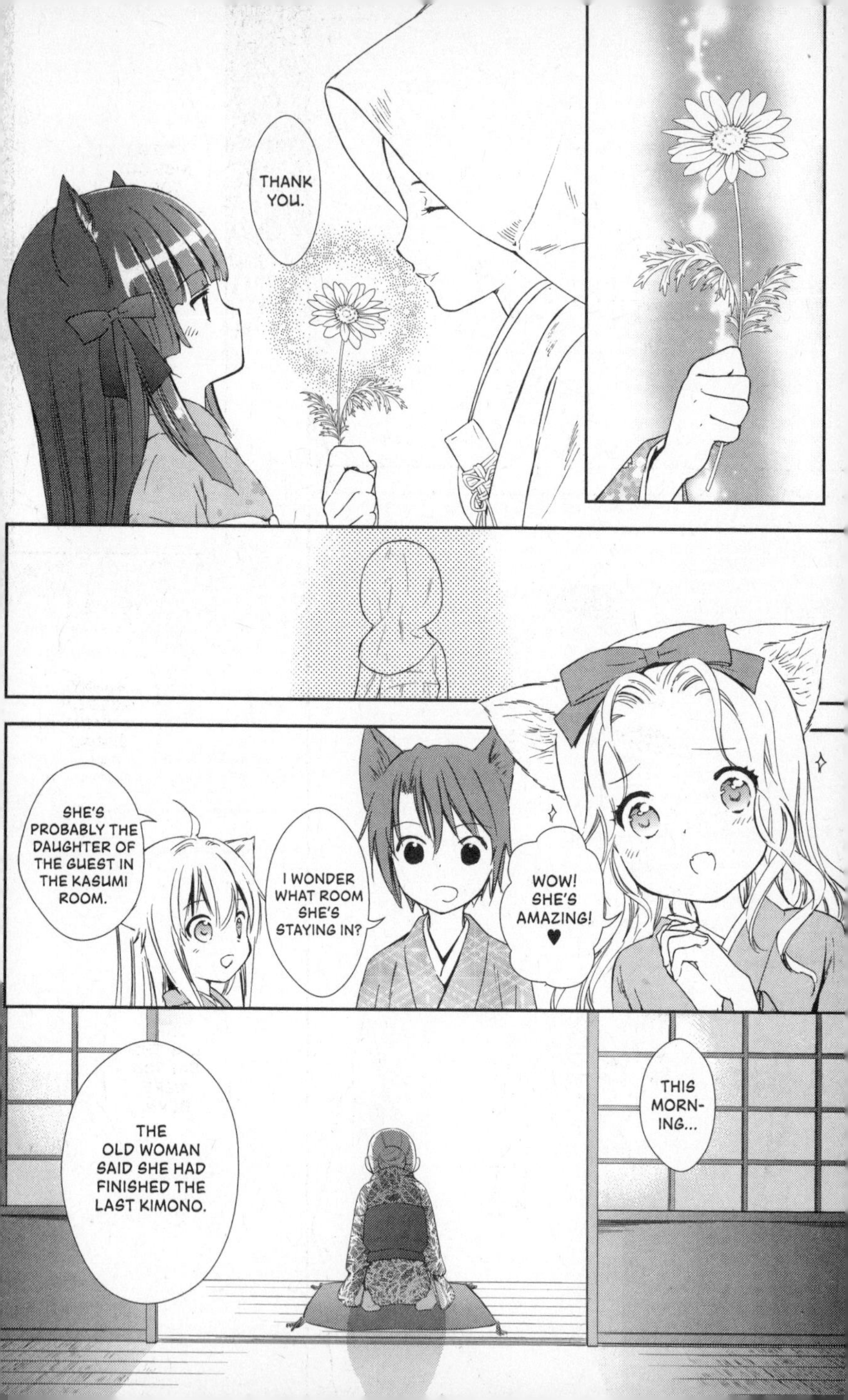
THANK YOU.
WOW! SHE'S AMAZING! ♥
I WONDER WHAT ROOM SHE'S STAYING IN?
SHE'S PROBABLY THE DAUGHTER OF THE GUEST IN THE KASUMI ROOM.
THIS MORN-ING...
THE OLD WOMAN SAID SHE HAD FINISHED THE LAST KIMONO.

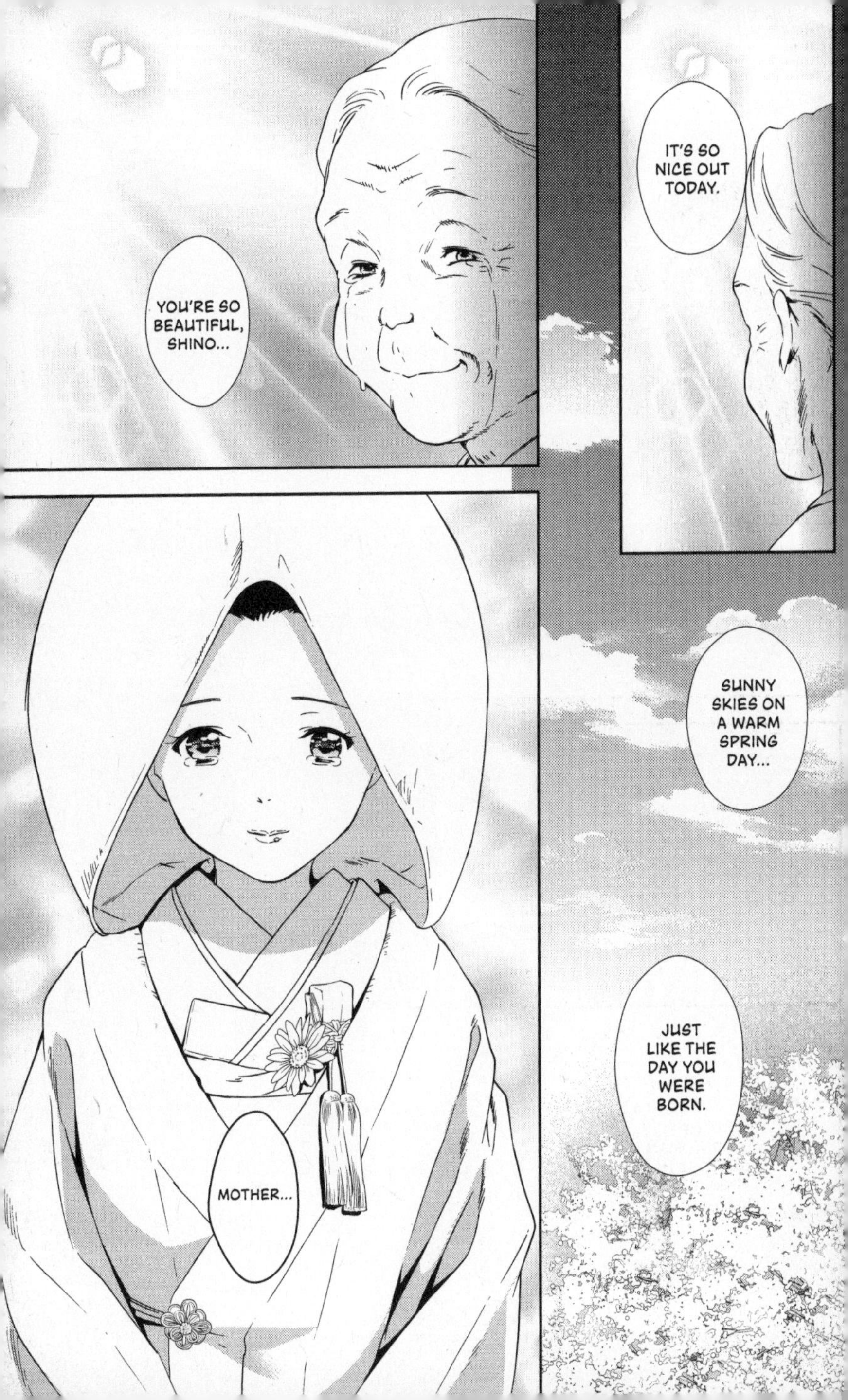
IT'S SO NICE OUT TODAY.
YOU'RE SO BEAUTIFUL, SHINO...
SUNNY SKIES ON A WARM SPRING DAY...
JUST LIKE THE DAY YOU WERE BORN.
MOTHER...

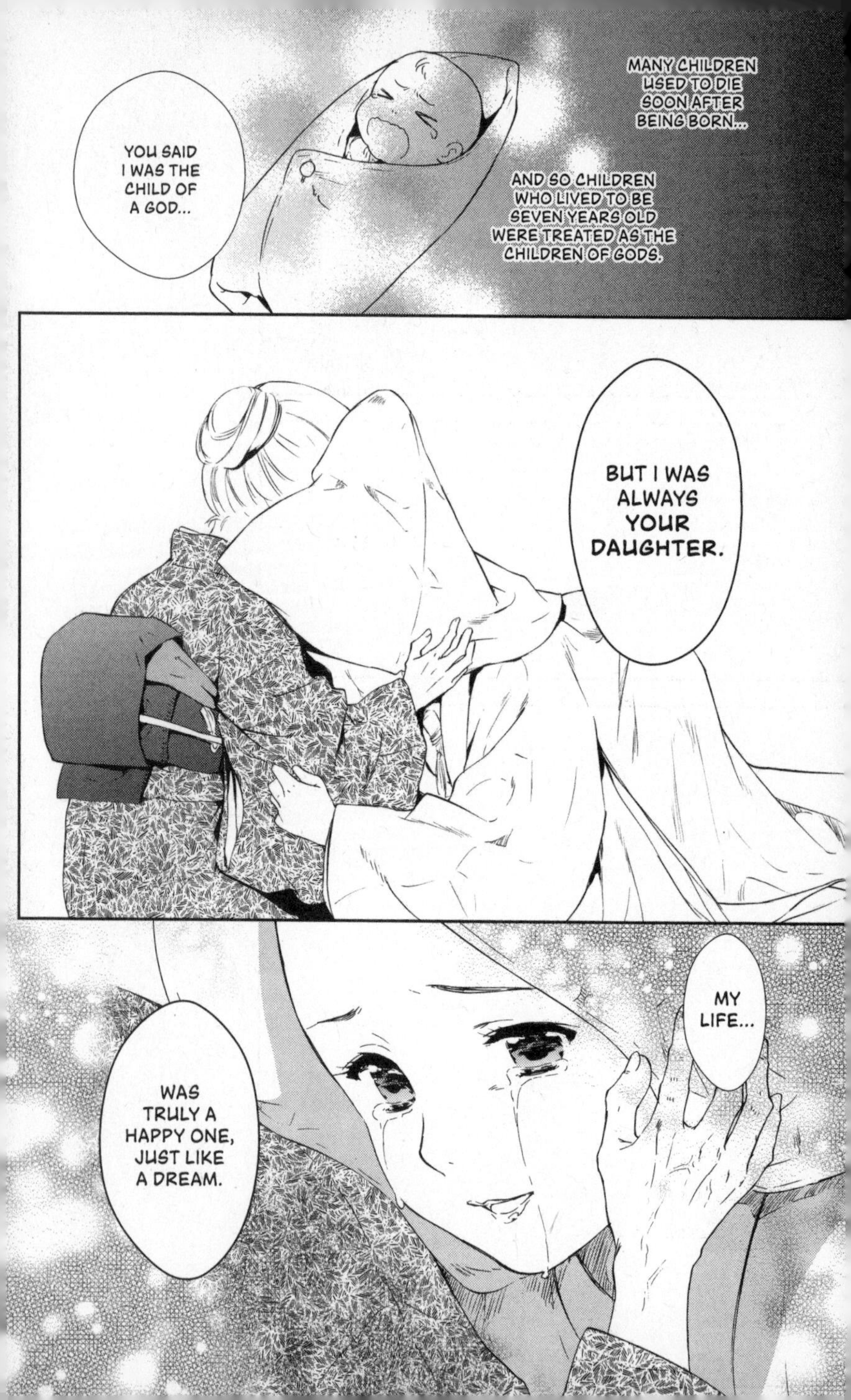
MANY CHILDREN USED TO DIE SOON AFTER BEING BORN...
AND SO CHILDREN WHO LIVED TO BE SEVEN YEARS OLD WERE TREATED AS THE CHILDREN OF GODS.
YOU SAID I WAS THE CHILD OF A GOD...
BUT I WAS ALWAYS YOUR DAUGHTER.
MY LIFE...
WAS TRULY A HAPPY ONE, JUST LIKE A DREAM.

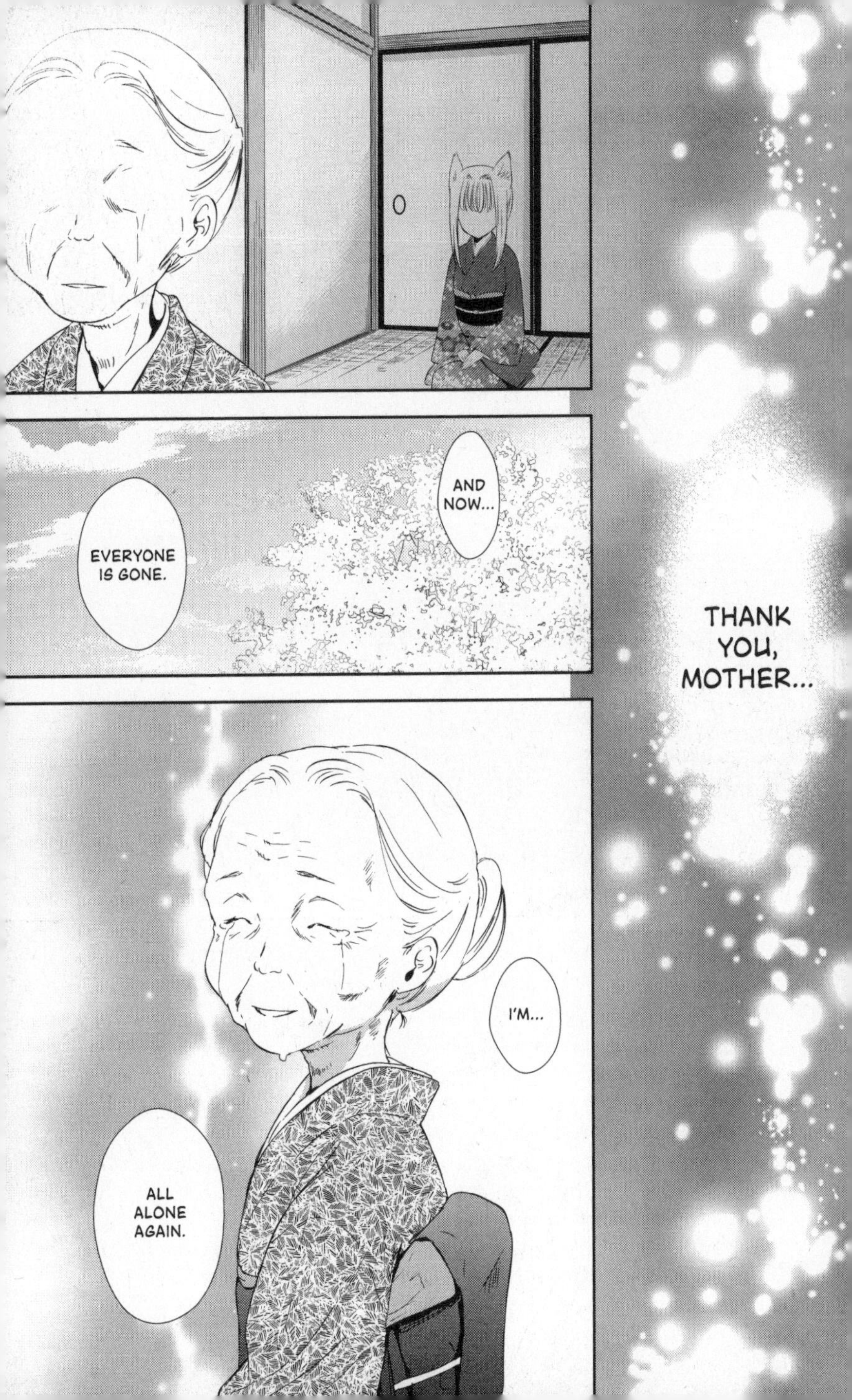
THANK YOU, MOTHER...
AND NOW...
EVERYONE IS GONE.
I'M...
ALL ALONE AGAIN.

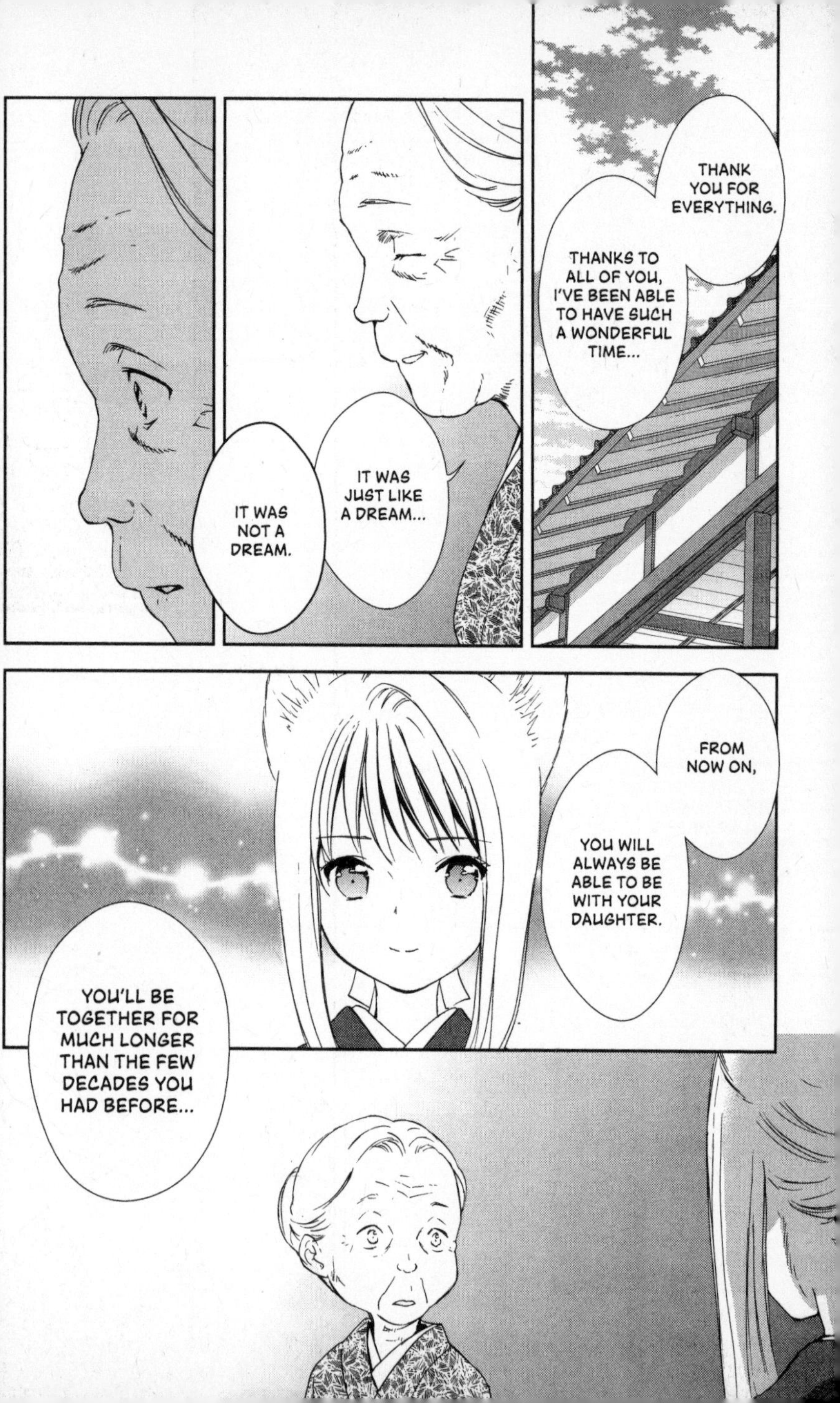
THANK YOU FOR EVERYTHING.
THANKS TO ALL OF YOU, I'VE BEEN ABLE TO HAVE SUCH A WONDERFUL TIME...
IT WAS JUST LIKE A DREAM...
IT WAS NOT A DREAM.
FROM NOW ON,
YOU WILL ALWAYS BE ABLE TO BE WITH YOUR DAUGHTER.
YOU'LL BE TOGETHER FOR MUCH LONGER THAN THE FEW DECADES YOU HAD BEFORE...

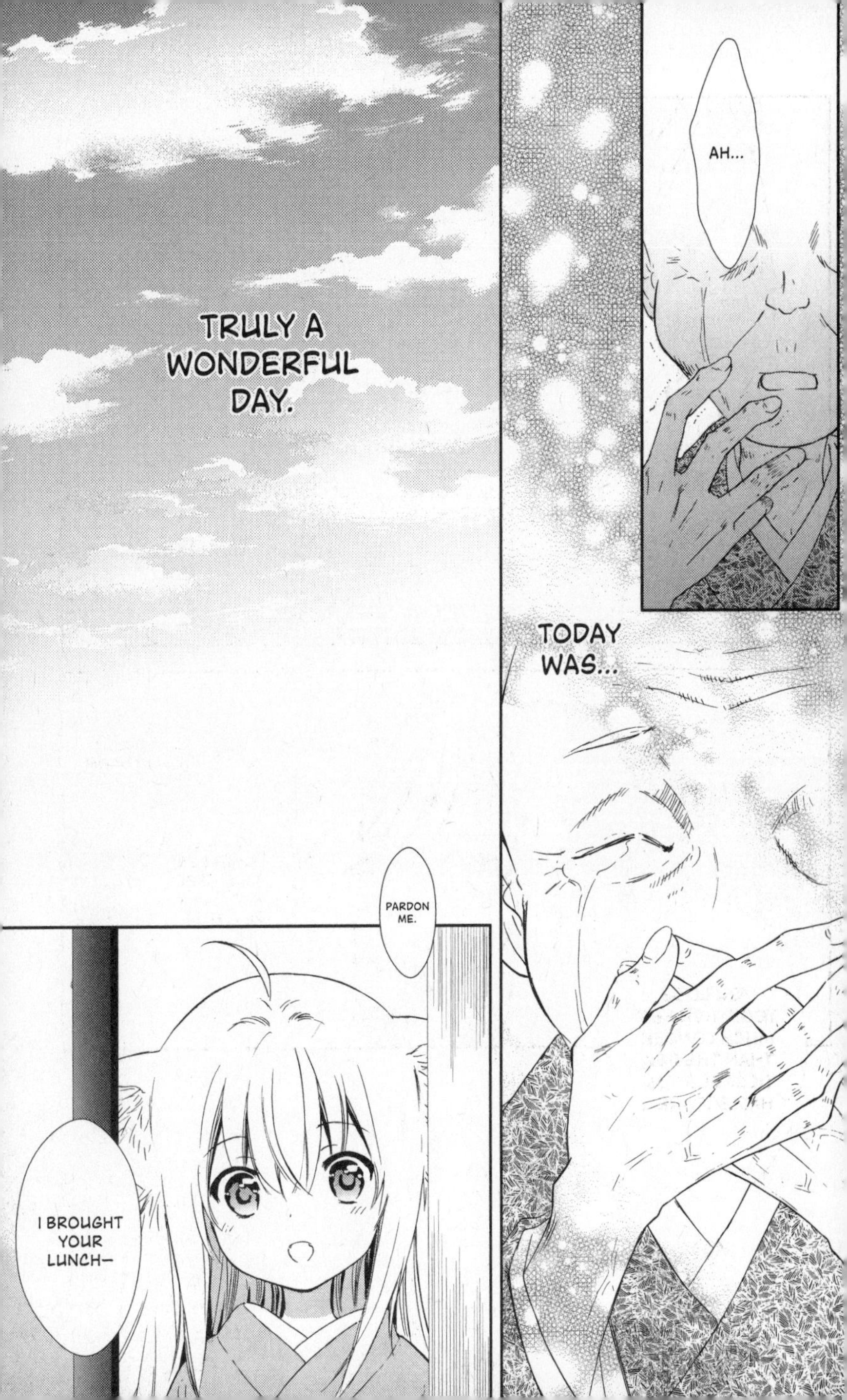
AH...
TODAY WAS...
TRULY A WONDERFUL DAY.
PARDON ME.
I BROUGHT YOUR LUNCH—

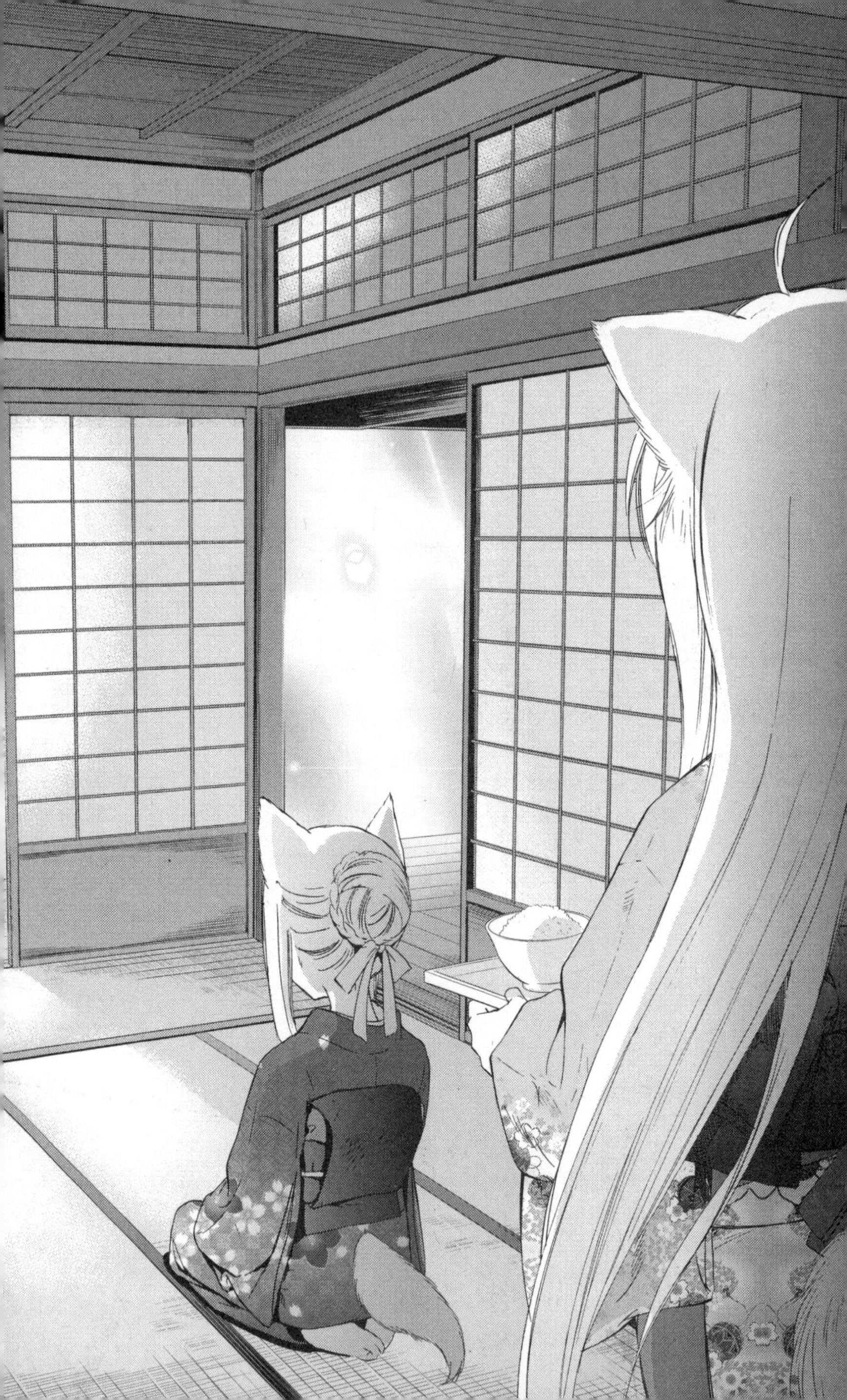

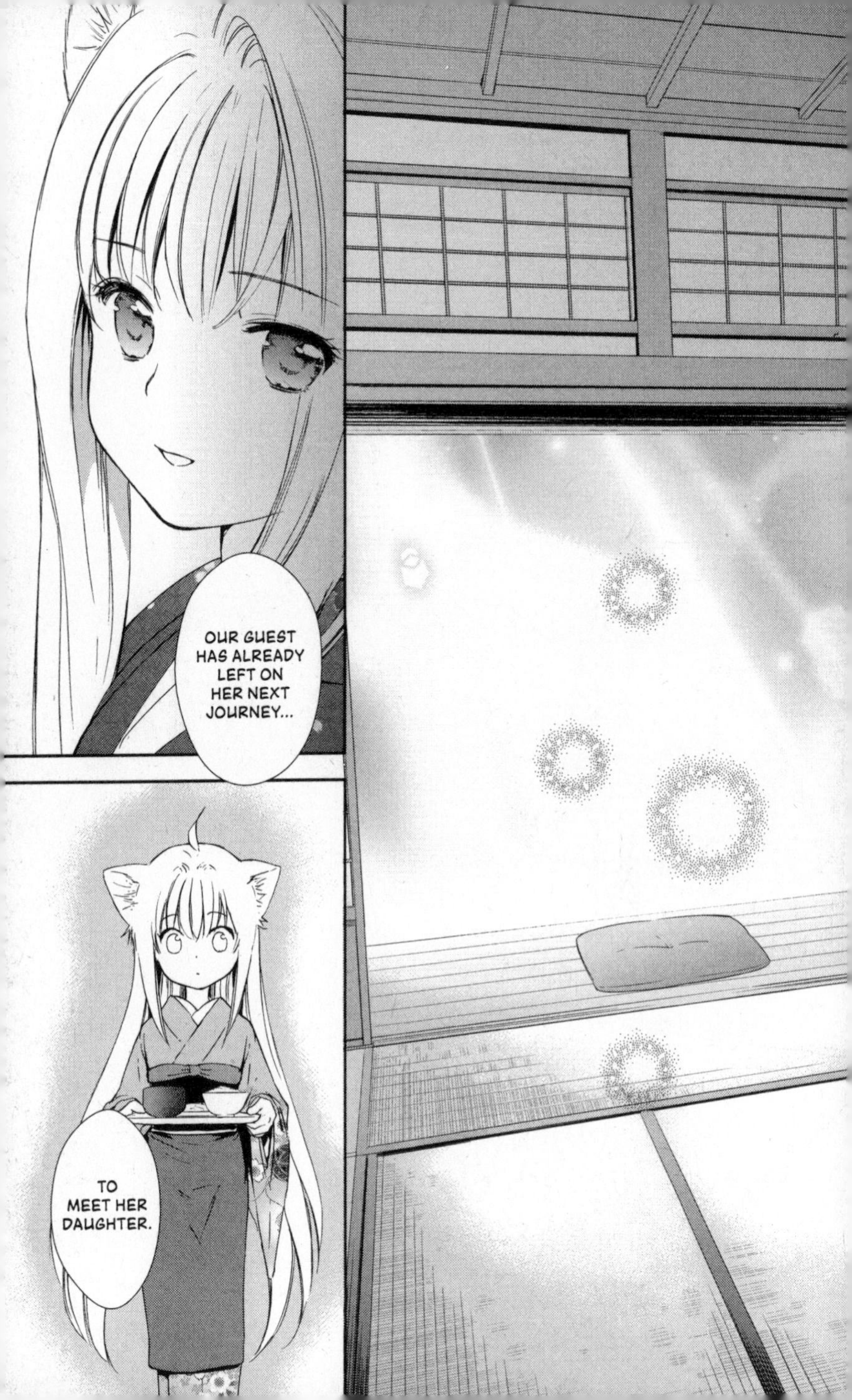
OUR GUEST HAS ALREADY LEFT ON HER NEXT JOURNEY...
TO MEET HER DAUGHTER.

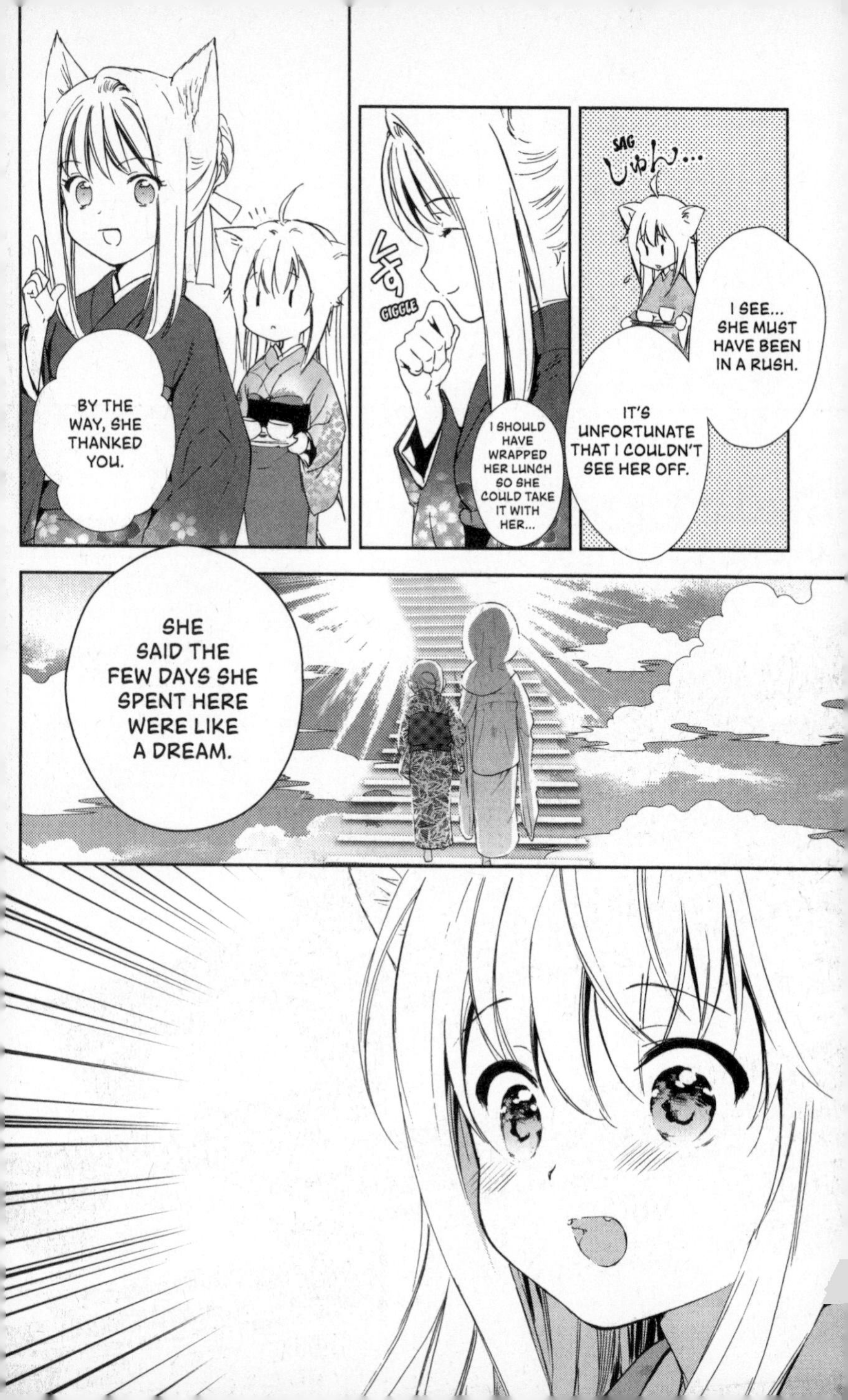
SAG
じゅん…
I SEE... SHE MUST HAVE BEEN IN A RUSH.
IT'S UNFORTUNATE THAT I COULDN'T SEE HER OFF.
くす
GIGGLE
I SHOULD HAVE WRAPPED HER LUNCH SO SHE COULD TAKE IT WITH HER...
BY THE WAY, SHE THANKED YOU.
SHE SAID THE FEW DAYS SHE SPENT HERE WERE LIKE A DREAM.

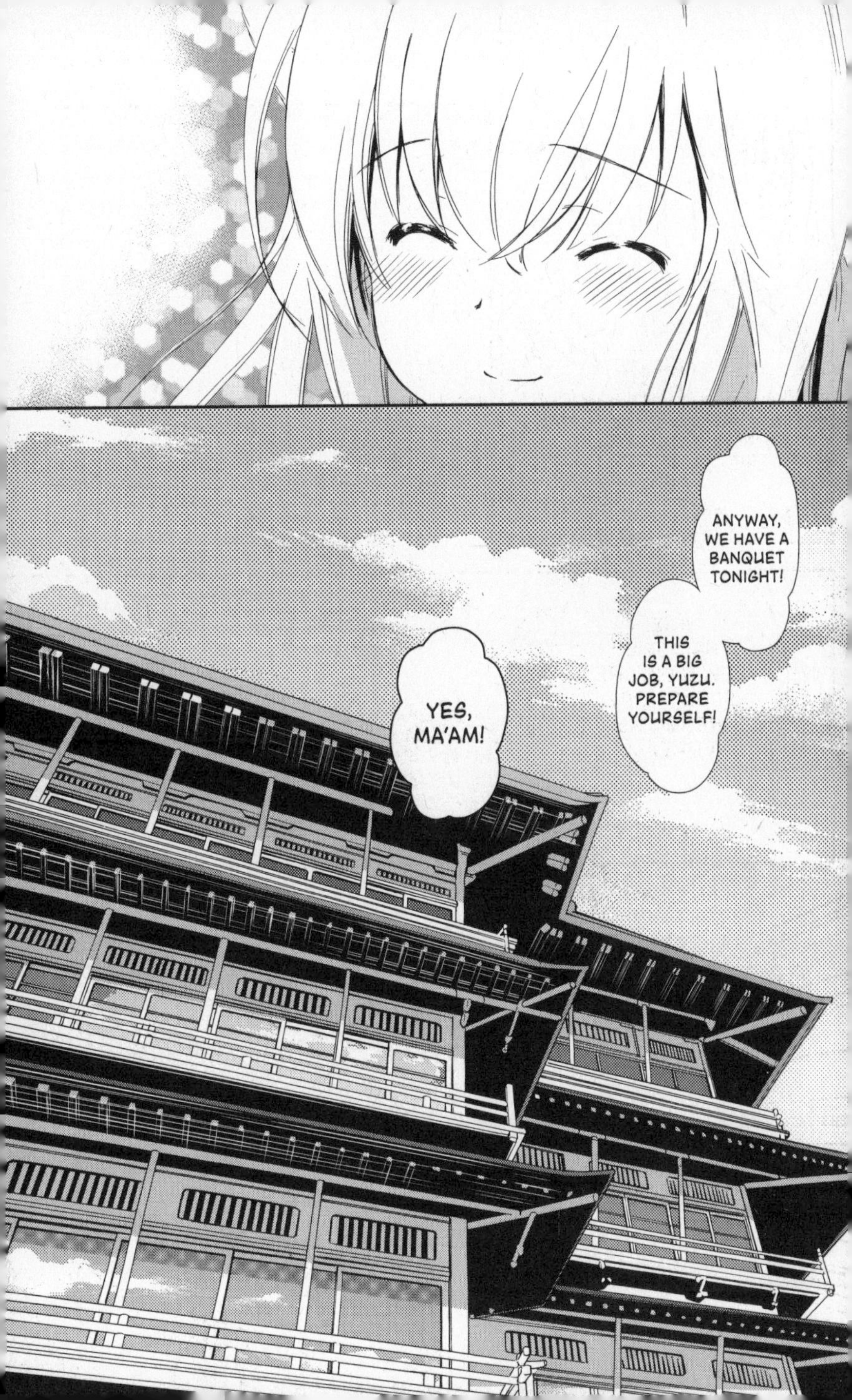
ANYWAY, WE HAVE A BANQUET TONIGHT!
THIS IS A BIG JOB, YUZU. PREPARE YOURSELF!
YES, MA'AM!

KONOHANA KITAN

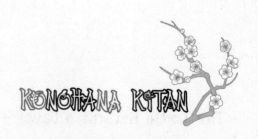

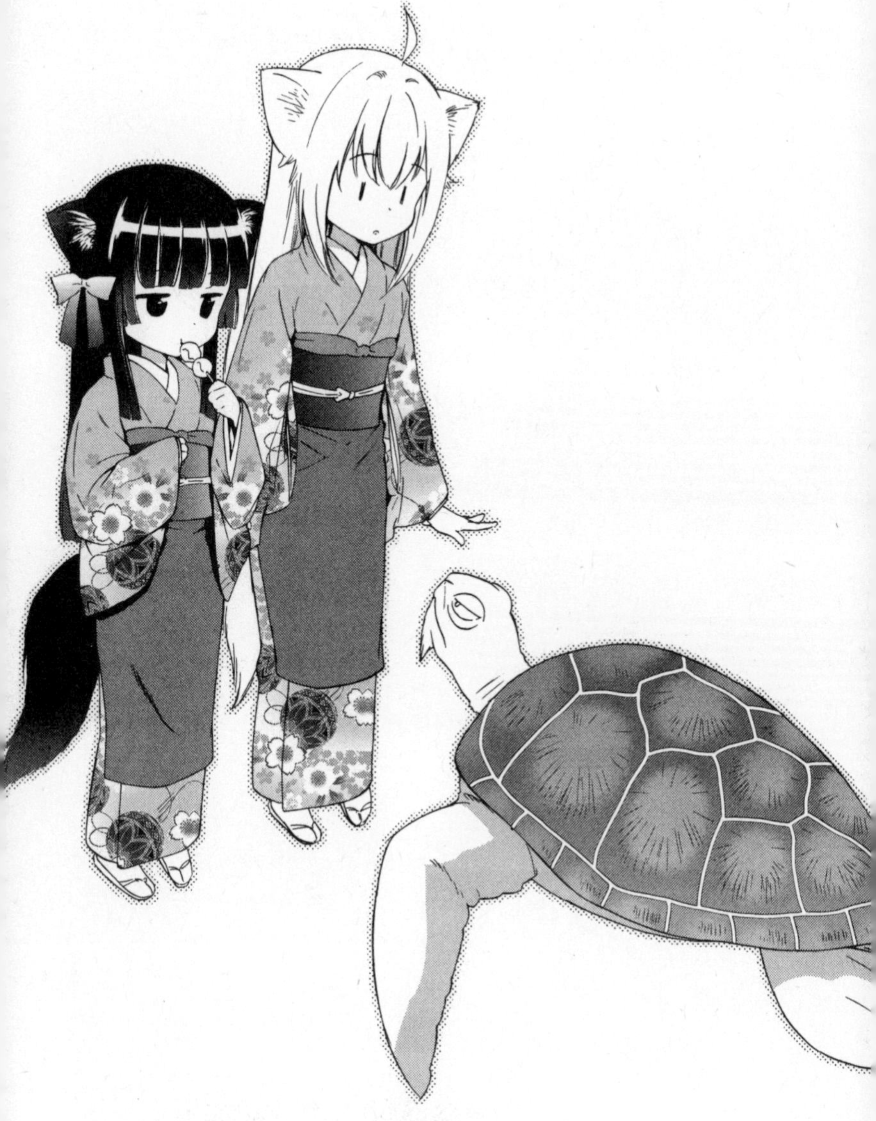

The Turtle Returns a Favor

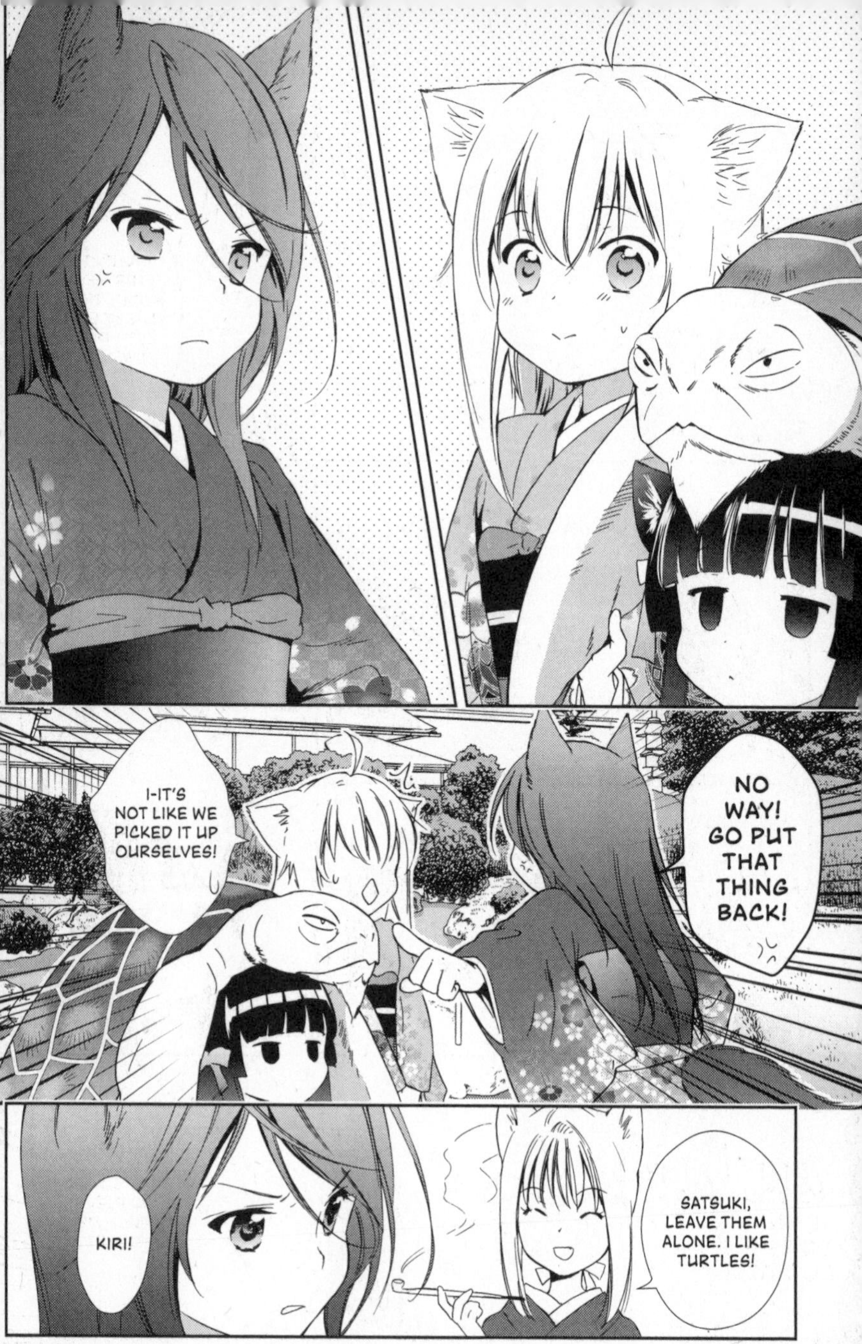
NO WAY! GO PUT THAT THING BACK!
I-IT'S NOT LIKE WE PICKED IT UP OURSELVES!
SATSUKI, LEAVE THEM ALONE. I LIKE TURTLES!
KIRI!

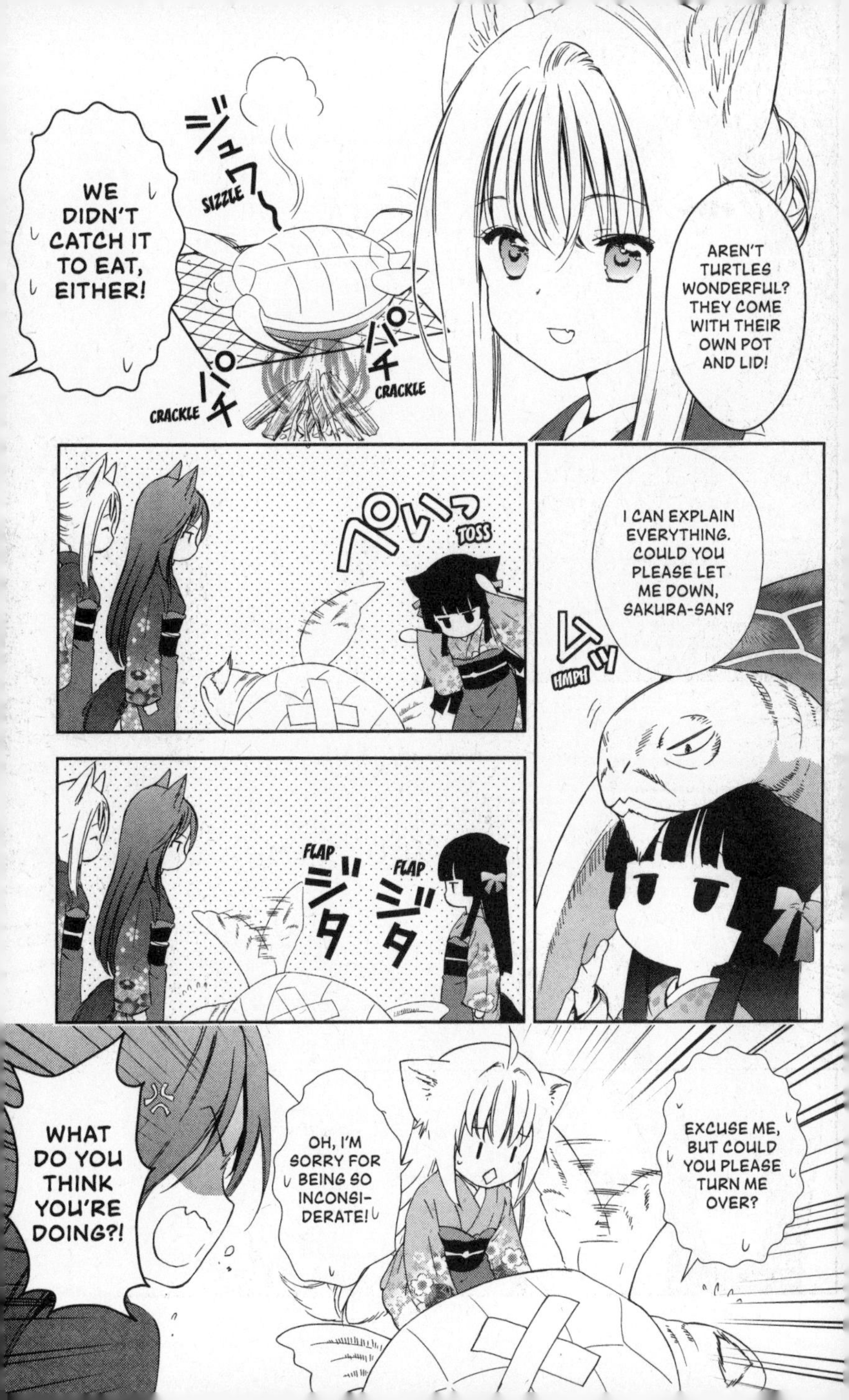
AREN'T TURTLES WONDERFUL? THEY COME WITH THEIR OWN POT AND LID!
ジュワ〜 SIZZLE
パチ CRACKLE
パチ CRACKLE
WE DIDN'T CATCH IT TO EAT, EITHER!
I CAN EXPLAIN EVERYTHING. COULD YOU PLEASE LET ME DOWN, SAKURA-SAN?
ムッ HMPH
ペいっ TOSS
ジタ FLAP
ジタ FLAP
EXCUSE ME, BUT COULD YOU PLEASE TURN ME OVER?
OH, I'M SORRY FOR BEING SO INCONSI-DERATE!
WHAT DO YOU THINK YOU'RE DOING?!

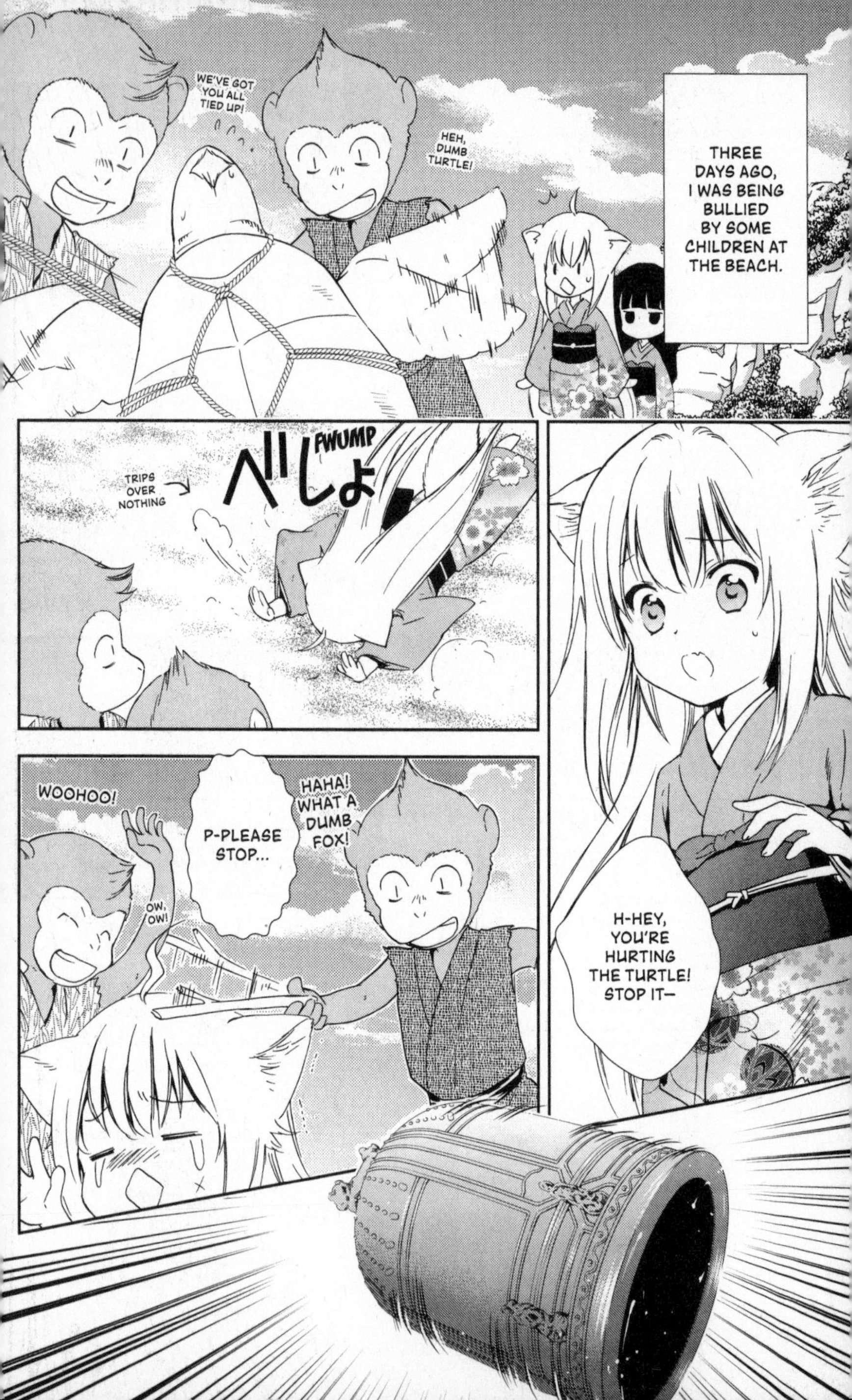
THREE DAYS AGO, I WAS BEING BULLIED BY SOME CHILDREN AT THE BEACH.
HEH, DUMB TURTLE!
WE'VE GOT YOU ALL TIED UP!
H-HEY, YOU'RE HURTING THE TURTLE! STOP IT—
べしょ
FWUMP
TRIPS OVER NOTHING
HAHA! WHAT A DUMB FOX!
P-PLEASE STOP...
WOOHOO!
OW, OW!

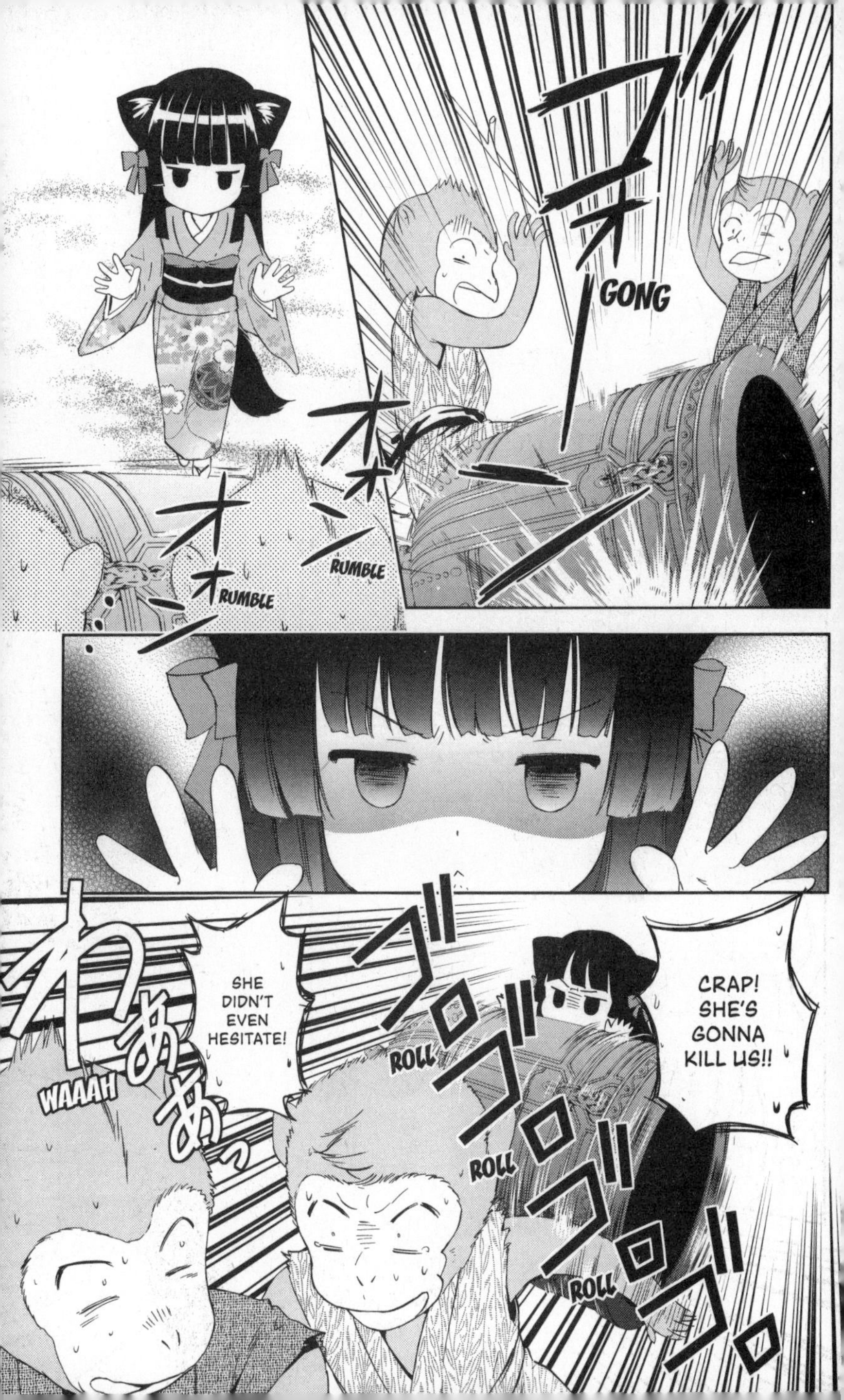
GONG
RUMBLE
RUMBLE
CRAP! SHE'S GONNA KILL US!!
ROLL
ROLL
ROLL
SHE DIDN'T EVEN HESITATE!
WAAAH

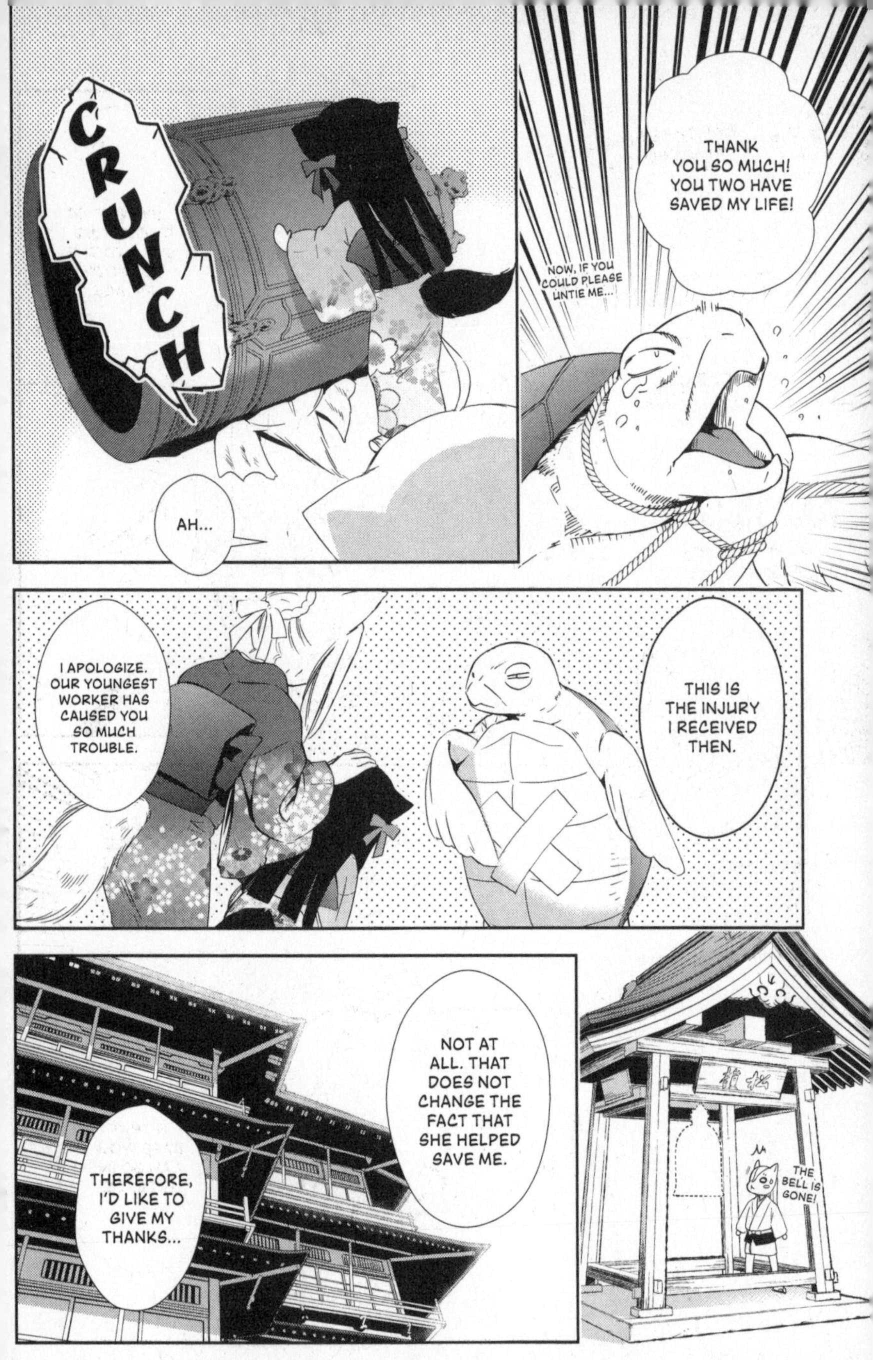
THANK YOU SO MUCH! YOU TWO HAVE SAVED MY LIFE!
NOW, IF YOU COULD PLEASE UNTIE ME...
CRUNCH
AH...
THIS IS THE INJURY I RECEIVED THEN.
I APOLOGIZE. OUR YOUNGEST WORKER HAS CAUSED YOU SO MUCH TROUBLE.
THE BELL IS GONE!
NOT AT ALL. THAT DOES NOT CHANGE THE FACT THAT SHE HELPED SAVE ME.
THEREFORE, I'D LIKE TO GIVE MY THANKS...

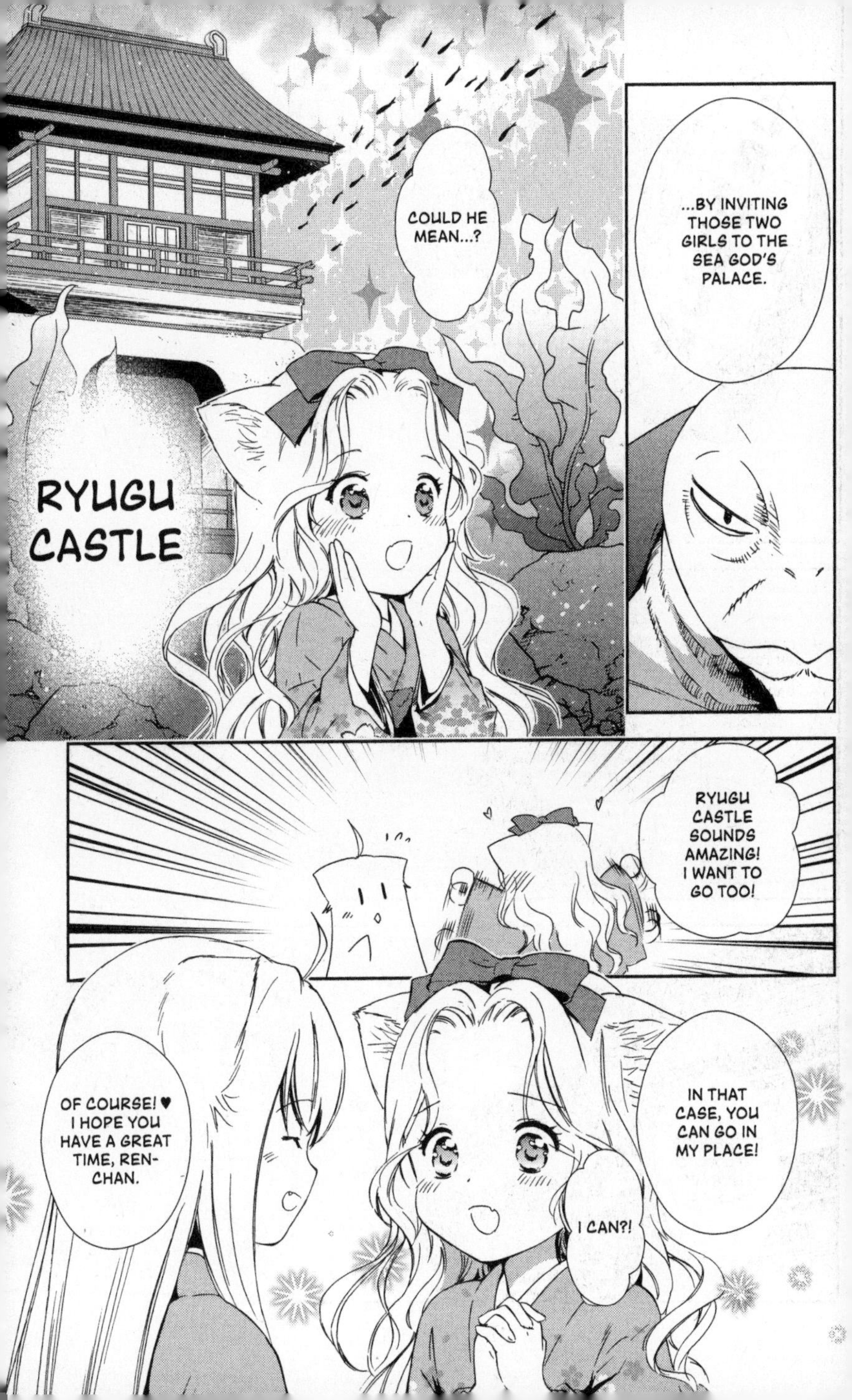
...BY INVITING THOSE TWO GIRLS TO THE SEA GOD'S PALACE.
COULD HE MEAN...?
RYUGU CASTLE
RYUGU CASTLE SOUNDS AMAZING! I WANT TO GO TOO!
IN THAT CASE, YOU CAN GO IN MY PLACE!
I CAN?!
OF COURSE! ♥ I HOPE YOU HAVE A GREAT TIME, REN-CHAN.

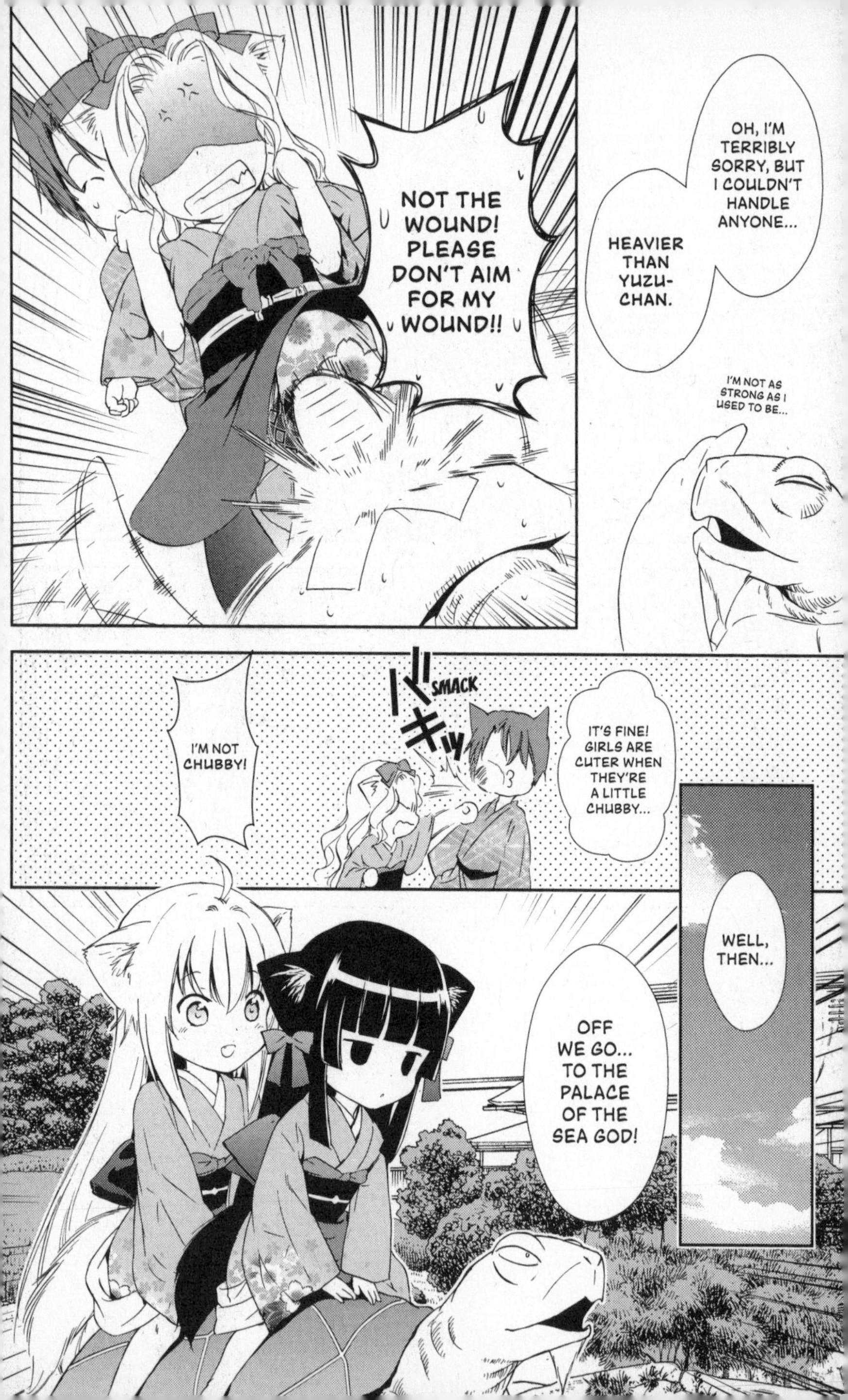
OH, I'M TERRIBLY SORRY, BUT I COULDN'T HANDLE ANYONE...
HEAVIER THAN YUZU-CHAN.
I'M NOT AS STRONG AS I USED TO BE...
NOT THE WOUND! PLEASE DON'T AIM FOR MY WOUND!!
IT'S FINE! GIRLS ARE CUTER WHEN THEY'RE A LITTLE CHUBBY...
SMACK
I'M NOT CHUBBY!
WELL, THEN...
OFF WE GO... TO THE PALACE OF THE SEA GOD!

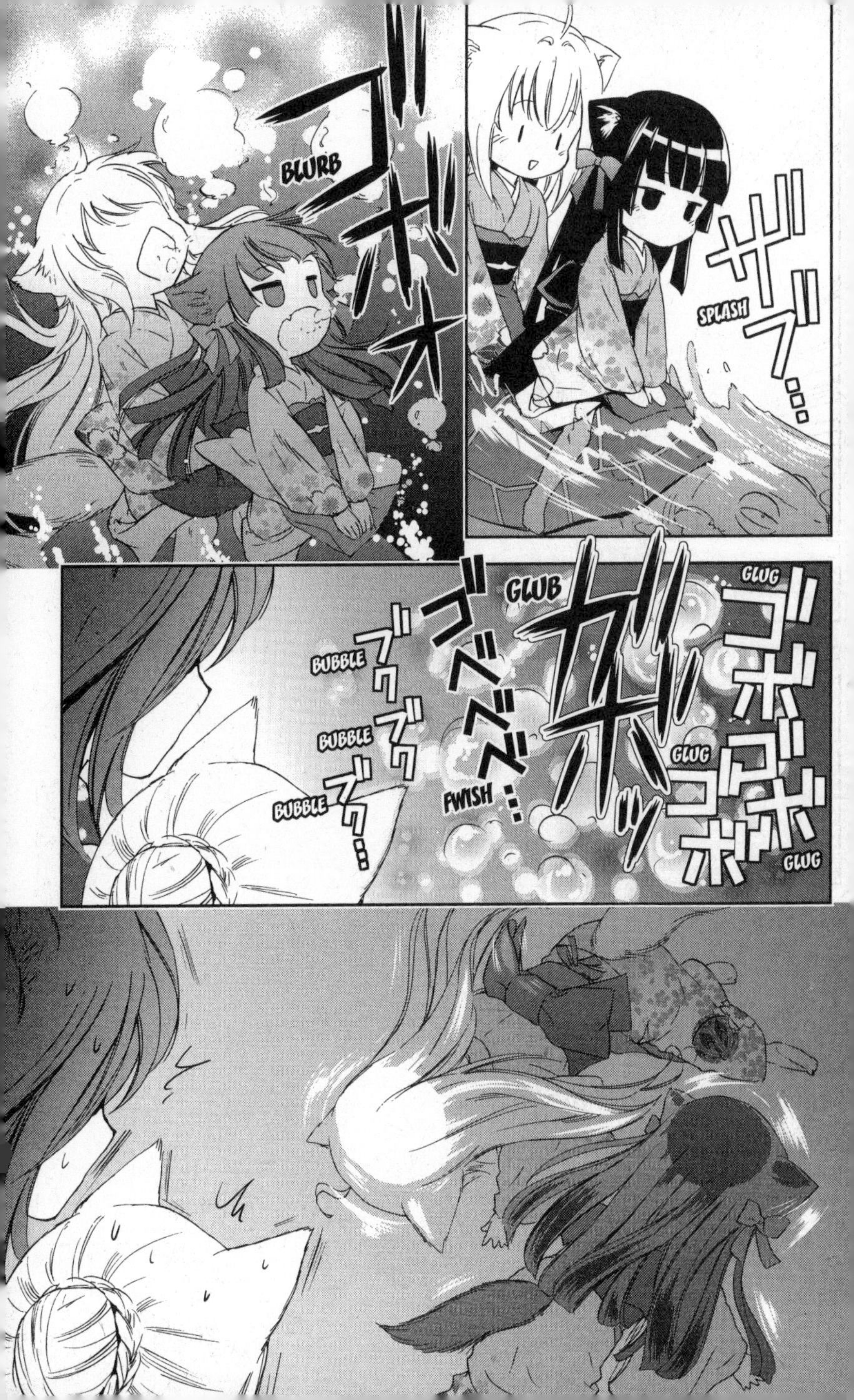
ザブ…
SPLASH
BLURB
ゴボォ
ゴボゴボゴボ
GLUG
GLUG
GLUG
ガバッ
GLUB
ごべべ…
FWISH
ブクブクブク…
BUBBLE
BUBBLE
BUBBLE

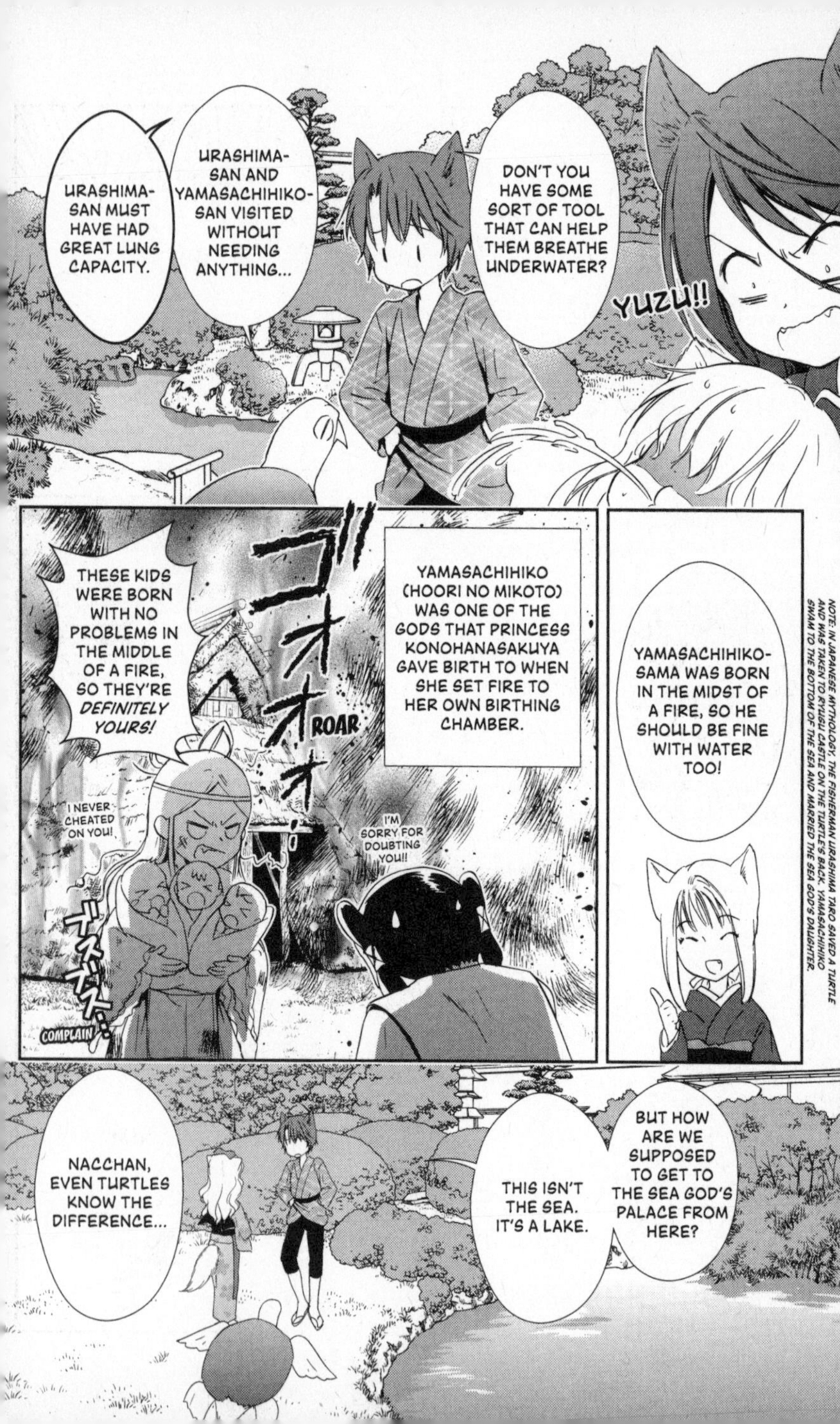
DON'T YOU HAVE SOME SORT OF TOOL THAT CAN HELP THEM BREATHE UNDERWATER?
YUZU!!
URASHIMA-SAN AND YAMASACHIHIKO-SAN VISITED WITHOUT NEEDING ANYTHING...
URASHIMA-SAN MUST HAVE HAD GREAT LUNG CAPACITY.
YAMASACHIHIKO-SAMA WAS BORN IN THE MIDST OF A FIRE, SO HE SHOULD BE FINE WITH WATER TOO!
YAMASACHIHIKO (HOORI NO MIKOTO) WAS ONE OF THE GODS THAT PRINCESS KONOHANASAKUYA GAVE BIRTH TO WHEN SHE SET FIRE TO HER OWN BIRTHING CHAMBER.
ROAR
THESE KIDS WERE BORN WITH NO PROBLEMS IN THE MIDDLE OF A FIRE, SO THEY'RE *DEFINITELY* YOURS!
I'M SORRY FOR DOUBTING YOU!!
I NEVER CHEATED ON YOU!
COMPLAIN
BUT HOW ARE WE SUPPOSED TO GET TO THE SEA GOD'S PALACE FROM HERE?
THIS ISN'T THE SEA. IT'S A LAKE.
NACCHAN, EVEN TURTLES KNOW THE DIFFERENCE...

NOTE: IN JAPANESE MYTHOLOGY, THE FISHERMAN URASHIMA TARO SAVED A TURTLE AND WAS TAKEN TO RYUGU CASTLE ON THE TURTLE'S BACK. YAMASACHIHIKO SWAM TO THE BOTTOM OF THE SEA AND MARRIED THE SEA GOD'S DAUGHTER.

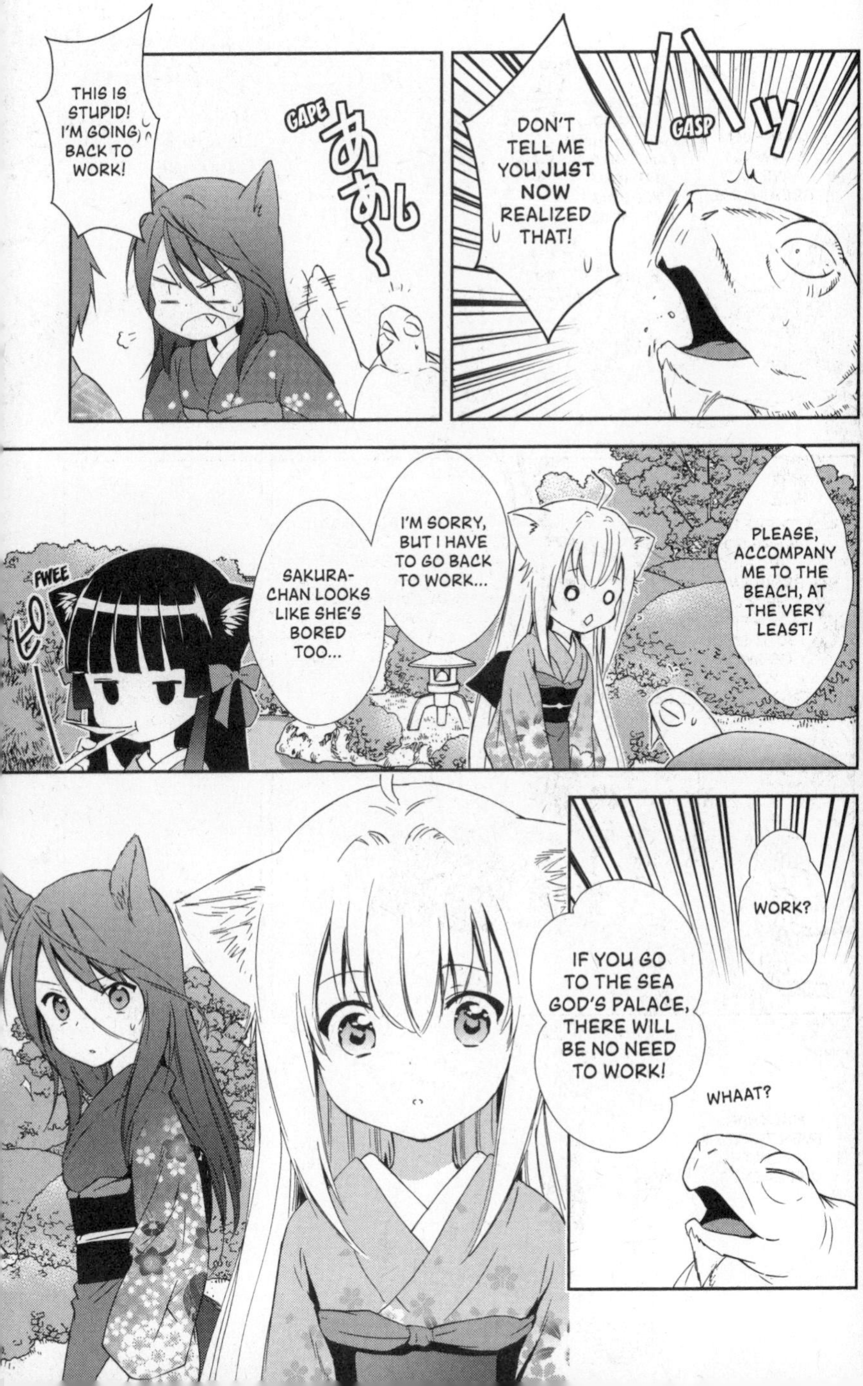
DON'T TELL ME YOU JUST NOW REALIZED THAT!
GASP
ハッ
THIS IS STUPID! I'M GOING BACK TO WORK!
GAPE
PLEASE, ACCOMPANY ME TO THE BEACH, AT THE VERY LEAST!
I'M SORRY, BUT I HAVE TO GO BACK TO WORK...
SAKURA-CHAN LOOKS LIKE SHE'S BORED TOO...
FWEE
ピー
WORK?
IF YOU GO TO THE SEA GOD'S PALACE, THERE WILL BE NO NEED TO WORK!
WHAAT?

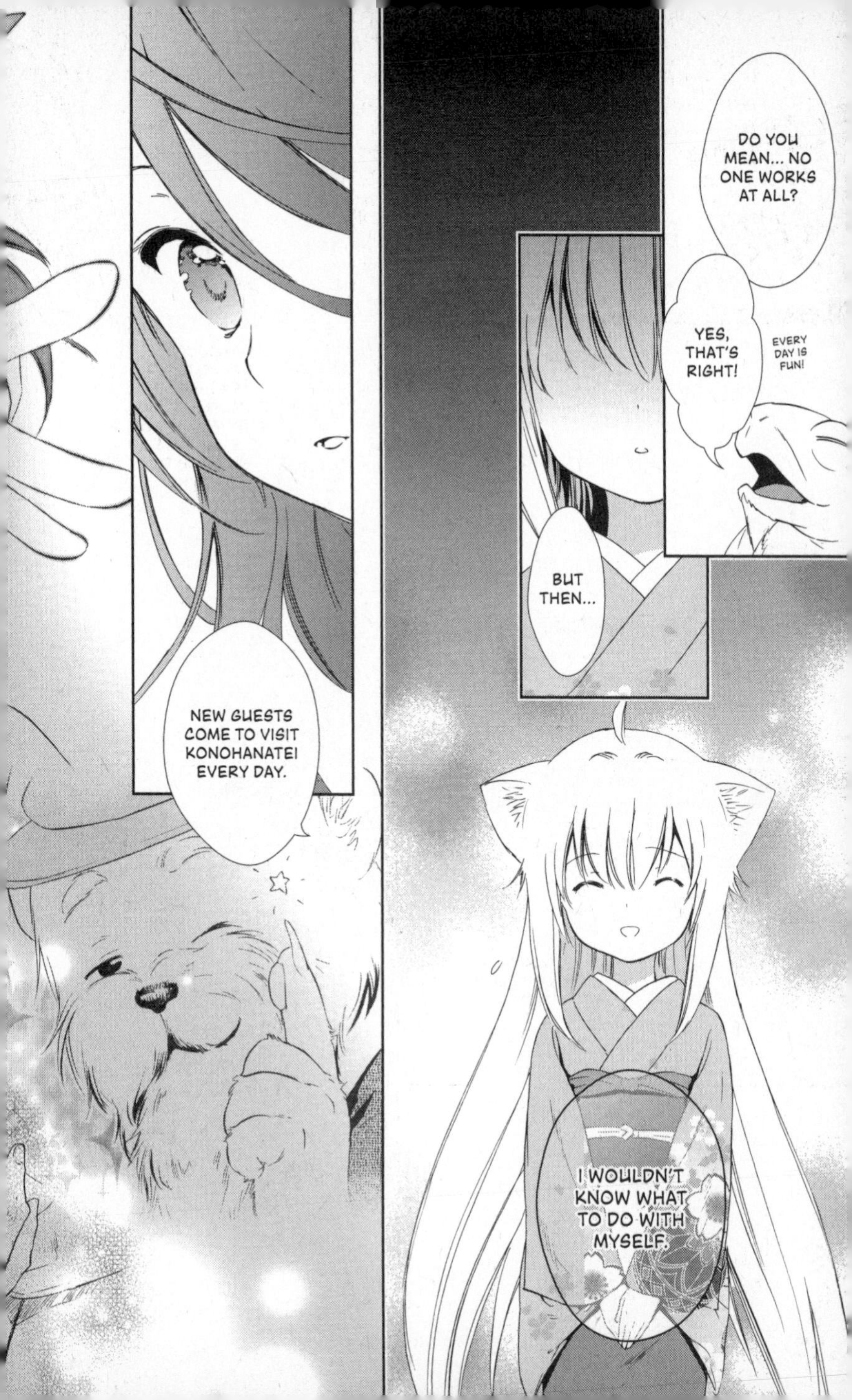
DO YOU MEAN... NO ONE WORKS AT ALL?
YES, THAT'S RIGHT!
EVERY DAY IS FUN!
BUT THEN...
I WOULDN'T KNOW WHAT TO DO WITH MYSELF.
NEW GUESTS COME TO VISIT KONOHANATEI EVERY DAY.

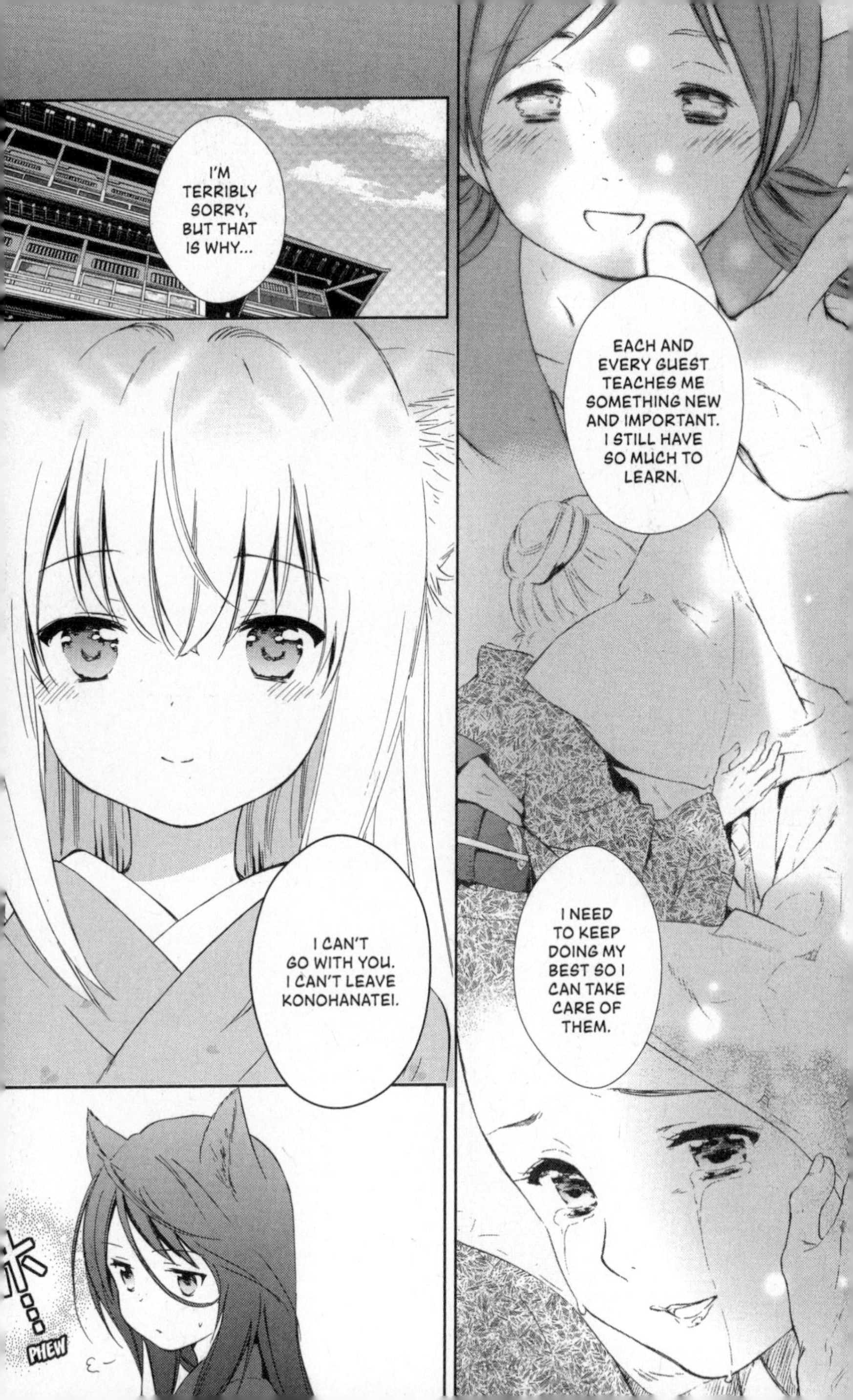
EACH AND EVERY GUEST TEACHES ME SOMETHING NEW AND IMPORTANT. I STILL HAVE SO MUCH TO LEARN.
I NEED TO KEEP DOING MY BEST SO I CAN TAKE CARE OF THEM.
I'M TERRIBLY SORRY, BUT THAT IS WHY...
I CAN'T GO WITH YOU. I CAN'T LEAVE KONOHANATEI.
PHEW

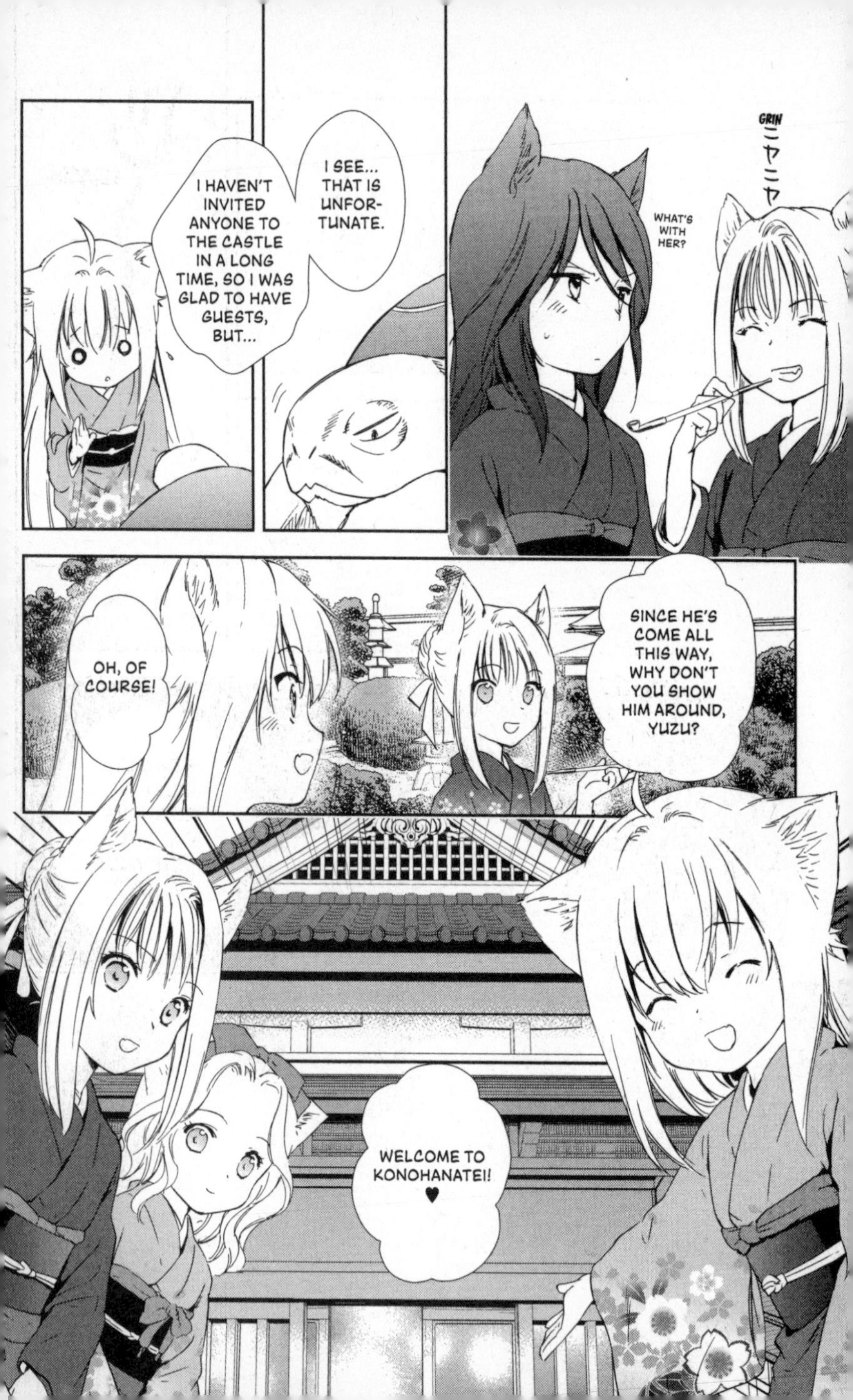
GRIN
ニヤニヤ
WHAT'S WITH HER?
I SEE... THAT IS UNFORTUNATE.
I HAVEN'T INVITED ANYONE TO THE CASTLE IN A LONG TIME, SO I WAS GLAD TO HAVE GUESTS, BUT...
SINCE HE'S COME ALL THIS WAY, WHY DON'T YOU SHOW HIM AROUND, YUZU?
OH, OF COURSE!
WELCOME TO KONOHANATEI!! ♥

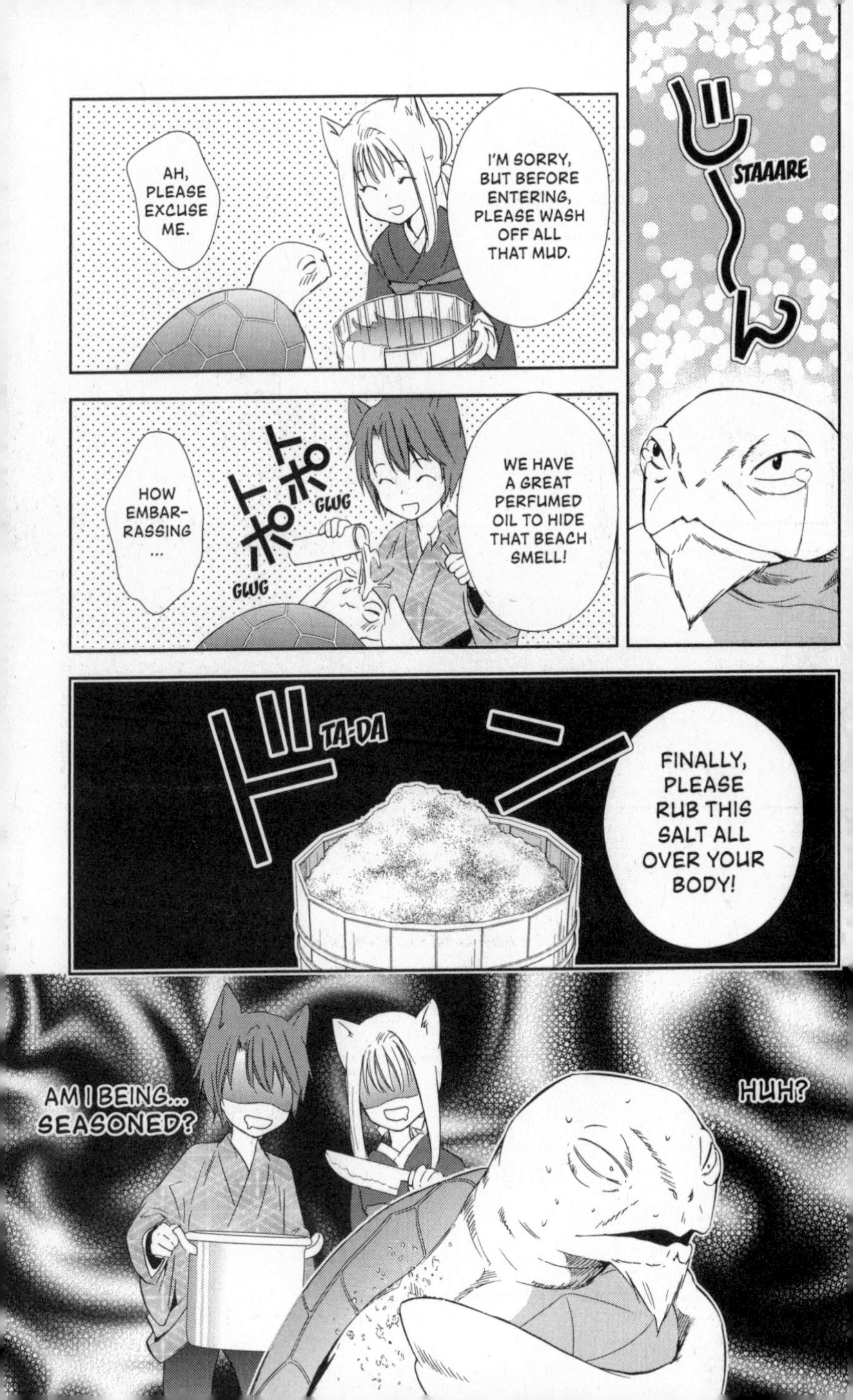
じーん
STAAARE
I'M SORRY, BUT BEFORE ENTERING, PLEASE WASH OFF ALL THAT MUD.
AH, PLEASE EXCUSE ME.
WE HAVE A GREAT PERFUMED OIL TO HIDE THAT BEACH SMELL!
ポトポト
GLUG
GLUG
HOW EMBAR-RASSING ...
FINALLY, PLEASE RUB THIS SALT ALL OVER YOUR BODY!
ドーン
TA-DA
HUH?
AM I BEING... SEASONED?

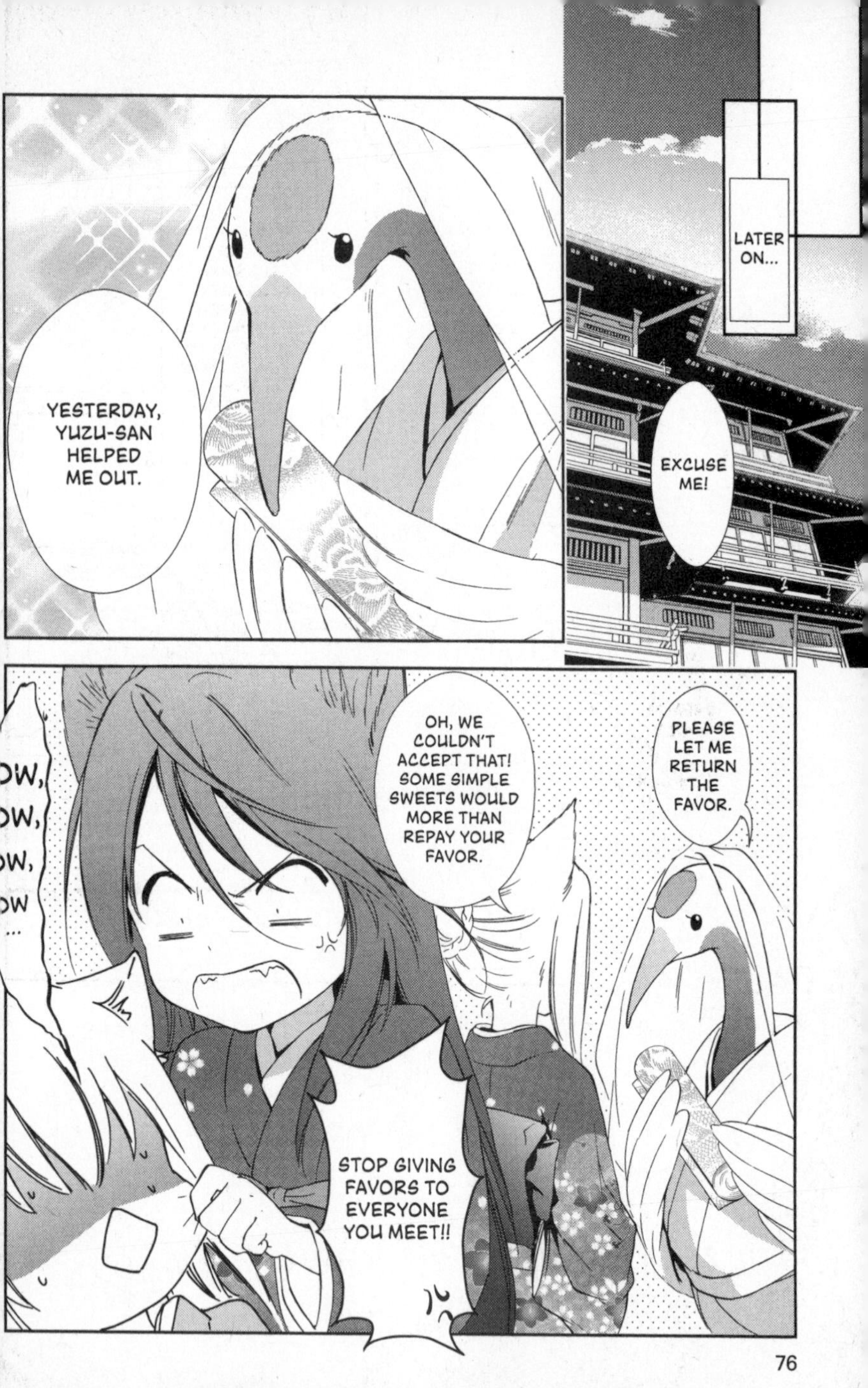
LATER ON...
EXCUSE ME!
YESTERDAY, YUZU-SAN HELPED ME OUT.
PLEASE LET ME RETURN THE FAVOR.
OH, WE COULDN'T ACCEPT THAT! SOME SIMPLE SWEETS WOULD MORE THAN REPAY YOUR FAVOR.
STOP GIVING FAVORS TO EVERYONE YOU MEET!!

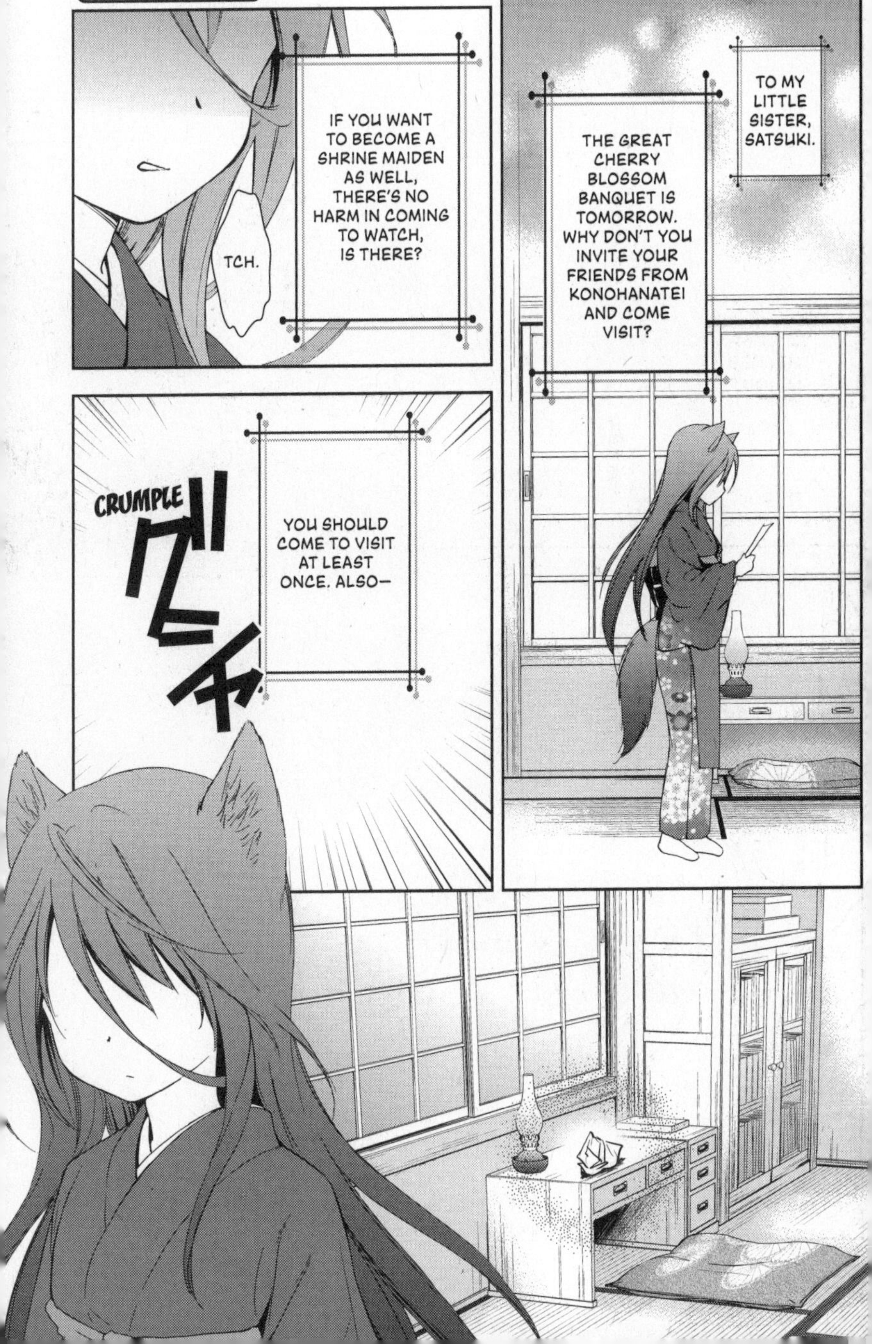
TO MY LITTLE SISTER, SATSUKI.
THE GREAT CHERRY BLOSSOM BANQUET IS TOMORROW. WHY DON'T YOU INVITE YOUR FRIENDS FROM KONOHANATEI AND COME VISIT?
IF YOU WANT TO BECOME A SHRINE MAIDEN AS WELL, THERE'S NO HARM IN COMING TO WATCH, IS THERE?
TCH.
YOU SHOULD COME TO VISIT AT LEAST ONCE. ALSO—
CRUMPLE

The Dream Egg

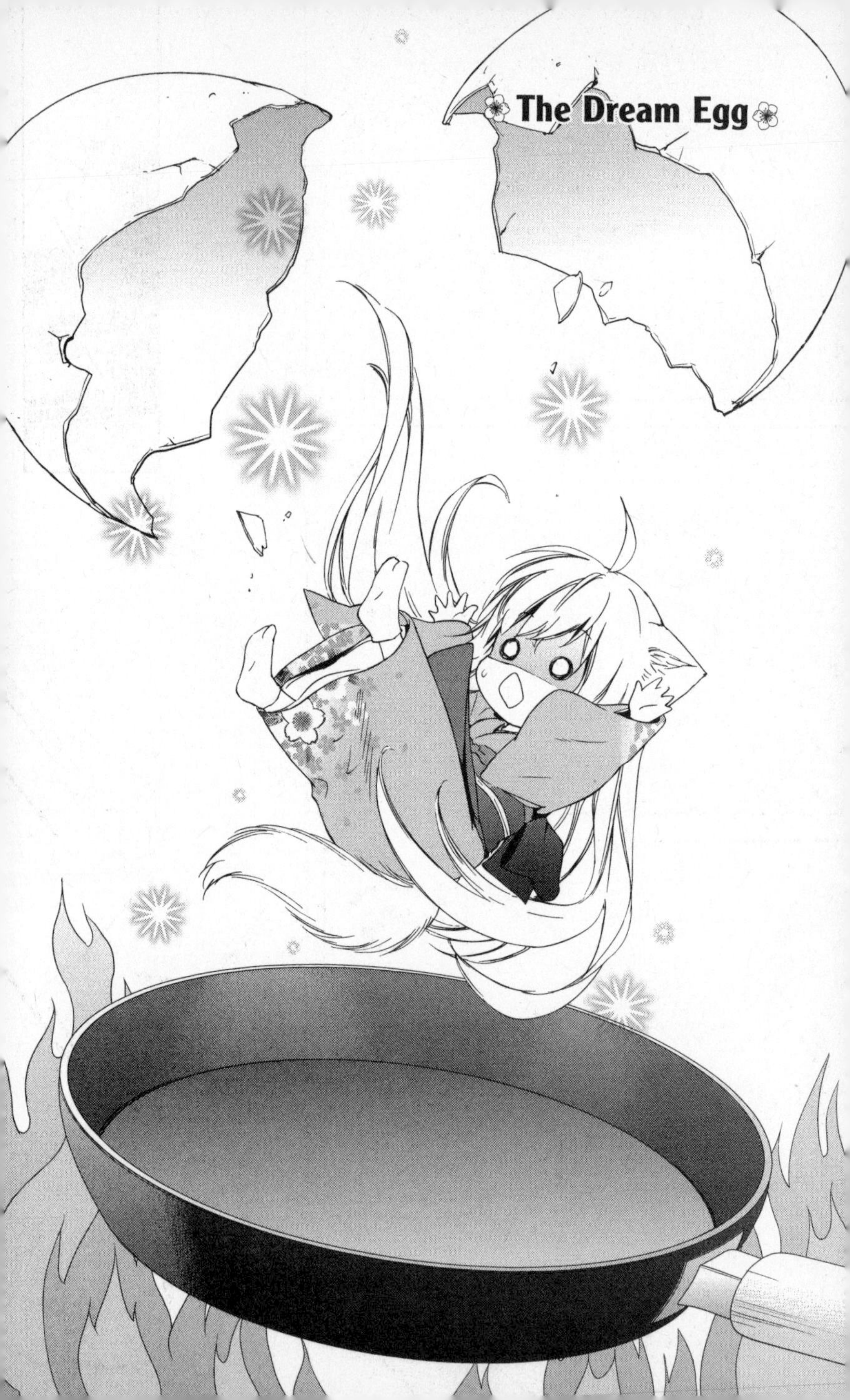

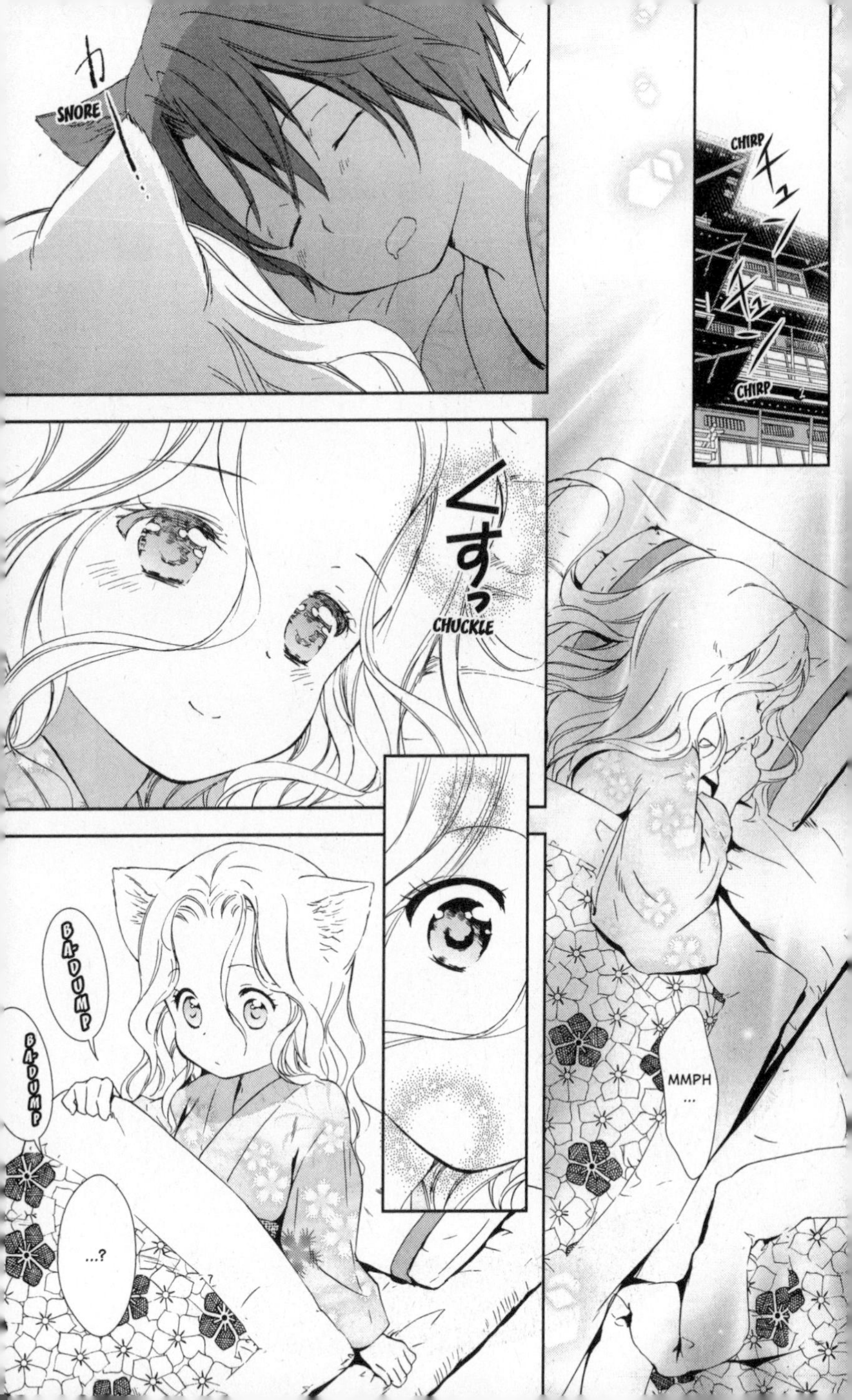
CHIRP
CHIRP
MMPH ...
SNORE
くすっ
CHUCKLE
BA-DUMP
BA-DUMP
...?

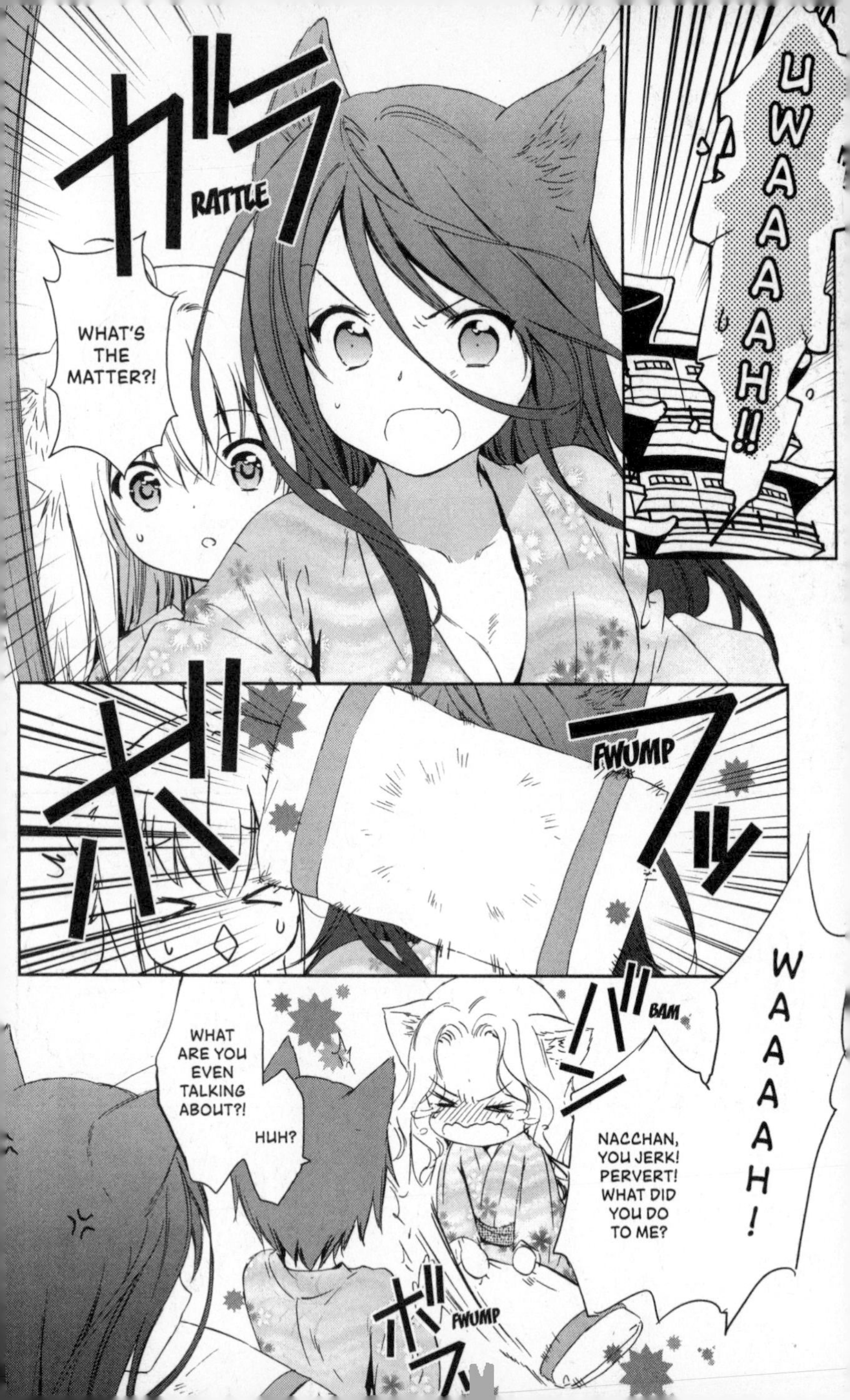
UWAAAAH!!
RATTLE
WHAT'S THE MATTER?!
FWUMP
WAAAAH!
BAM
NACCHAN, YOU JERK! PERVERT! WHAT DID YOU DO TO ME?
HUH?
WHAT ARE YOU EVEN TALKING ABOUT?!
FWUMP

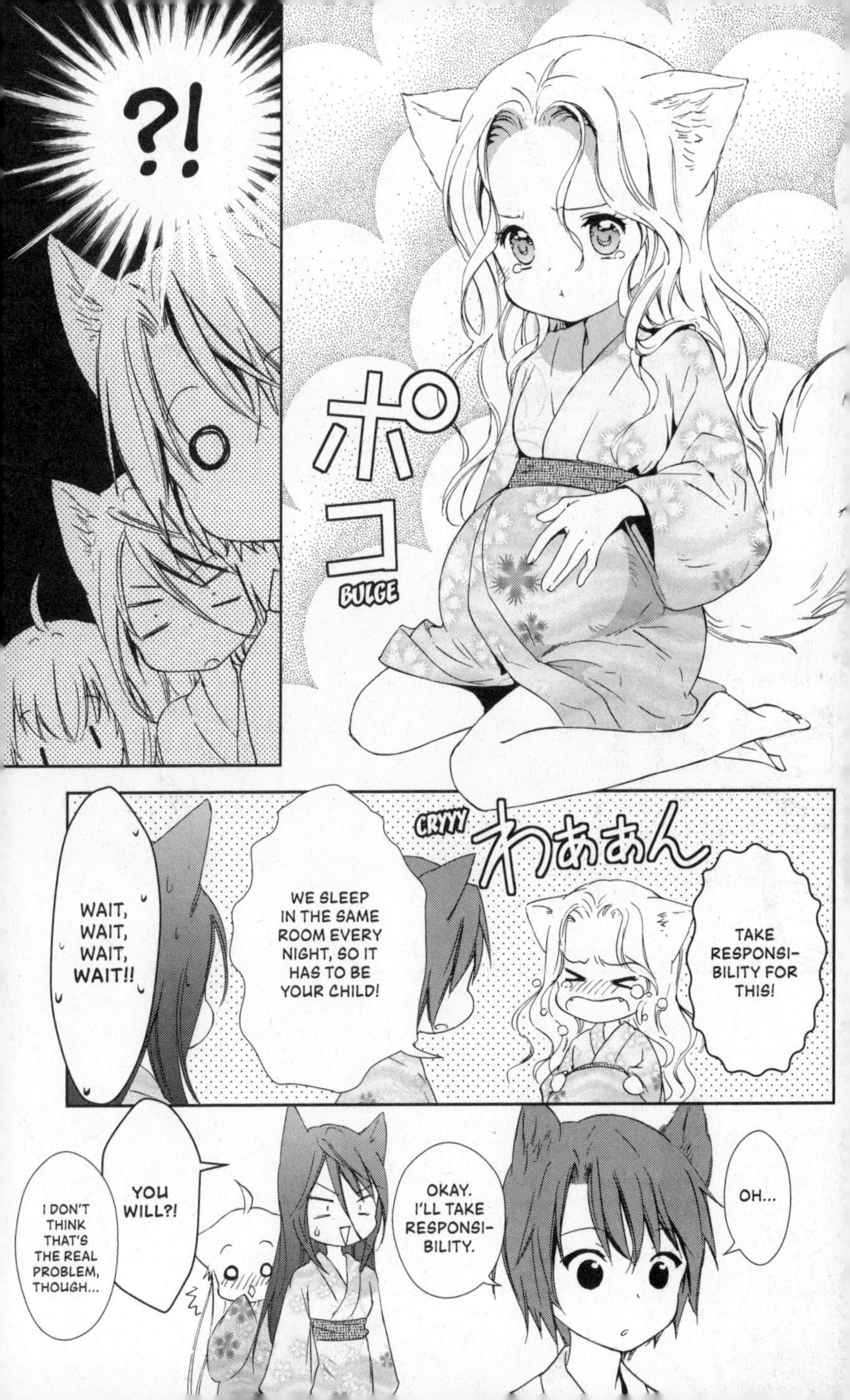
ポコ
BULGE
?!
わあぁん
CRYYY
TAKE RESPONSI-BILITY FOR THIS!
WE SLEEP IN THE SAME ROOM EVERY NIGHT, SO IT HAS TO BE YOUR CHILD!
WAIT, WAIT, WAIT, WAIT!!
OH...
OKAY. I'LL TAKE RESPONSI-BILITY.
YOU WILL?!
I DON'T THINK THAT'S THE REAL PROBLEM, THOUGH...

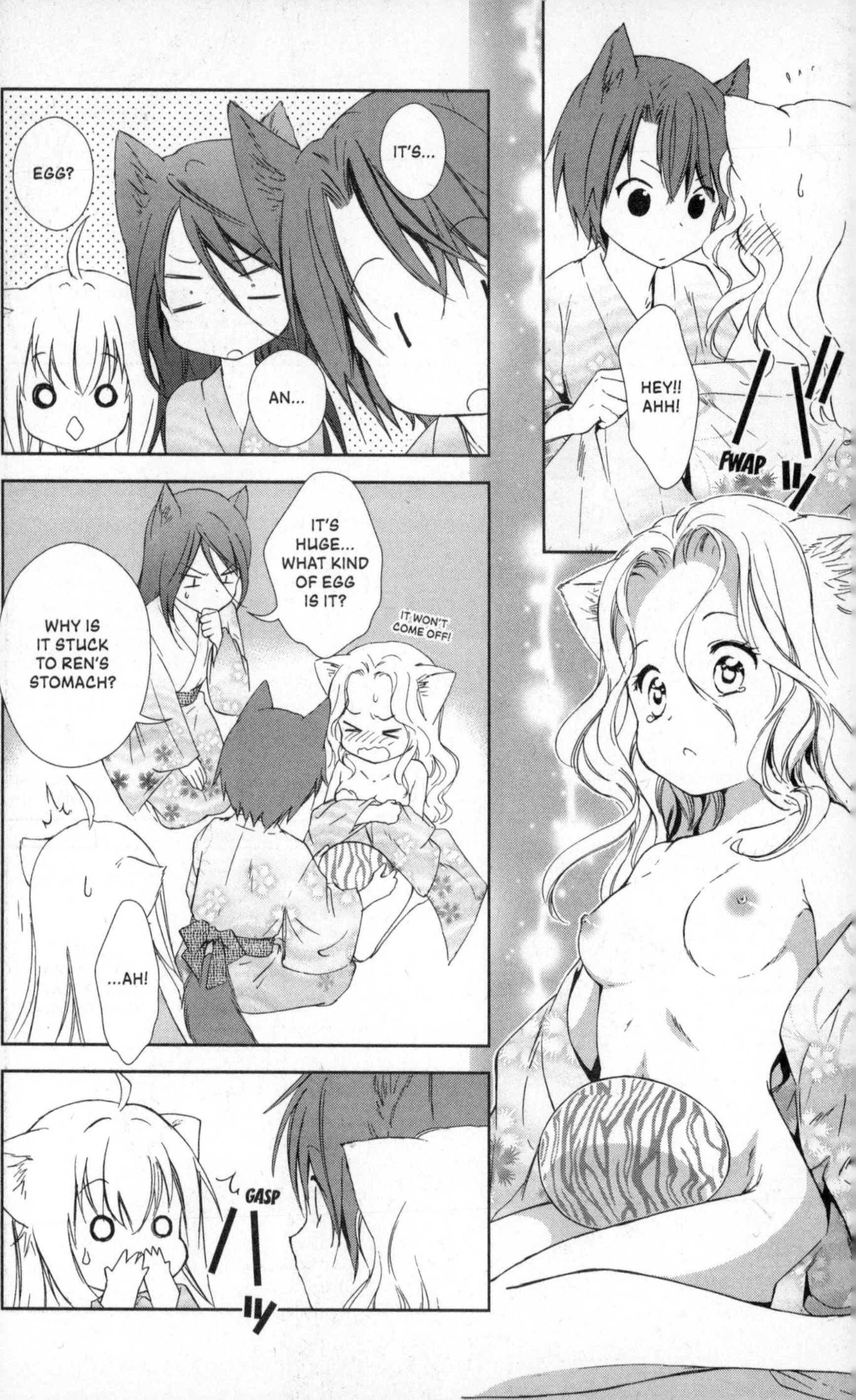
IT'S...
AN...
EGG?
IT'S HUGE... WHAT KIND OF EGG IS IT?
IT WON'T COME OFF!
WHY IS IT STUCK TO REN'S STOMACH?
...AH!
GASP
HEY!! AHH!
FWAP

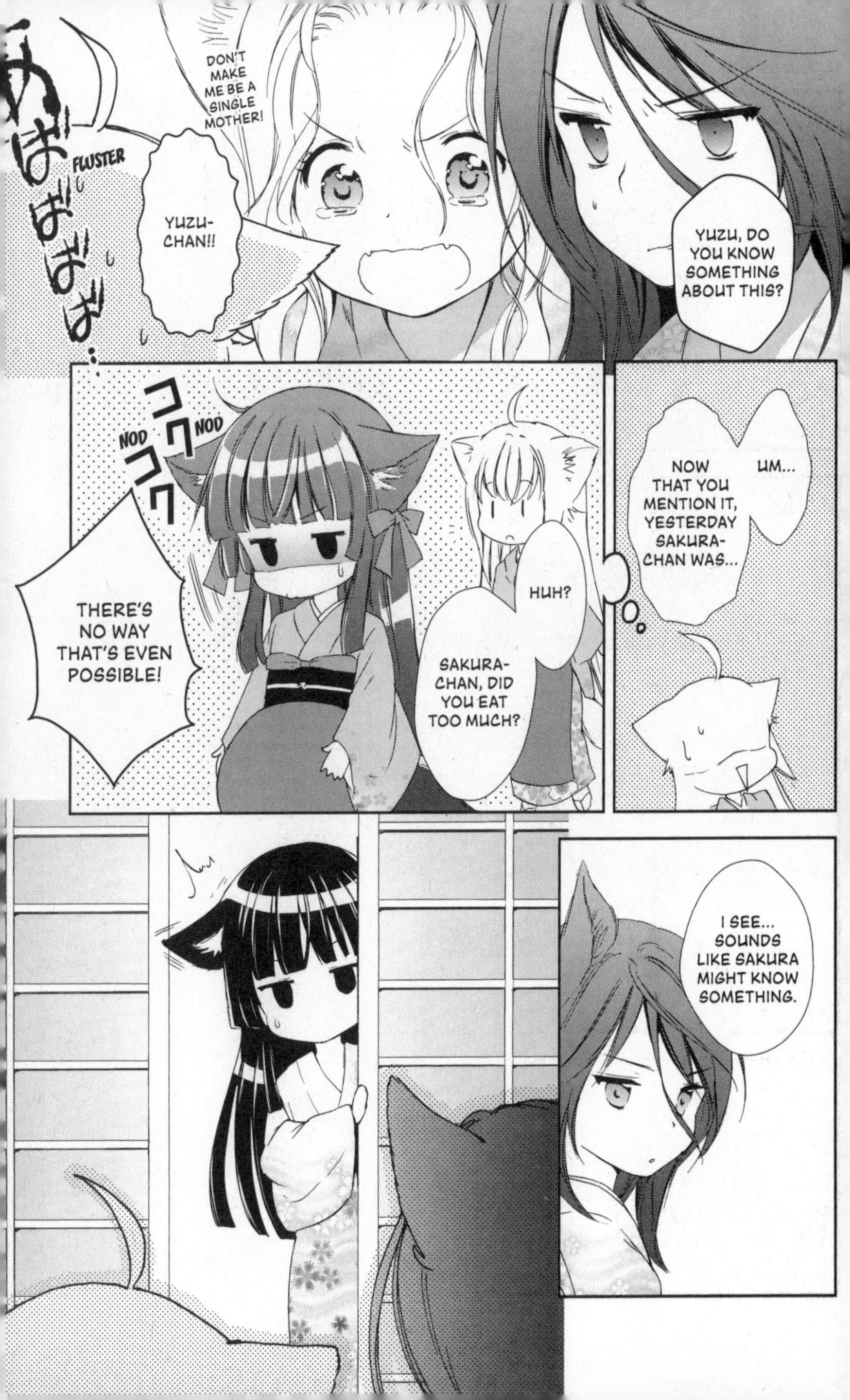
YUZU, DO YOU KNOW SOMETHING ABOUT THIS?
DON'T MAKE ME BE A SINGLE MOTHER!
YUZU-CHAN!!
FLUSTER
あばばばば…
NOW THAT YOU MENTION IT, YESTERDAY SAKURA-CHAN WAS...
UM...
HUH?
SAKURA-CHAN, DID YOU EAT TOO MUCH?
NOD
NOD
コクコク
THERE'S NO WAY THAT'S EVEN POSSIBLE!
I SEE... SOUNDS LIKE SAKURA MIGHT KNOW SOMETHING.

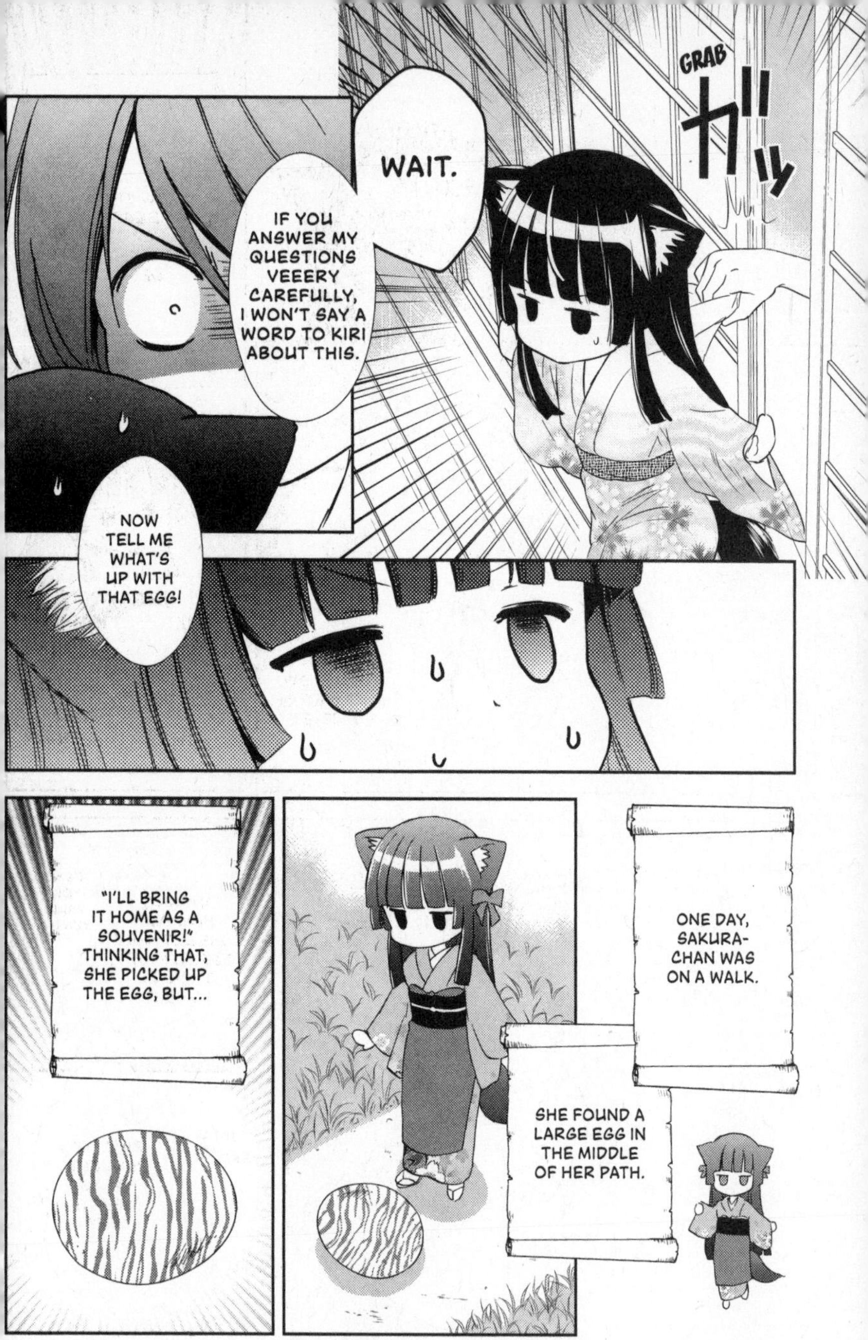
GRAB
ガッ
WAIT.
IF YOU ANSWER MY QUESTIONS VEEERY CAREFULLY, I WON'T SAY A WORD TO KIRI ABOUT THIS.
NOW TELL ME WHAT'S UP WITH THAT EGG!
ONE DAY, SAKURA-CHAN WAS ON A WALK.
SHE FOUND A LARGE EGG IN THE MIDDLE OF HER PATH.
"I'LL BRING IT HOME AS A SOUVENIR!" THINKING THAT, SHE PICKED UP THE EGG, BUT...

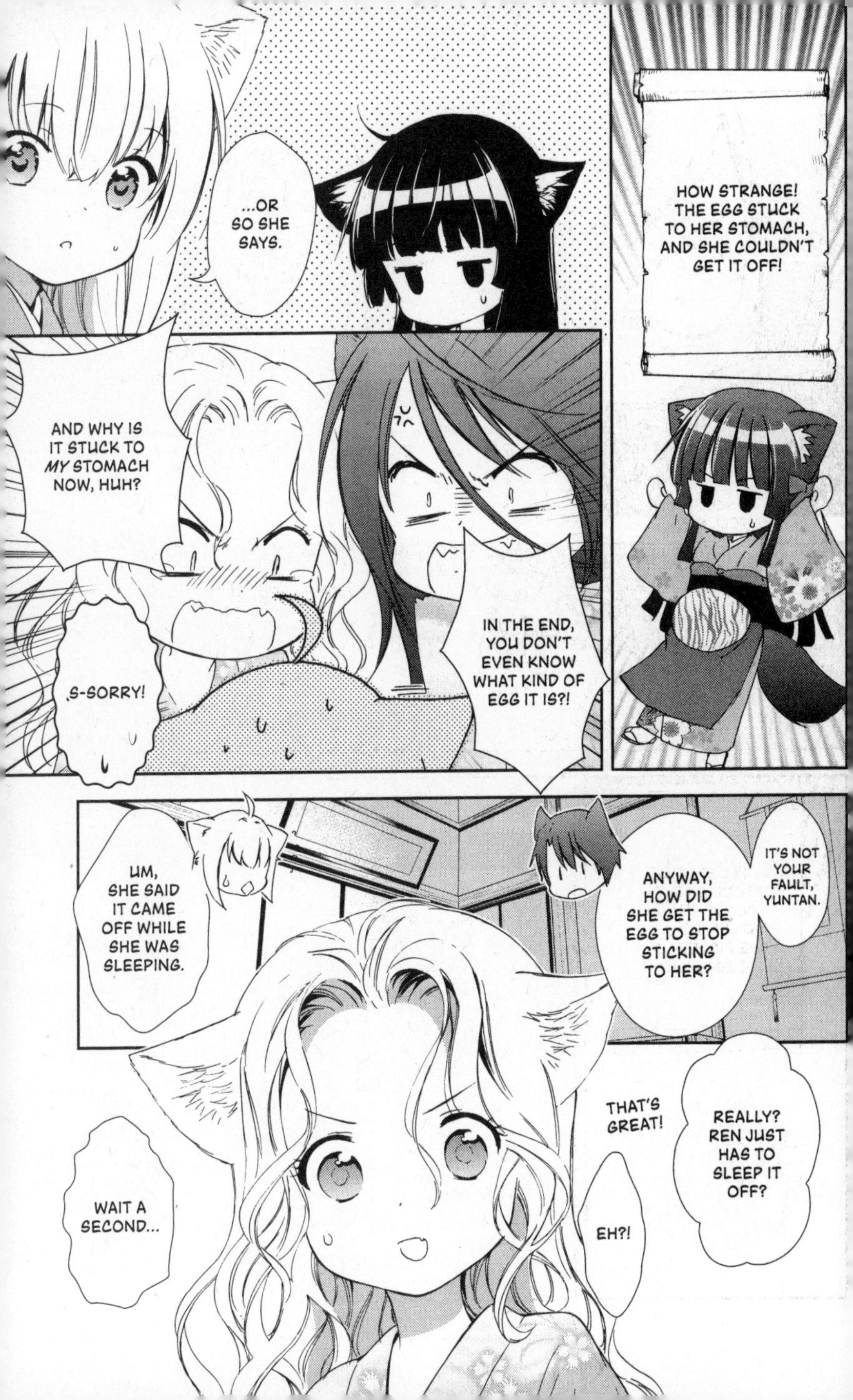
HOW STRANGE! THE EGG STUCK TO HER STOMACH, AND SHE COULDN'T GET IT OFF!
...OR SO SHE SAYS.
IN THE END, YOU DON'T EVEN KNOW WHAT KIND OF EGG IT IS?!
AND WHY IS IT STUCK TO *MY* STOMACH NOW, HUH?
S-SORRY!
IT'S NOT YOUR FAULT, YUNTAN.
ANYWAY, HOW DID SHE GET THE EGG TO STOP STICKING TO HER?
UM, SHE SAID IT CAME OFF WHILE SHE WAS SLEEPING.
REALLY? REN JUST HAS TO SLEEP IT OFF?
THAT'S GREAT!
EH?!
WAIT A SECOND...

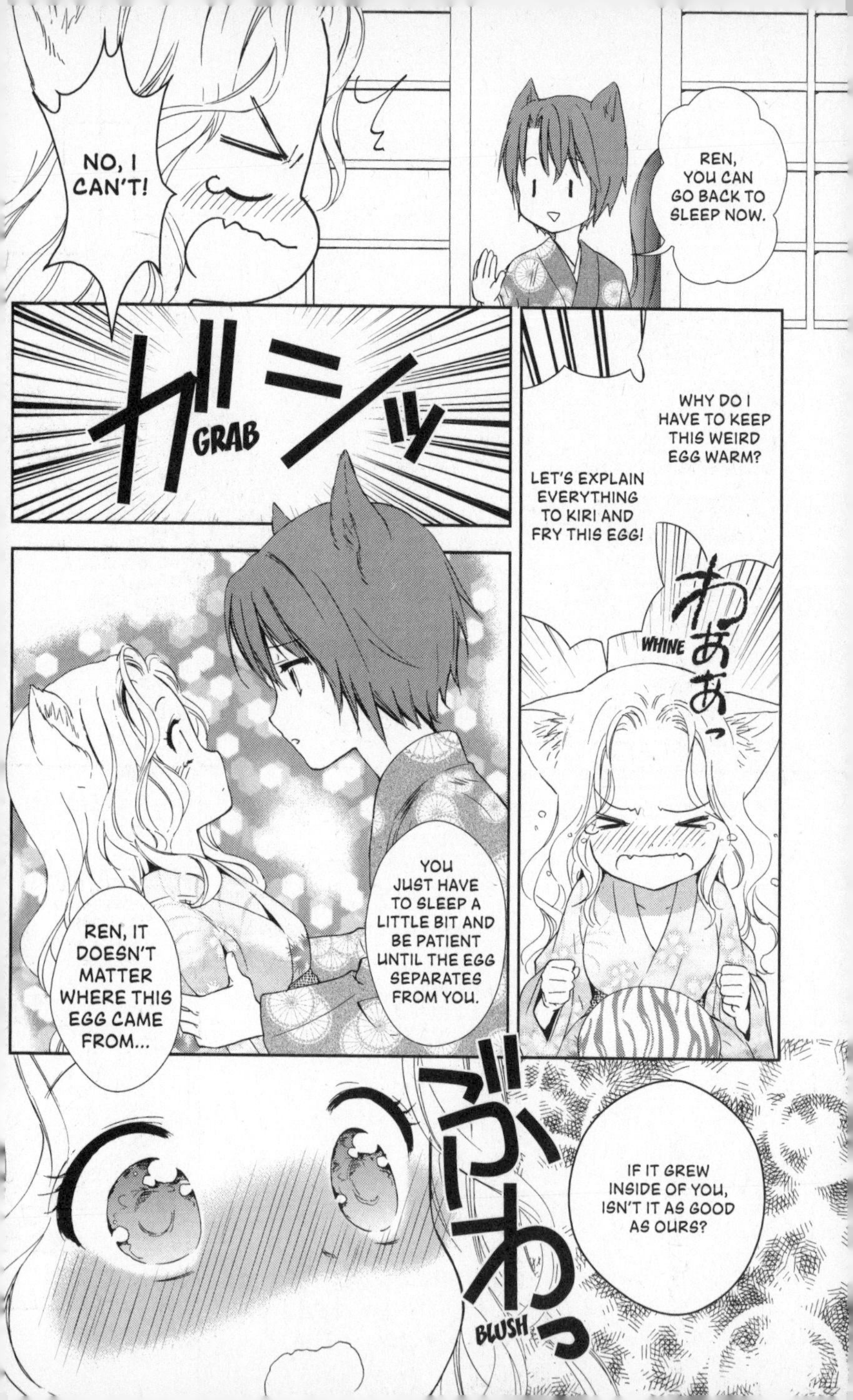
REN, YOU CAN GO BACK TO SLEEP NOW.
NO, I CAN'T!
WHY DO I HAVE TO KEEP THIS WEIRD EGG WARM?
LET'S EXPLAIN EVERYTHING TO KIRI AND FRY THIS EGG!
わああっ
WHINE
ガシッ
GRAB
YOU JUST HAVE TO SLEEP A LITTLE BIT AND BE PATIENT UNTIL THE EGG SEPARATES FROM YOU.
REN, IT DOESN'T MATTER WHERE THIS EGG CAME FROM...
IF IT GREW INSIDE OF YOU, ISN'T IT AS GOOD AS OURS?
ぶわっ
BLUSH

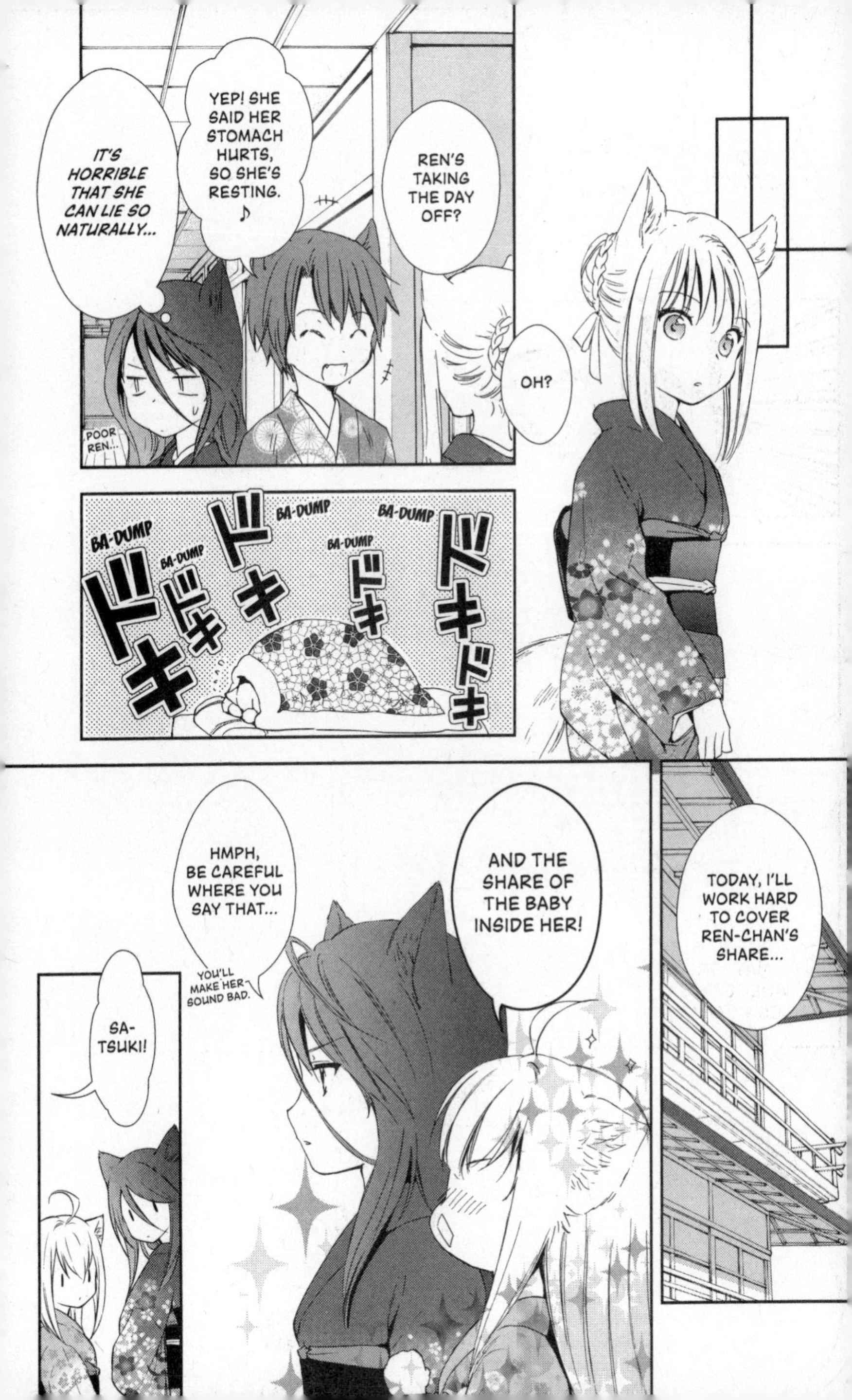
OH?
REN'S TAKING THE DAY OFF?
YEP! SHE SAID HER STOMACH HURTS, SO SHE'S RESTING. ♪
IT'S HORRIBLE THAT SHE CAN LIE SO NATURALLY...
POOR REN...
BA-DUMP
ドキドキ
BA-DUMP
ドキ
BA-DUMP
ドキ
BA-DUMP
ドキ
BA-DUMP
ドキ
TODAY, I'LL WORK HARD TO COVER REN-CHAN'S SHARE...
AND THE SHARE OF THE BABY INSIDE HER!
HMPH, BE CAREFUL WHERE YOU SAY THAT...
YOU'LL MAKE HER SOUND BAD.
SA-TSUKI!

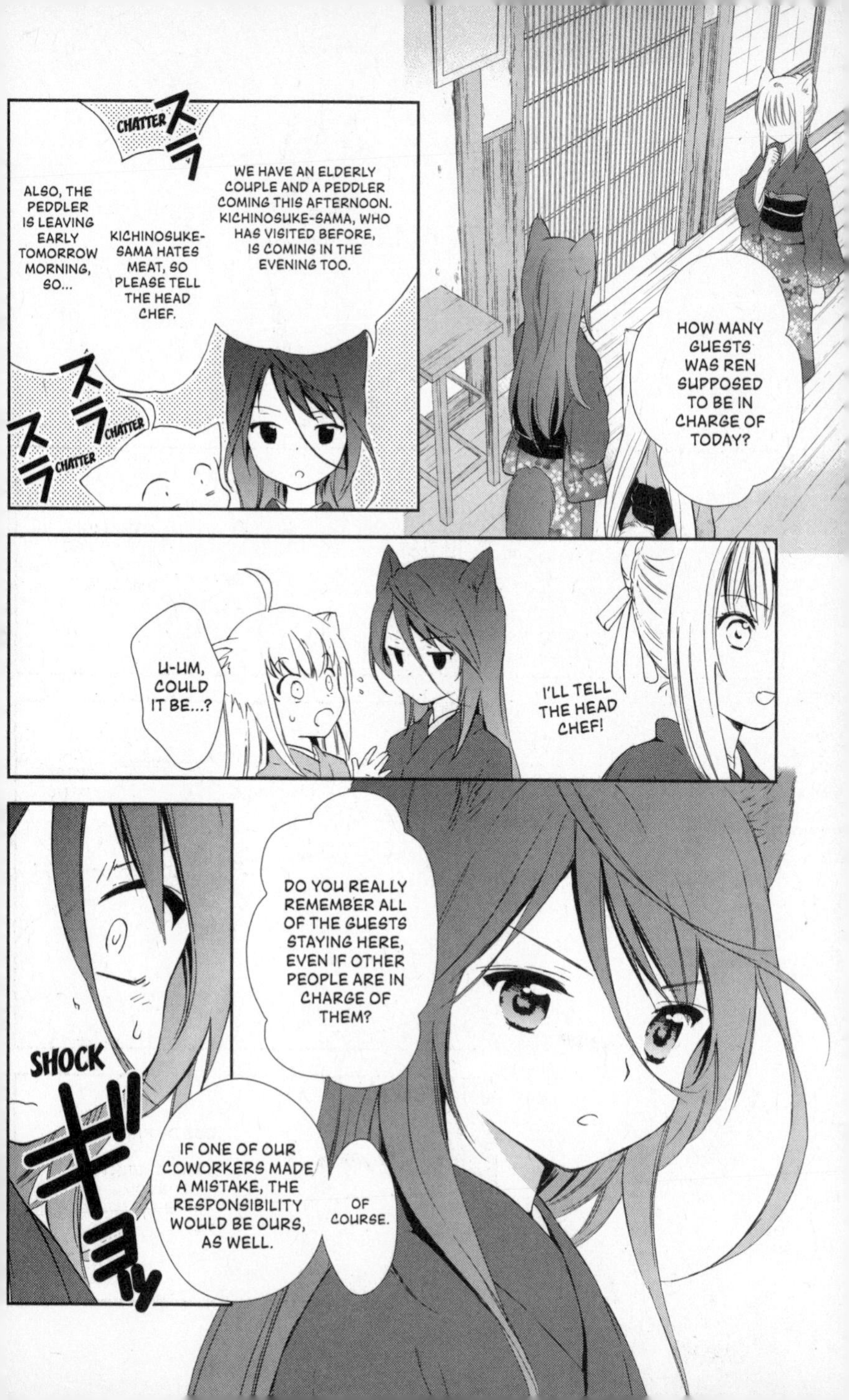
HOW MANY GUESTS WAS REN SUPPOSED TO BE IN CHARGE OF TODAY?
CHATTER スラ
WE HAVE AN ELDERLY COUPLE AND A PEDDLER COMING THIS AFTERNOON. KICHINOSUKE-SAMA, WHO HAS VISITED BEFORE, IS COMING IN THE EVENING TOO.
KICHINOSUKE-SAMA HATES MEAT, SO PLEASE TELL THE HEAD CHEF.
ALSO, THE PEDDLER IS LEAVING EARLY TOMORROW MORNING, SO...
スラ CHATTER
スラ CHATTER
I'LL TELL THE HEAD CHEF!
U-UM, COULD IT BE...?
DO YOU REALLY REMEMBER ALL OF THE GUESTS STAYING HERE, EVEN IF OTHER PEOPLE ARE IN CHARGE OF THEM?
OF COURSE.
IF ONE OF OUR COWORKERS MADE A MISTAKE, THE RESPONSIBILITY WOULD BE OURS, AS WELL.
SHOCK ギョッ

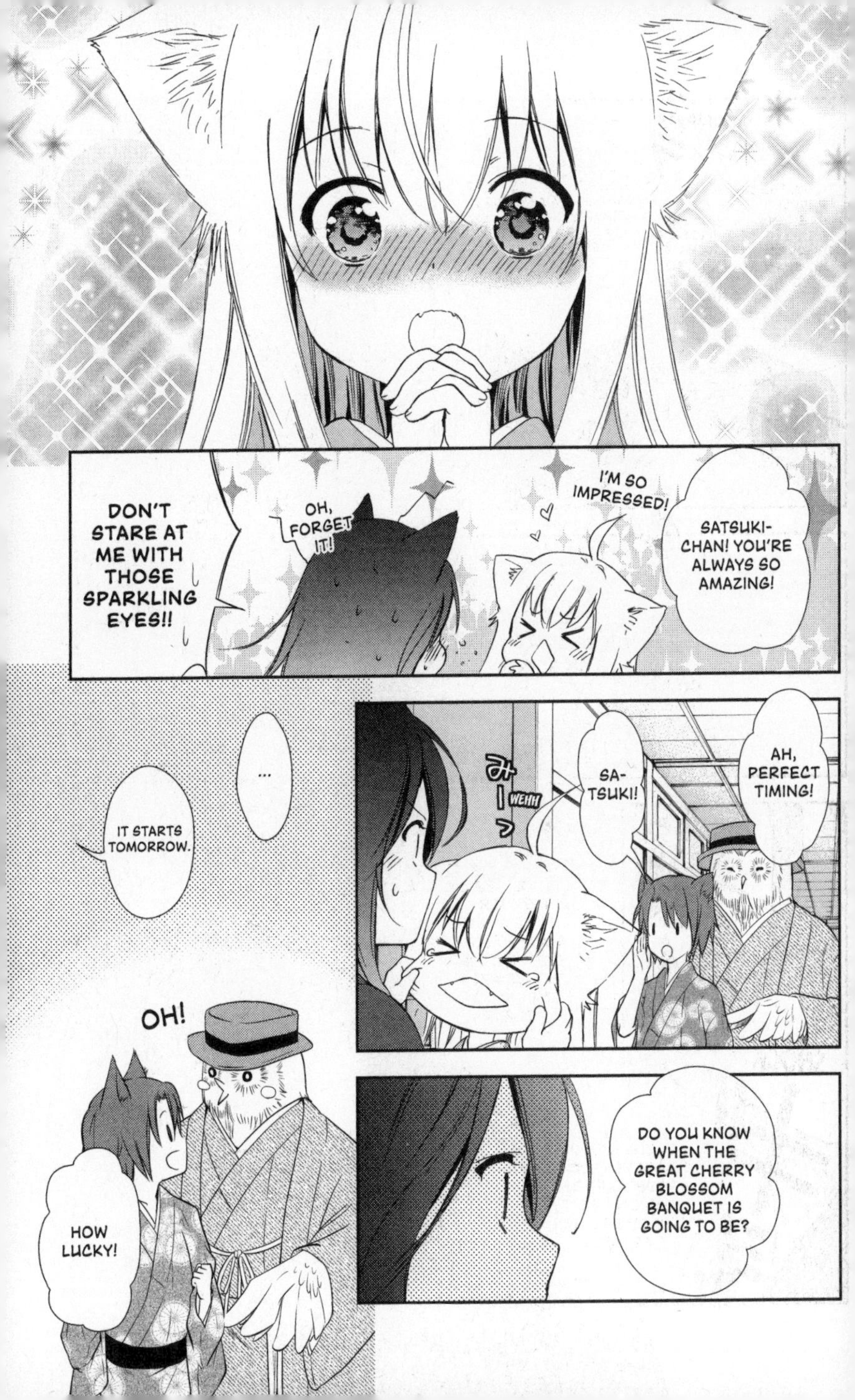
SATSUKI-CHAN! YOU'RE ALWAYS SO AMAZING!
I'M SO IMPRESSED!
OH, FORGET IT!
DON'T STARE AT ME WITH THOSE SPARKLING EYES!!
AH, PERFECT TIMING!
SA-TSUKI!
WEHH
DO YOU KNOW WHEN THE GREAT CHERRY BLOSSOM BANQUET IS GOING TO BE?
...
IT STARTS TOMORROW.
OH!
HOW LUCKY!

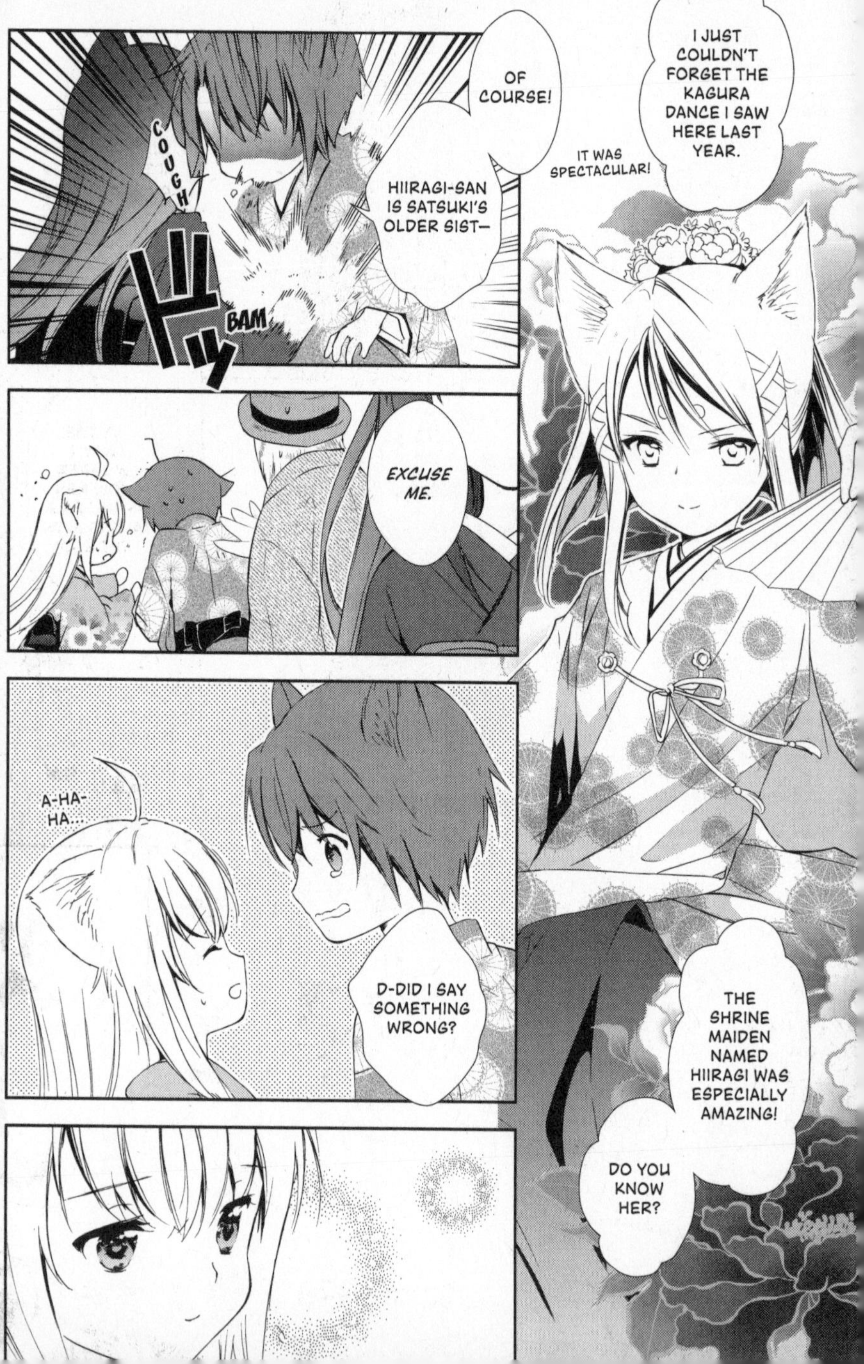
I JUST COULDN'T FORGET THE KAGURA DANCE I SAW HERE LAST YEAR.
IT WAS SPECTACULAR!
THE SHRINE MAIDEN NAMED HIIRAGI WAS ESPECIALLY AMAZING!
DO YOU KNOW HER?
OF COURSE!
HIIRAGI-SAN IS SATSUKI'S OLDER SIST—
COUGH
ドッ
BAM
EXCUSE ME.
D-DID I SAY SOMETHING WRONG?
A-HA-HA...

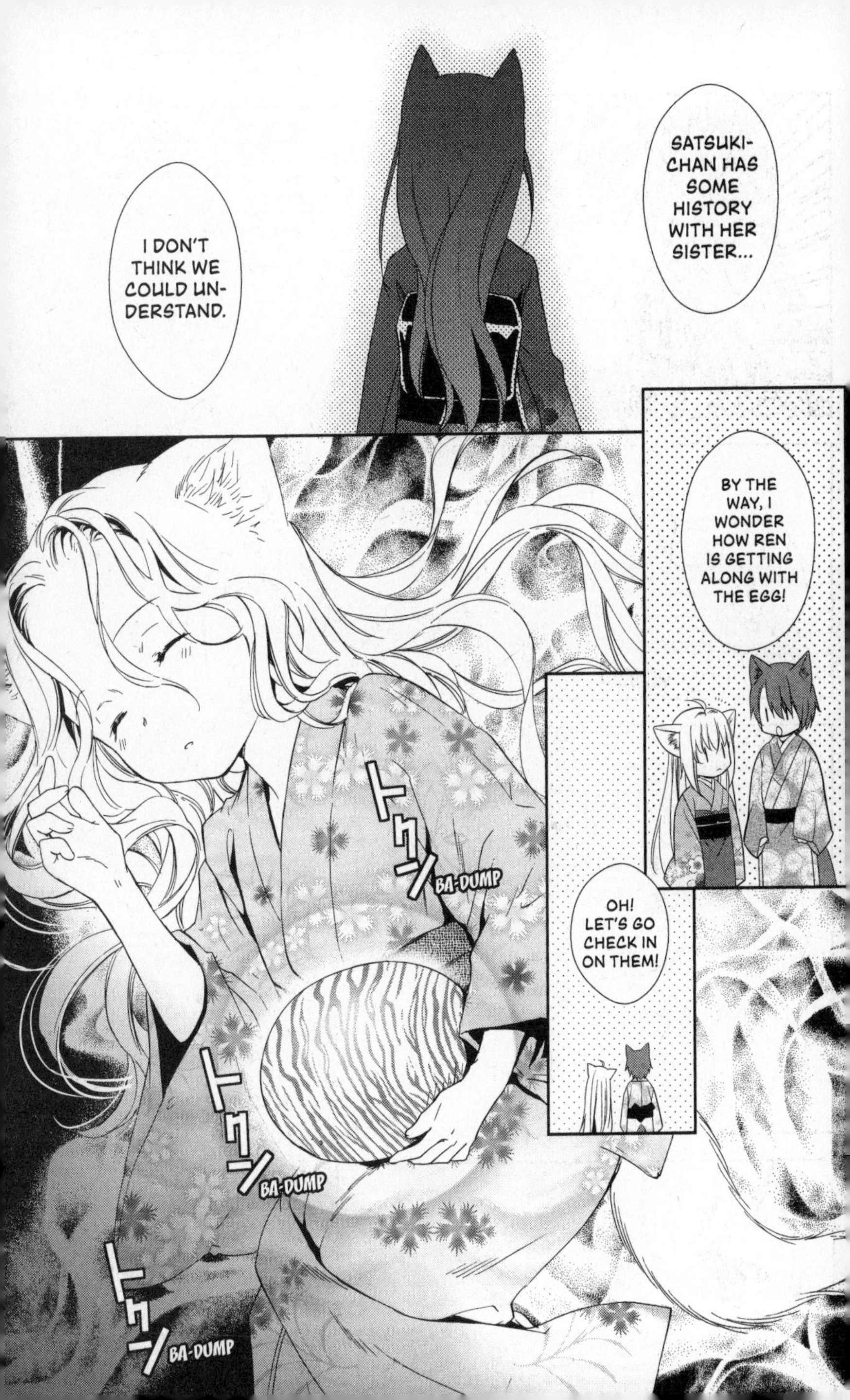

SATSUKI-CHAN HAS SOME HISTORY WITH HER SISTER...
I DON'T THINK WE COULD UNDERSTAND.
BY THE WAY, I WONDER HOW REN IS GETTING ALONG WITH THE EGG!
OH! LET'S GO CHECK IN ON THEM!
トクン
BA-DUMP
トクン
BA-DUMP
トクン
BA-DUMP

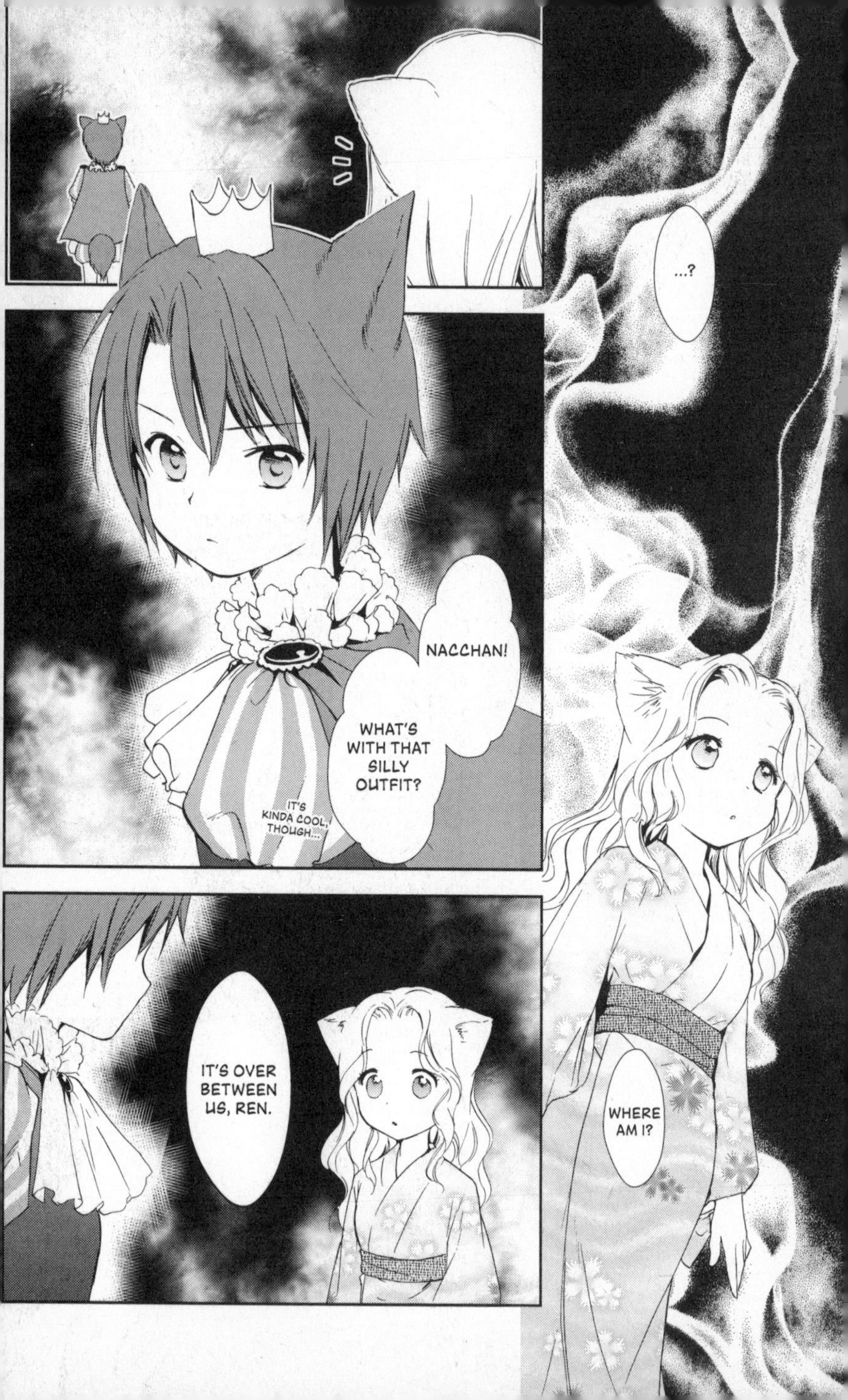
...?
WHERE AM I?
NACCHAN!
WHAT'S WITH THAT SILLY OUTFIT?
IT'S KINDA COOL, THOUGH...
IT'S OVER BETWEEN US, REN.

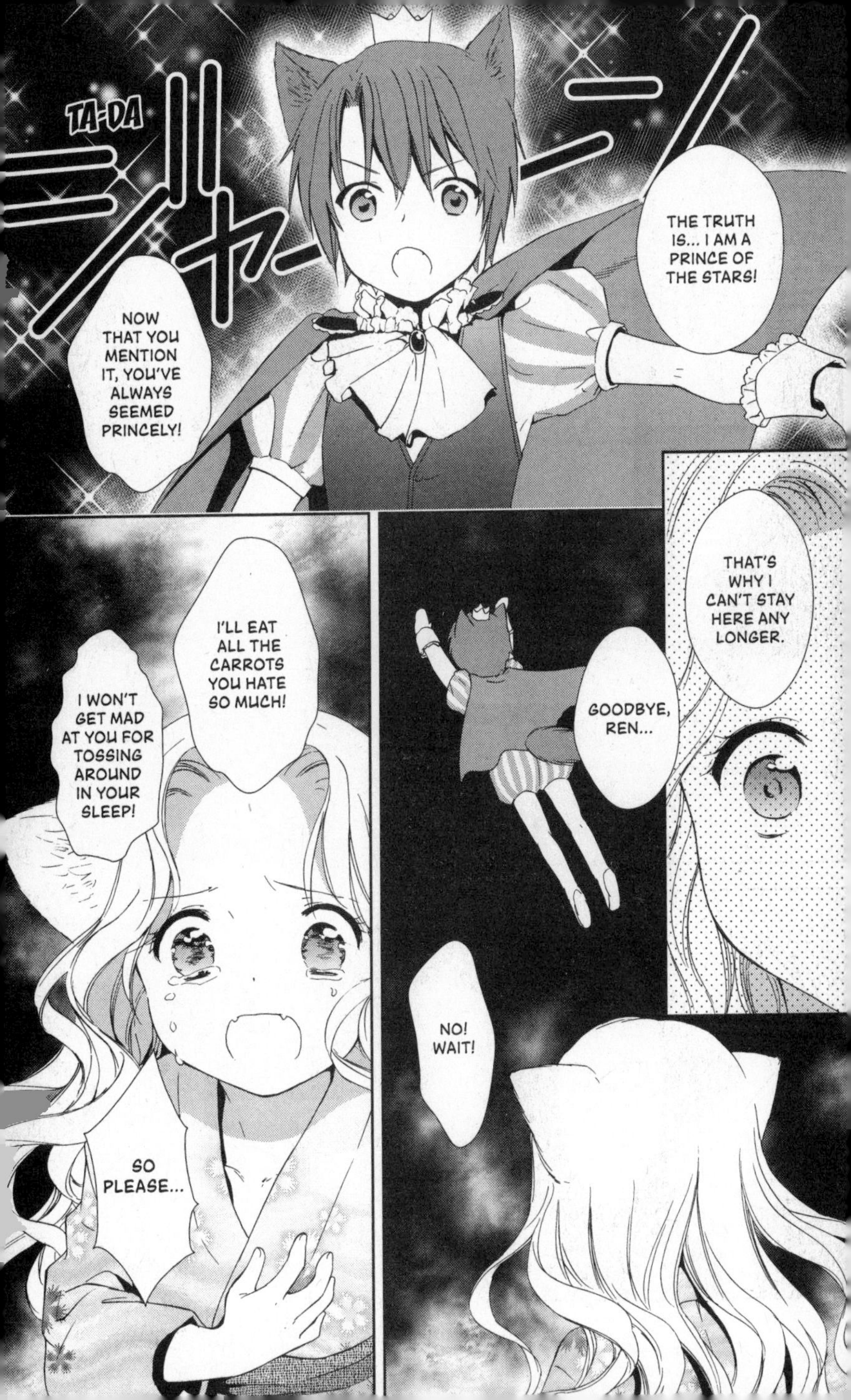
TA-DA
THE TRUTH IS... I AM A PRINCE OF THE STARS!
NOW THAT YOU MENTION IT, YOU'VE ALWAYS SEEMED PRINCELY!
THAT'S WHY I CAN'T STAY HERE ANY LONGER.
GOODBYE, REN...
NO! WAIT!
I'LL EAT ALL THE CARROTS YOU HATE SO MUCH!
I WON'T GET MAD AT YOU FOR TOSSING AROUND IN YOUR SLEEP!
SO PLEASE...

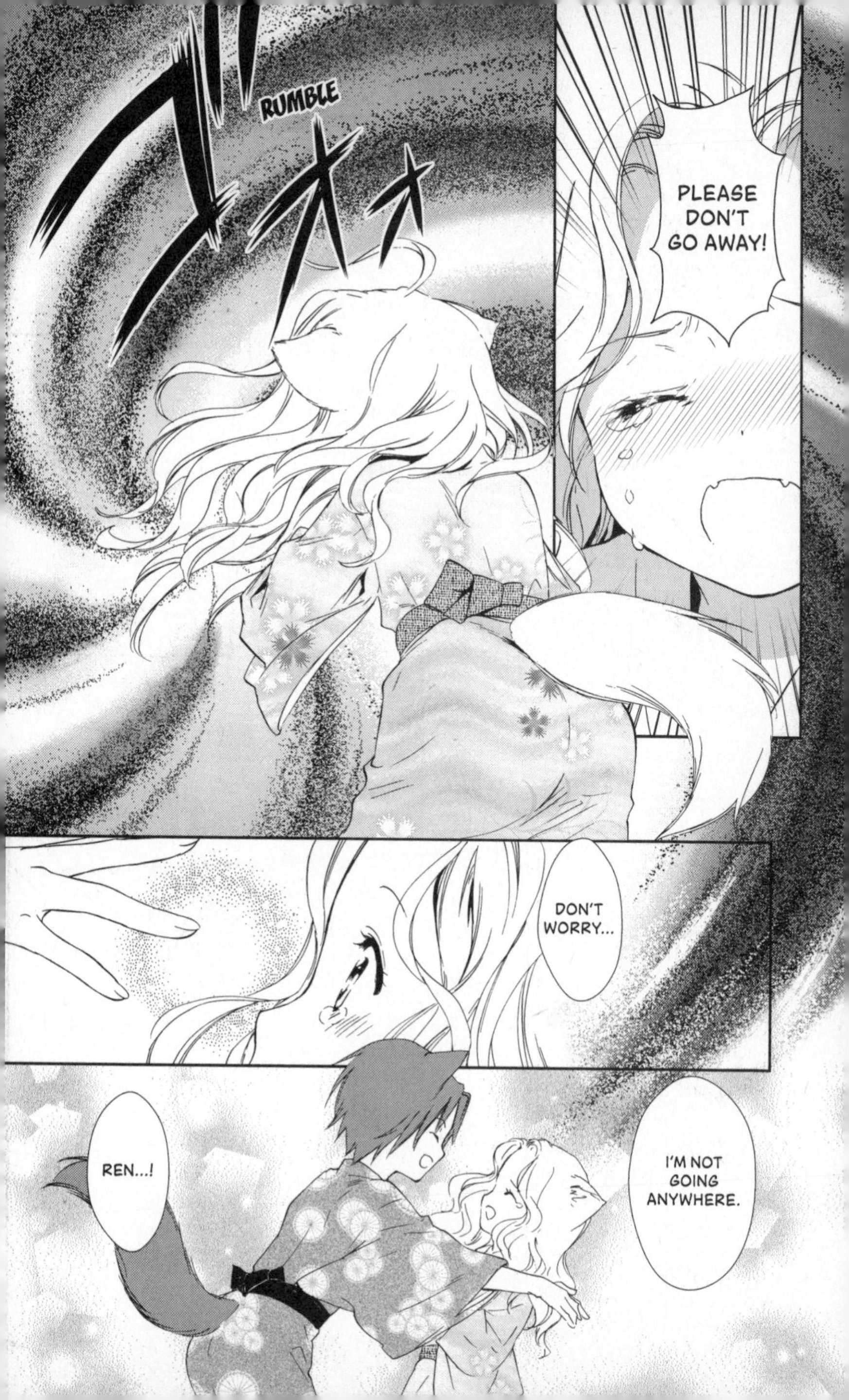
PLEASE DON'T GO AWAY!
RUMBLE
DON'T WORRY...
I'M NOT GOING ANYWHERE.
REN...!

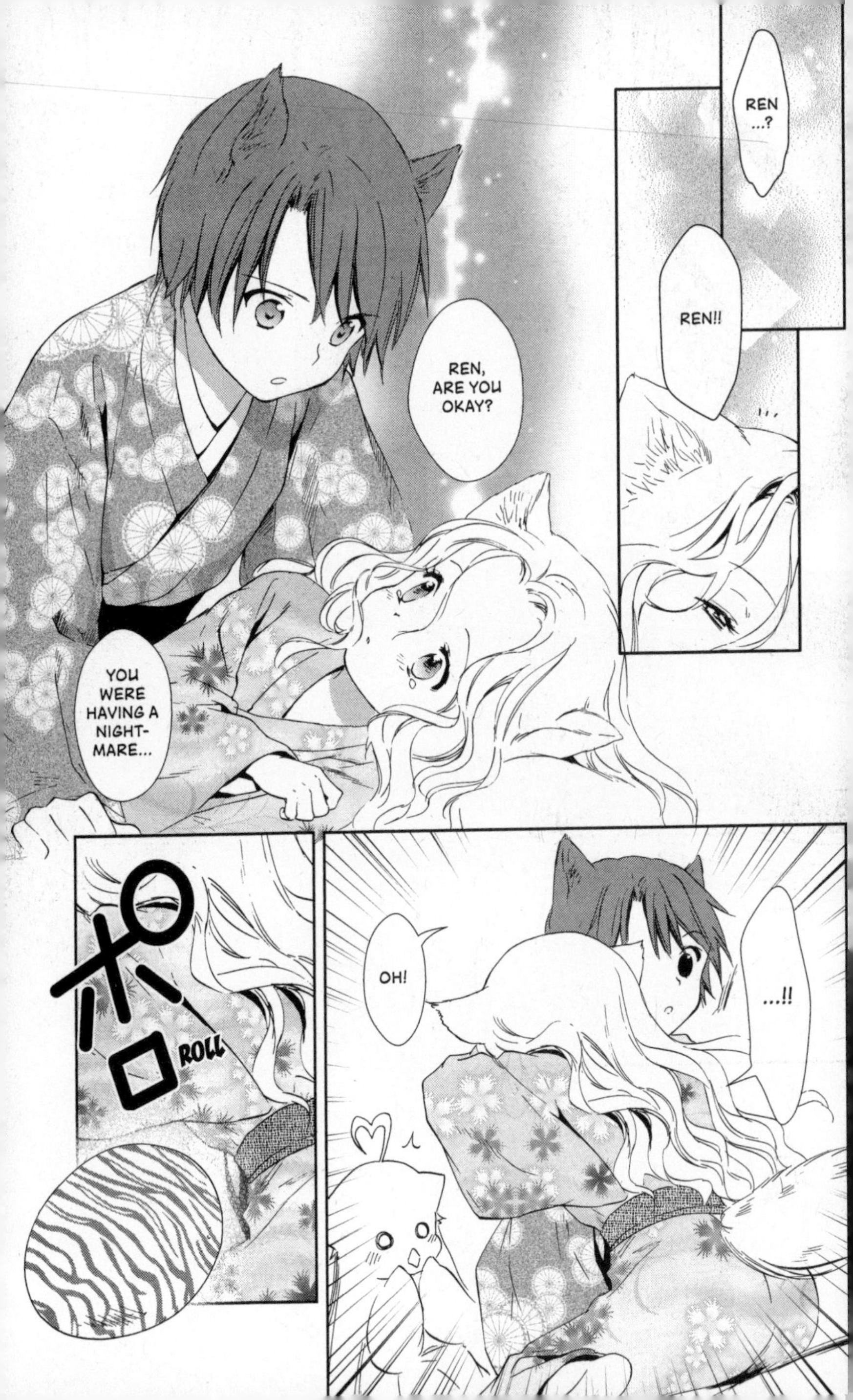
REN ...?
REN!!
REN, ARE YOU OKAY?
YOU WERE HAVING A NIGHT-MARE...
...!!
OH!
ポロ
ROLL

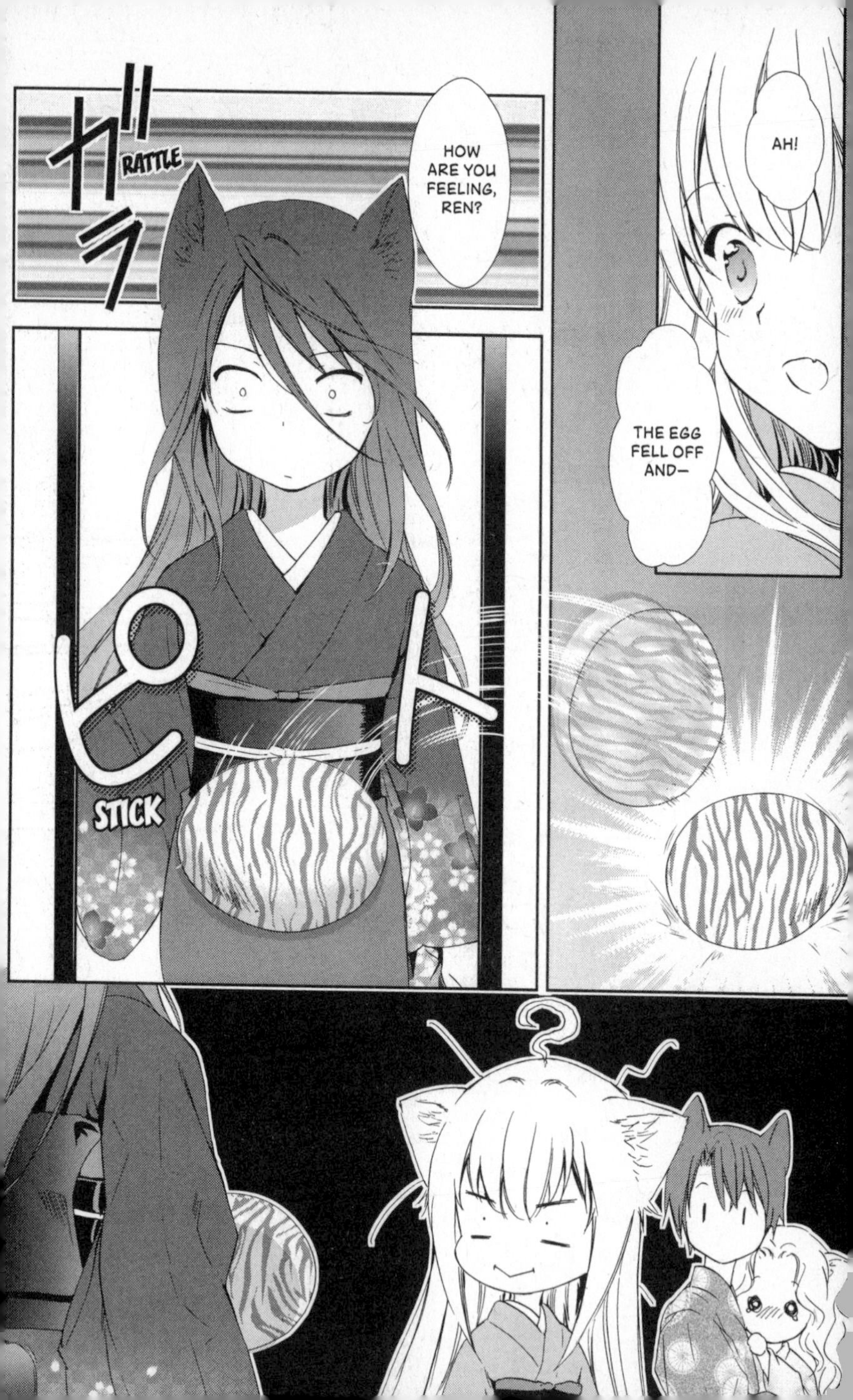
AH!
THE EGG FELL OFF AND—
ガラ
RATTLE
HOW ARE YOU FEELING, REN?
ピト
STICK

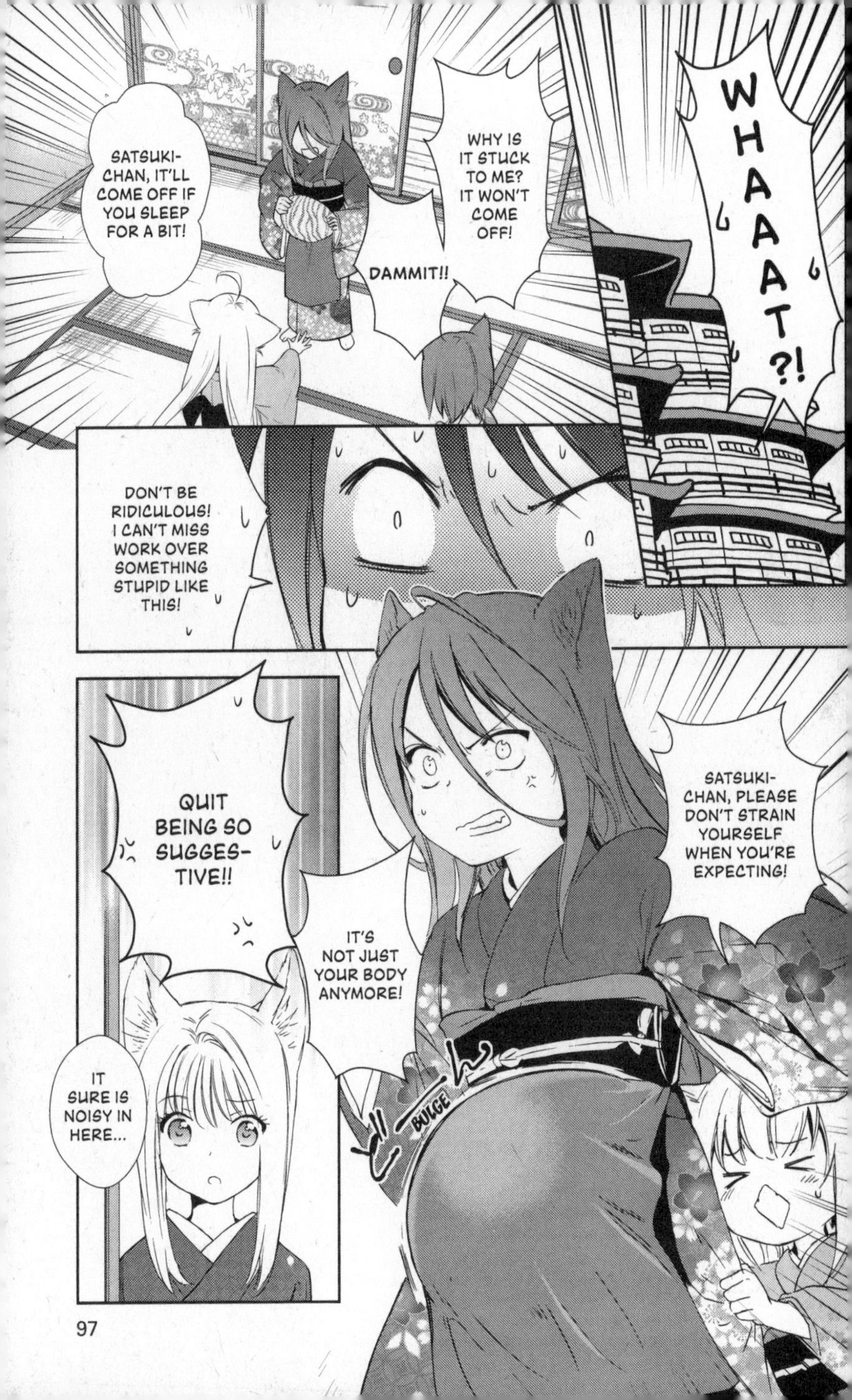
WHAAAT?!
WHY IS IT STUCK TO ME? IT WON'T COME OFF!
DAMMIT!!
SATSUKI-CHAN, IT'LL COME OFF IF YOU SLEEP FOR A BIT!
DON'T BE RIDICULOUS! I CAN'T MISS WORK OVER SOMETHING STUPID LIKE THIS!
SATSUKI-CHAN, PLEASE DON'T STRAIN YOURSELF WHEN YOU'RE EXPECTING!
IT'S NOT JUST YOUR BODY ANYMORE!
BULGE
QUIT BEING SO SUGGES-TIVE!!
IT SURE IS NOISY IN HERE...

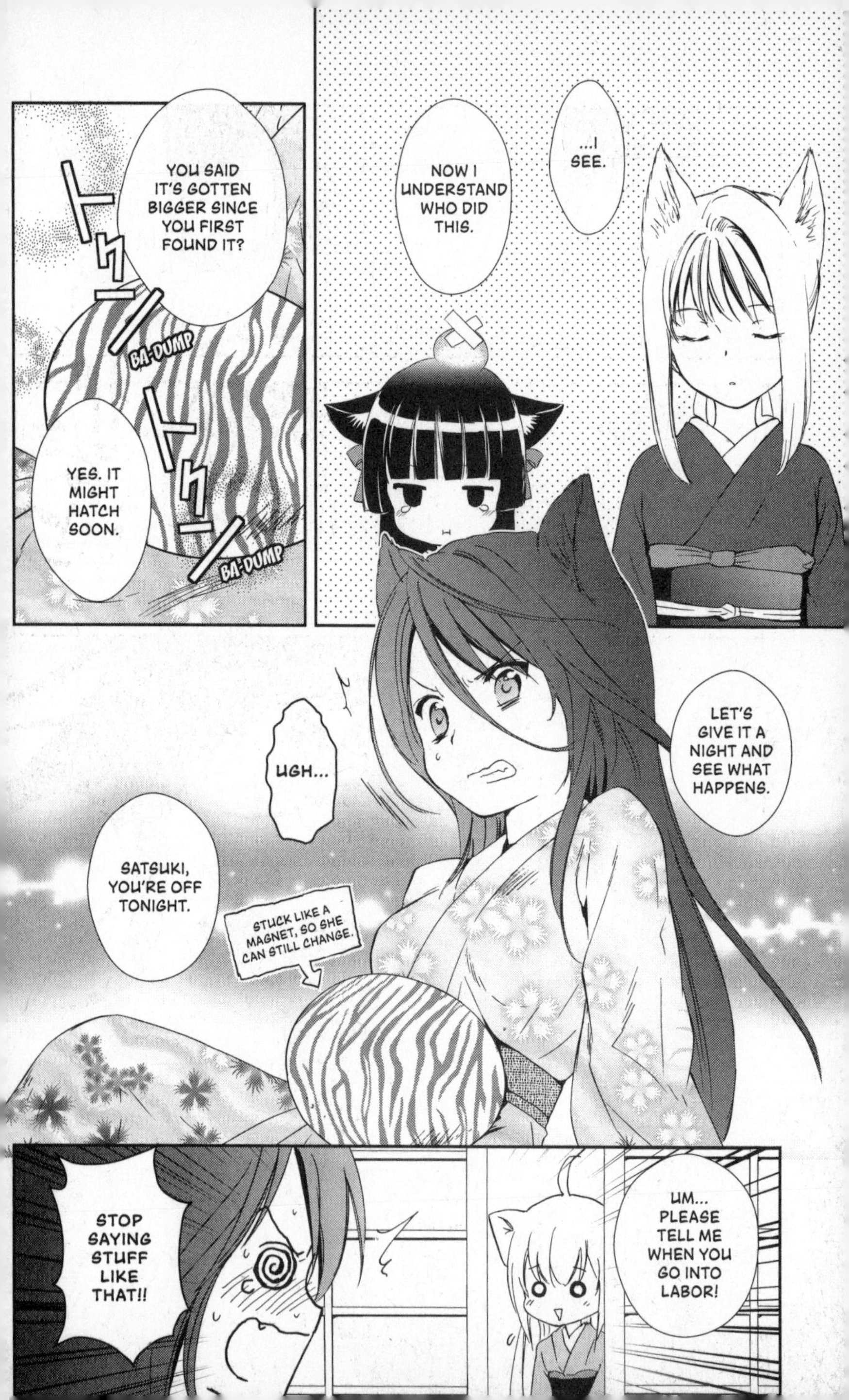
...I SEE.
NOW I UNDERSTAND WHO DID THIS.
YOU SAID IT'S GOTTEN BIGGER SINCE YOU FIRST FOUND IT?
BA-DUMP
YES. IT MIGHT HATCH SOON.
BA-DUMP
LET'S GIVE IT A NIGHT AND SEE WHAT HAPPENS.
UGH...
SATSUKI, YOU'RE OFF TONIGHT.
STUCK LIKE A MAGNET, SO SHE CAN STILL CHANGE.
UM... PLEASE TELL ME WHEN YOU GO INTO LABOR!
STOP SAYING STUFF LIKE THAT!!

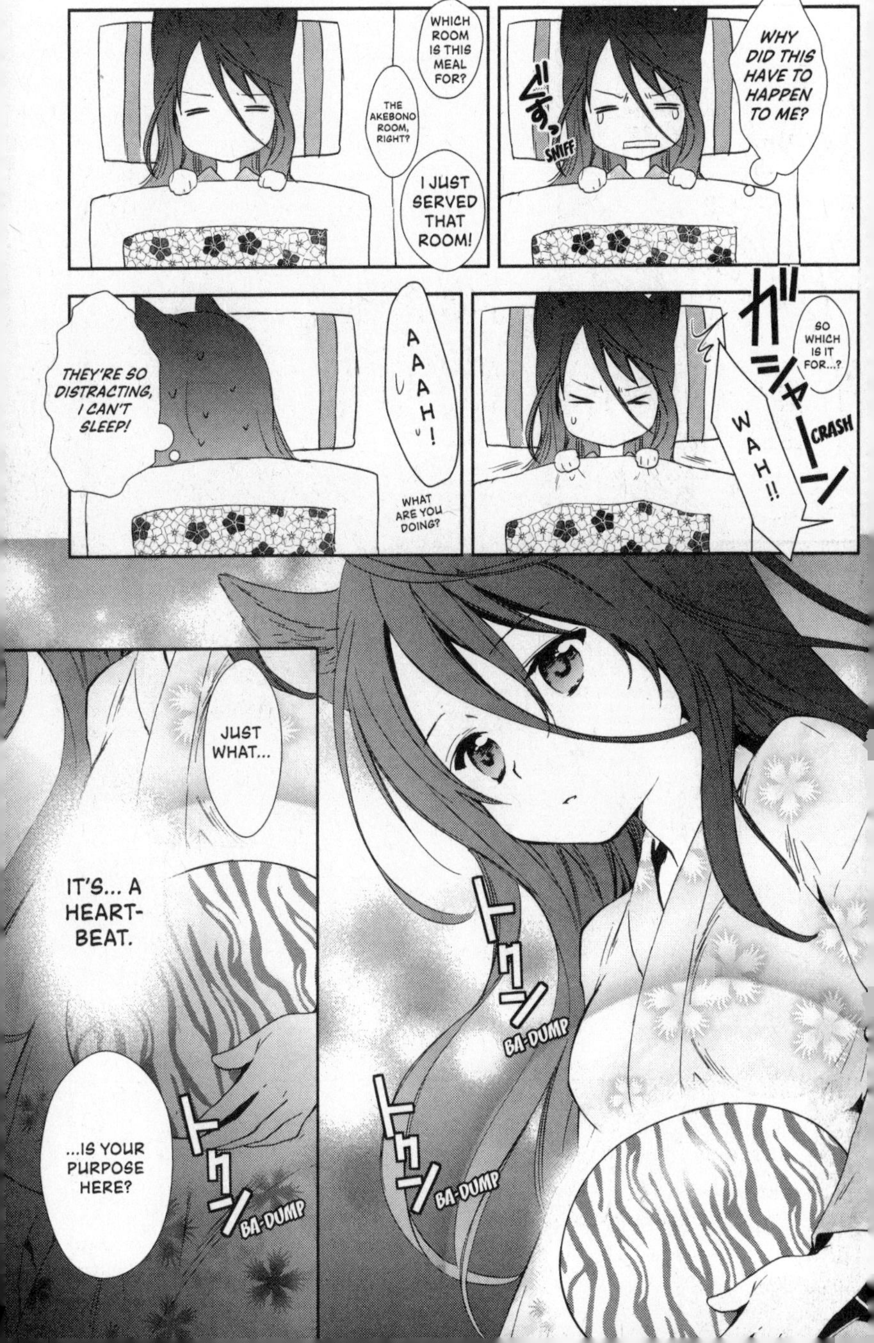
WHY DID THIS HAVE TO HAPPEN TO ME?
ぐすっ
SNIFF
WHICH ROOM IS THIS MEAL FOR?
THE AKEBONO ROOM, RIGHT?
I JUST SERVED THAT ROOM!
SO WHICH IS IT FOR...?
ガシャーン
CRASH
WAH!!
AAAH!
WHAT ARE YOU DOING?
THEY'RE SO DISTRACTING, I CAN'T SLEEP!
トクン
BA-DUMP
トクン
BA-DUMP
JUST WHAT...
IT'S... A HEART-BEAT.
...IS YOUR PURPOSE HERE?
トクン
BA-DUMP

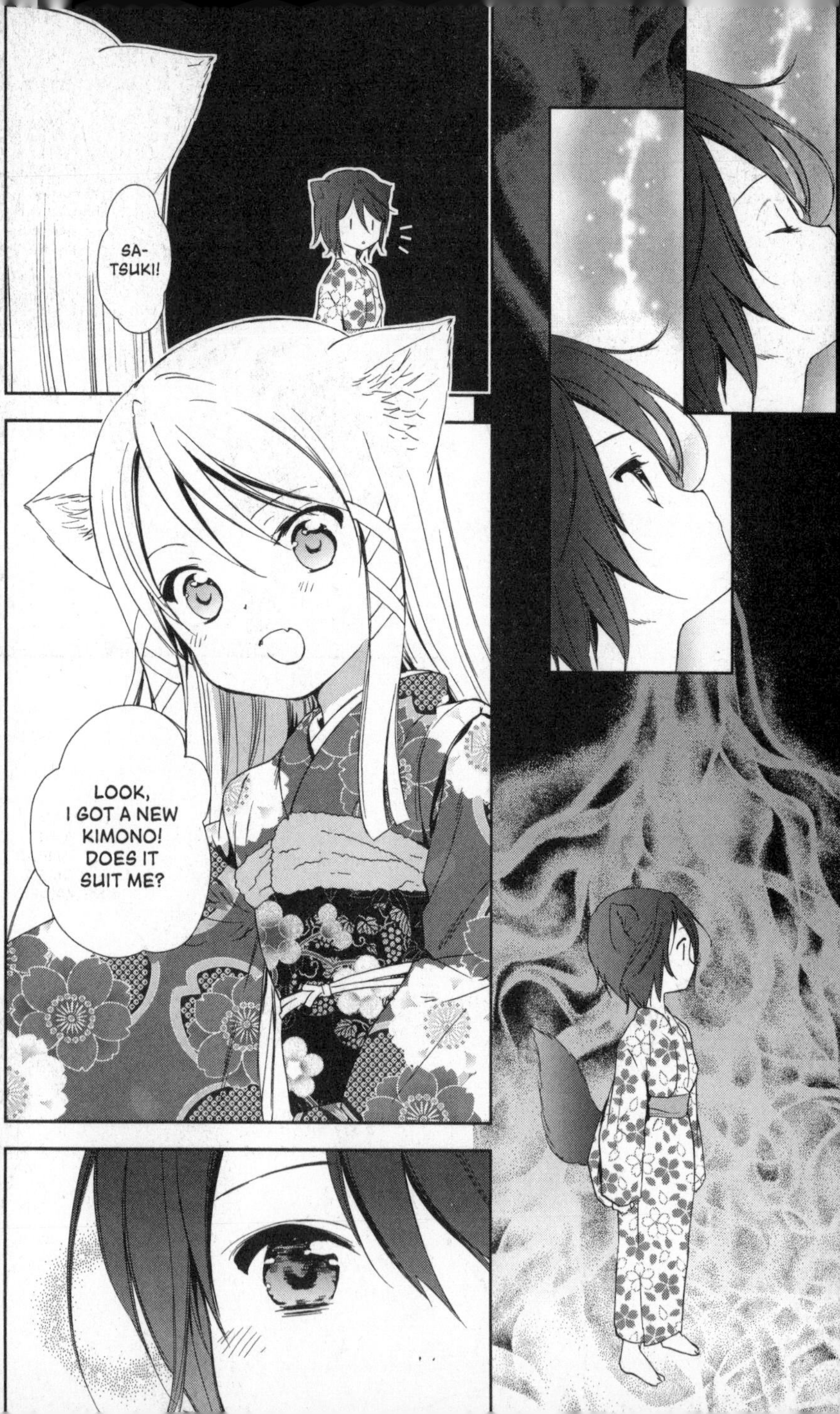
SA-TSUKI!
LOOK, I GOT A NEW KIMONO! DOES IT SUIT ME?

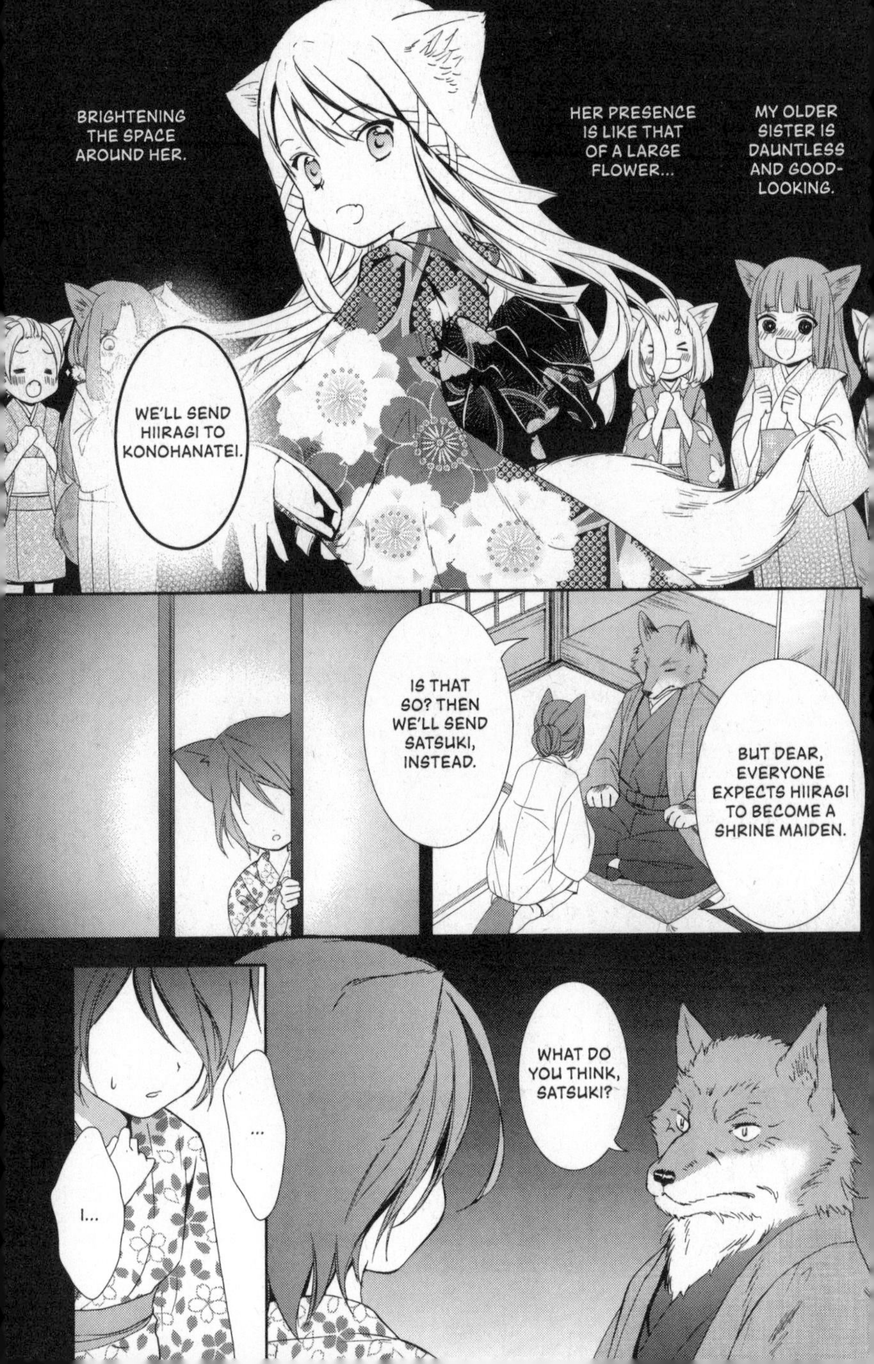
MY OLDER SISTER IS DAUNTLESS AND GOOD-LOOKING.
HER PRESENCE IS LIKE THAT OF A LARGE FLOWER...
BRIGHTENING THE SPACE AROUND HER.
WE'LL SEND HIIRAGI TO KONOHANATEI.
BUT DEAR, EVERYONE EXPECTS HIIRAGI TO BECOME A SHRINE MAIDEN.
IS THAT SO? THEN WE'LL SEND SATSUKI, INSTEAD.
WHAT DO YOU THINK, SATSUKI?
...
I...

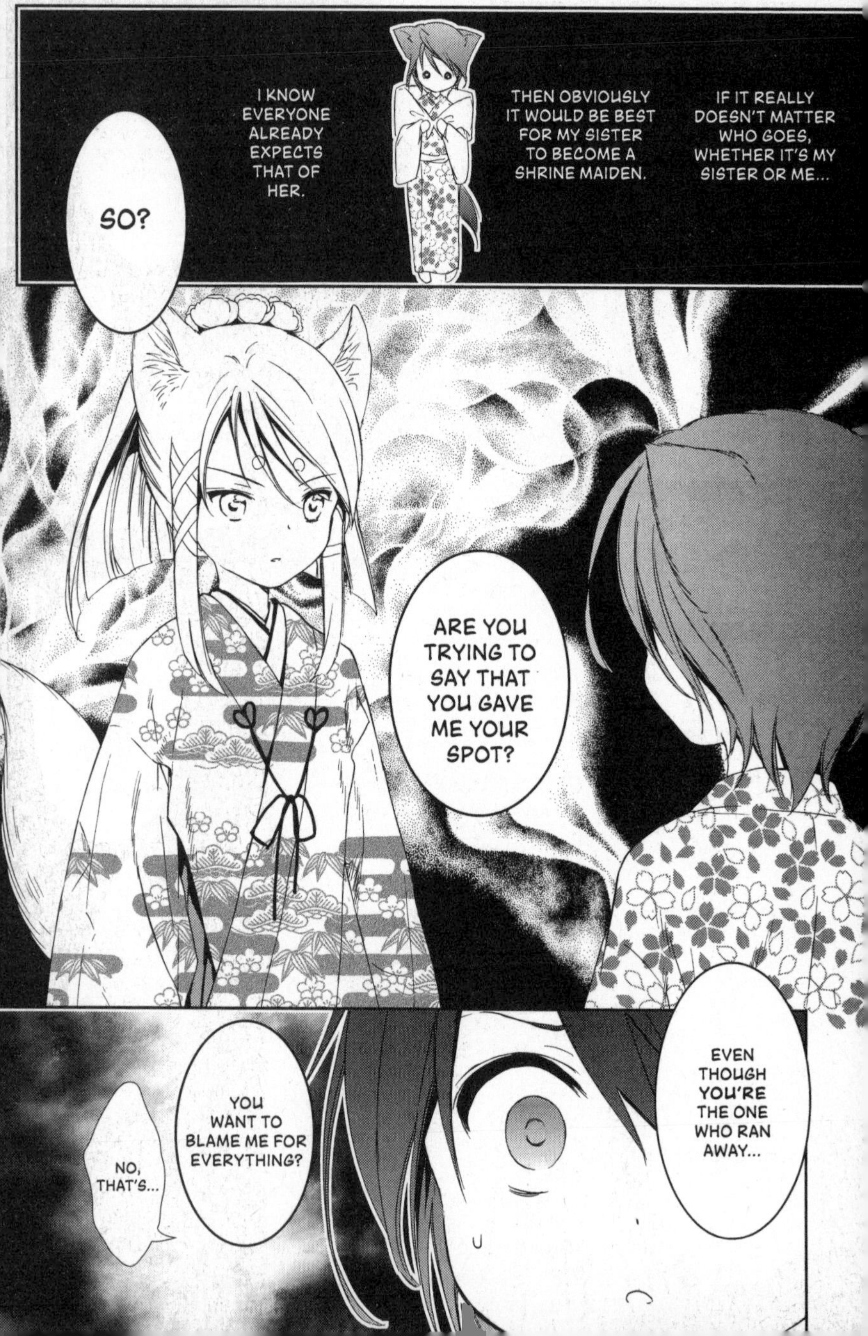
IF IT REALLY DOESN'T MATTER WHO GOES, WHETHER IT'S MY SISTER OR ME...
THEN OBVIOUSLY IT WOULD BE BEST FOR MY SISTER TO BECOME A SHRINE MAIDEN.
I KNOW EVERYONE ALREADY EXPECTS THAT OF HER.
SO?
ARE YOU TRYING TO SAY THAT YOU GAVE ME YOUR SPOT?
EVEN THOUGH YOU'RE THE ONE WHO RAN AWAY...
YOU WANT TO BLAME ME FOR EVERYTHING?
NO, THAT'S...

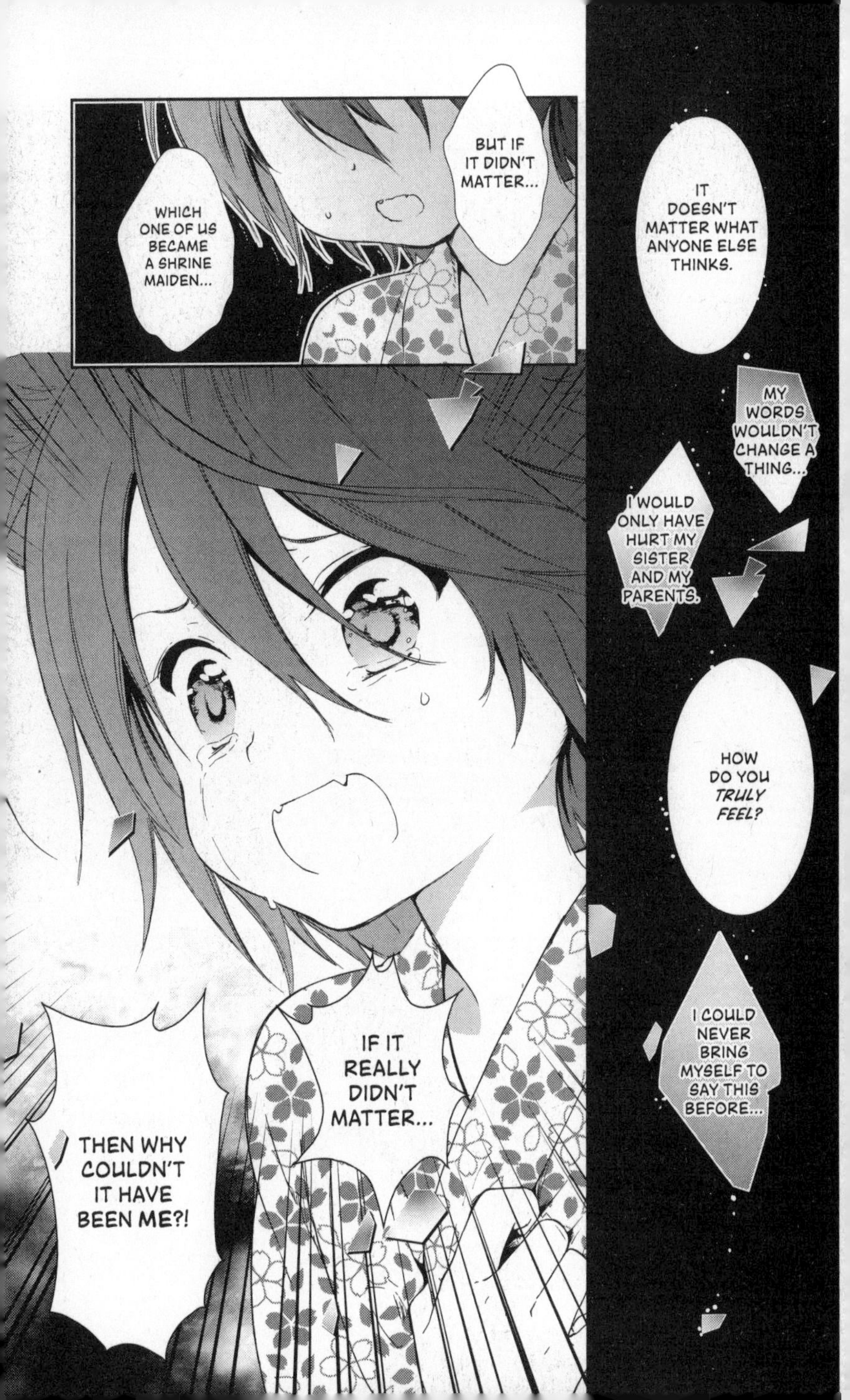
IT DOESN'T MATTER WHAT ANYONE ELSE THINKS.
MY WORDS WOULDN'T CHANGE A THING...
I WOULD ONLY HAVE HURT MY SISTER AND MY PARENTS.
HOW DO YOU *TRULY FEEL?*
I COULD NEVER BRING MYSELF TO SAY THIS BEFORE...
BUT IF IT DIDN'T MATTER...
WHICH ONE OF US BECAME A SHRINE MAIDEN...
IF IT REALLY DIDN'T MATTER...
THEN WHY COULDN'T IT HAVE BEEN ME?!

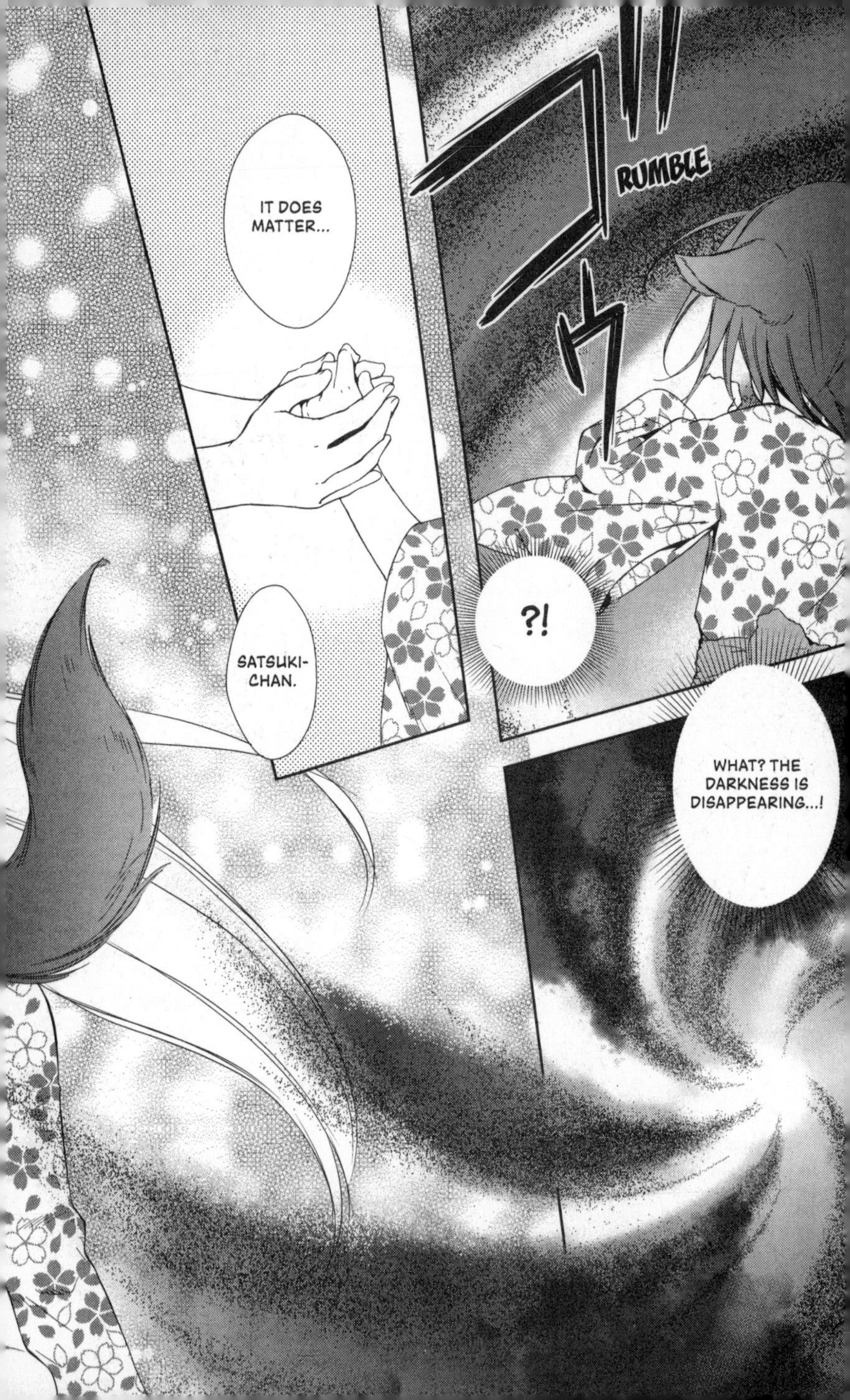
RUMBLE
?!
WHAT? THE DARKNESS IS DISAPPEARING...!
IT DOES MATTER...
SATSUKI-CHAN.

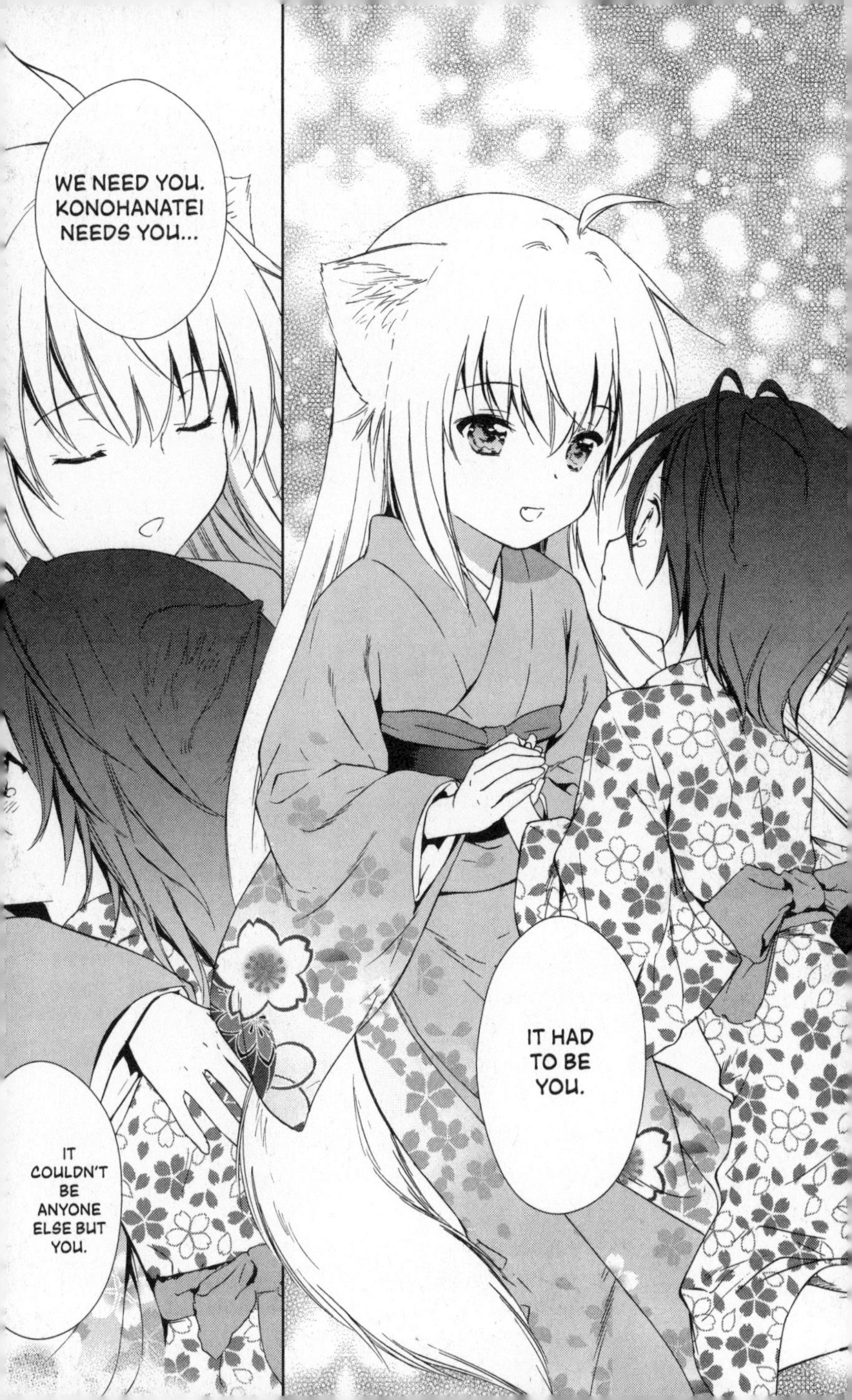
IT HAD TO BE YOU.
WE NEED YOU. KONOHANATEI NEEDS YOU...
IT COULDN'T BE ANYONE ELSE BUT YOU.

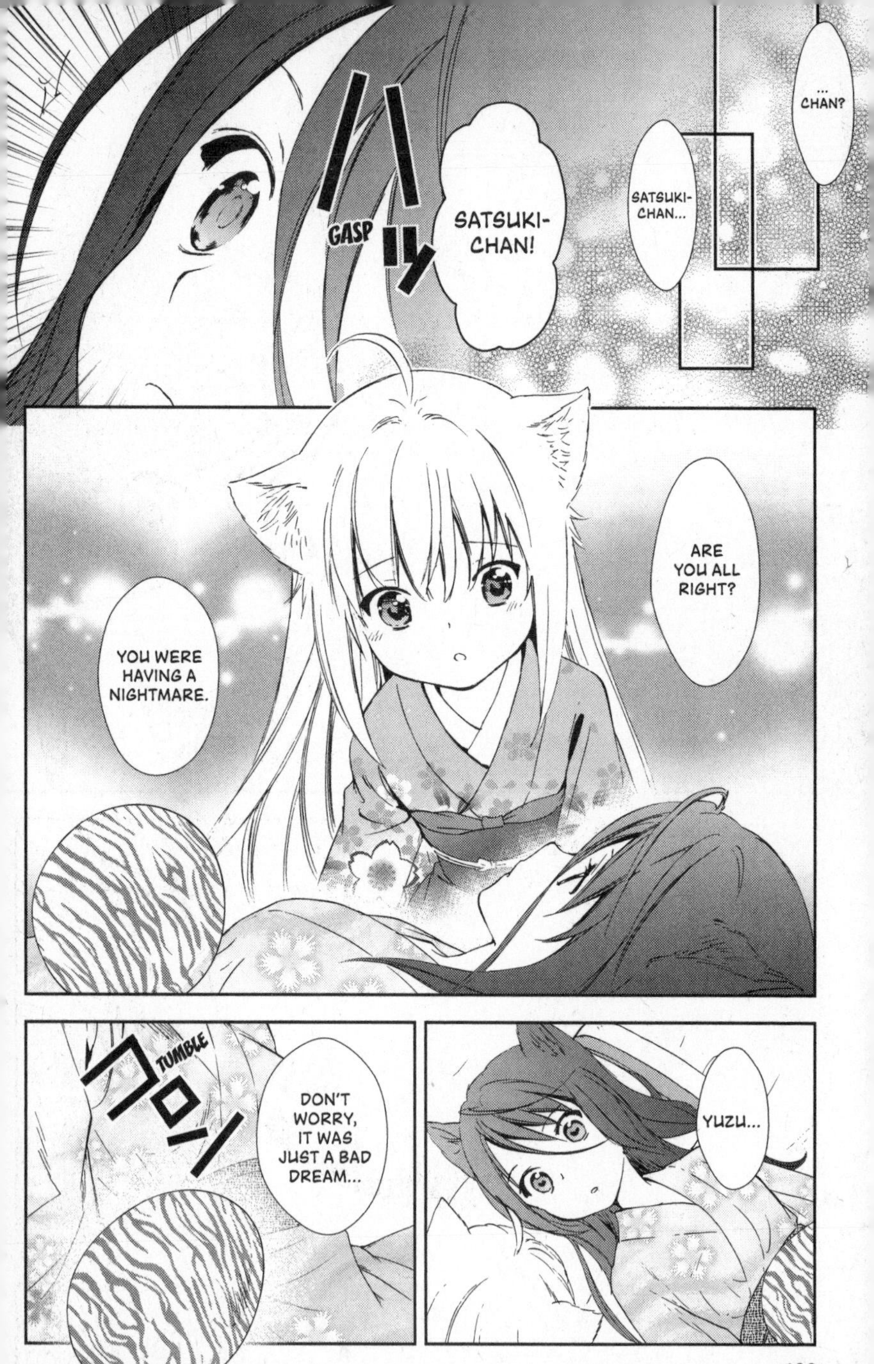
...CHAN?
SATSUKI-CHAN...
GASP
SATSUKI-CHAN!
ARE YOU ALL RIGHT?
YOU WERE HAVING A NIGHTMARE.
YUZU...
DON'T WORRY, IT WAS JUST A BAD DREAM...
TUMBLE

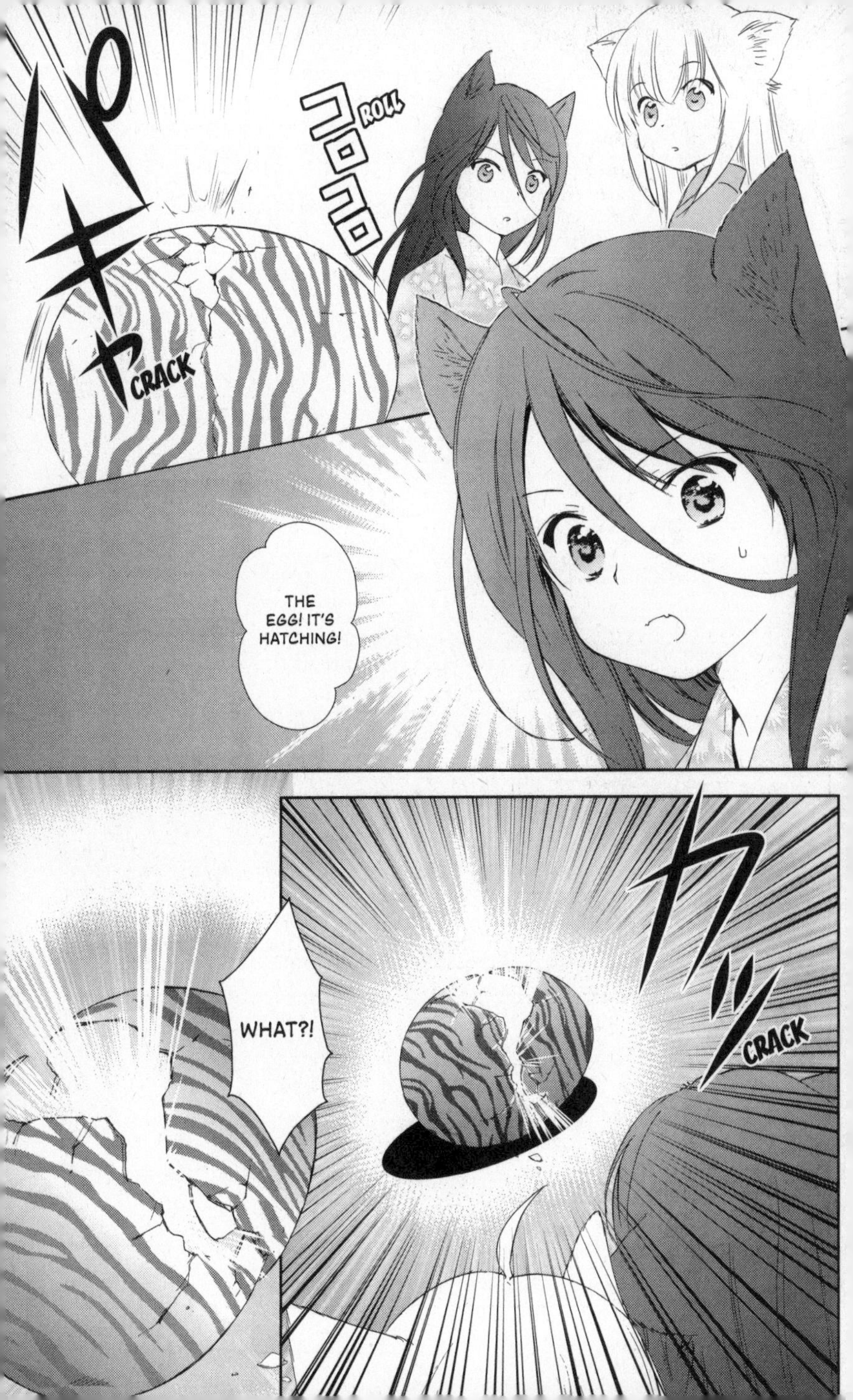
コロコロ
ROLL
パキャ
CRACK
THE EGG! IT'S HATCHING!
ガッ
CRACK
WHAT?!

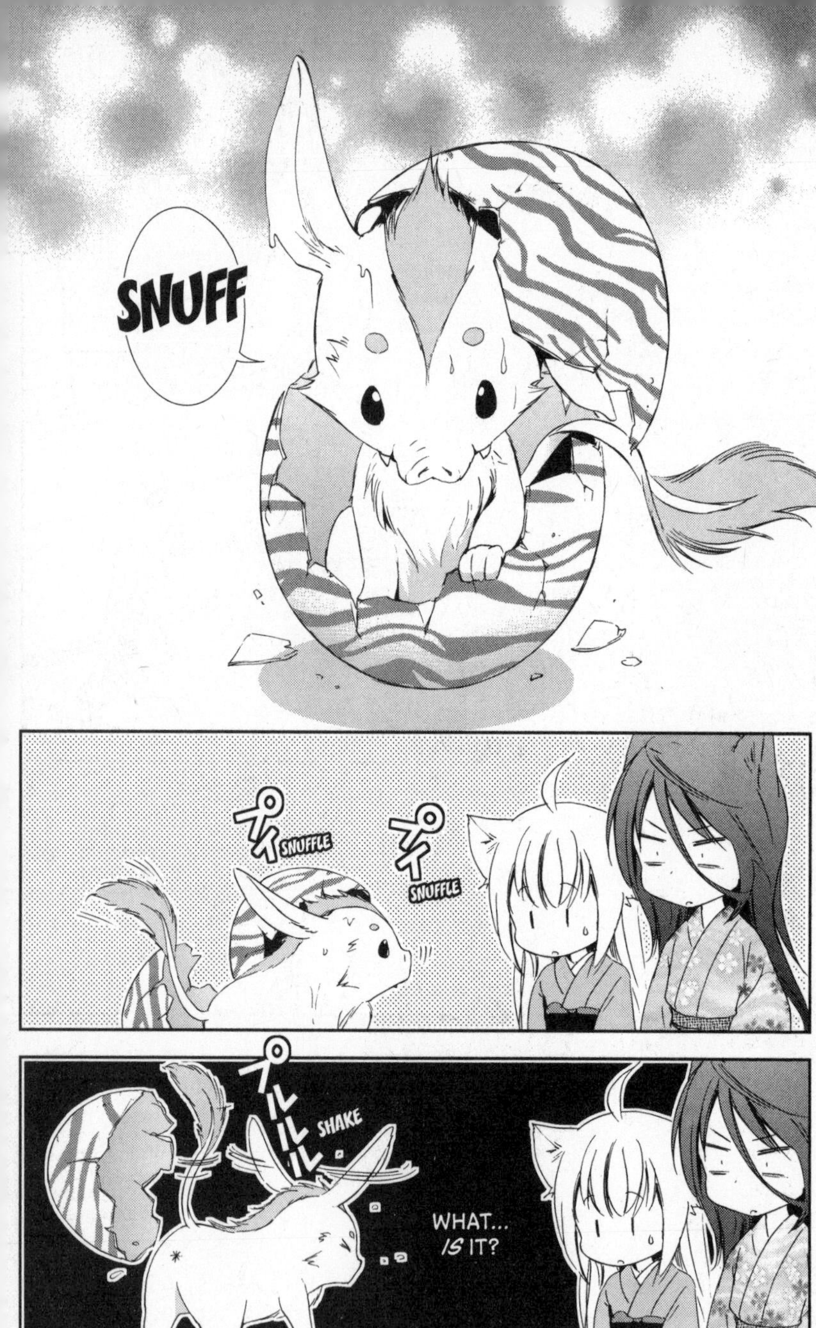
SNUFF
ピィ
SNUFFLE
ピィ
SNUFFLE
WHAT... *IS* IT?
プルルル
SHAKE

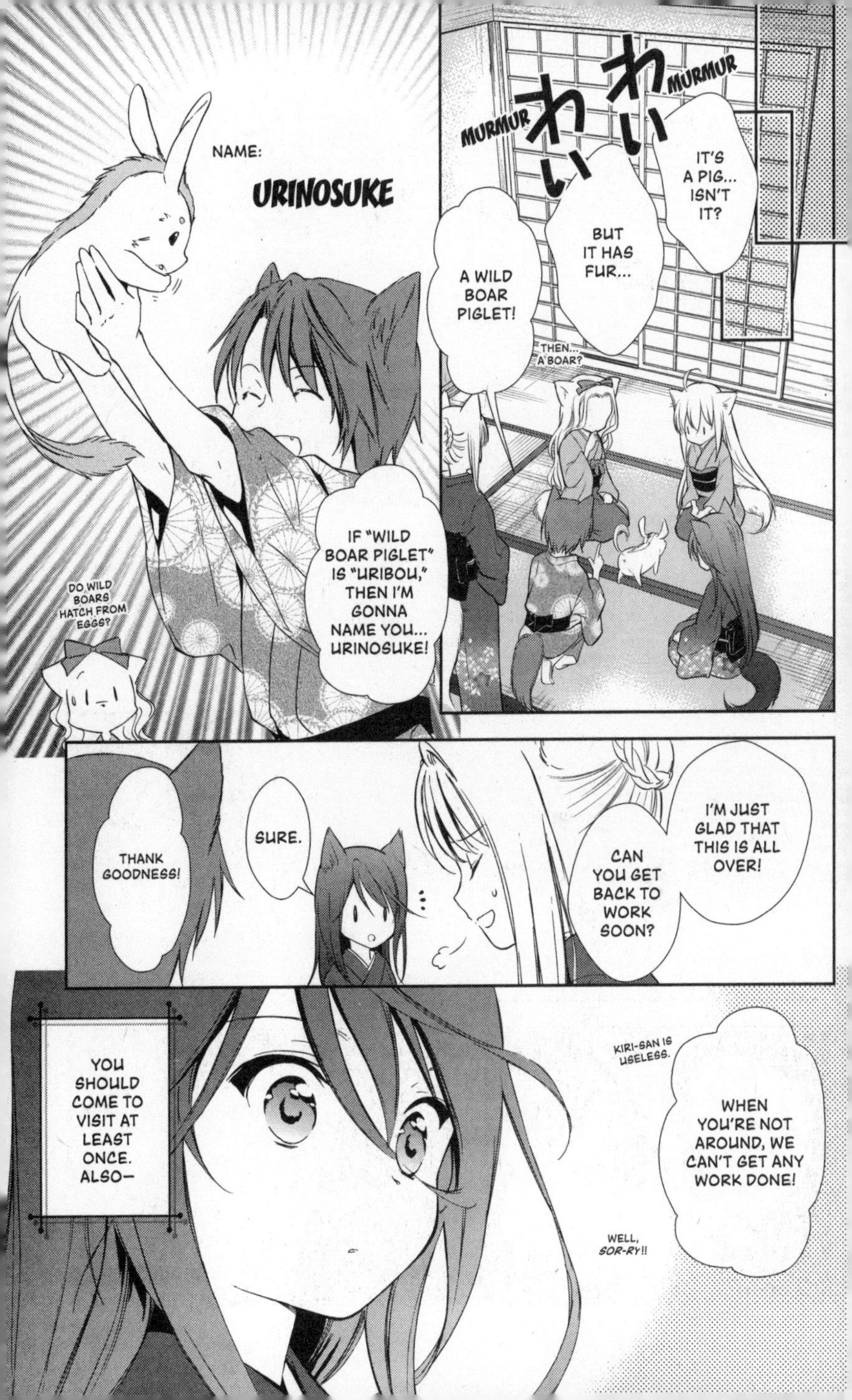

MURMUR
わいわい
MURMUR
IT'S A PIG... ISN'T IT?
BUT IT HAS FUR...
A WILD BOAR PIGLET!
THEN... A BOAR?
NAME:
URINOSUKE
IF "WILD BOAR PIGLET" IS "URIBOU," THEN I'M GONNA NAME YOU... URINOSUKE!
DO WILD BOARS HATCH FROM EGGS?
I'M JUST GLAD THAT THIS IS ALL OVER!
CAN YOU GET BACK TO WORK SOON?
SURE.
THANK GOODNESS!
KIRI-SAN IS USELESS.
WHEN YOU'RE NOT AROUND, WE CAN'T GET ANY WORK DONE!
WELL, *SOR-RY*!!
YOU SHOULD COME TO VISIT AT LEAST ONCE. ALSO—

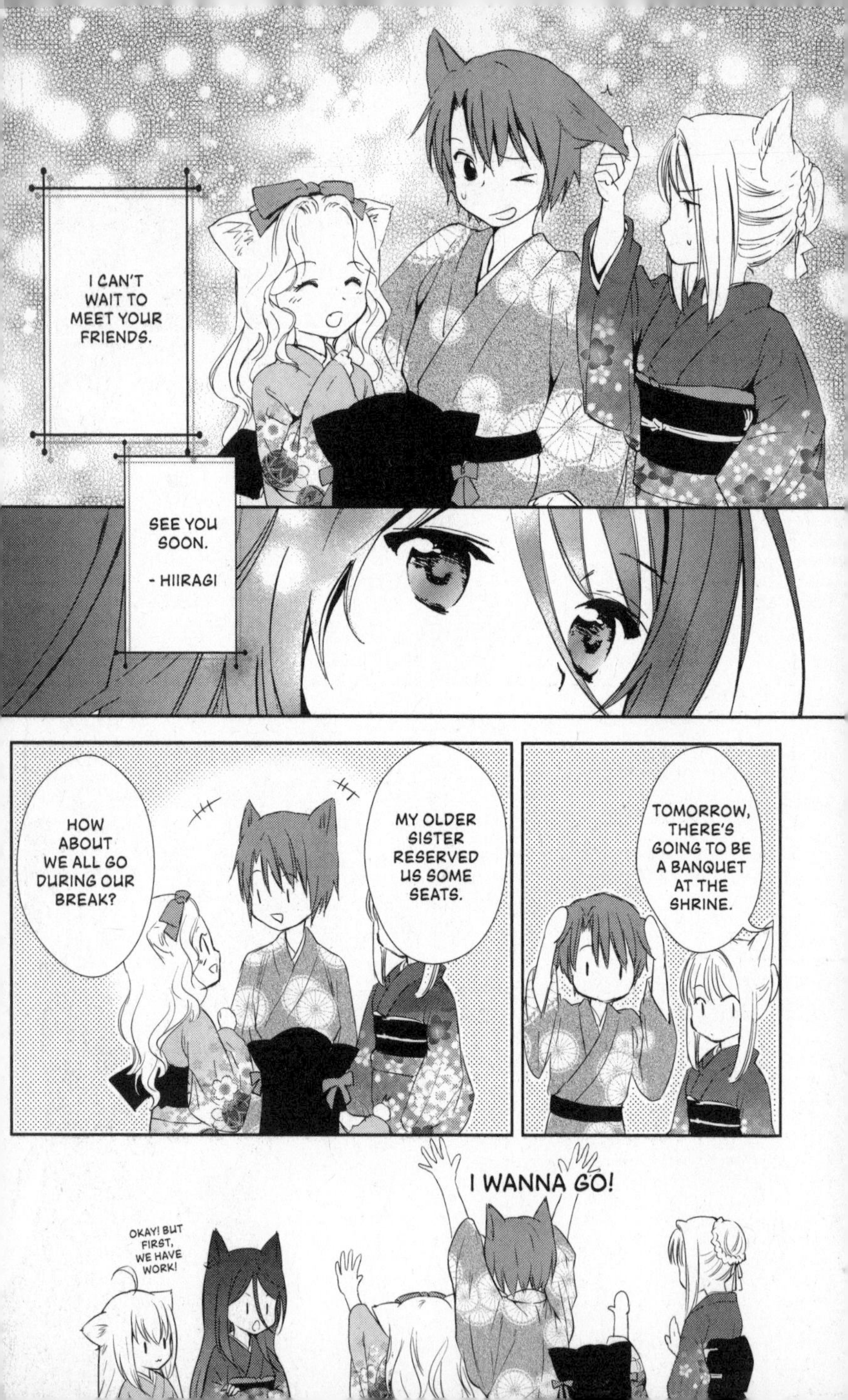
I CAN'T WAIT TO MEET YOUR FRIENDS.
SEE YOU SOON.
- HIIRAGI
TOMORROW, THERE'S GOING TO BE A BANQUET AT THE SHRINE.
MY OLDER SISTER RESERVED US SOME SEATS.
HOW ABOUT WE ALL GO DURING OUR BREAK?
I WANNA GO!
OKAY! BUT FIRST, WE HAVE WORK!

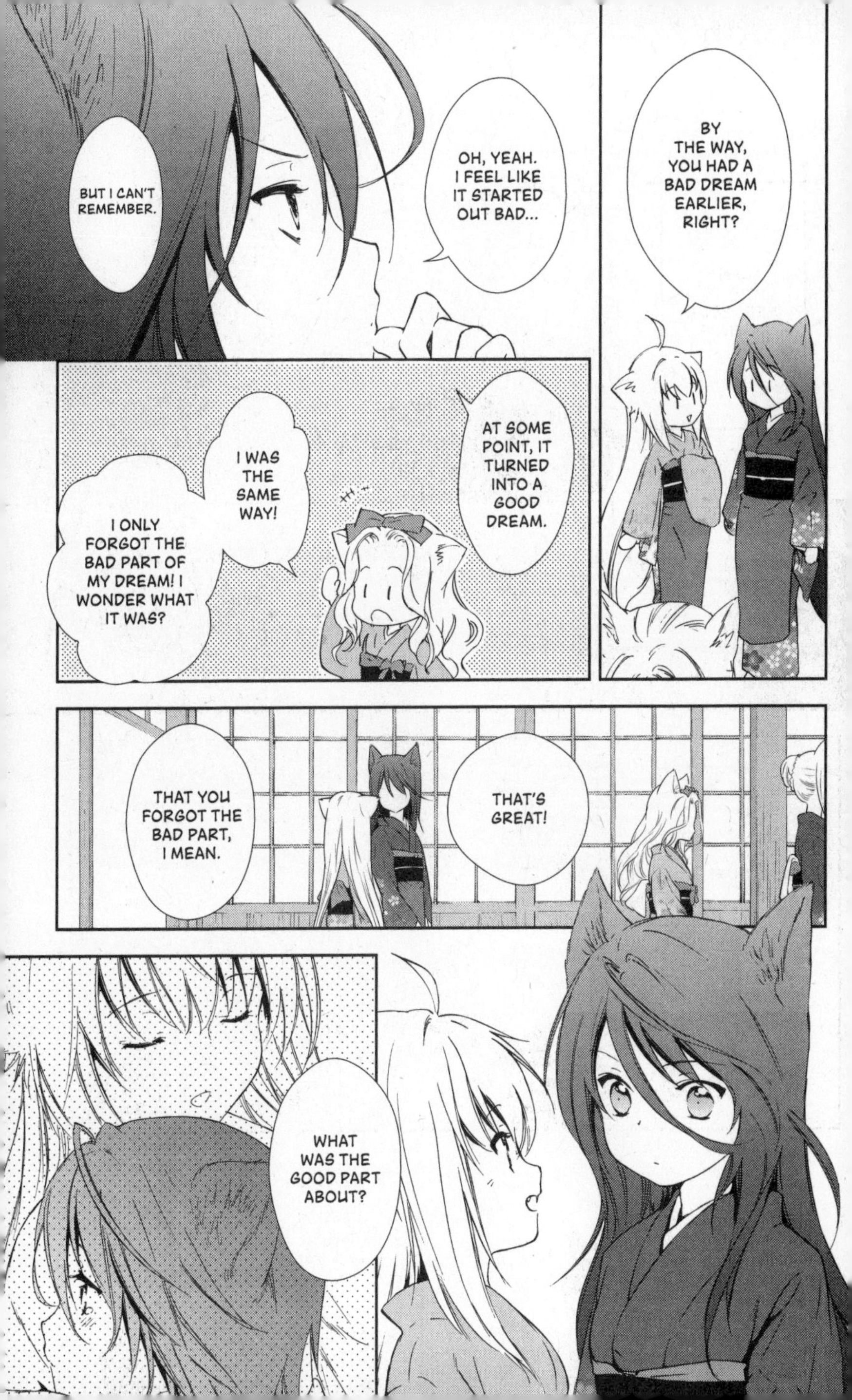
BY THE WAY, YOU HAD A BAD DREAM EARLIER, RIGHT?
OH, YEAH. I FEEL LIKE IT STARTED OUT BAD...
BUT I CAN'T REMEMBER.
AT SOME POINT, IT TURNED INTO A GOOD DREAM.
I WAS THE SAME WAY!
I ONLY FORGOT THE BAD PART OF MY DREAM! I WONDER WHAT IT WAS?
THAT'S GREAT!
THAT YOU FORGOT THE BAD PART, I MEAN.
WHAT WAS THE GOOD PART ABOUT?

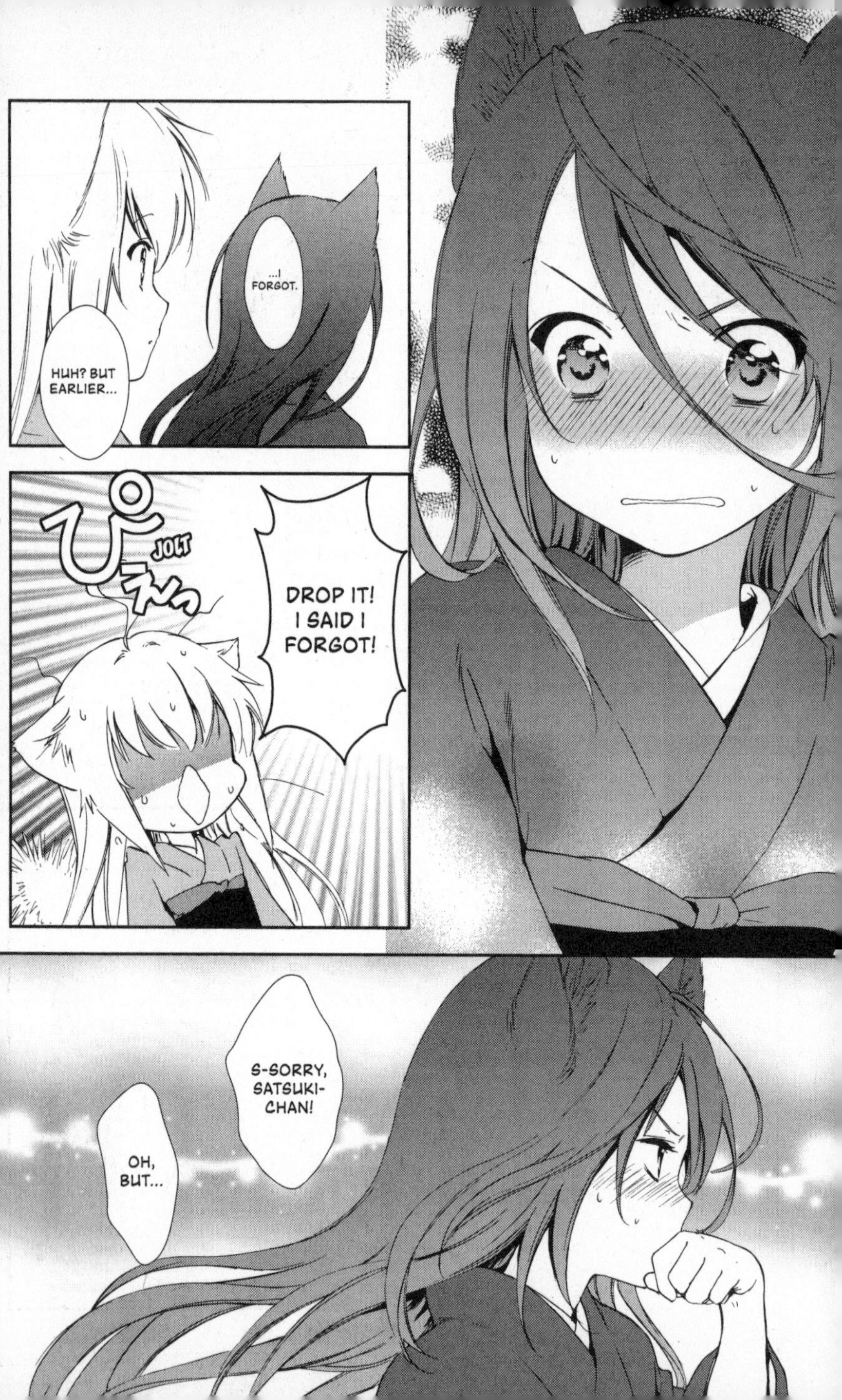
...I FORGOT.
HUH? BUT EARLIER...
DROP IT! I SAID I FORGOT!
ぴえっ
JOLT
S-SORRY, SATSUKI-CHAN!
OH, BUT...

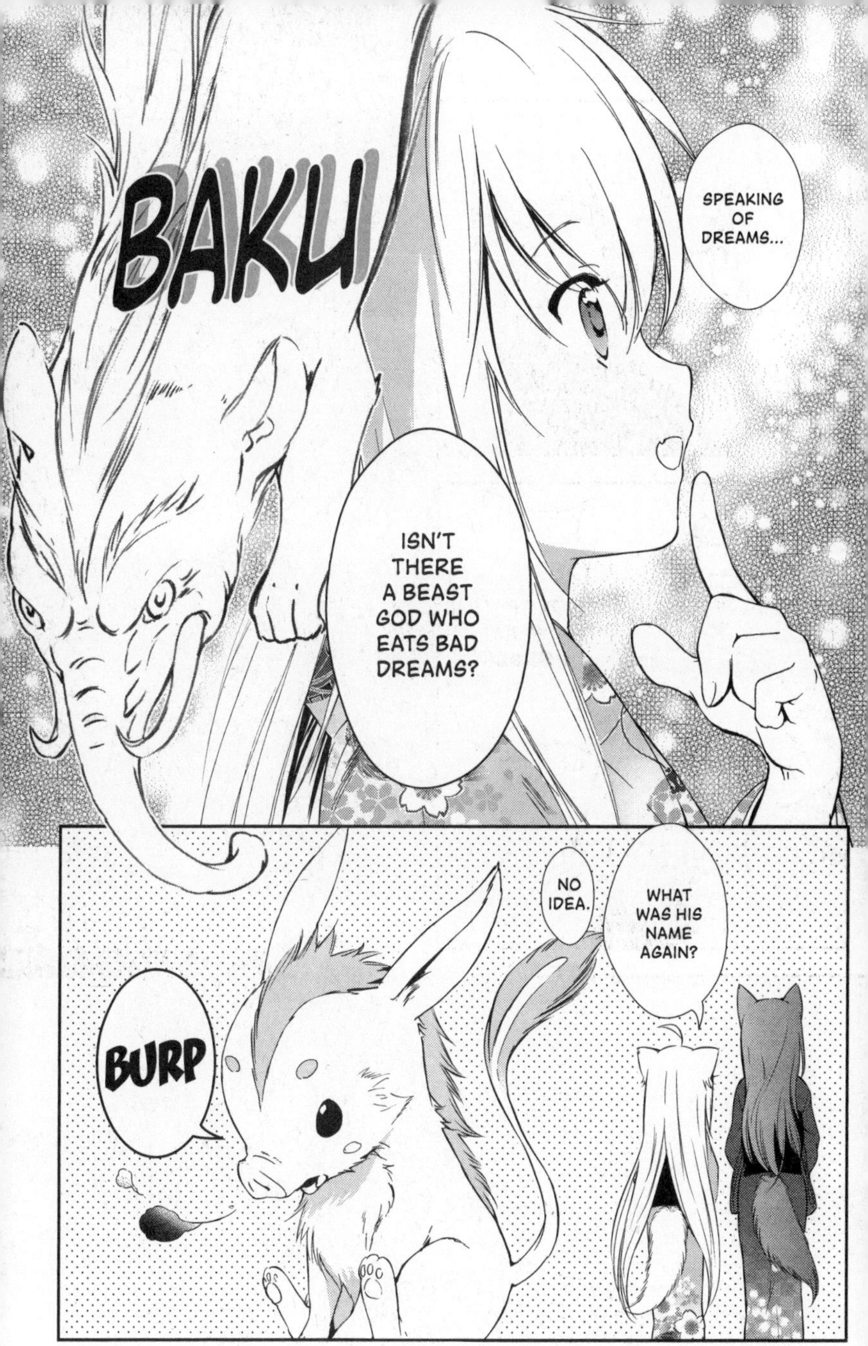
SPEAKING OF DREAMS...
ISN'T THERE A BEAST GOD WHO EATS BAD DREAMS?
BAKU
WHAT WAS HIS NAME AGAIN?
NO IDEA.
BURP

KONOHANA KITAN

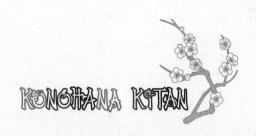

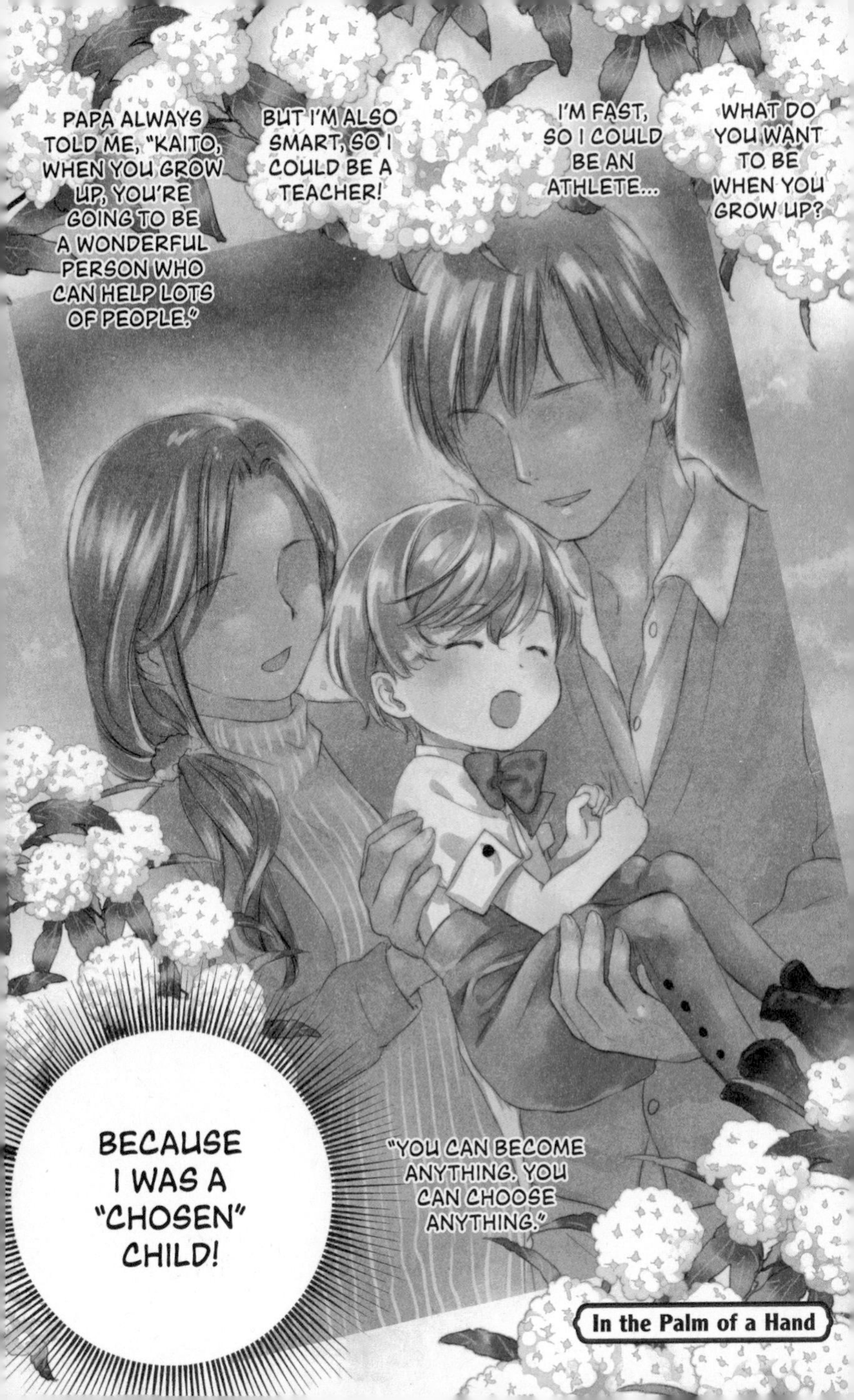
WHAT DO YOU WANT TO BE WHEN YOU GROW UP?
I'M FAST, SO I COULD BE AN ATHLETE...
BUT I'M ALSO SMART, SO I COULD BE A TEACHER!
PAPA ALWAYS TOLD ME, "KAITO, WHEN YOU GROW UP, YOU'RE GOING TO BE A WONDERFUL PERSON WHO CAN HELP LOTS OF PEOPLE."
"YOU CAN BECOME ANYTHING. YOU CAN CHOOSE ANYTHING."
BECAUSE I WAS A "CHOSEN" CHILD!

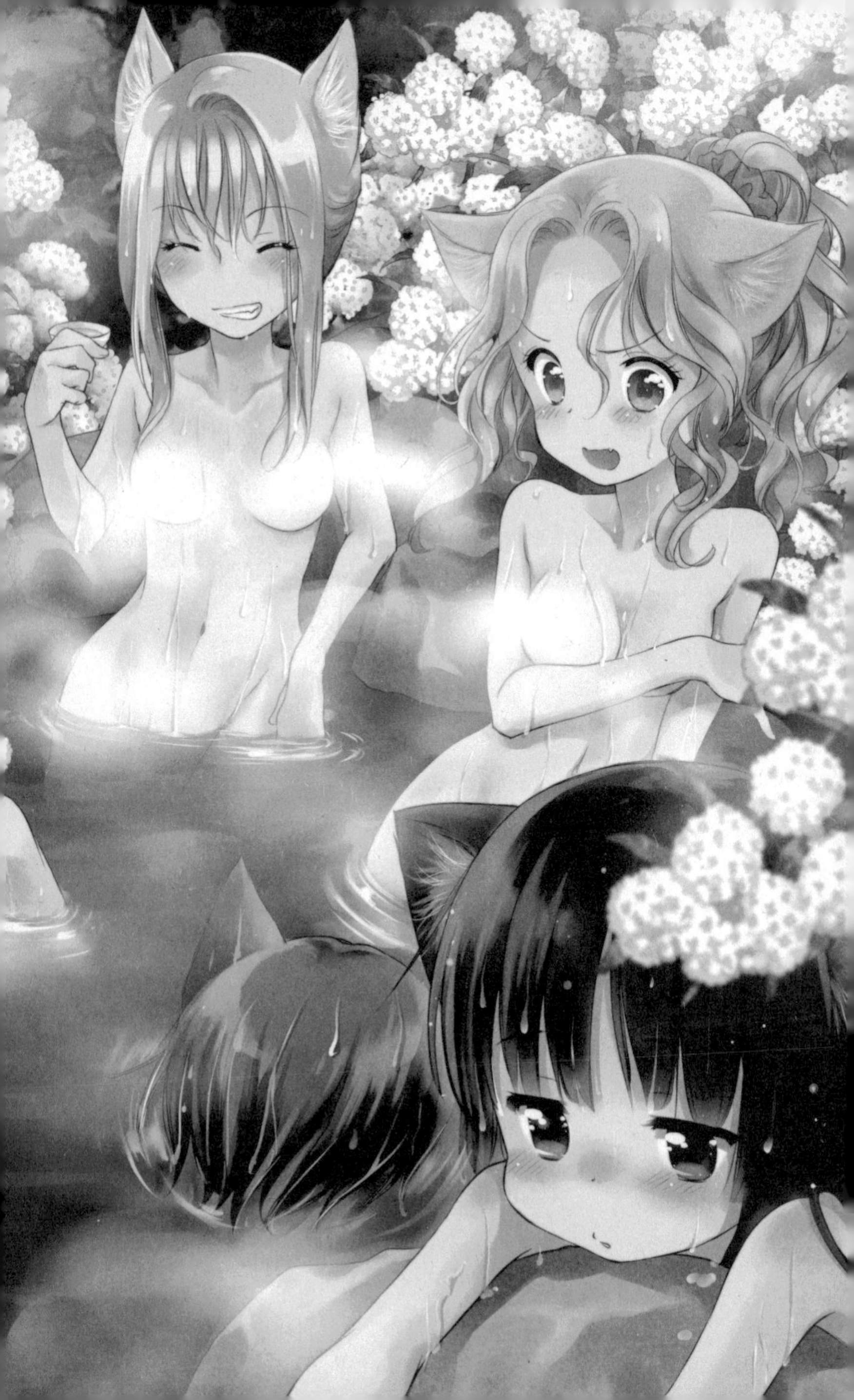

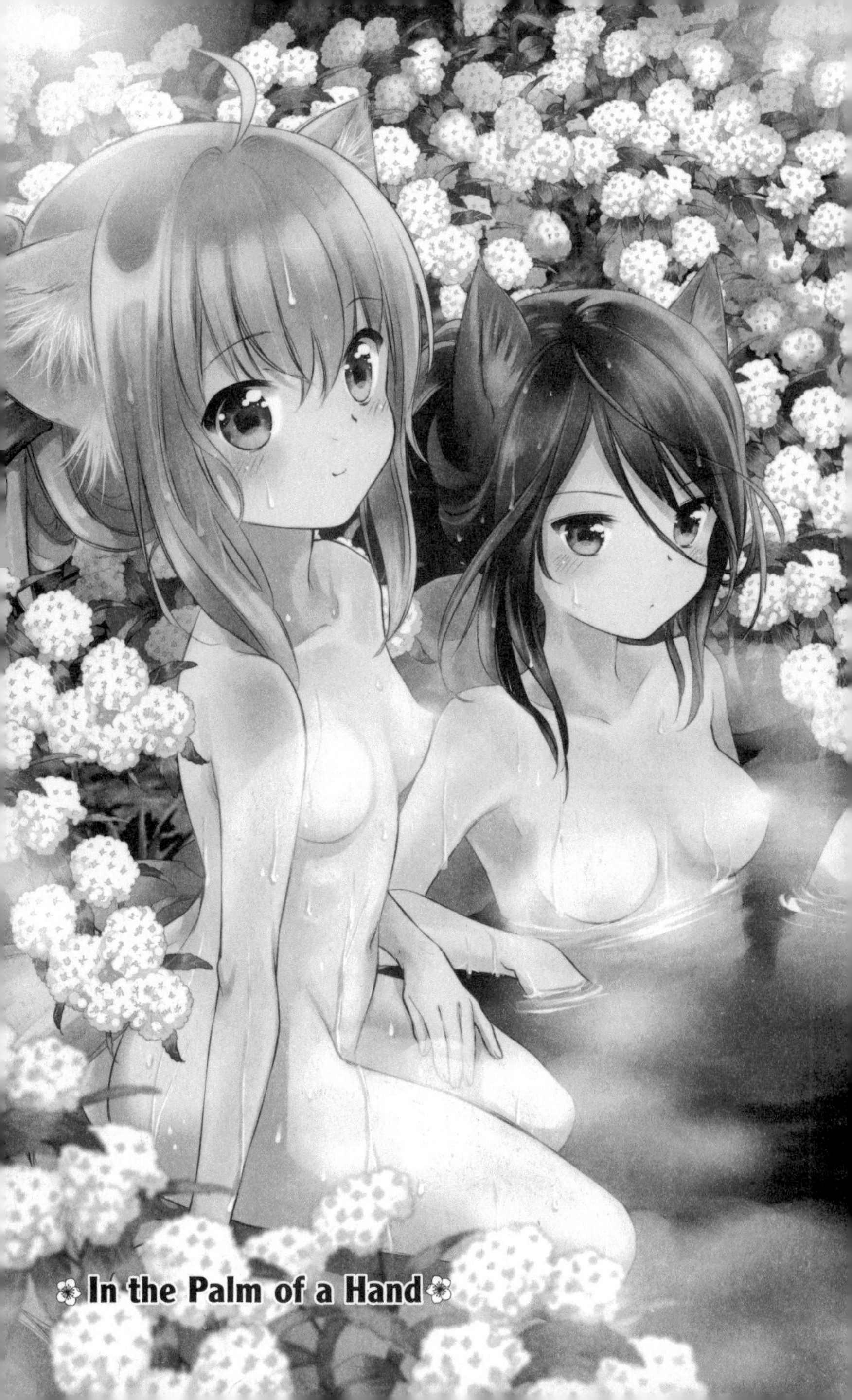
In the Palm of a Hand

KONOHANA KITAN

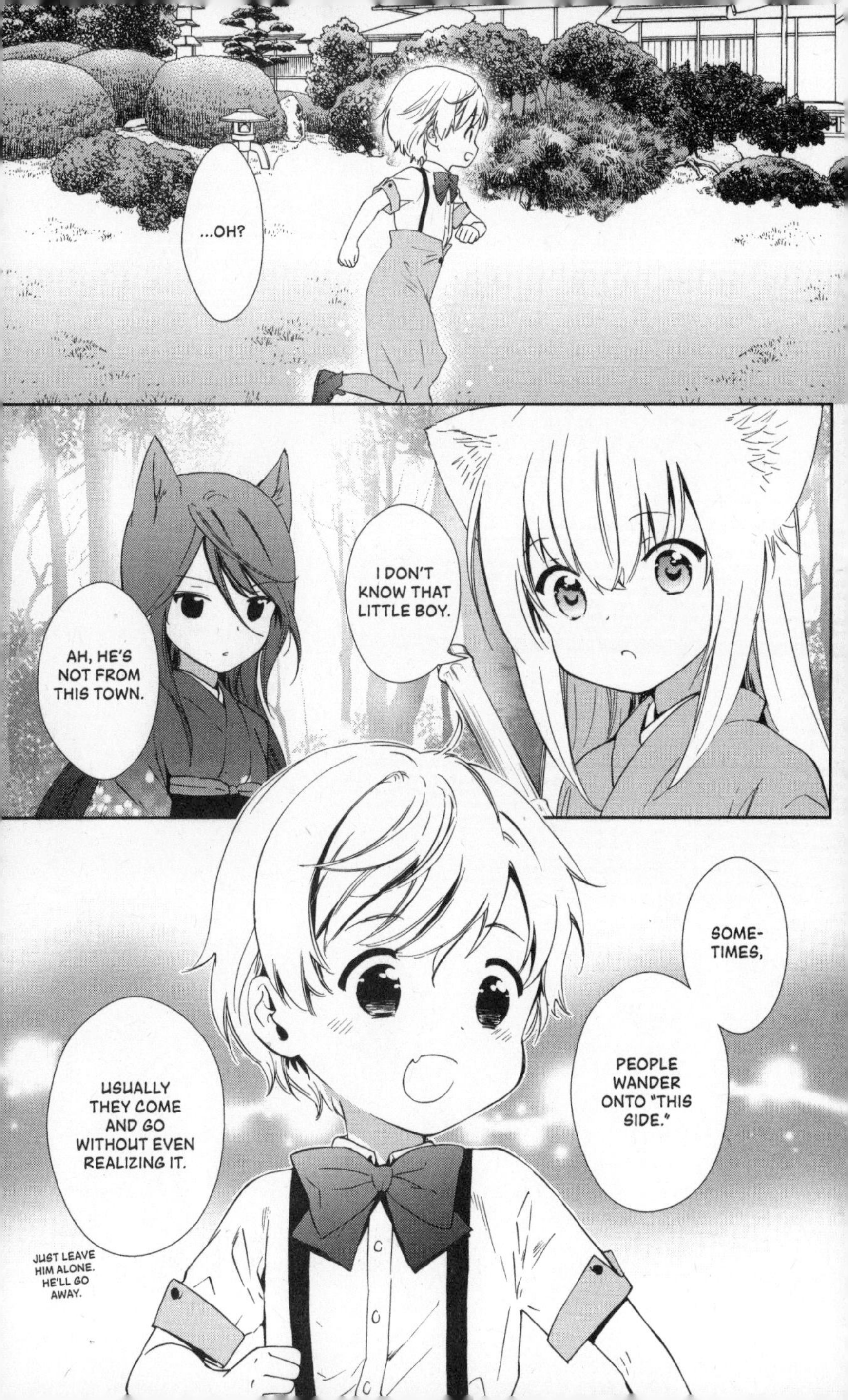
...OH?
I DON'T KNOW THAT LITTLE BOY.
AH, HE'S NOT FROM THIS TOWN.
SOME-TIMES,
PEOPLE WANDER ONTO "THIS SIDE."
USUALLY THEY COME AND GO WITHOUT EVEN REALIZING IT.
JUST LEAVE HIM ALONE. HE'LL GO AWAY.

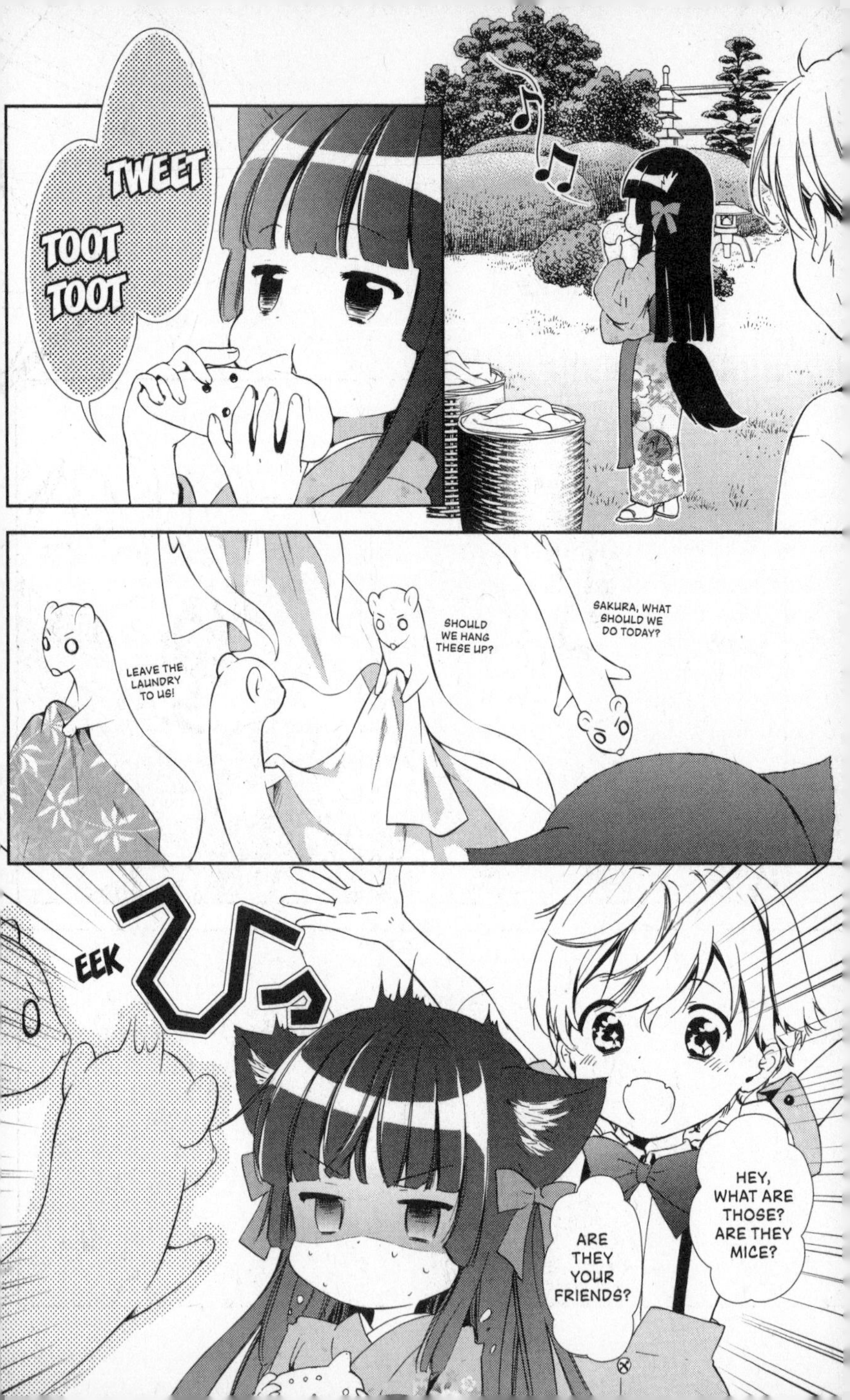
TWEET
TOOT TOOT
SAKURA, WHAT SHOULD WE DO TODAY?
SHOULD WE HANG THESE UP?
LEAVE THE LAUNDRY TO US!
HEY, WHAT ARE THOSE? ARE THEY MICE?
ARE THEY YOUR FRIENDS?
EEK
ひっ

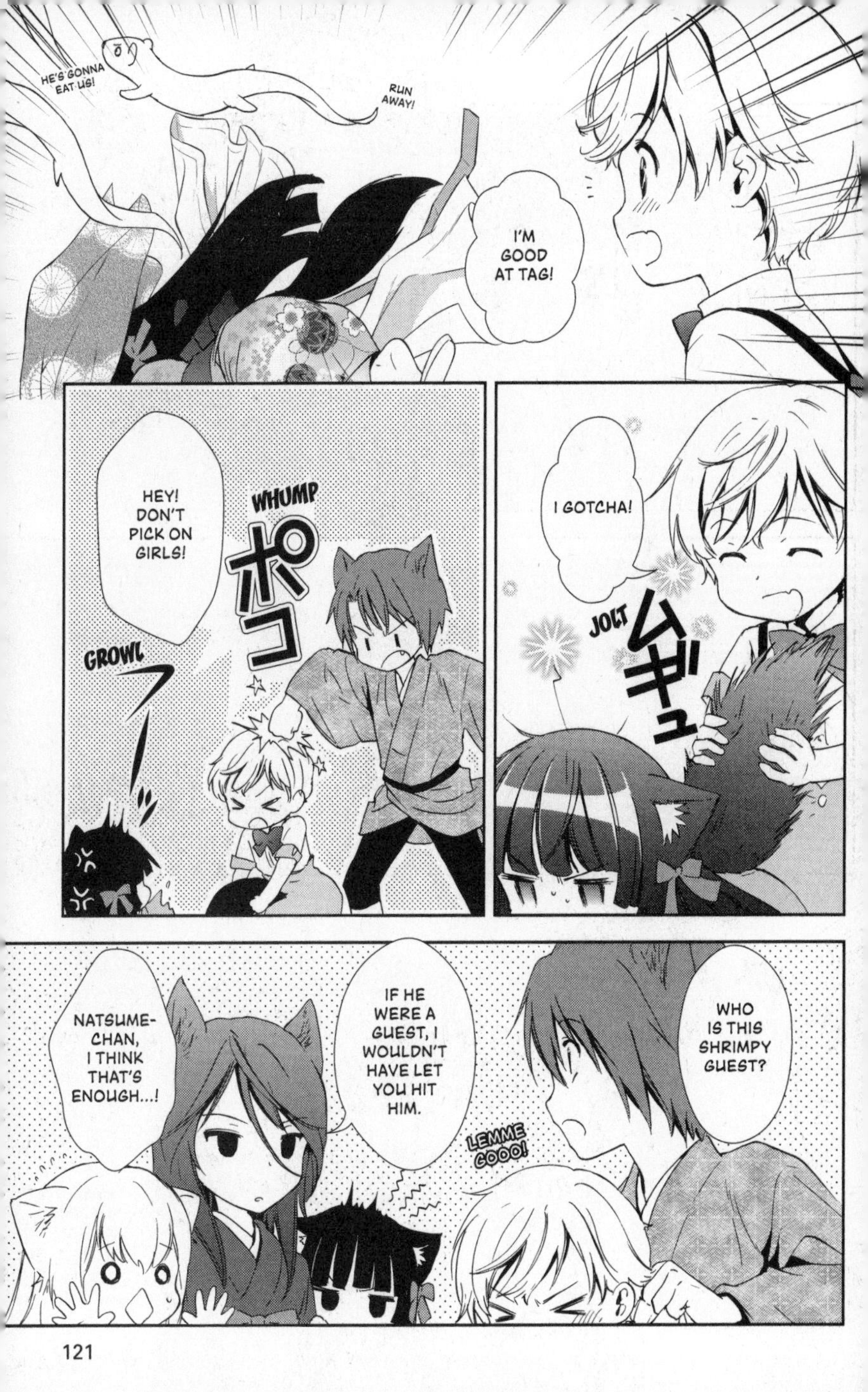
RUN AWAY!
HE'S GONNA EAT US!
I'M GOOD AT TAG!
I GOTCHA!
JOLT
ムギュ
HEY! DON'T PICK ON GIRLS!
WHUMP
ポコ
GROWL
WHO IS THIS SHRIMPY GUEST?
LEMME GOOO!
IF HE WERE A GUEST, I WOULDN'T HAVE LET YOU HIT HIM.
NATSUME-CHAN, I THINK THAT'S ENOUGH...!

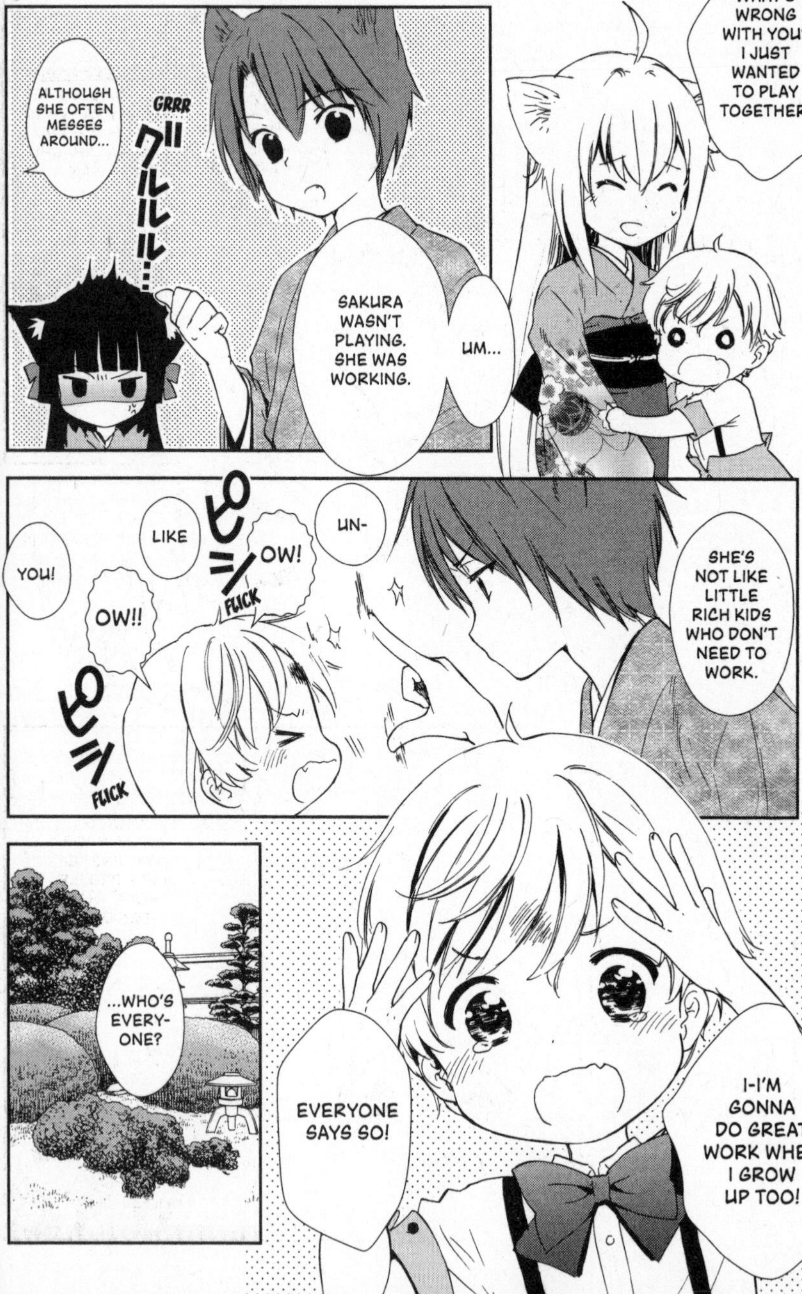
WHAT'S WRONG WITH YOU? I JUST WANTED TO PLAY TOGETHER!
UM...
SAKURA WASN'T PLAYING. SHE WAS WORKING.
ALTHOUGH SHE OFTEN MESSES AROUND...
GRRR
グルルル…
SHE'S NOT LIKE LITTLE RICH KIDS WHO DON'T NEED TO WORK.
UN-
OW!
ピシ
FLICK
LIKE
OW!!
YOU!
ピシ
FLICK
I-I'M GONNA DO GREAT WORK WHEN I GROW UP TOO!
EVERYONE SAYS SO!
...WHO'S EVERY-ONE?

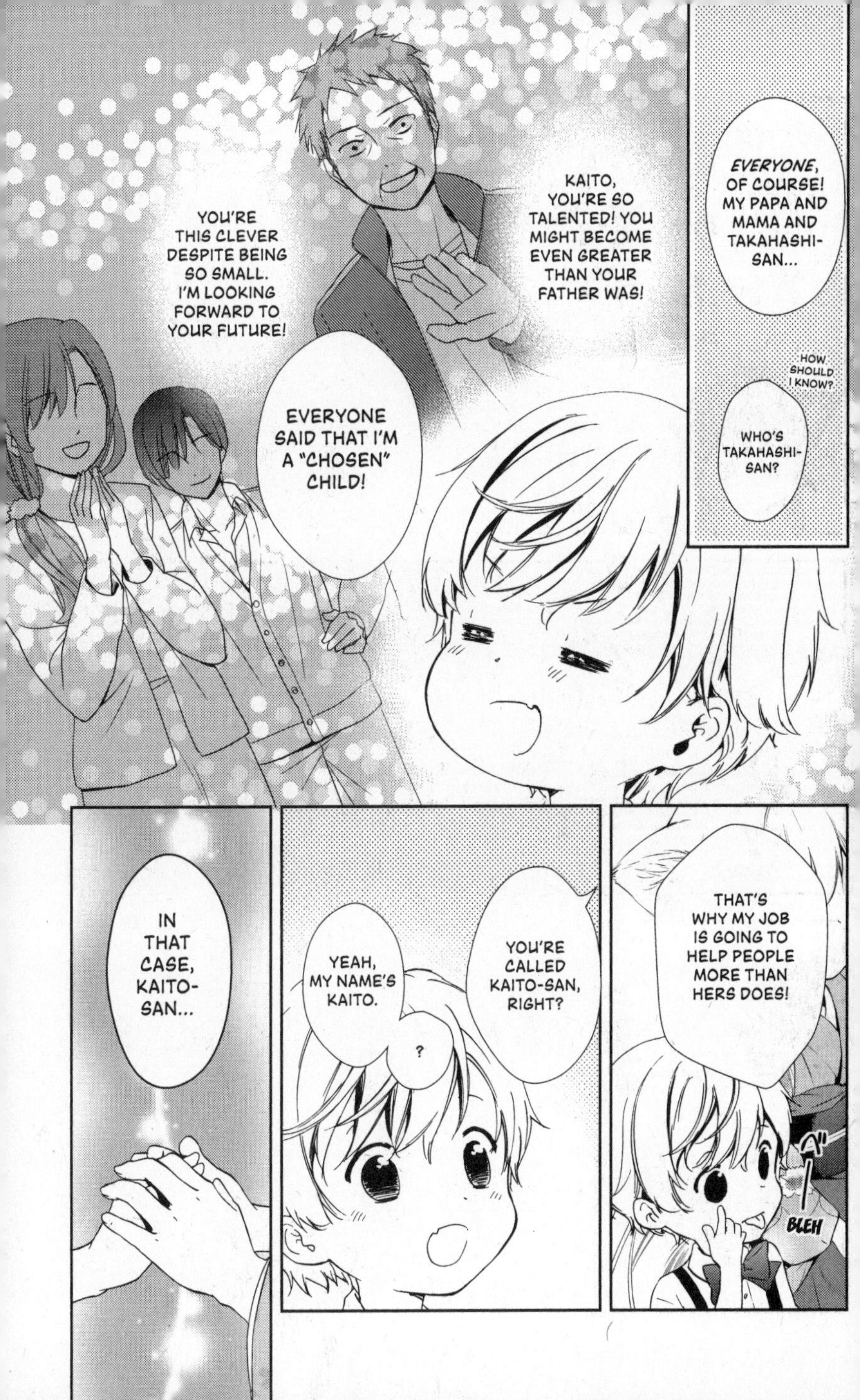
EVERYONE, OF COURSE! MY PAPA AND MAMA AND TAKAHASHI-SAN...
WHO'S TAKAHASHI-SAN?
HOW SHOULD I KNOW?
KAITO, YOU'RE SO TALENTED! YOU MIGHT BECOME EVEN GREATER THAN YOUR FATHER WAS!
YOU'RE THIS CLEVER DESPITE BEING SO SMALL. I'M LOOKING FORWARD TO YOUR FUTURE!
EVERYONE SAID THAT I'M A "CHOSEN" CHILD!
THAT'S WHY MY JOB IS GOING TO HELP PEOPLE MORE THAN HERS DOES!
BLEH
YOU'RE CALLED KAITO-SAN, RIGHT?
YEAH, MY NAME'S KAITO.
?
IN THAT CASE, KAITO-SAN...

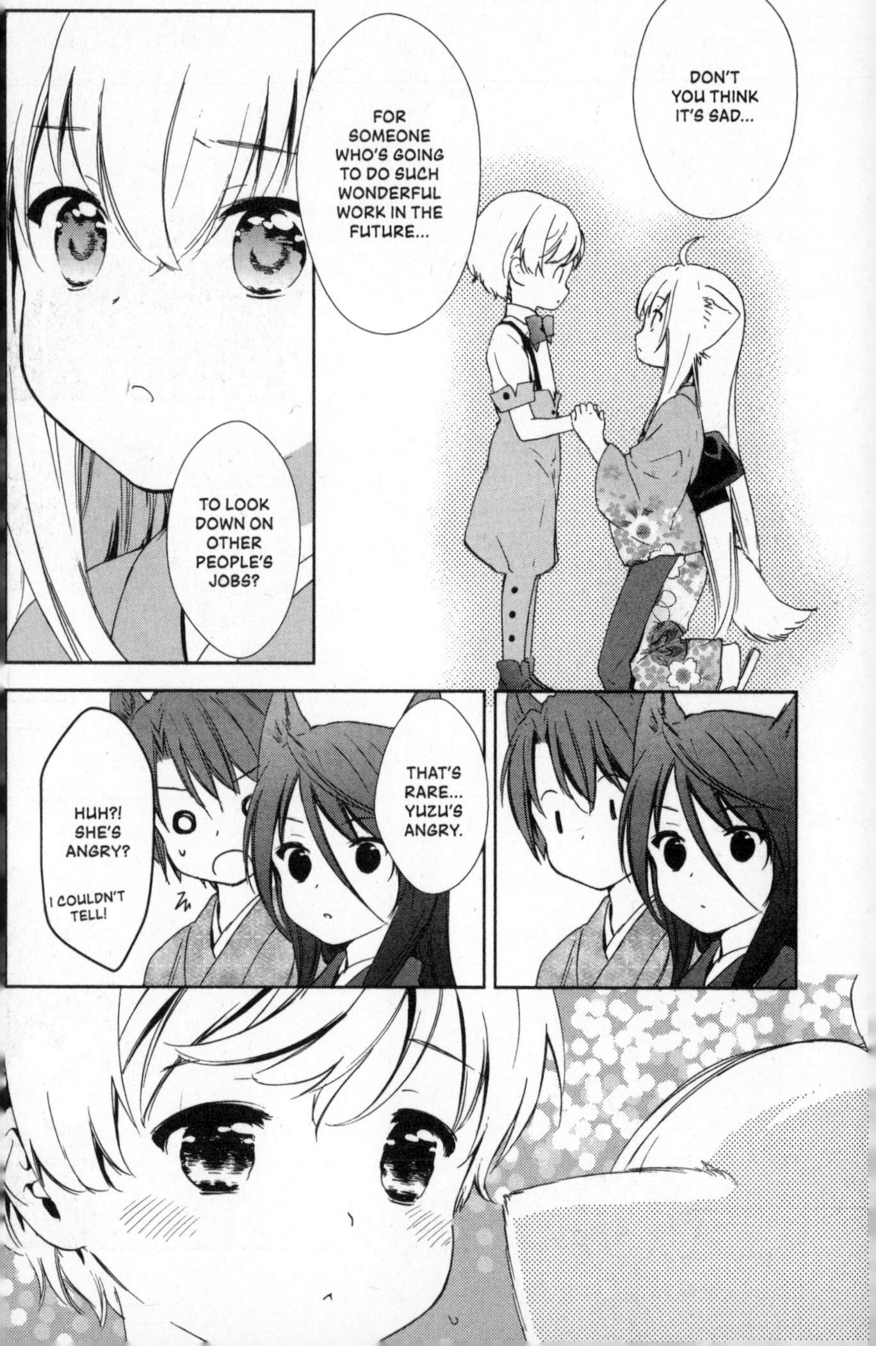
DON'T YOU THINK IT'S SAD...
FOR SOMEONE WHO'S GOING TO DO SUCH WONDERFUL WORK IN THE FUTURE...
TO LOOK DOWN ON OTHER PEOPLE'S JOBS?
THAT'S RARE... YUZU'S ANGRY.
HUH?! SHE'S ANGRY?
I COULDN'T TELL!

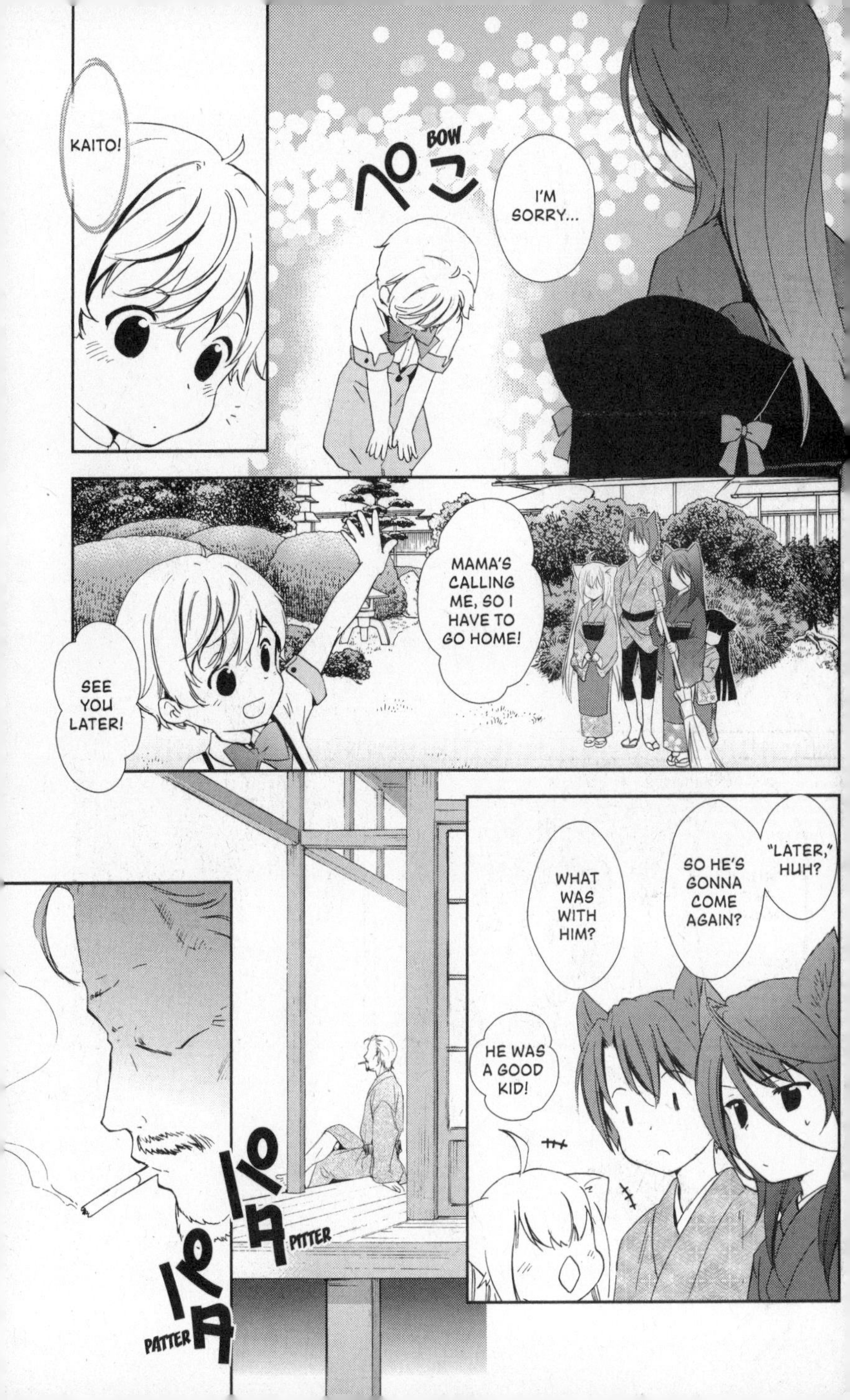
ペこ
BOW
I'M SORRY...
KAITO!
MAMA'S CALLING ME, SO I HAVE TO GO HOME!
SEE YOU LATER!
"LATER," HUH?
SO HE'S GONNA COME AGAIN?
WHAT WAS WITH HIM?
HE WAS A GOOD KID!
パタ
PITTER
パタ
PATTER

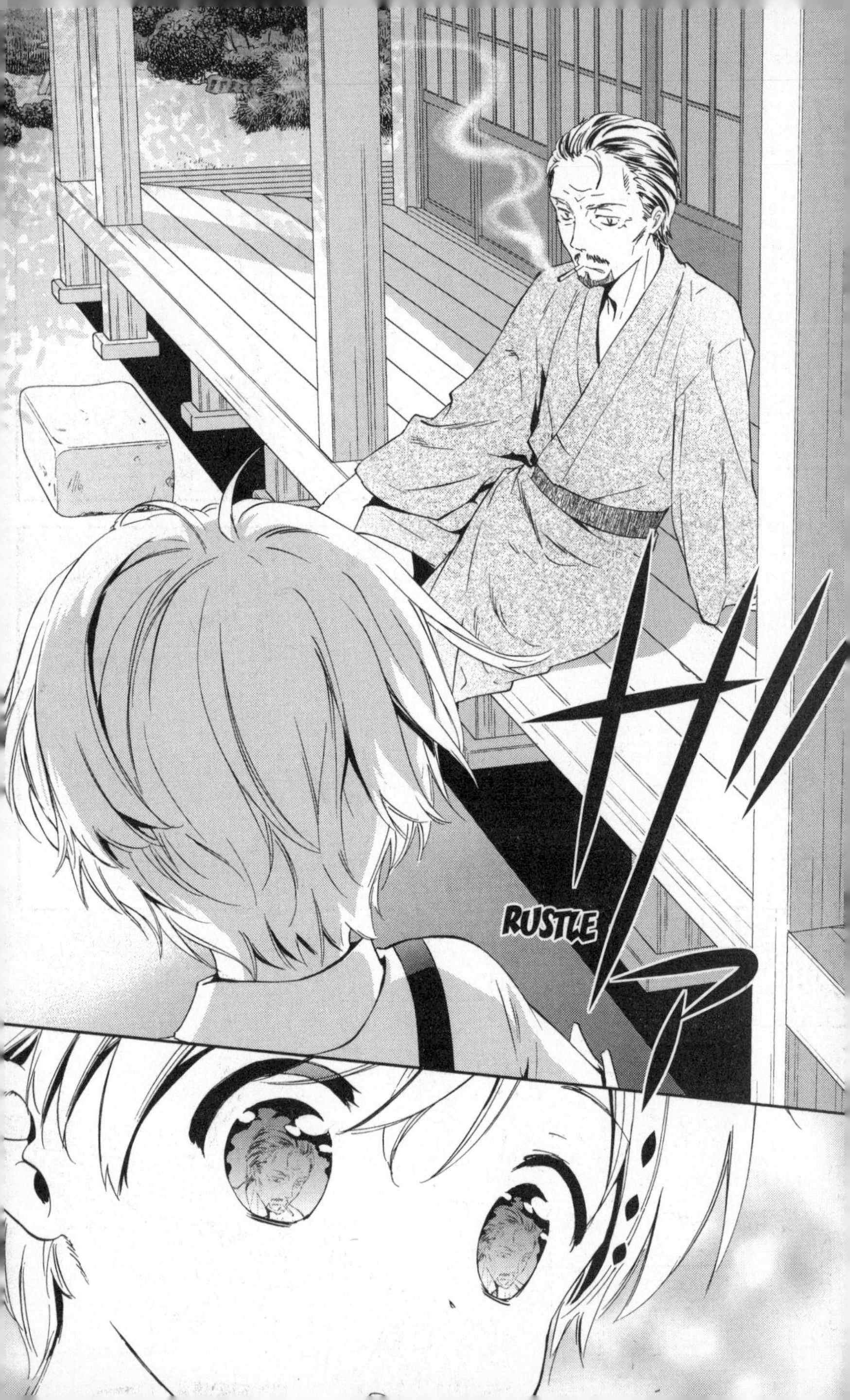
RUSTLE

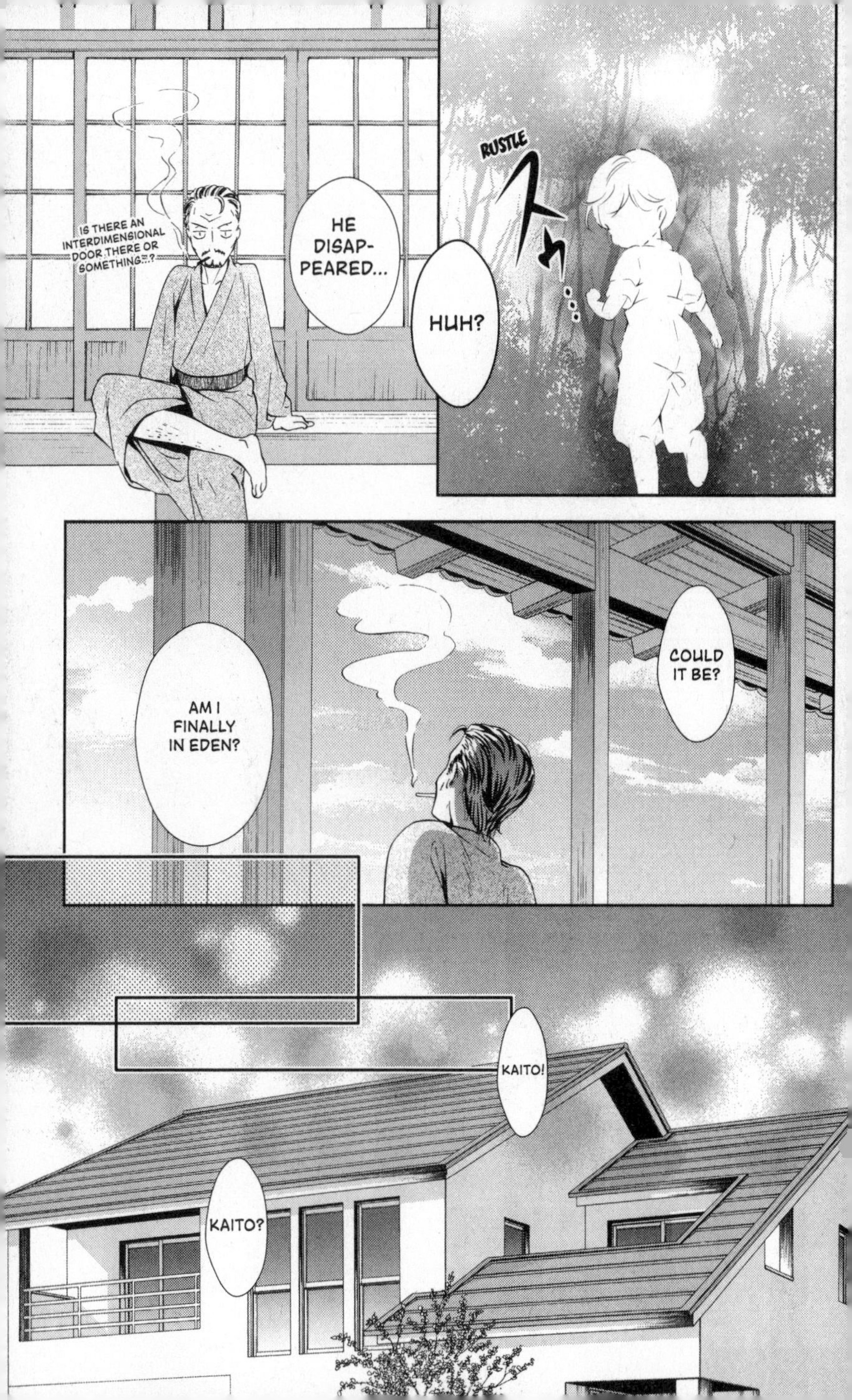
RUSTLE
HUH?
HE DISAP-PEARED...
IS THERE AN INTERDIMENSIONAL DOOR THERE OR SOMETHING...?
COULD IT BE?
AM I FINALLY IN EDEN?
KAITO!
KAITO?

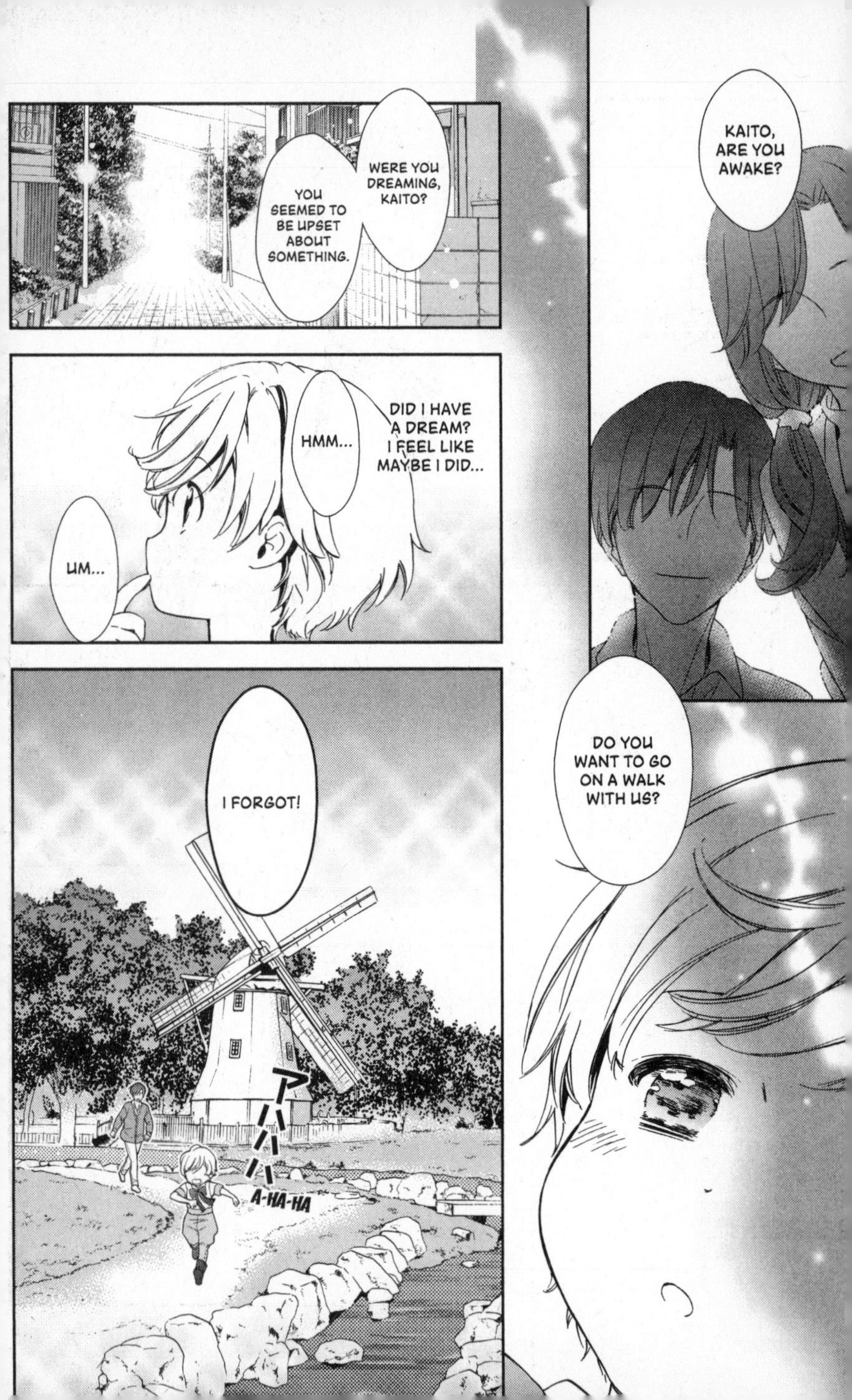
KAITO, ARE YOU AWAKE?
DO YOU WANT TO GO ON A WALK WITH US?
WERE YOU DREAMING, KAITO?
YOU SEEMED TO BE UPSET ABOUT SOMETHING.
DID I HAVE A DREAM? I FEEL LIKE MAYBE I DID...
HMM...
UM...
I FORGOT!
A-HA-HA

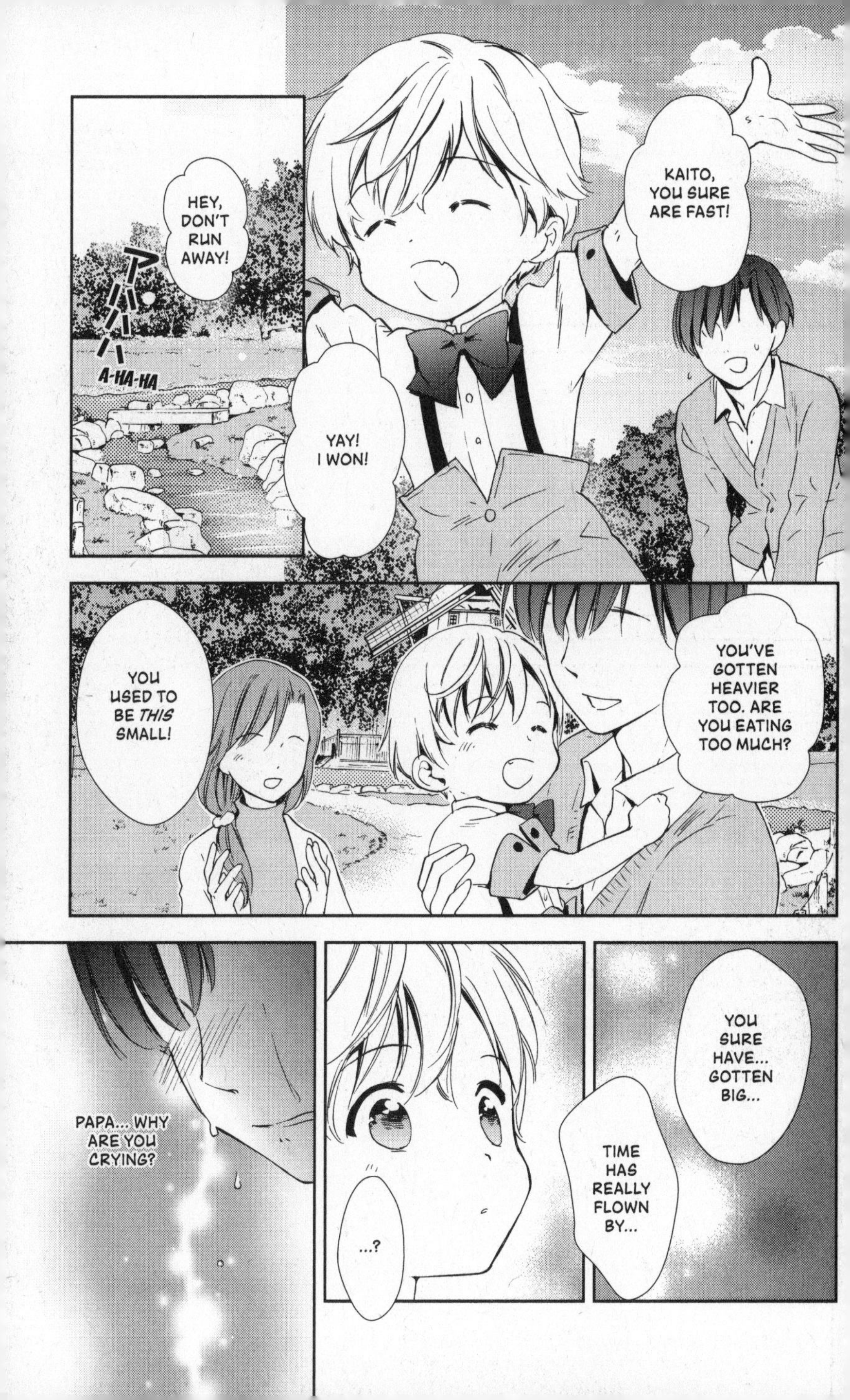
KAITO, YOU SURE ARE FAST!
YAY! I WON!
HEY, DON'T RUN AWAY!
A-HA-HA
YOU'VE GOTTEN HEAVIER TOO. ARE YOU EATING TOO MUCH?
YOU USED TO BE *THIS* SMALL!
YOU SURE HAVE... GOTTEN BIG...
TIME HAS REALLY FLOWN BY...
...?
PAPA... WHY ARE YOU CRYING?

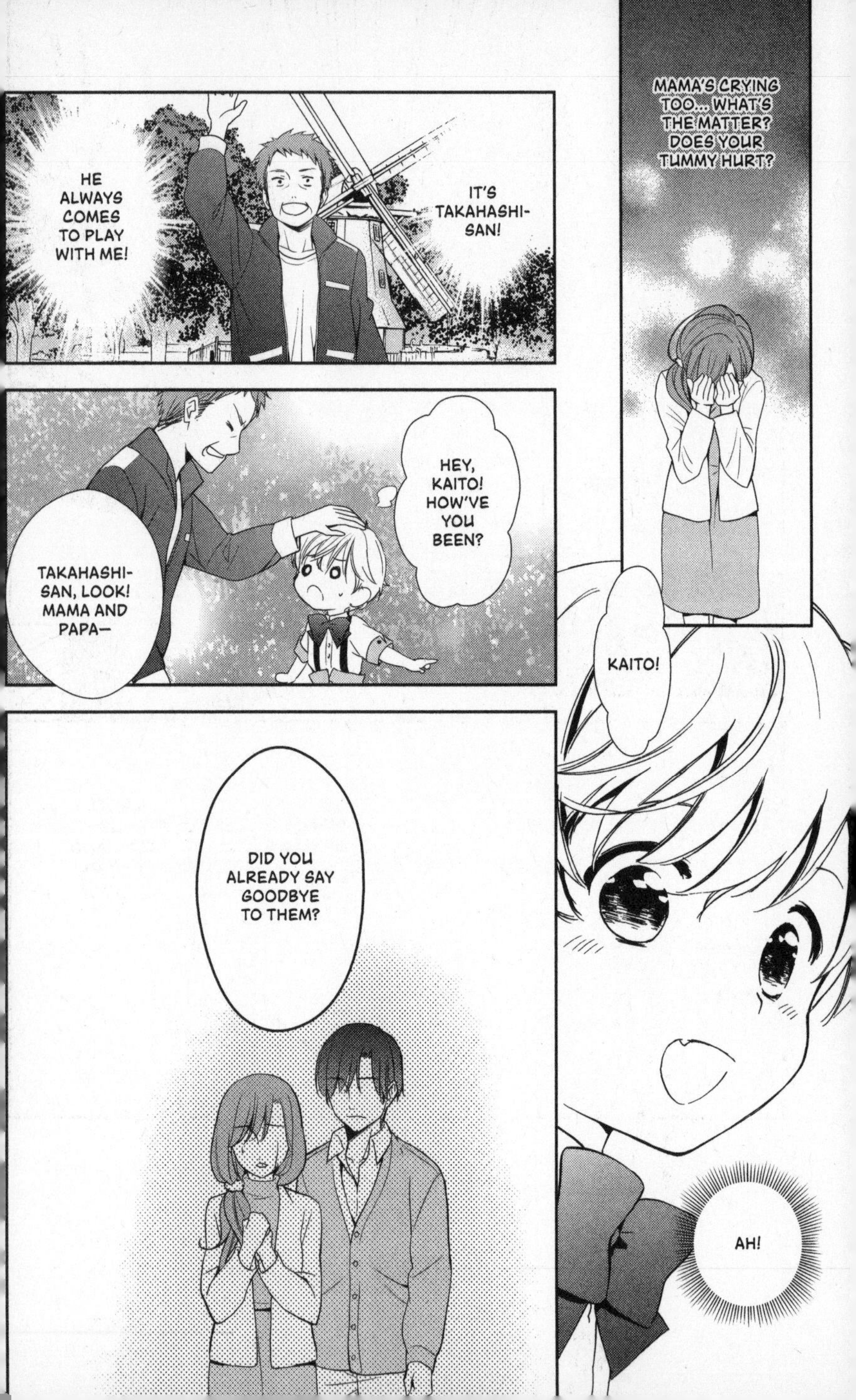
MAMA'S CRYING TOO... WHAT'S THE MATTER? DOES YOUR TUMMY HURT?
KAITO!
AH!
IT'S TAKAHASHI-SAN!
HE ALWAYS COMES TO PLAY WITH ME!
HEY, KAITO! HOW'VE YOU BEEN?
TAKAHASHI-SAN, LOOK! MAMA AND PAPA—
DID YOU ALREADY SAY GOODBYE TO THEM?

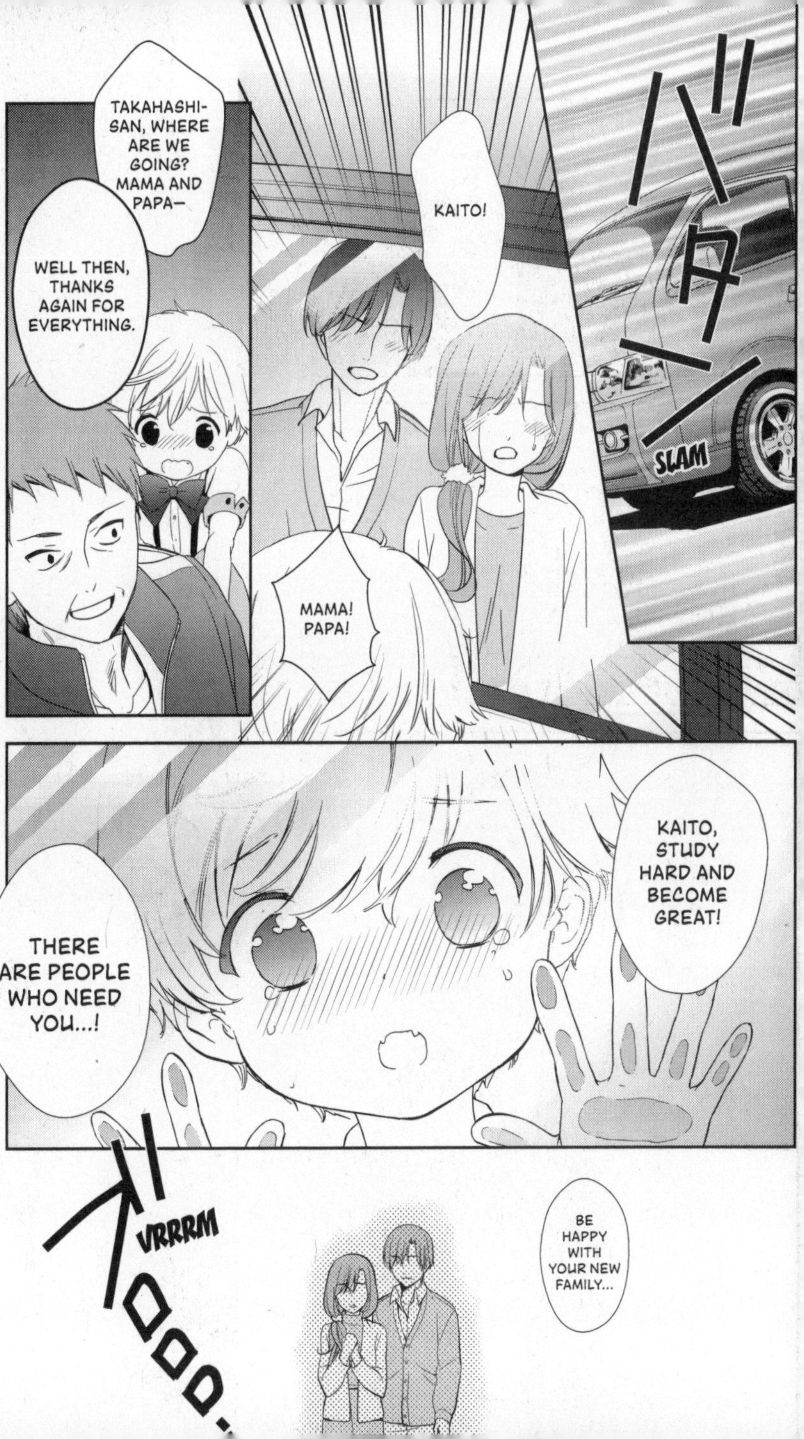
SLAM
KAITO!
MAMA! PAPA!
TAKAHASHI-SAN, WHERE ARE WE GOING? MAMA AND PAPA—
WELL THEN, THANKS AGAIN FOR EVERYTHING.
KAITO, STUDY HARD AND BECOME GREAT!
THERE ARE PEOPLE WHO NEED YOU...!
BE HAPPY WITH YOUR NEW FAMILY...
VRRRM

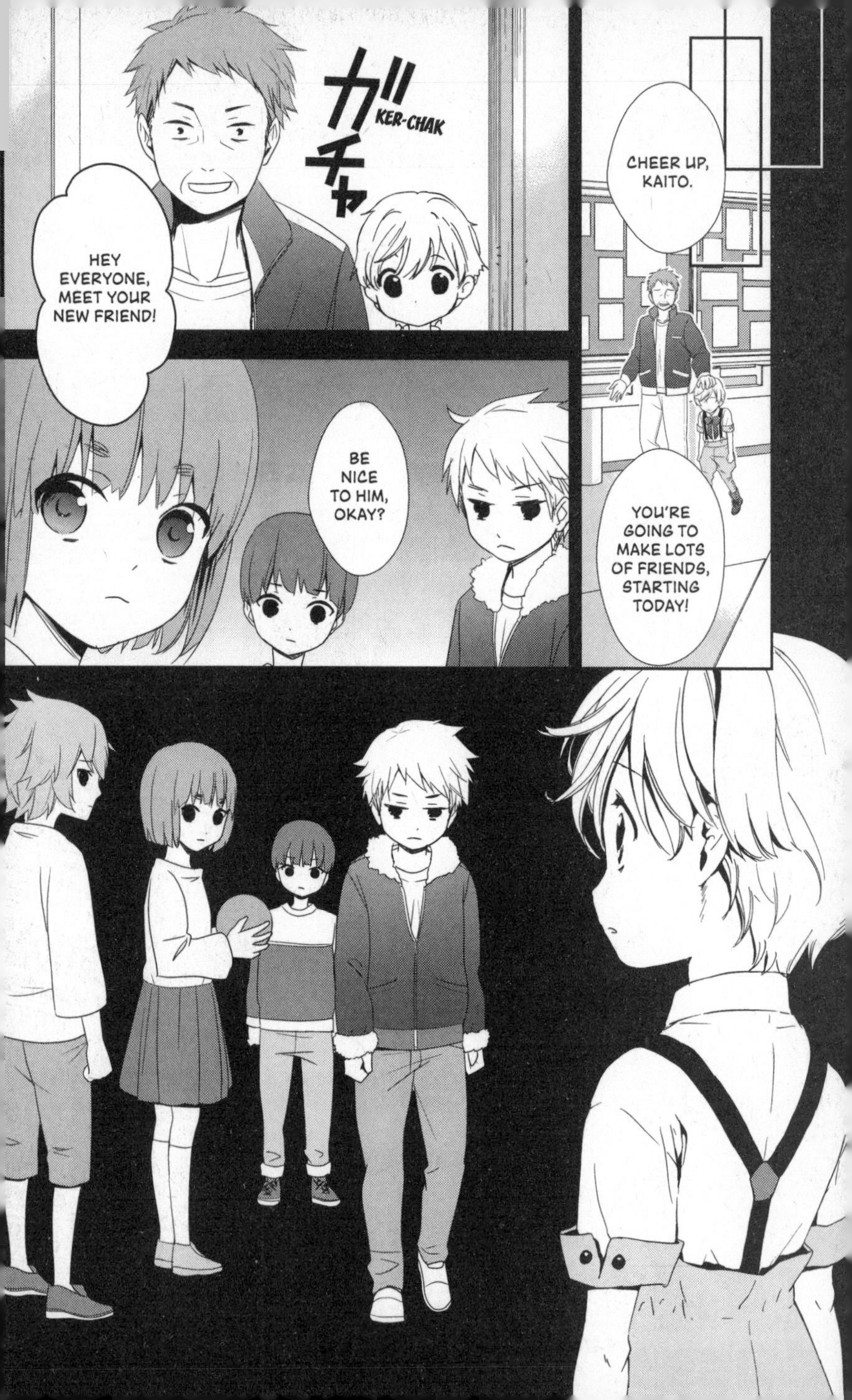

CHEER UP, KAITO.
YOU'RE GOING TO MAKE LOTS OF FRIENDS, STARTING TODAY!
ガチャ
KER-CHAK
HEY EVERYONE, MEET YOUR NEW FRIEND!
BE NICE TO HIM, OKAY?

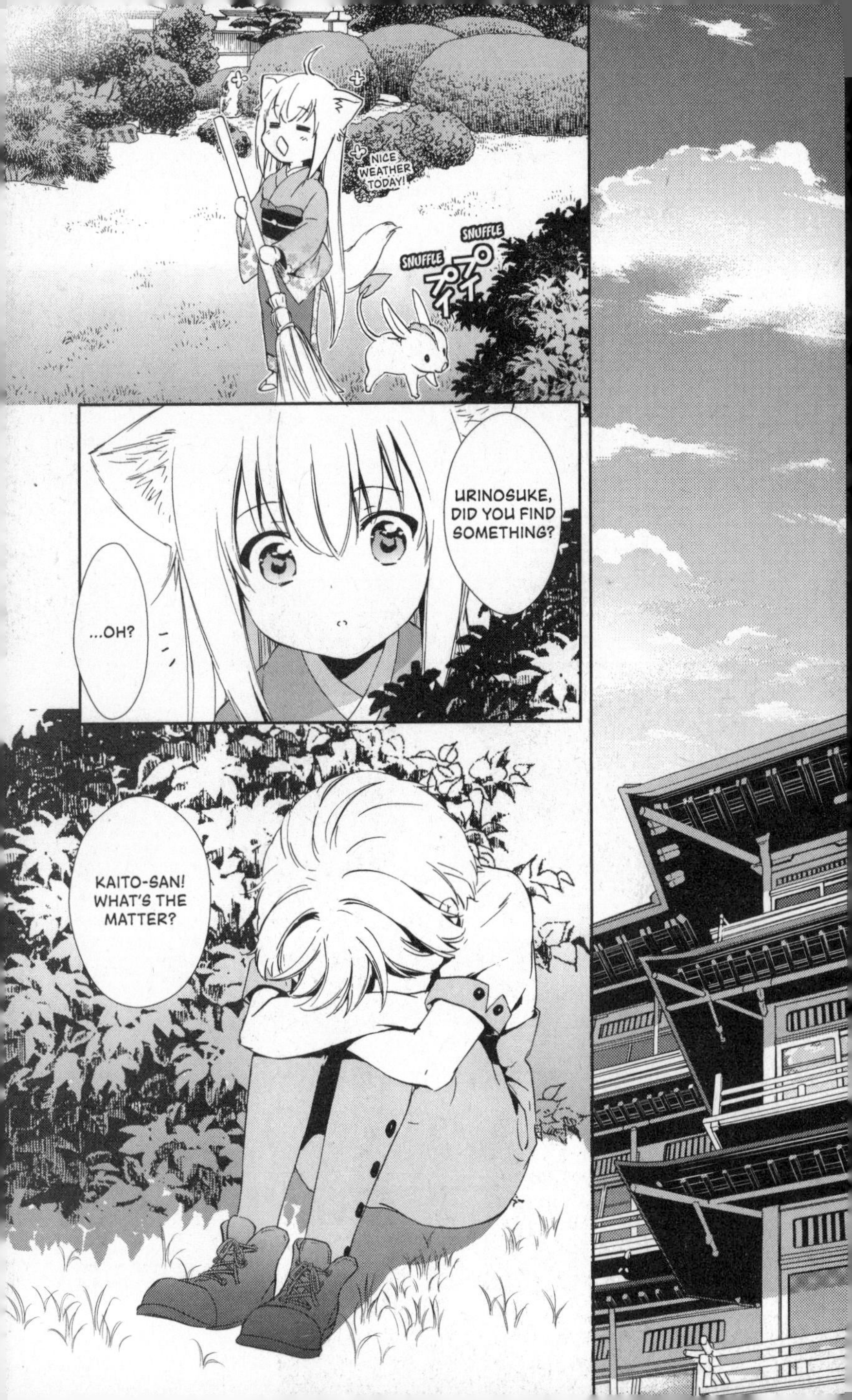
NICE WEATHER TODAY!
SNUFFLE
SNUFFLE
URINOSUKE, DID YOU FIND SOMETHING?
...OH?
KAITO-SAN! WHAT'S THE MATTER?

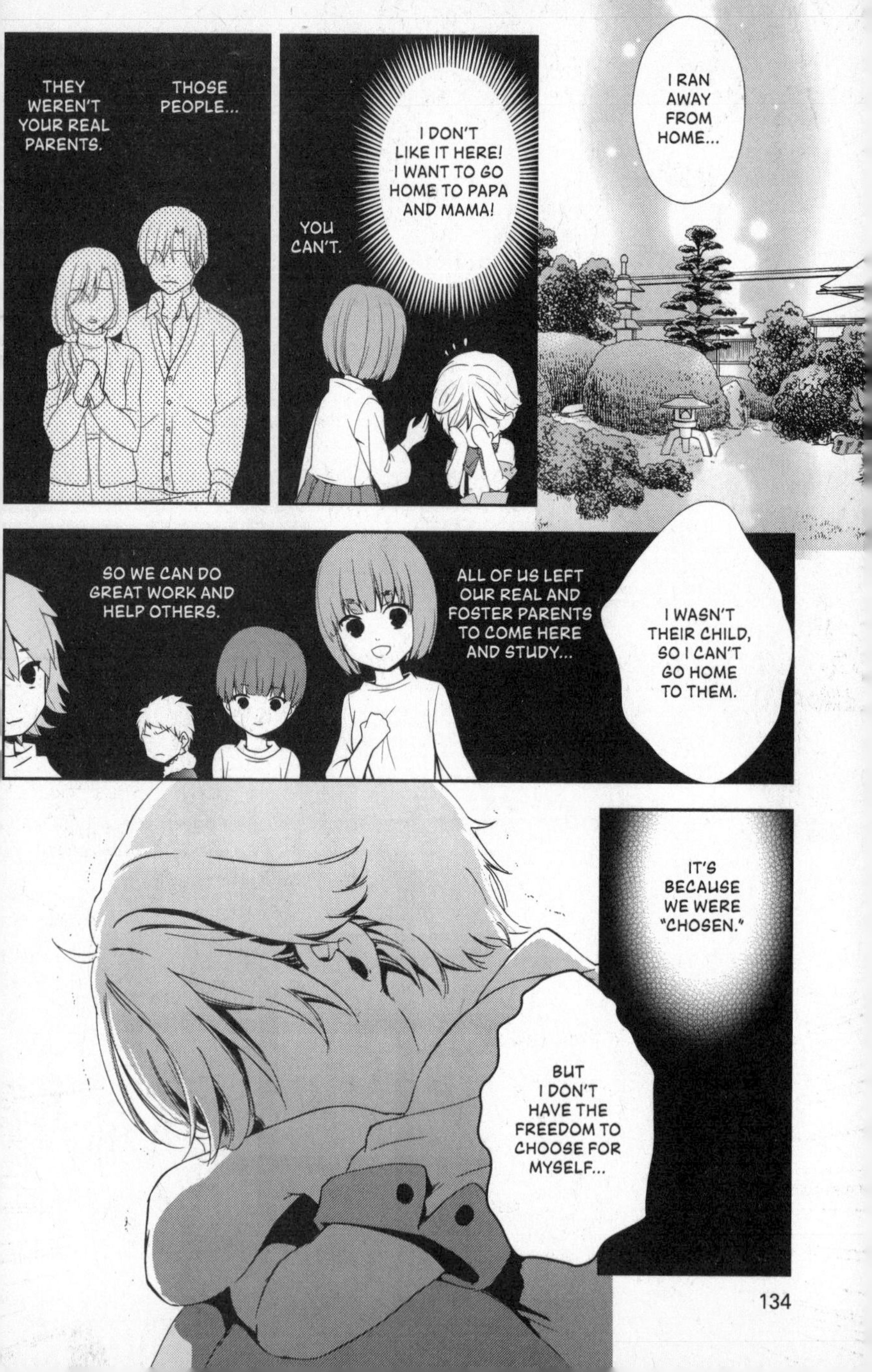
I RAN AWAY FROM HOME...
I DON'T LIKE IT HERE! I WANT TO GO HOME TO PAPA AND MAMA!
YOU CAN'T.
THOSE PEOPLE...
THEY WEREN'T YOUR REAL PARENTS.
I WASN'T THEIR CHILD, SO I CAN'T GO HOME TO THEM.
ALL OF US LEFT OUR REAL AND FOSTER PARENTS TO COME HERE AND STUDY...
SO WE CAN DO GREAT WORK AND HELP OTHERS.
IT'S BECAUSE WE WERE "CHOSEN."
BUT I DON'T HAVE THE FREEDOM TO CHOOSE FOR MYSELF...

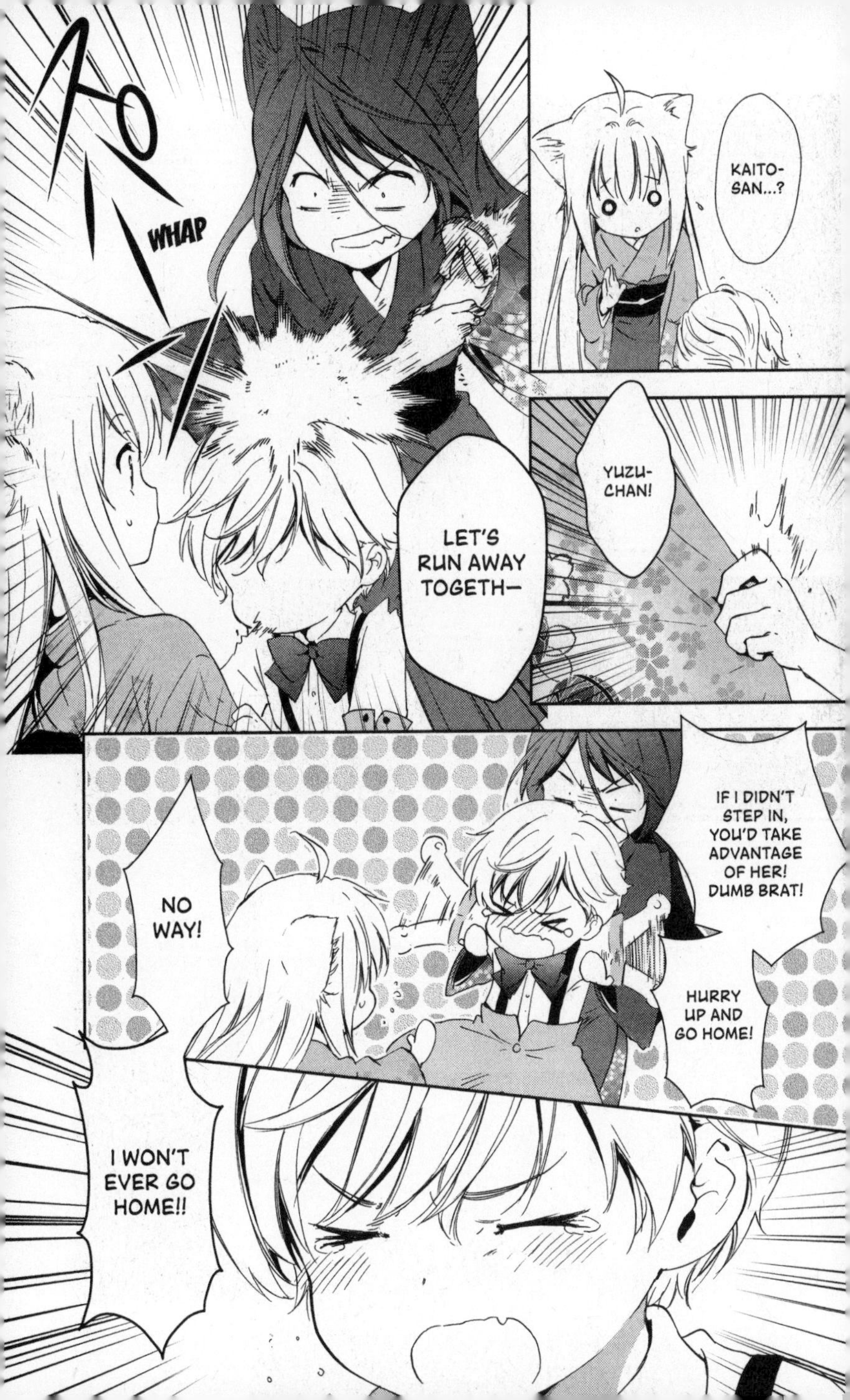
KAITO-SAN...?
YUZU-CHAN!
WHAP
LET'S RUN AWAY TOGETH—
IF I DIDN'T STEP IN, YOU'D TAKE ADVANTAGE OF HER! DUMB BRAT!
HURRY UP AND GO HOME!
NO WAY!
I WON'T EVER GO HOME!!

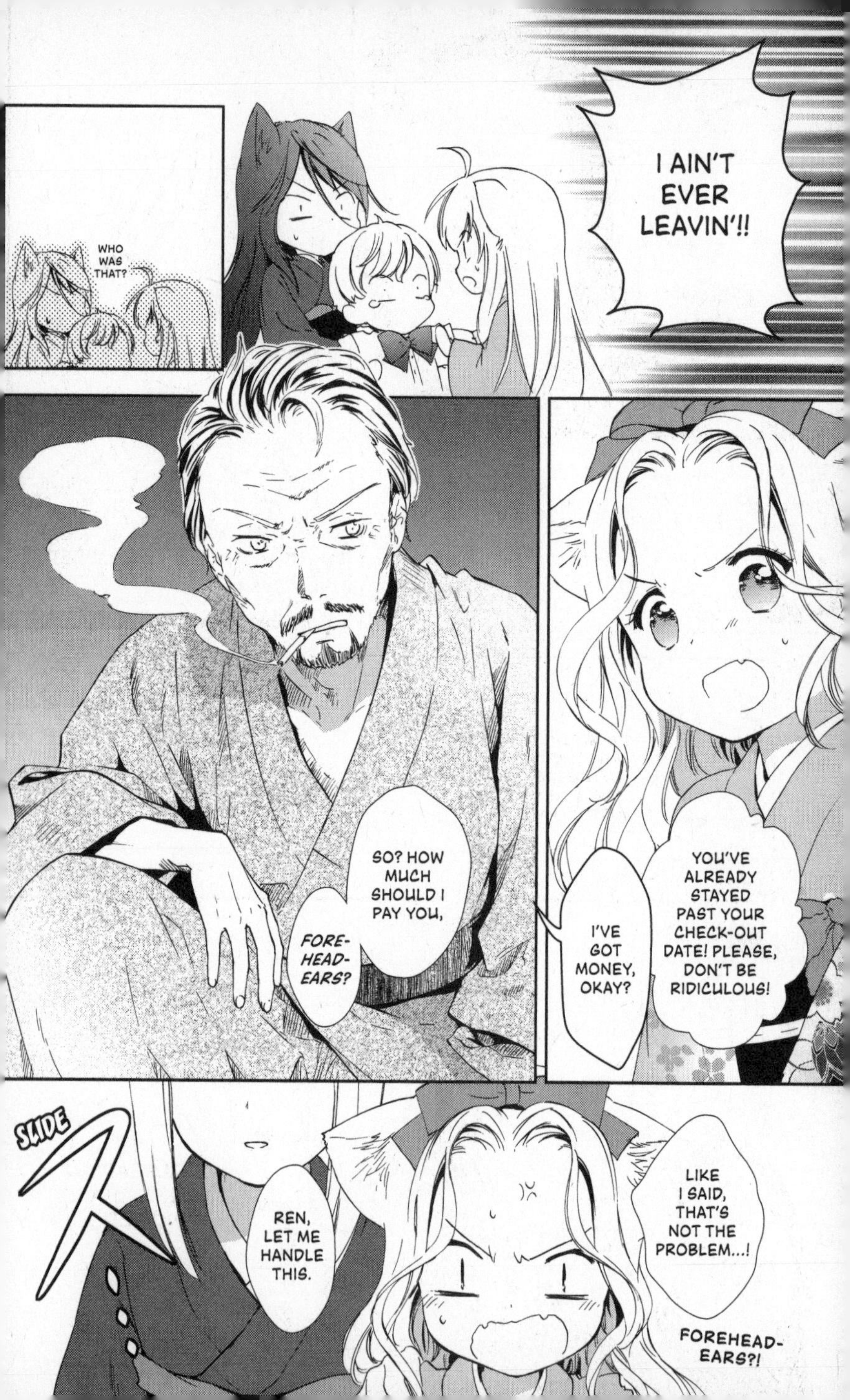
I AIN'T EVER LEAVIN'!!
WHO WAS THAT?
YOU'VE ALREADY STAYED PAST YOUR CHECK-OUT DATE! PLEASE, DON'T BE RIDICULOUS!
I'VE GOT MONEY, OKAY?
SO? HOW MUCH SHOULD I PAY YOU,
FORE-HEAD-EARS?
LIKE I SAID, THAT'S NOT THE PROBLEM...!
FOREHEAD-EARS?!
REN, LET ME HANDLE THIS.
SLIDE

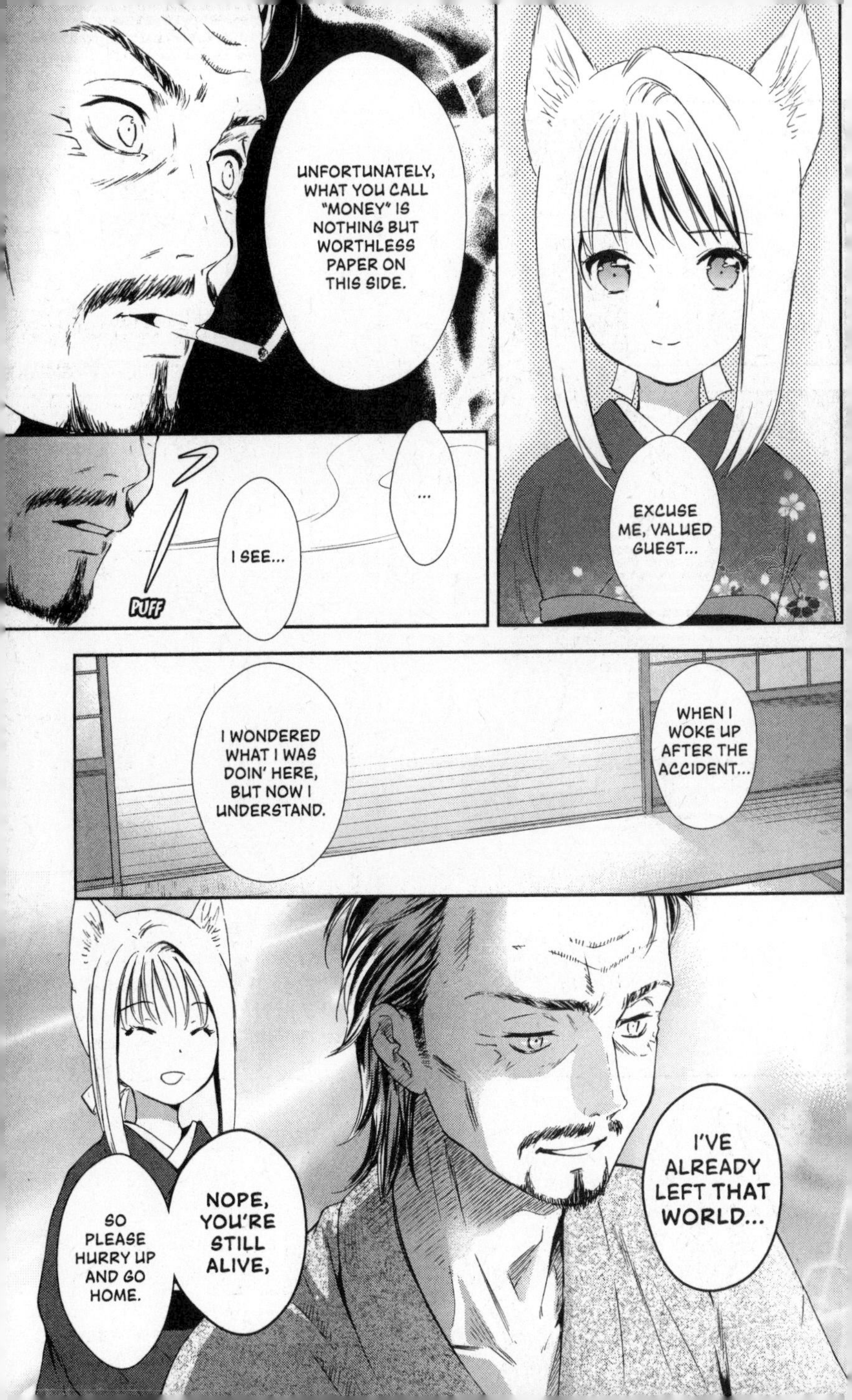
EXCUSE ME, VALUED GUEST...
UNFORTUNATELY, WHAT YOU CALL "MONEY" IS NOTHING BUT WORTHLESS PAPER ON THIS SIDE.
...
I SEE...
PUFF
WHEN I WOKE UP AFTER THE ACCIDENT...
I WONDERED WHAT I WAS DOIN' HERE, BUT NOW I UNDERSTAND.
I'VE ALREADY LEFT THAT WORLD...
NOPE, YOU'RE STILL ALIVE,
SO PLEASE HURRY UP AND GO HOME.

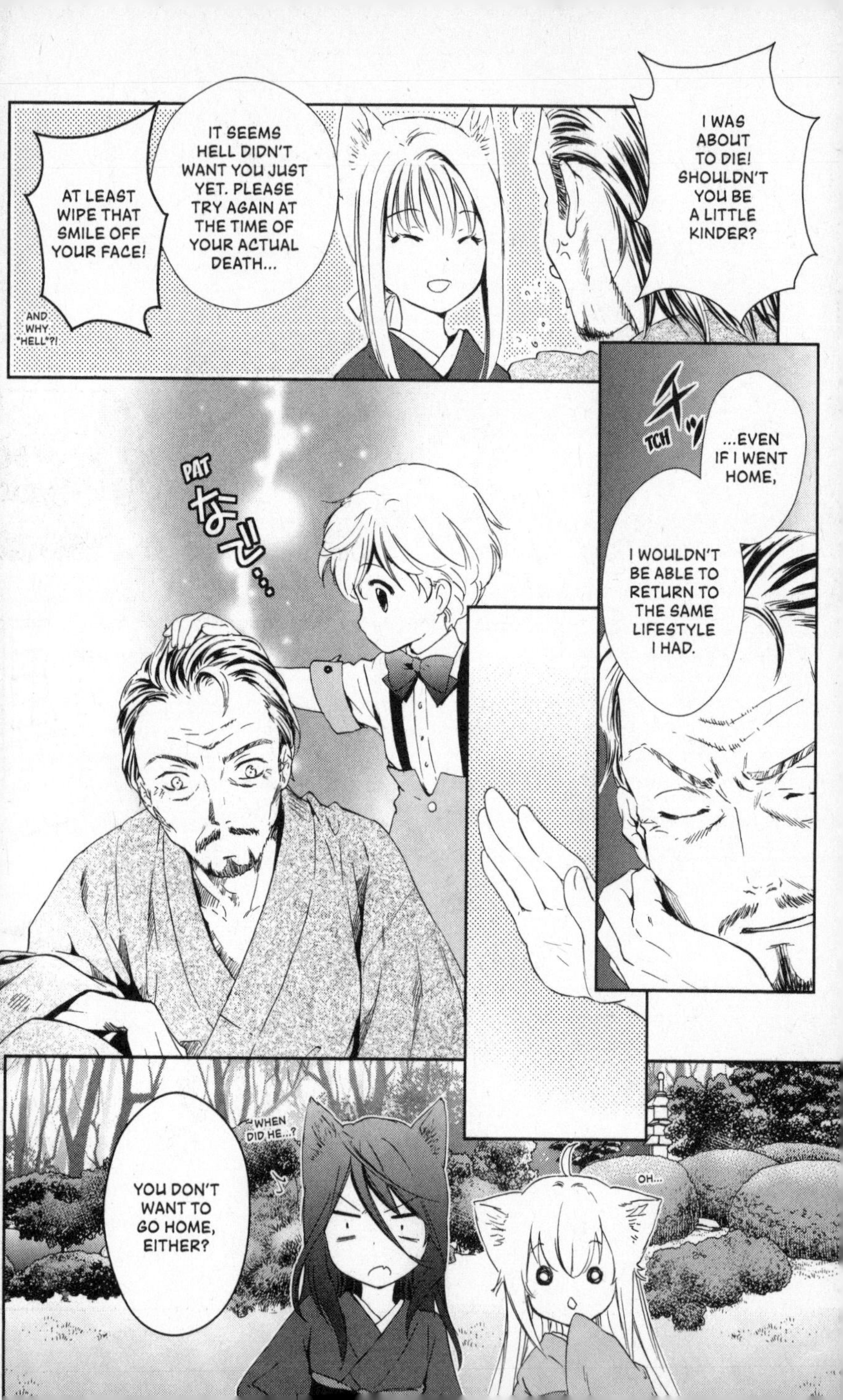
I WAS ABOUT TO DIE! SHOULDN'T YOU BE A LITTLE KINDER?
IT SEEMS HELL DIDN'T WANT YOU JUST YET. PLEASE TRY AGAIN AT THE TIME OF YOUR ACTUAL DEATH...
AT LEAST WIPE THAT SMILE OFF YOUR FACE!
AND WHY *HELL*?!
TCH
...EVEN IF I WENT HOME,
I WOULDN'T BE ABLE TO RETURN TO THE SAME LIFESTYLE I HAD.
PAT
OH...
WHEN DID HE...?
YOU DON'T WANT TO GO HOME, EITHER?

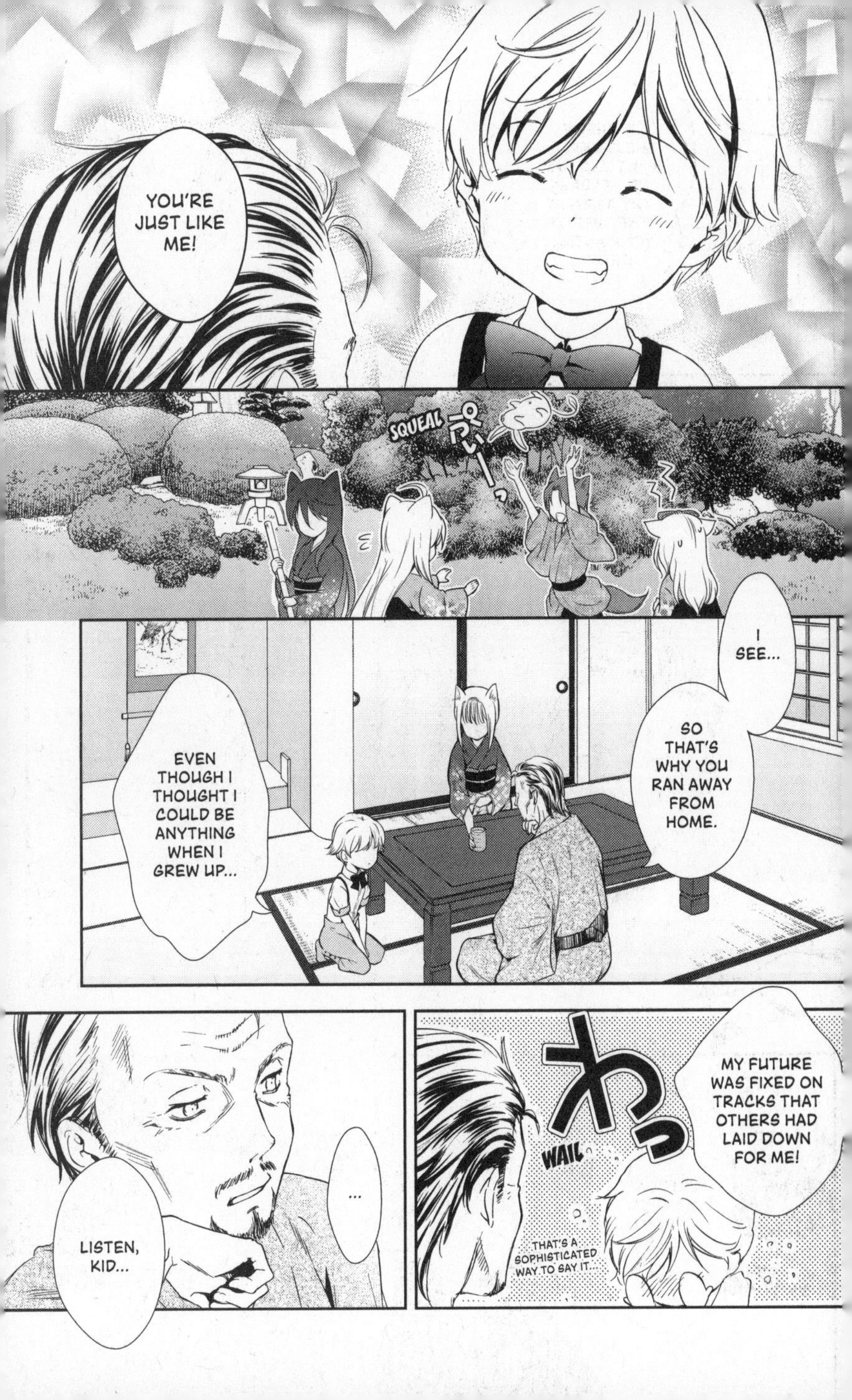
YOU'RE JUST LIKE ME!
SQUEAL
I SEE...
SO THAT'S WHY YOU RAN AWAY FROM HOME.
EVEN THOUGH I THOUGHT I COULD BE ANYTHING WHEN I GREW UP...
MY FUTURE WAS FIXED ON TRACKS THAT OTHERS HAD LAID DOWN FOR ME!
WAIL
THAT'S A SOPHISTICATED WAY TO SAY IT...
...
LISTEN, KID...

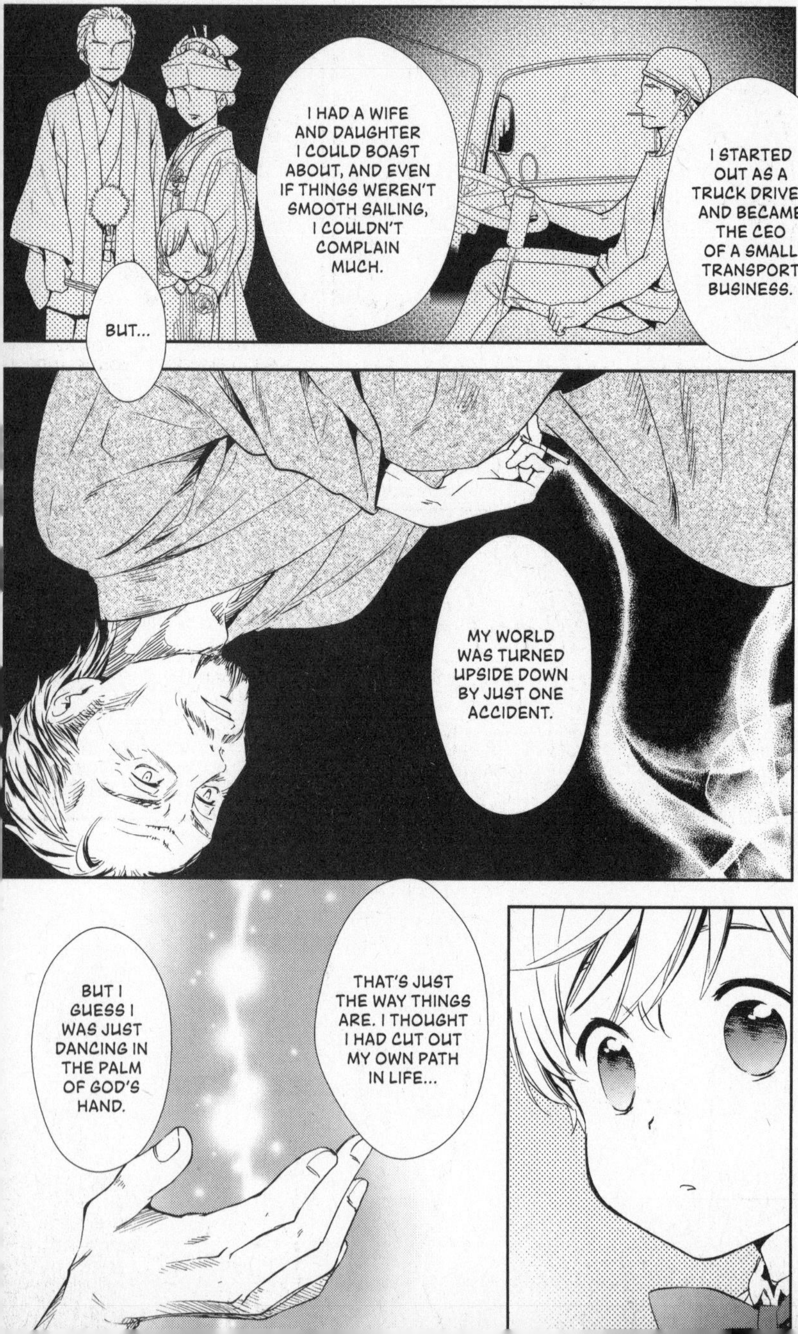
I STARTED OUT AS A TRUCK DRIVER AND BECAME THE CEO OF A SMALL TRANSPORT BUSINESS.
I HAD A WIFE AND DAUGHTER I COULD BOAST ABOUT, AND EVEN IF THINGS WEREN'T SMOOTH SAILING, I COULDN'T COMPLAIN MUCH.
BUT...
MY WORLD WAS TURNED UPSIDE DOWN BY JUST ONE ACCIDENT.
THAT'S JUST THE WAY THINGS ARE. I THOUGHT I HAD CUT OUT MY OWN PATH IN LIFE...
BUT I GUESS I WAS JUST DANCING IN THE PALM OF GOD'S HAND.

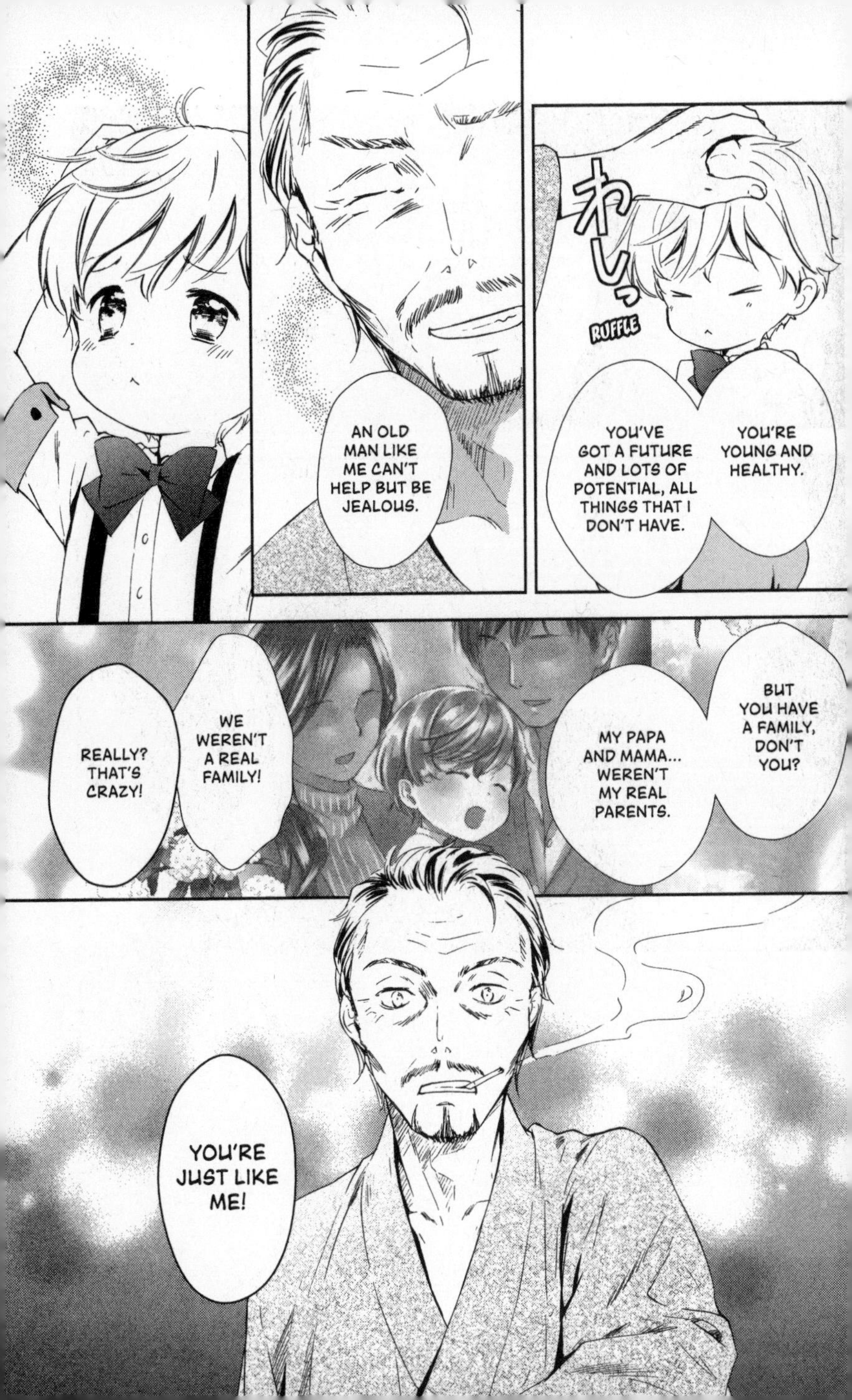
わしっ
RUFFLE
YOU'RE YOUNG AND HEALTHY.
YOU'VE GOT A FUTURE AND LOTS OF POTENTIAL, ALL THINGS THAT I DON'T HAVE.
AN OLD MAN LIKE ME CAN'T HELP BUT BE JEALOUS.
BUT YOU HAVE A FAMILY, DON'T YOU?
MY PAPA AND MAMA... WEREN'T MY REAL PARENTS.
WE WEREN'T A REAL FAMILY!
REALLY? THAT'S CRAZY!
YOU'RE JUST LIKE ME!

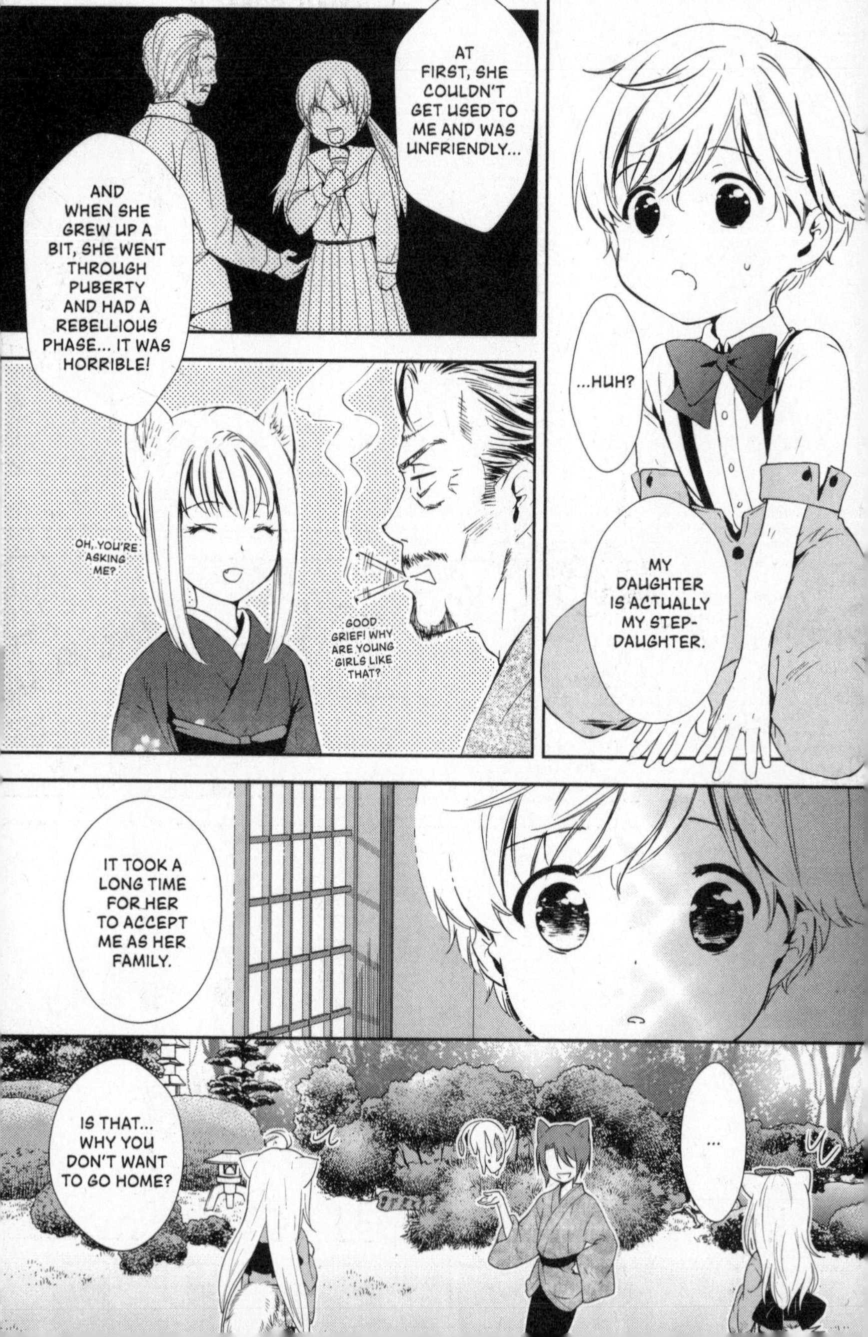
...HUH?
MY DAUGHTER IS ACTUALLY MY STEP-DAUGHTER.
AT FIRST, SHE COULDN'T GET USED TO ME AND WAS UNFRIENDLY...
AND WHEN SHE GREW UP A BIT, SHE WENT THROUGH PUBERTY AND HAD A REBELLIOUS PHASE... IT WAS HORRIBLE!
GOOD GRIEF! WHY ARE YOUNG GIRLS LIKE THAT?
OH, YOU'RE ASKING ME?
IT TOOK A LONG TIME FOR HER TO ACCEPT ME AS HER FAMILY.
...
IS THAT... WHY YOU DON'T WANT TO GO HOME?

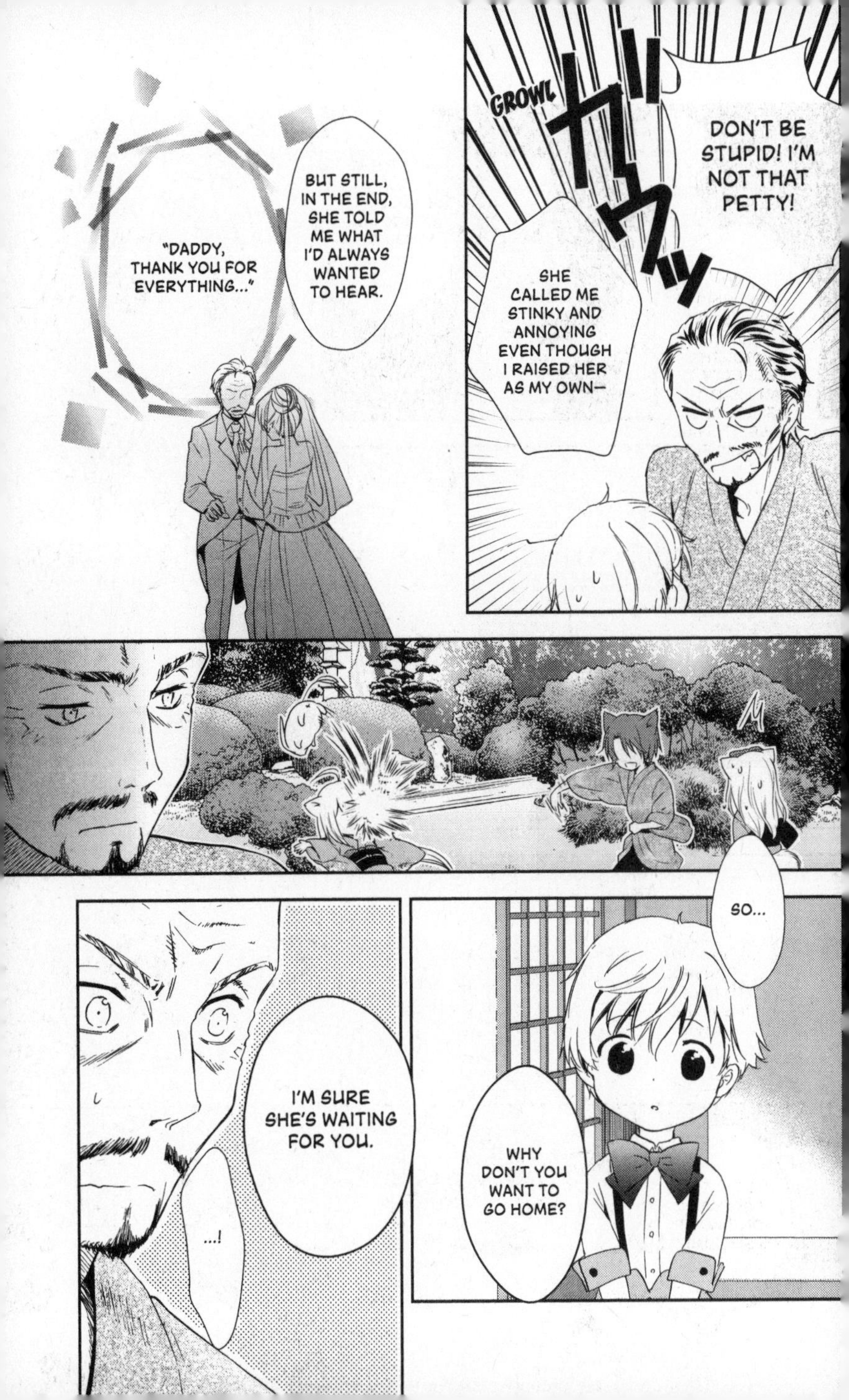
DON'T BE STUPID! I'M NOT THAT PETTY!
GROWL
SHE CALLED ME STINKY AND ANNOYING EVEN THOUGH I RAISED HER AS MY OWN—
BUT STILL, IN THE END, SHE TOLD ME WHAT I'D ALWAYS WANTED TO HEAR.
"DADDY, THANK YOU FOR EVERYTHING..."
SO...
WHY DON'T YOU WANT TO GO HOME?
I'M SURE SHE'S WAITING FOR YOU.
...!

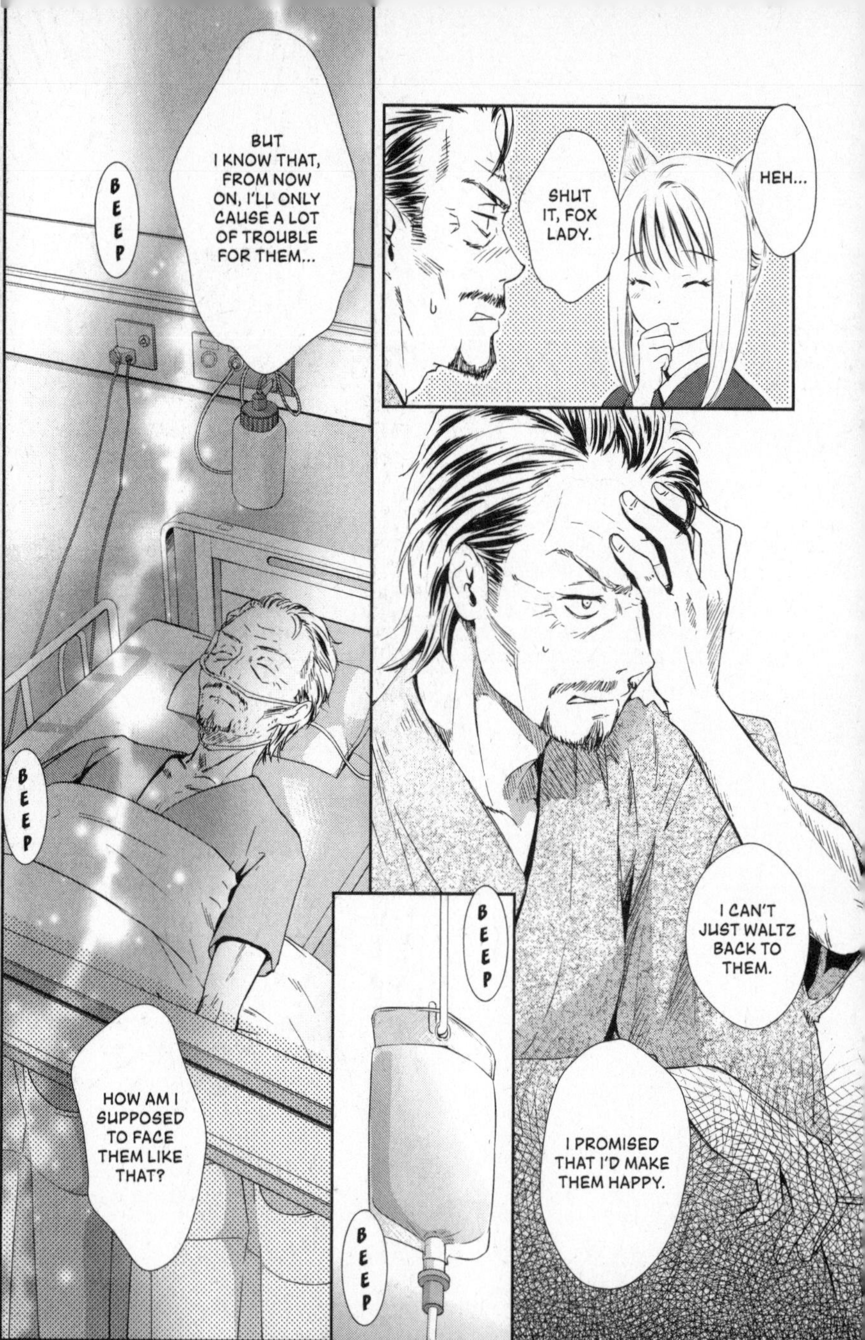
HEH...
SHUT IT, FOX LADY.
I CAN'T JUST WALTZ BACK TO THEM.
I PROMISED THAT I'D MAKE THEM HAPPY.
BEEP
BEEP
BUT I KNOW THAT, FROM NOW ON, I'LL ONLY CAUSE A LOT OF TROUBLE FOR THEM...
BEEP
BEEP
HOW AM I SUPPOSED TO FACE THEM LIKE THAT?

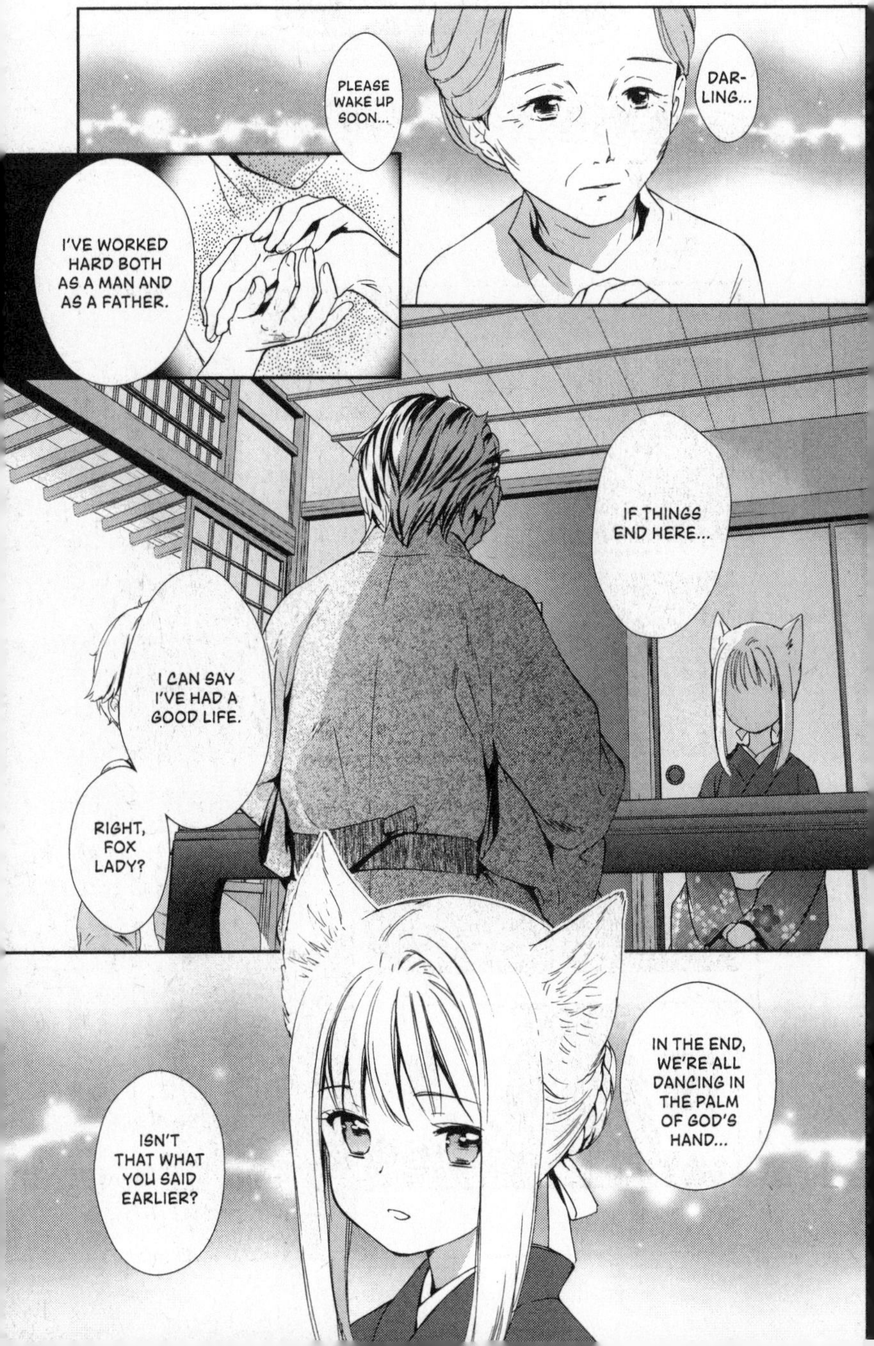
DAR-LING...
PLEASE WAKE UP SOON...
I'VE WORKED HARD BOTH AS A MAN AND AS A FATHER.
IF THINGS END HERE...
I CAN SAY I'VE HAD A GOOD LIFE.
RIGHT, FOX LADY?
IN THE END, WE'RE ALL DANCING IN THE PALM OF GOD'S HAND...
ISN'T THAT WHAT YOU SAID EARLIER?

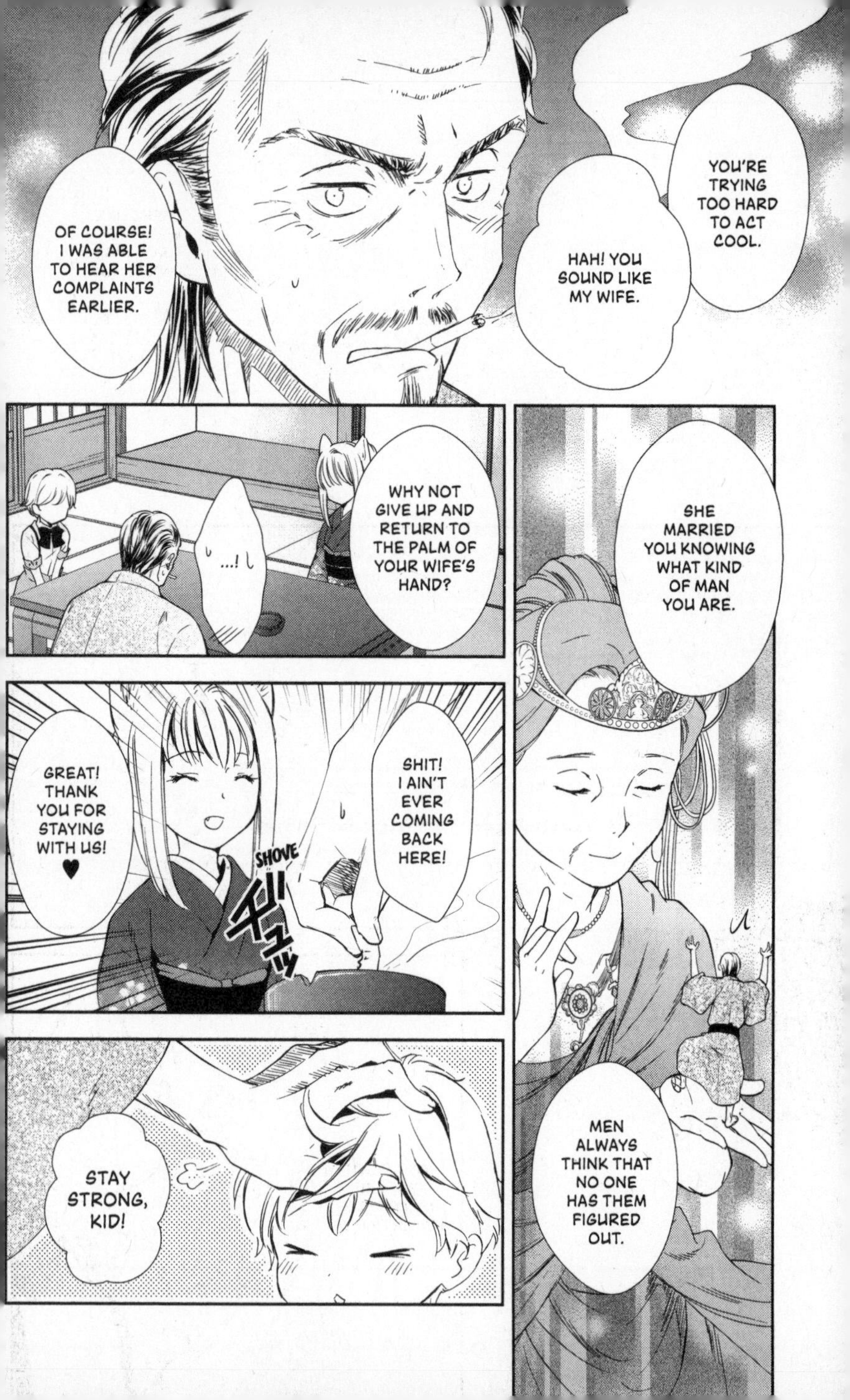
YOU'RE TRYING TOO HARD TO ACT COOL.
HAH! YOU SOUND LIKE MY WIFE.
OF COURSE! I WAS ABLE TO HEAR HER COMPLAINTS EARLIER.
SHE MARRIED YOU KNOWING WHAT KIND OF MAN YOU ARE.
MEN ALWAYS THINK THAT NO ONE HAS THEM FIGURED OUT.
WHY NOT GIVE UP AND RETURN TO THE PALM OF YOUR WIFE'S HAND?
...!
SHIT! I AIN'T EVER COMING BACK HERE!
SHOVE
GREAT! THANK YOU FOR STAYING WITH US! ♥
STAY STRONG, KID!

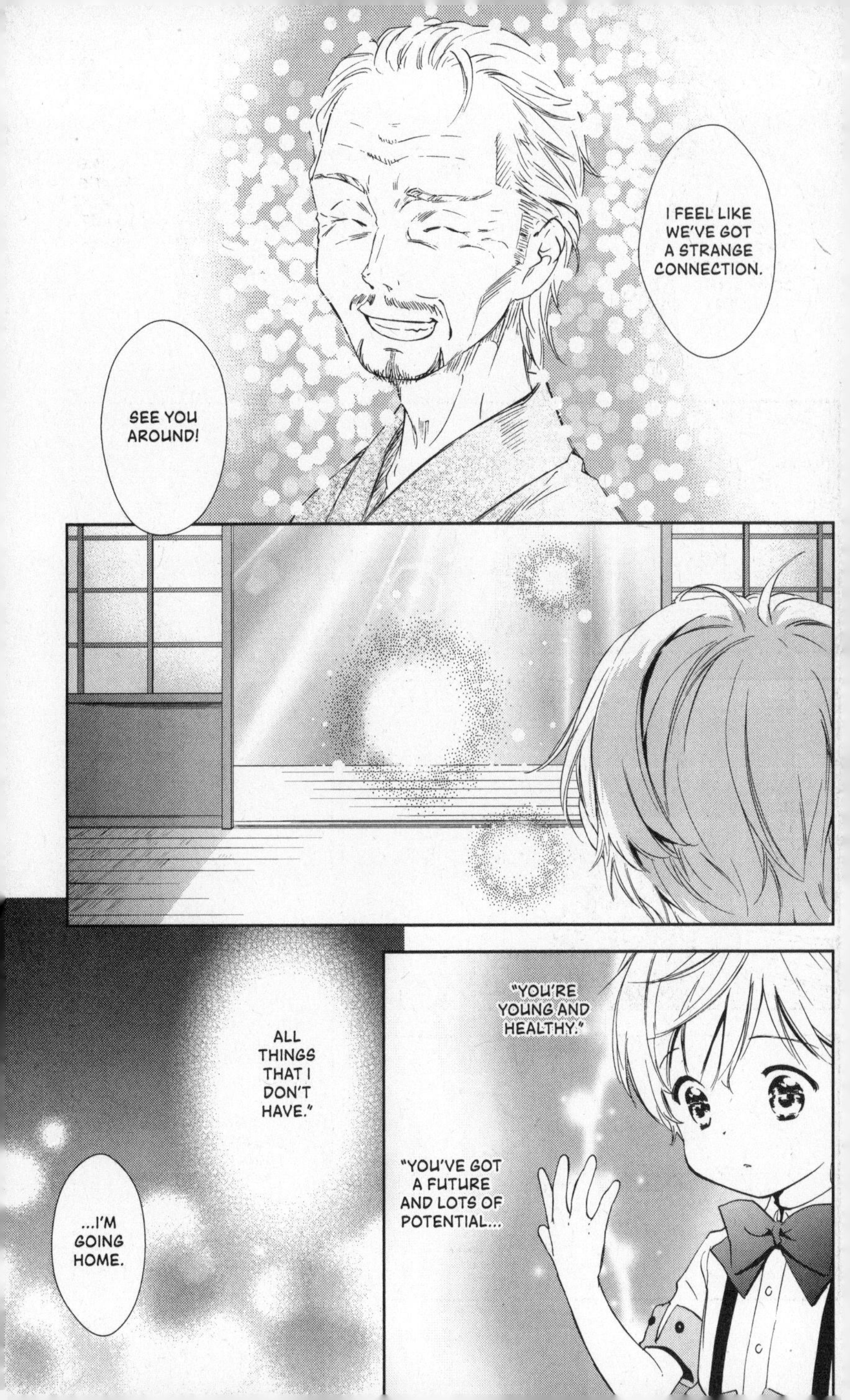
I FEEL LIKE WE'VE GOT A STRANGE CONNECTION.
SEE YOU AROUND!
"YOU'RE YOUNG AND HEALTHY."
"YOU'VE GOT A FUTURE AND LOTS OF POTENTIAL...
ALL THINGS THAT I DON'T HAVE."
...I'M GOING HOME.

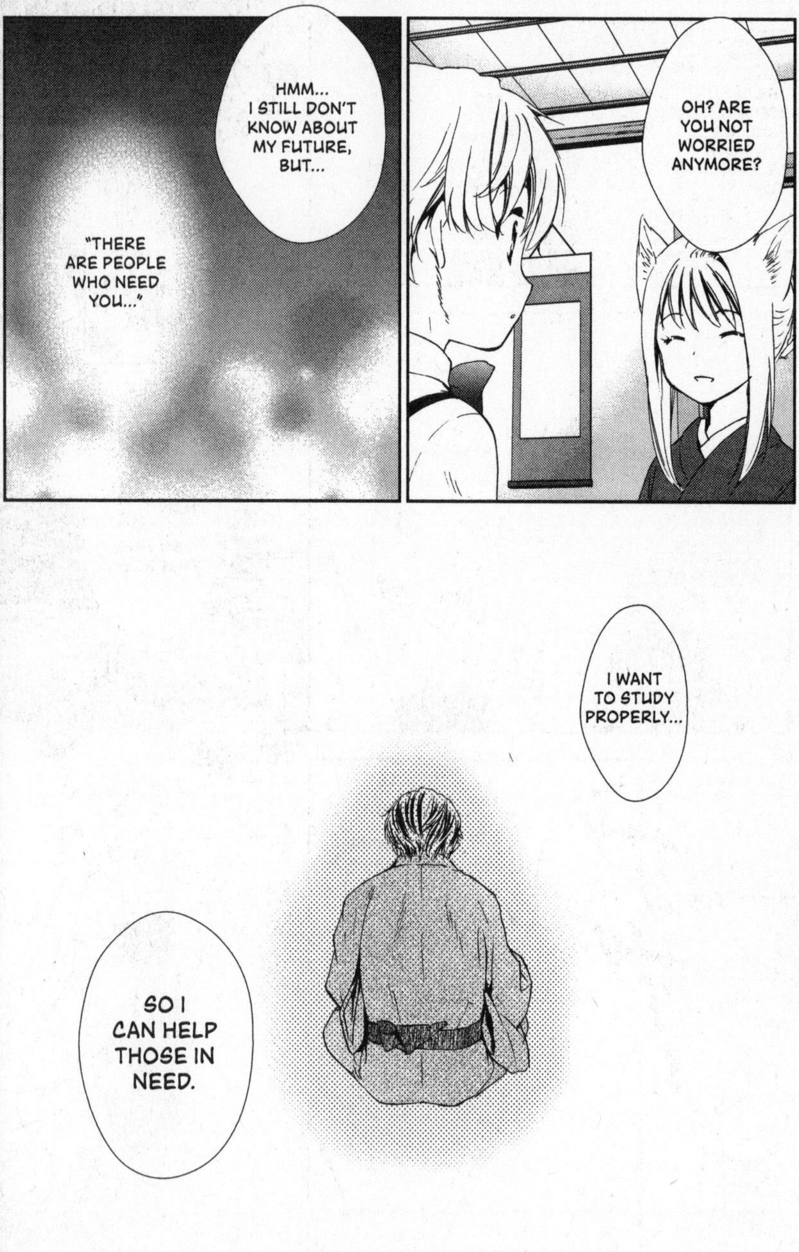
OH? ARE YOU NOT WORRIED ANYMORE?
HMM... I STILL DON'T KNOW ABOUT MY FUTURE, BUT...
"THERE ARE PEOPLE WHO NEED YOU..."
I WANT TO STUDY PROPERLY...
SO I CAN HELP THOSE IN NEED.

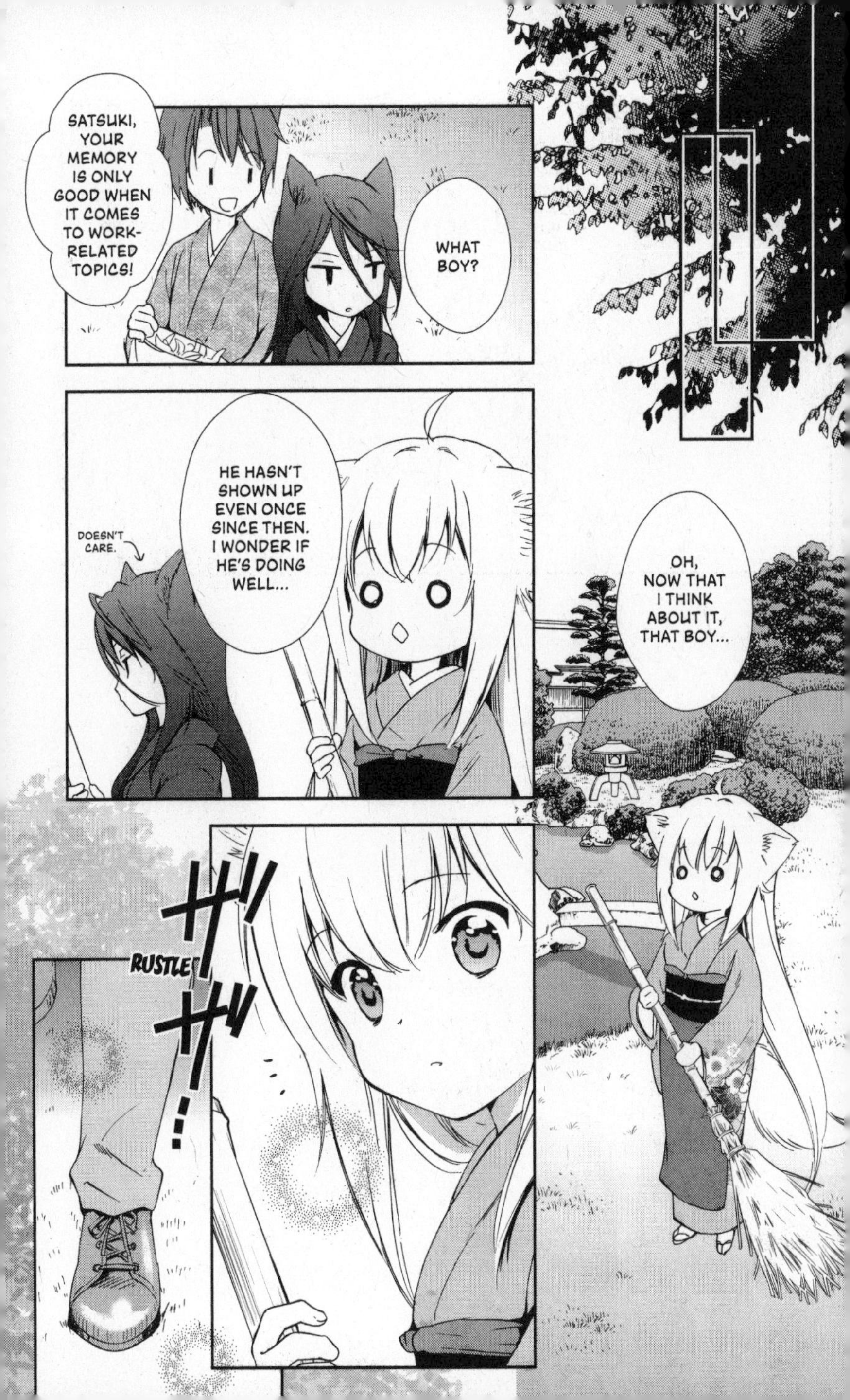
OH, NOW THAT I THINK ABOUT IT, THAT BOY...
WHAT BOY?
SATSUKI, YOUR MEMORY IS ONLY GOOD WHEN IT COMES TO WORK-RELATED TOPICS!
HE HASN'T SHOWN UP EVEN ONCE SINCE THEN. I WONDER IF HE'S DOING WELL...
DOESN'T CARE.
RUSTLE

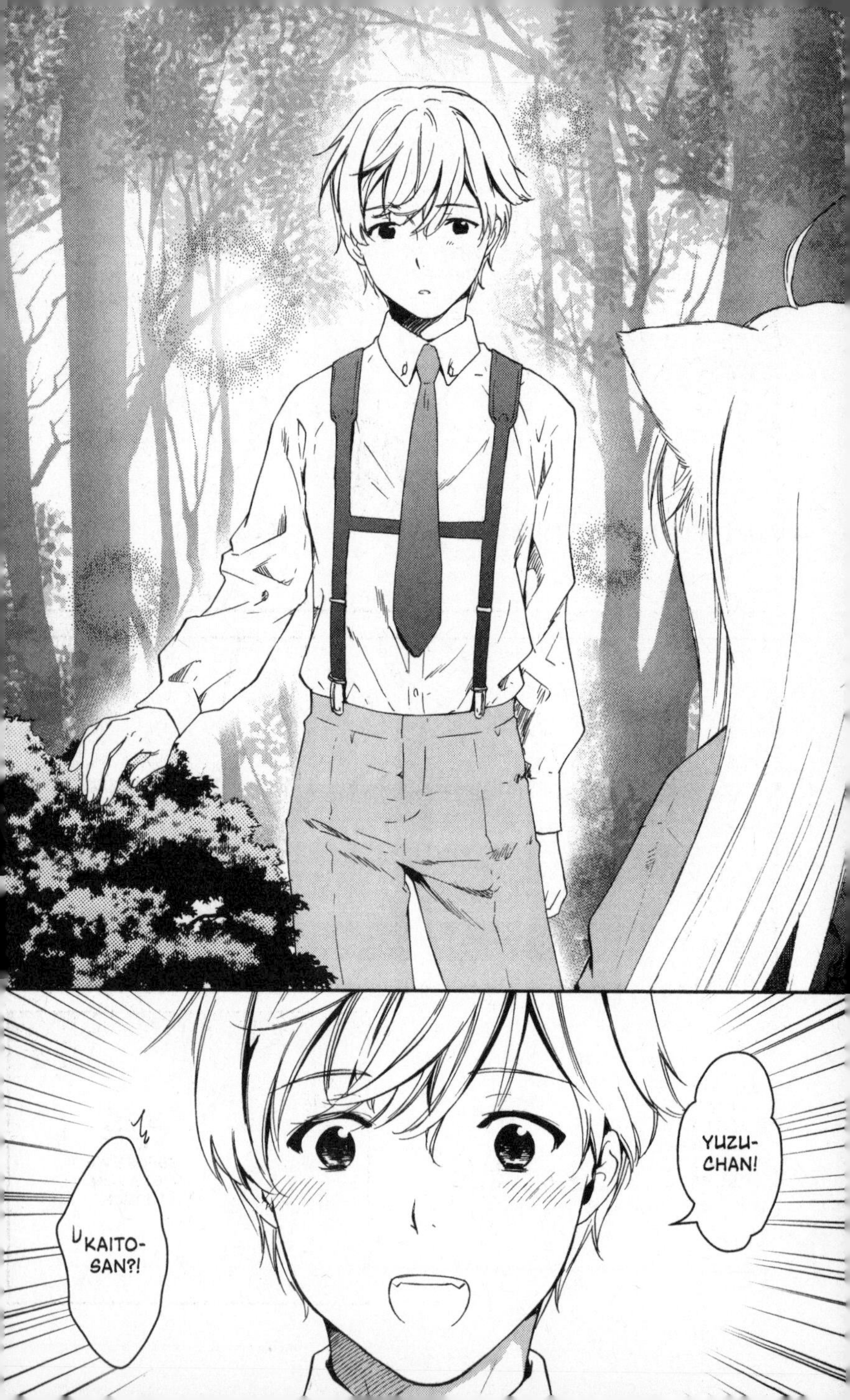
YUZU-CHAN!
U KAITO-SAN?!

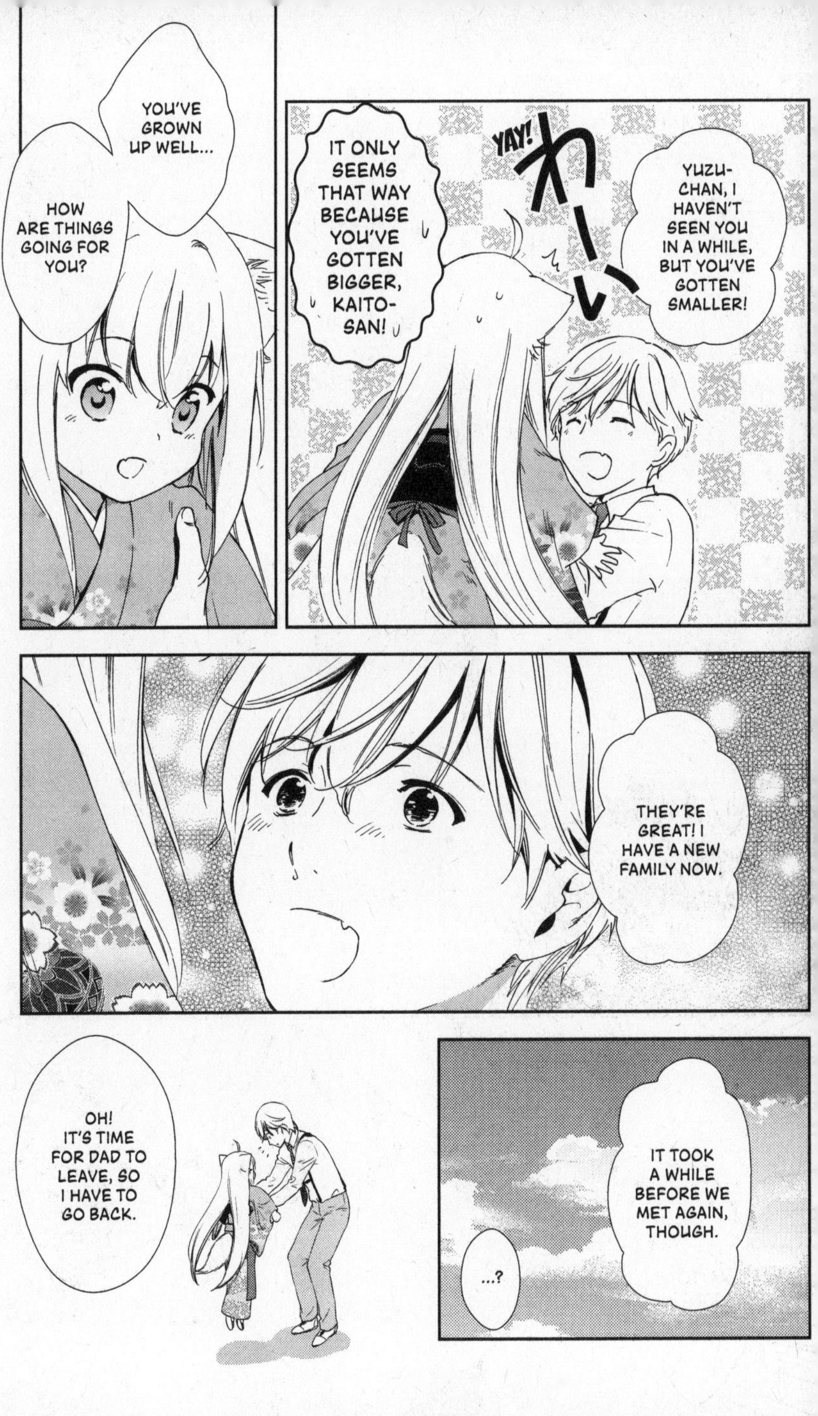
YAY!
わーい
YUZU-CHAN, I HAVEN'T SEEN YOU IN A WHILE, BUT YOU'VE GOTTEN SMALLER!
IT ONLY SEEMS THAT WAY BECAUSE YOU'VE GOTTEN BIGGER, KAITO-SAN!
YOU'VE GROWN UP WELL...
HOW ARE THINGS GOING FOR YOU?
THEY'RE GREAT! I HAVE A NEW FAMILY NOW.
IT TOOK A WHILE BEFORE WE MET AGAIN, THOUGH.
...?
OH! IT'S TIME FOR DAD TO LEAVE, SO I HAVE TO GO BACK.

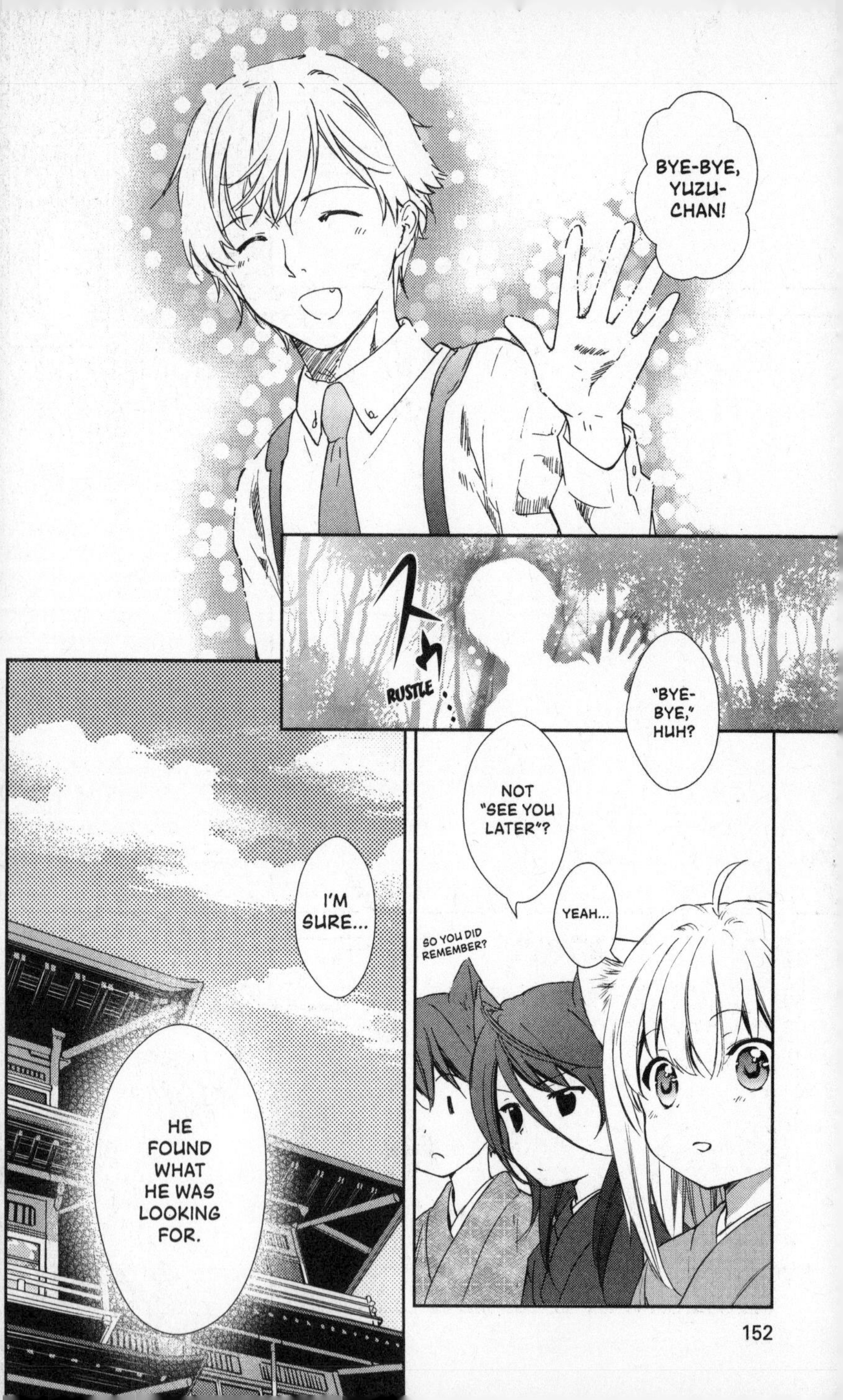
BYE-BYE, YUZU-CHAN!
RUSTLE
"BYE-BYE," HUH?
NOT "SEE YOU LATER"?
YEAH...
SO YOU DID REMEMBER?
I'M SURE...
HE FOUND WHAT HE WAS LOOKING FOR.

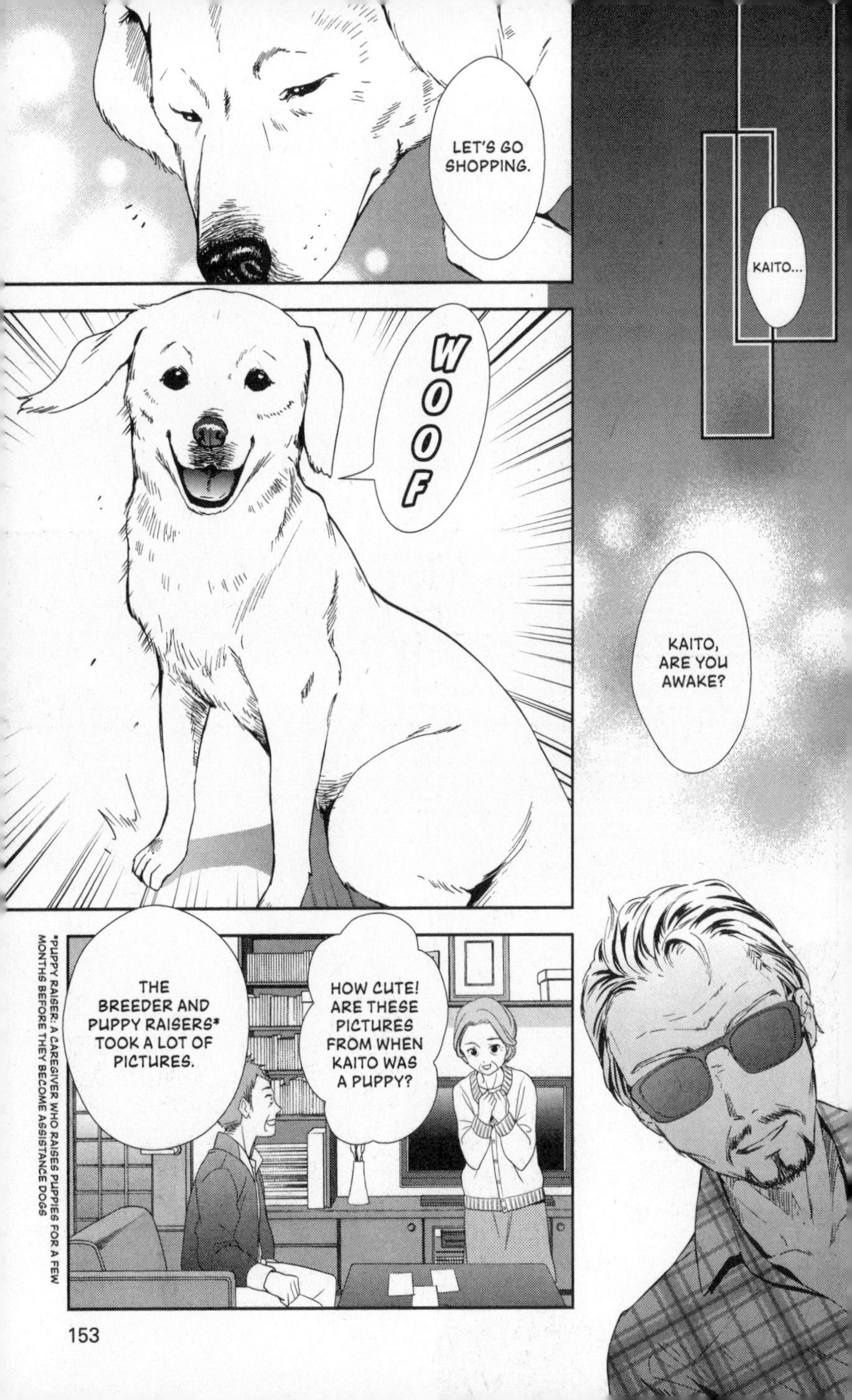
KAITO...
KAITO, ARE YOU AWAKE?
LET'S GO SHOPPING.
WOOF
HOW CUTE! ARE THESE PICTURES FROM WHEN KAITO WAS A PUPPY?
THE BREEDER AND PUPPY RAISERS* TOOK A LOT OF PICTURES.

*PUPPY RAISER: A CAREGIVER WHO RAISES PUPPIES FOR A FEW MONTHS BEFORE THEY BECOME ASSISTANCE DOGS

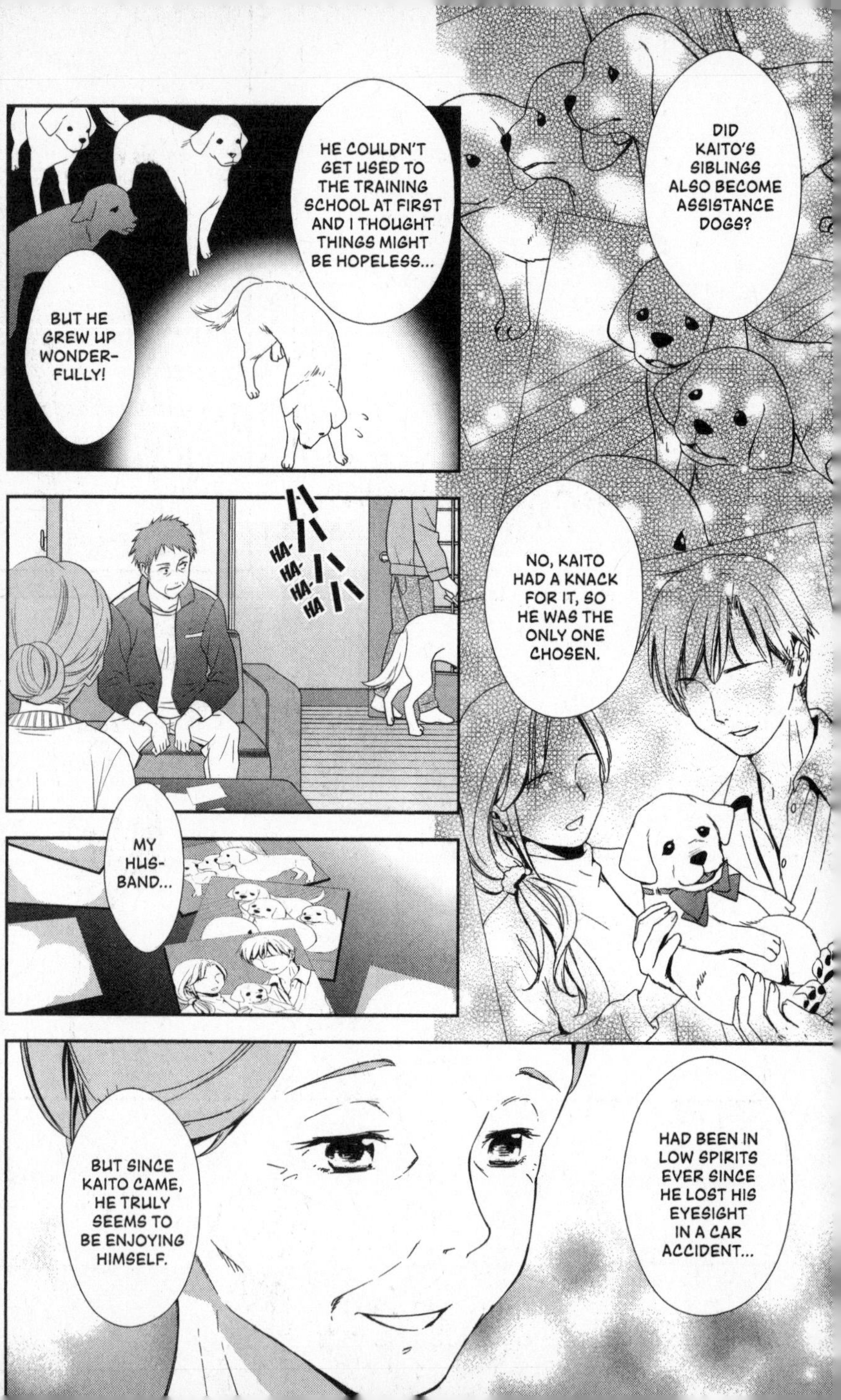
DID KAITO'S SIBLINGS ALSO BECOME ASSISTANCE DOGS?
NO, KAITO HAD A KNACK FOR IT, SO HE WAS THE ONLY ONE CHOSEN.
HE COULDN'T GET USED TO THE TRAINING SCHOOL AT FIRST AND I THOUGHT THINGS MIGHT BE HOPELESS...
BUT HE GREW UP WONDER-FULLY!
ハハハハ
HA-HA-HA-HA
MY HUS-BAND...
HAD BEEN IN LOW SPIRITS EVER SINCE HE LOST HIS EYESIGHT IN A CAR ACCIDENT...
BUT SINCE KAITO CAME, HE TRULY SEEMS TO BE ENJOYING HIMSELF.

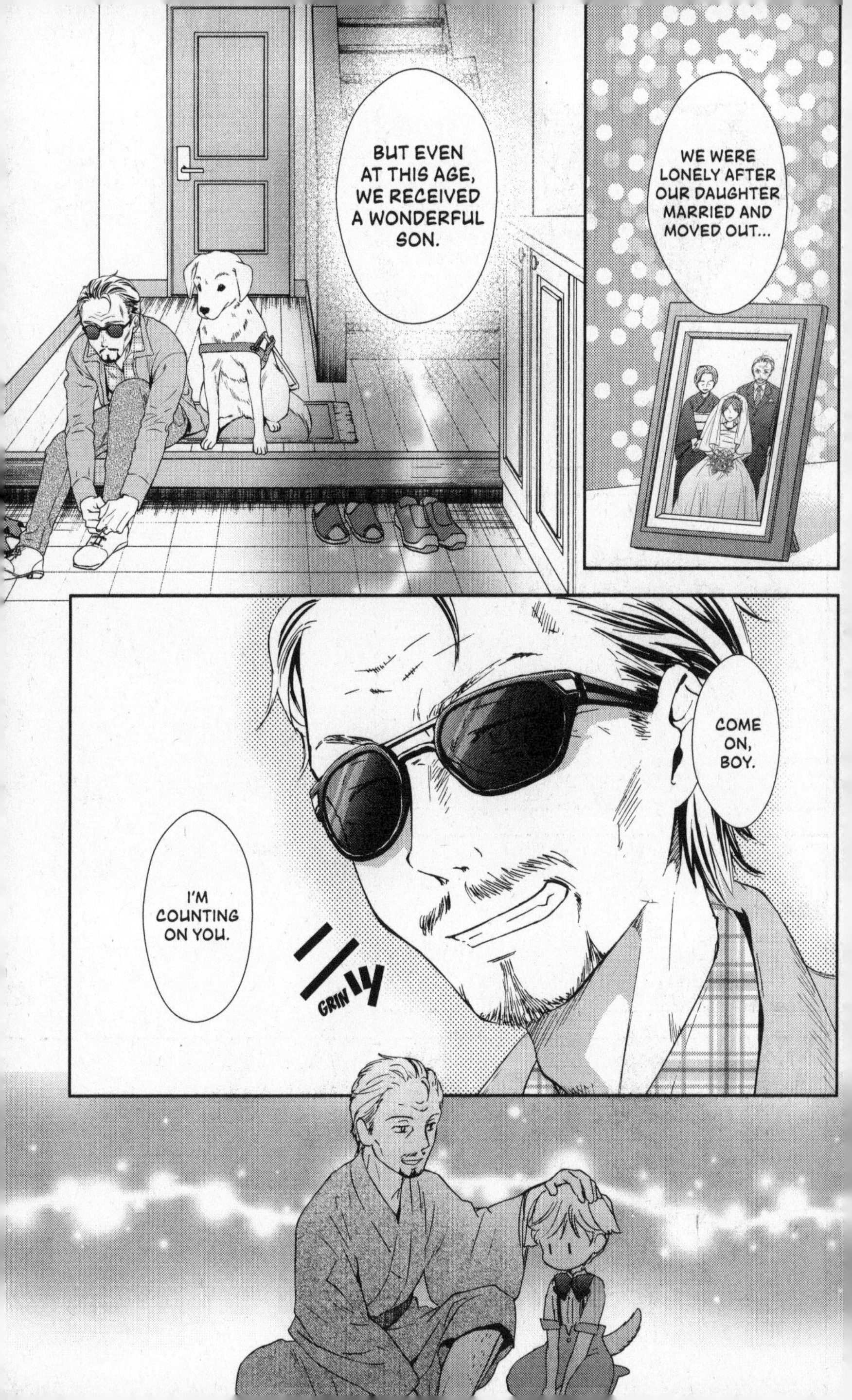
WE WERE LONELY AFTER OUR DAUGHTER MARRIED AND MOVED OUT...
BUT EVEN AT THIS AGE, WE RECEIVED A WONDERFUL SON.
COME ON, BOY.
I'M COUNTING ON YOU.
GRIN

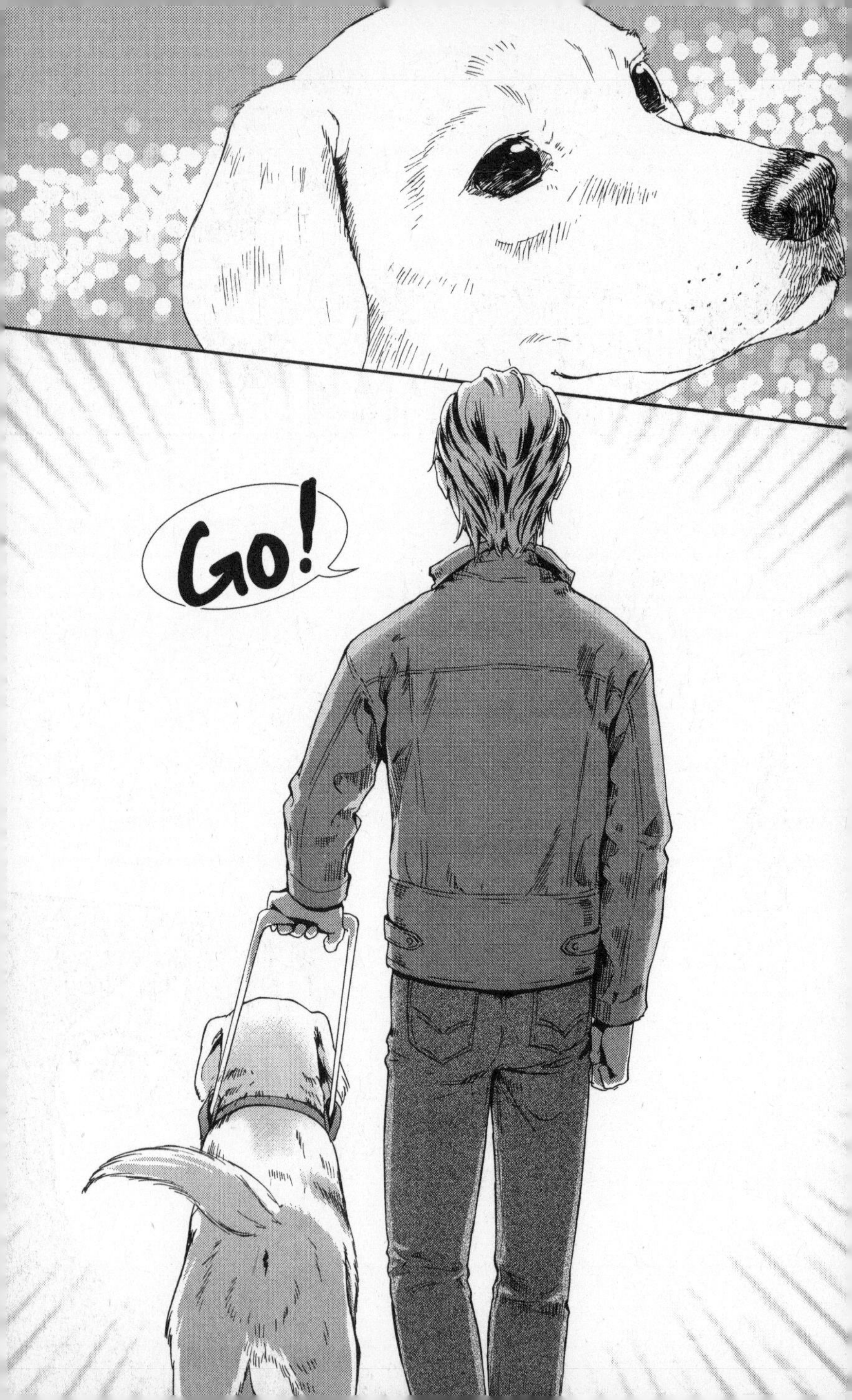
GO!

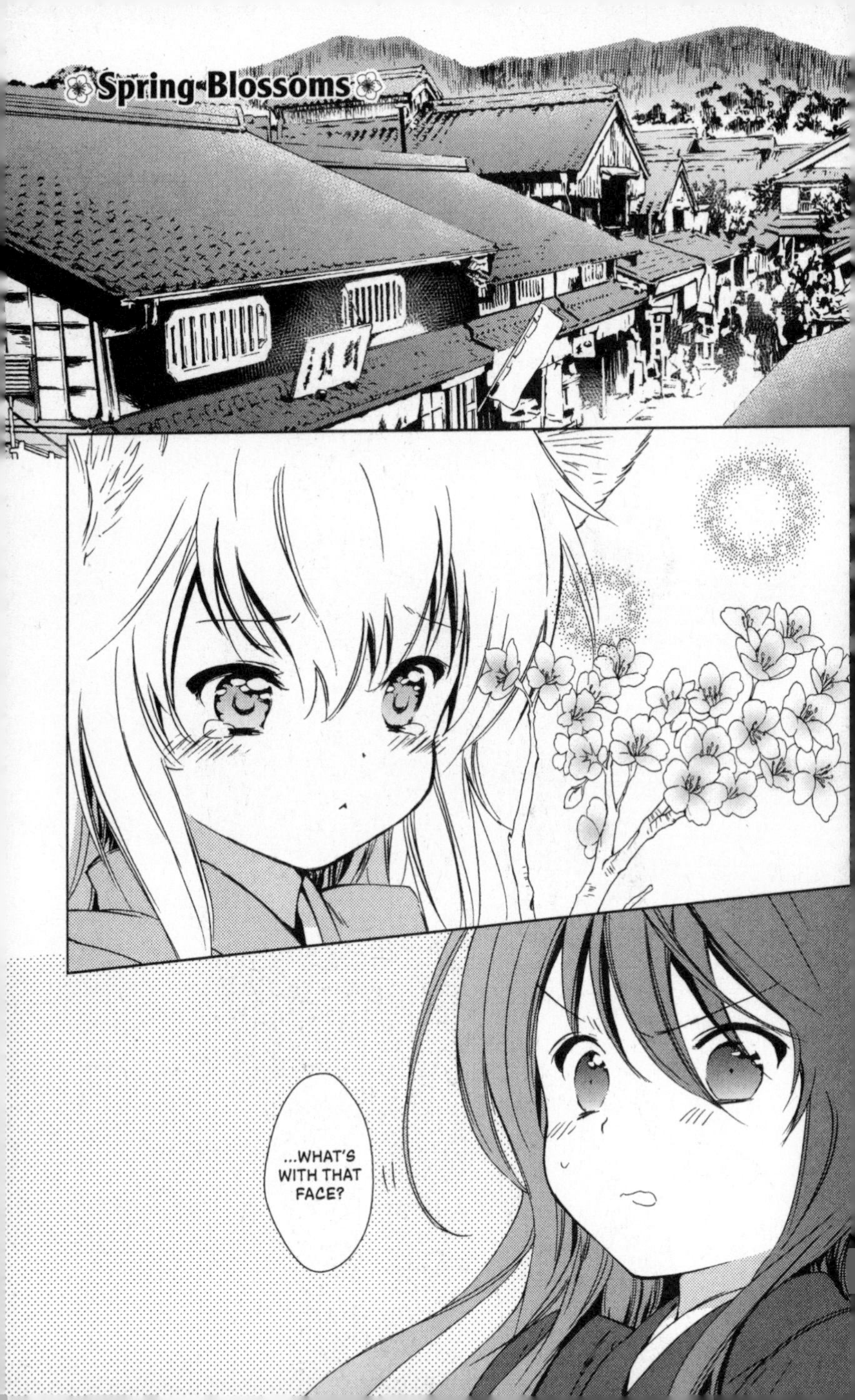
Spring Blossoms
...WHAT'S WITH THAT FACE?

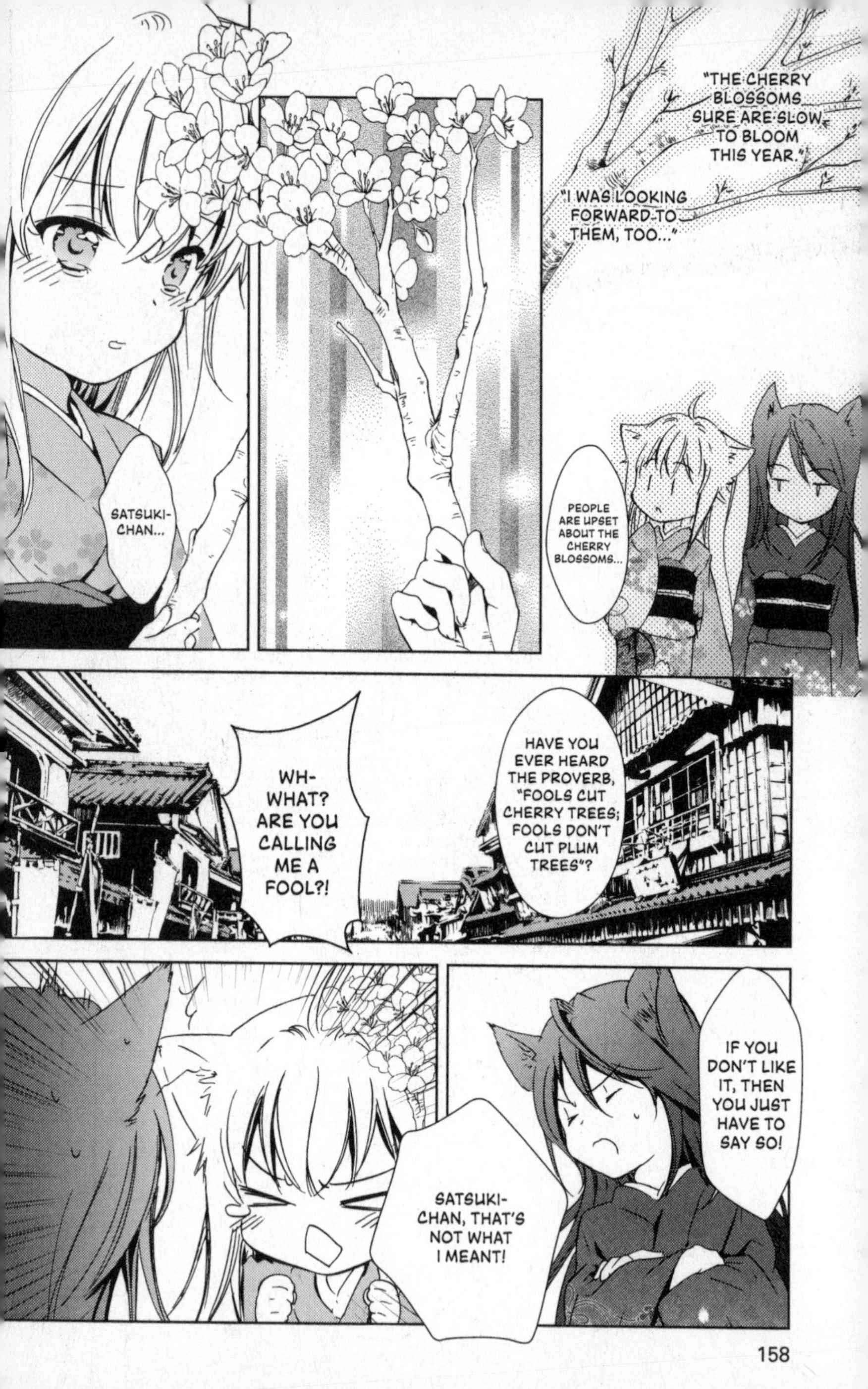
"THE CHERRY BLOSSOMS SURE ARE SLOW TO BLOOM THIS YEAR."
"I WAS LOOKING FORWARD TO THEM, TOO..."
PEOPLE ARE UPSET ABOUT THE CHERRY BLOSSOMS...
SATSUKI-CHAN...
HAVE YOU EVER HEARD THE PROVERB, "FOOLS CUT CHERRY TREES; FOOLS DON'T CUT PLUM TREES"?
WH-WHAT? ARE YOU CALLING ME A FOOL?!
IF YOU DON'T LIKE IT, THEN YOU JUST HAVE TO SAY SO!
SATSUKI-CHAN, THAT'S NOT WHAT I MEANT!

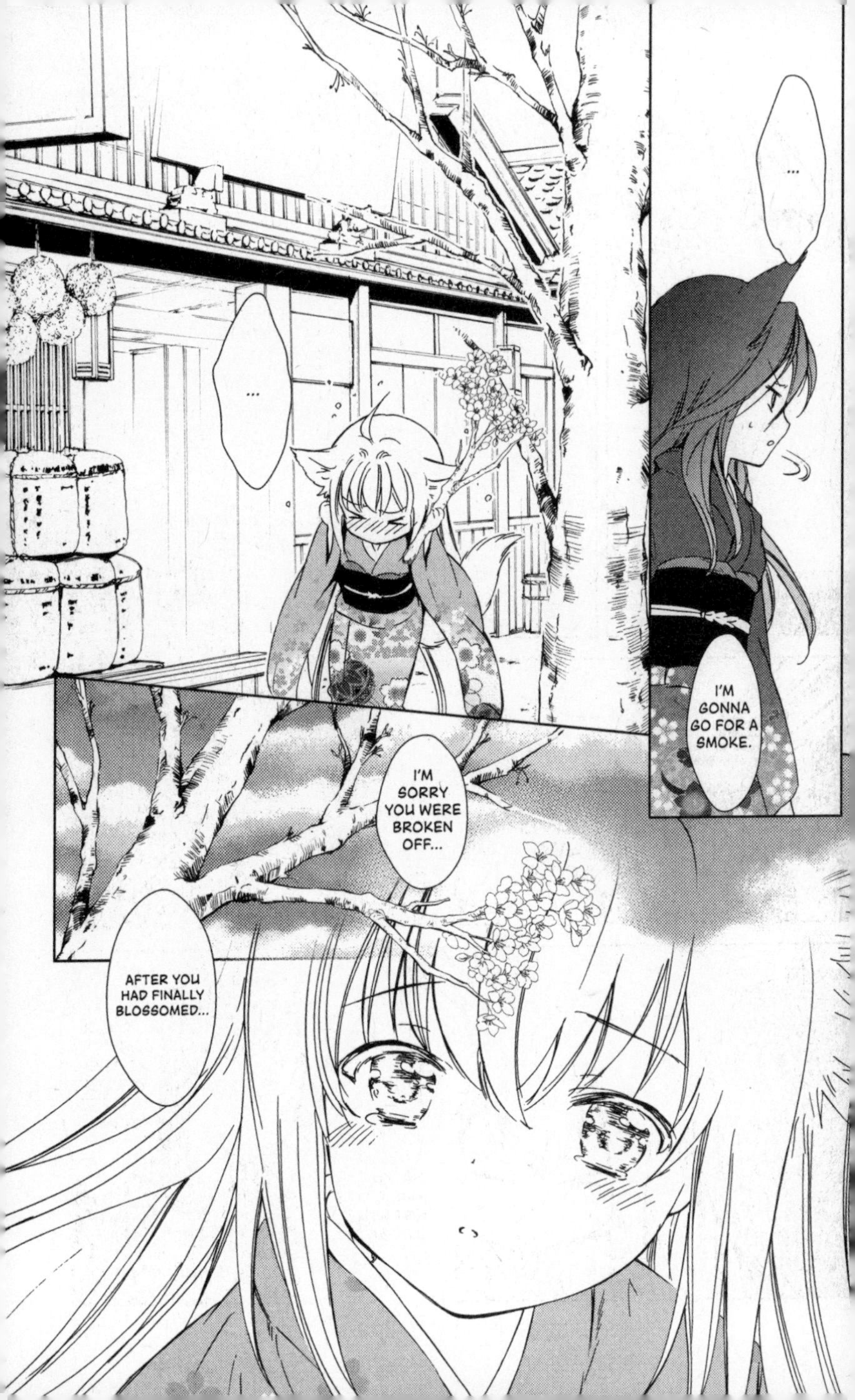
...
I'M GONNA GO FOR A SMOKE.
...
I'M SORRY YOU WERE BROKEN OFF...
AFTER YOU HAD FINALLY BLOSSOMED...

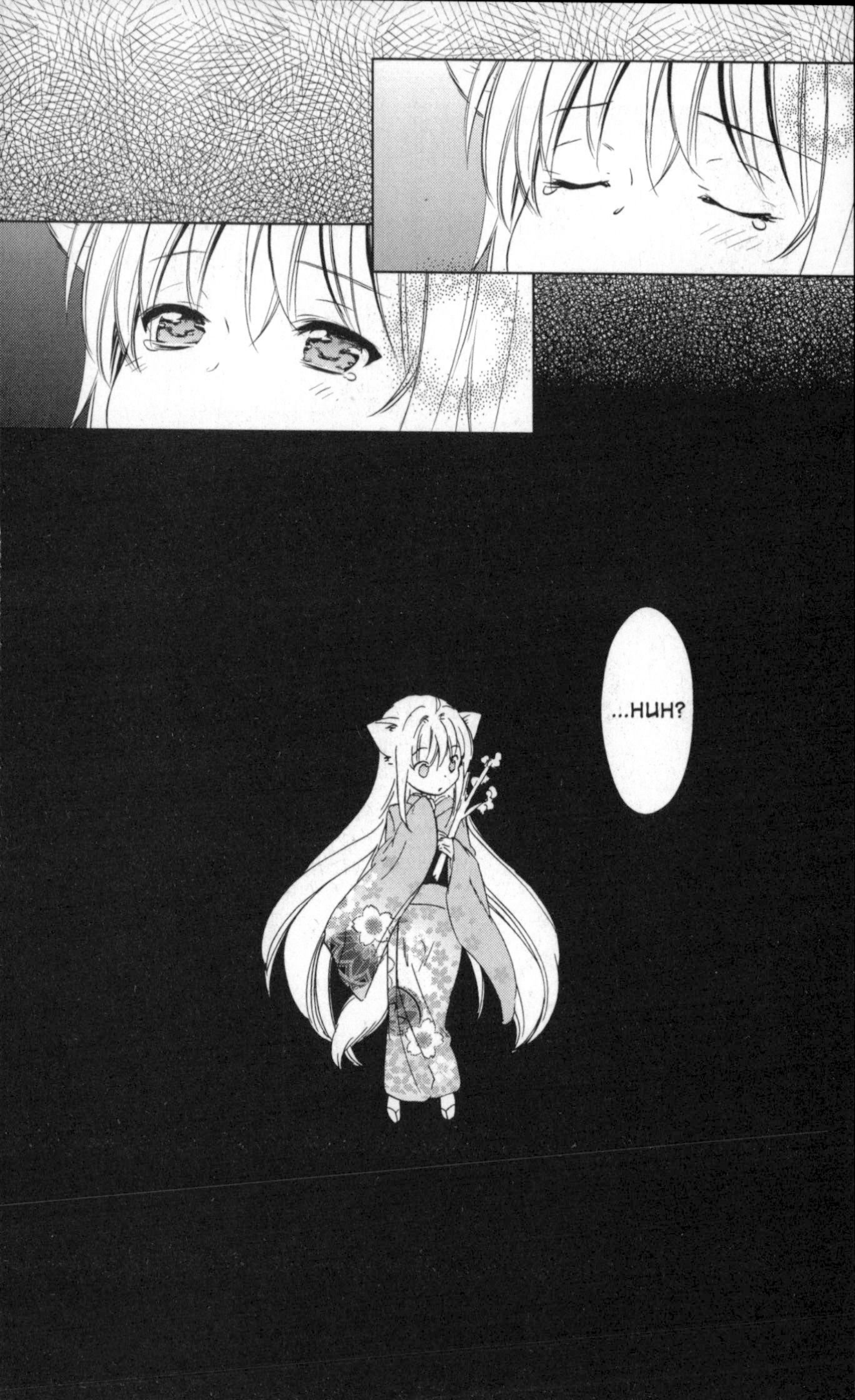
...HUH?

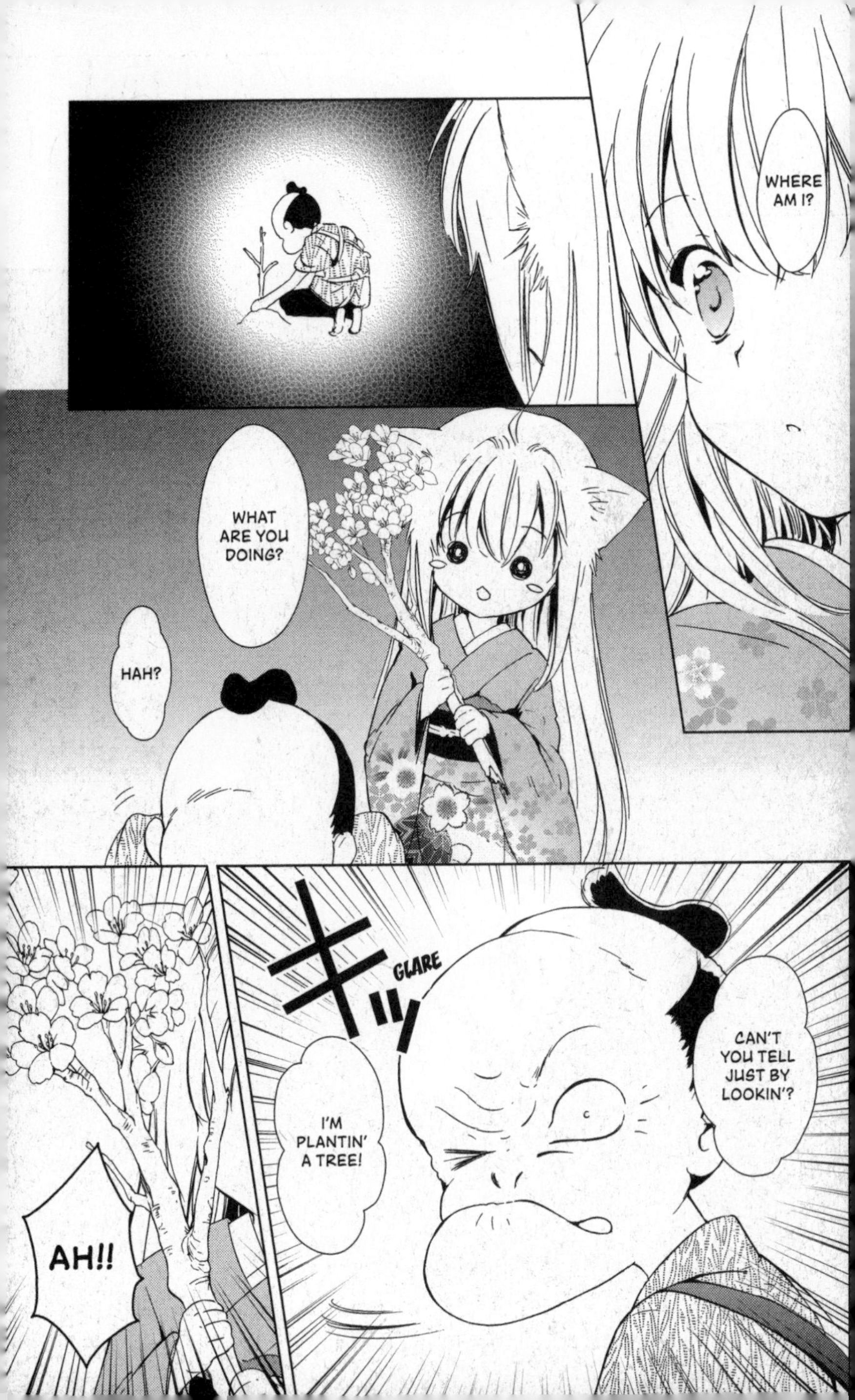
WHERE AM I?
WHAT ARE YOU DOING?
HAH?
GLARE
CAN'T YOU TELL JUST BY LOOKIN'?
I'M PLANTIN' A TREE!
AH!!

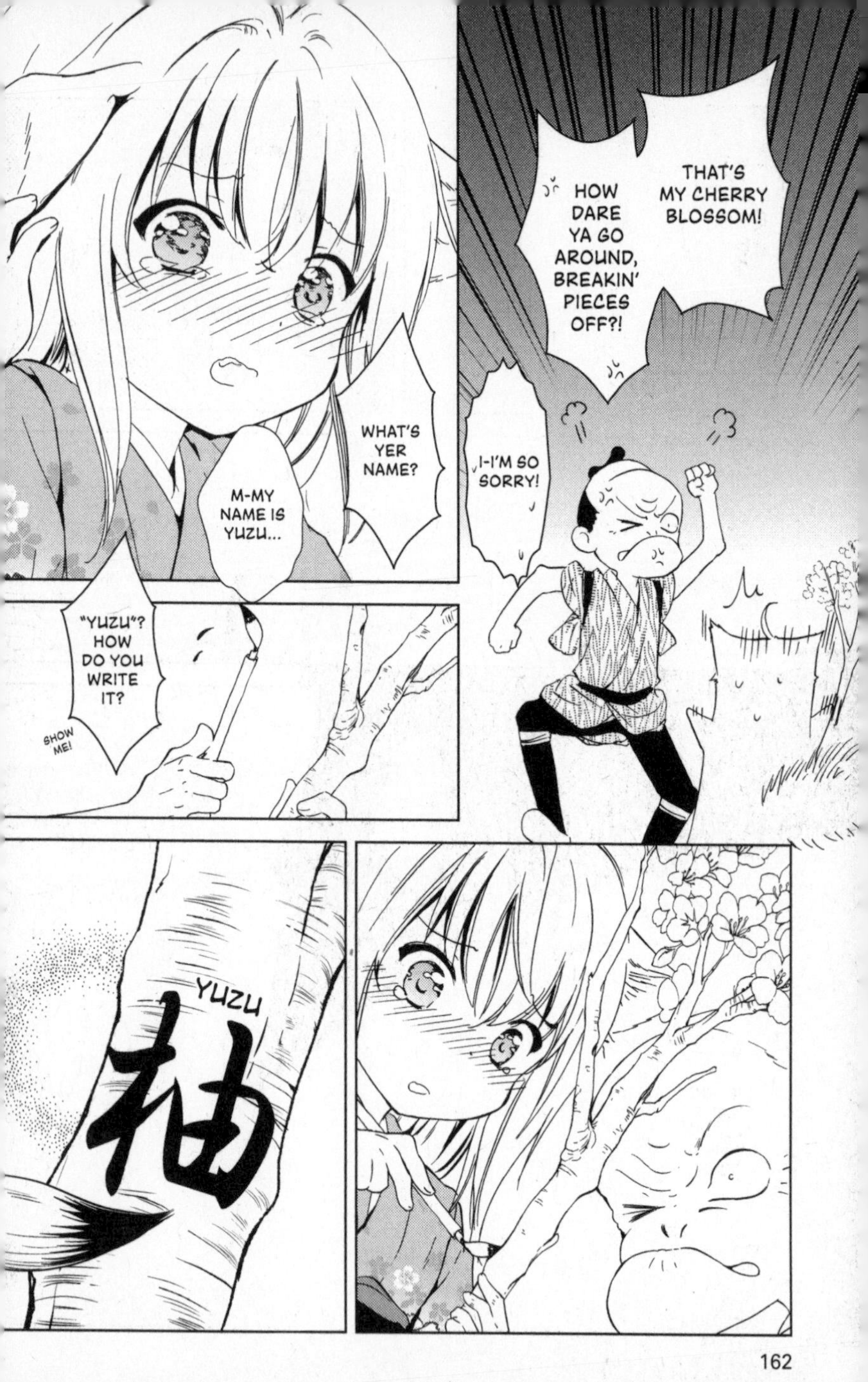
THAT'S MY CHERRY BLOSSOM!
HOW DARE YA GO AROUND, BREAKIN' PIECES OFF?!
I-I'M SO SORRY!
WHAT'S YER NAME?
M-MY NAME IS YUZU...
"YUZU"? HOW DO YOU WRITE IT?
SHOW ME!
柚
YUZU

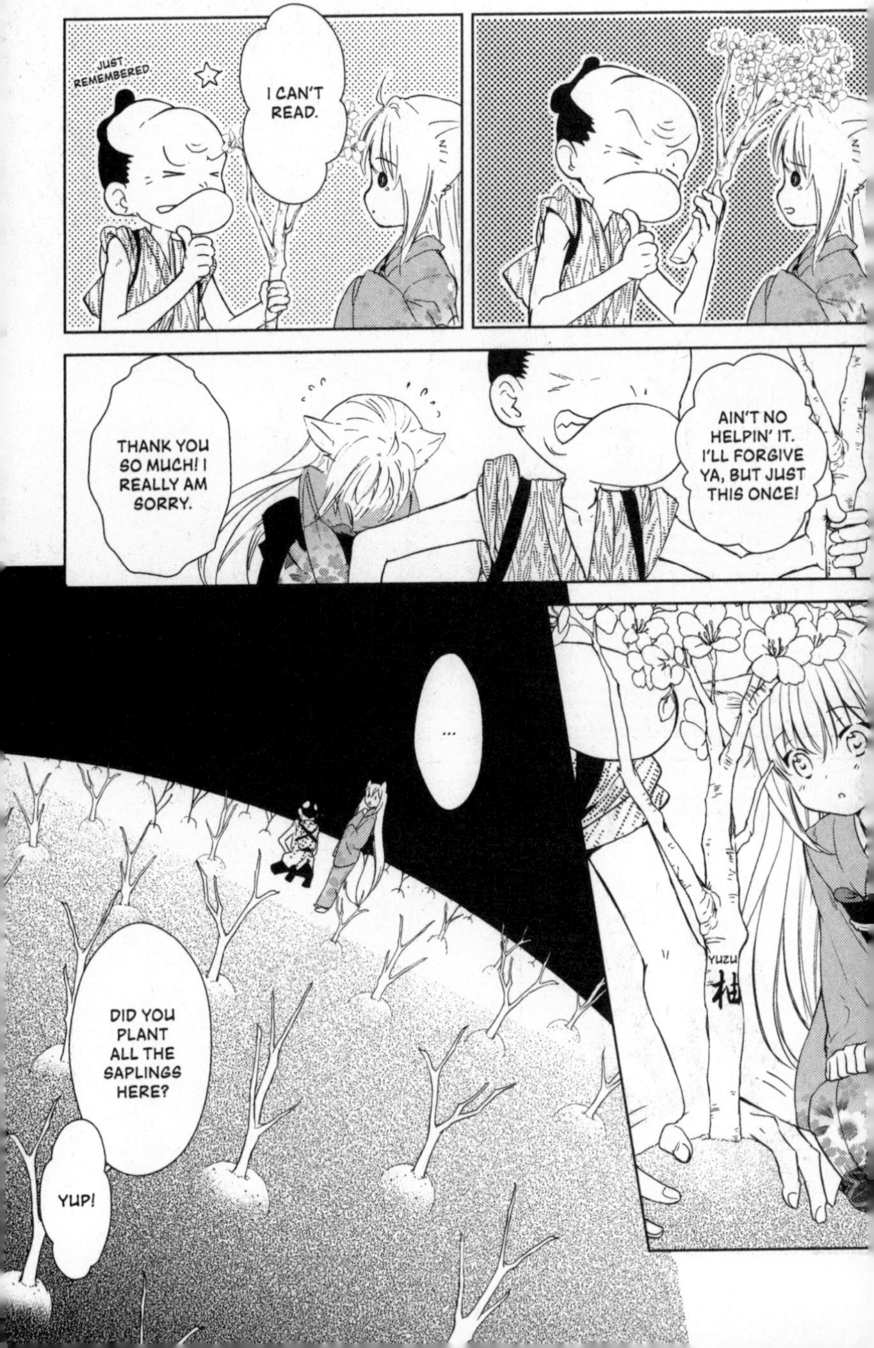
I CAN'T READ.
JUST REMEMBERED.
AIN'T NO HELPIN' IT. I'LL FORGIVE YA, BUT JUST THIS ONCE!
THANK YOU SO MUCH! I REALLY AM SORRY.
YUZU
柚
...
DID YOU PLANT ALL THE SAPLINGS HERE?
YUP!

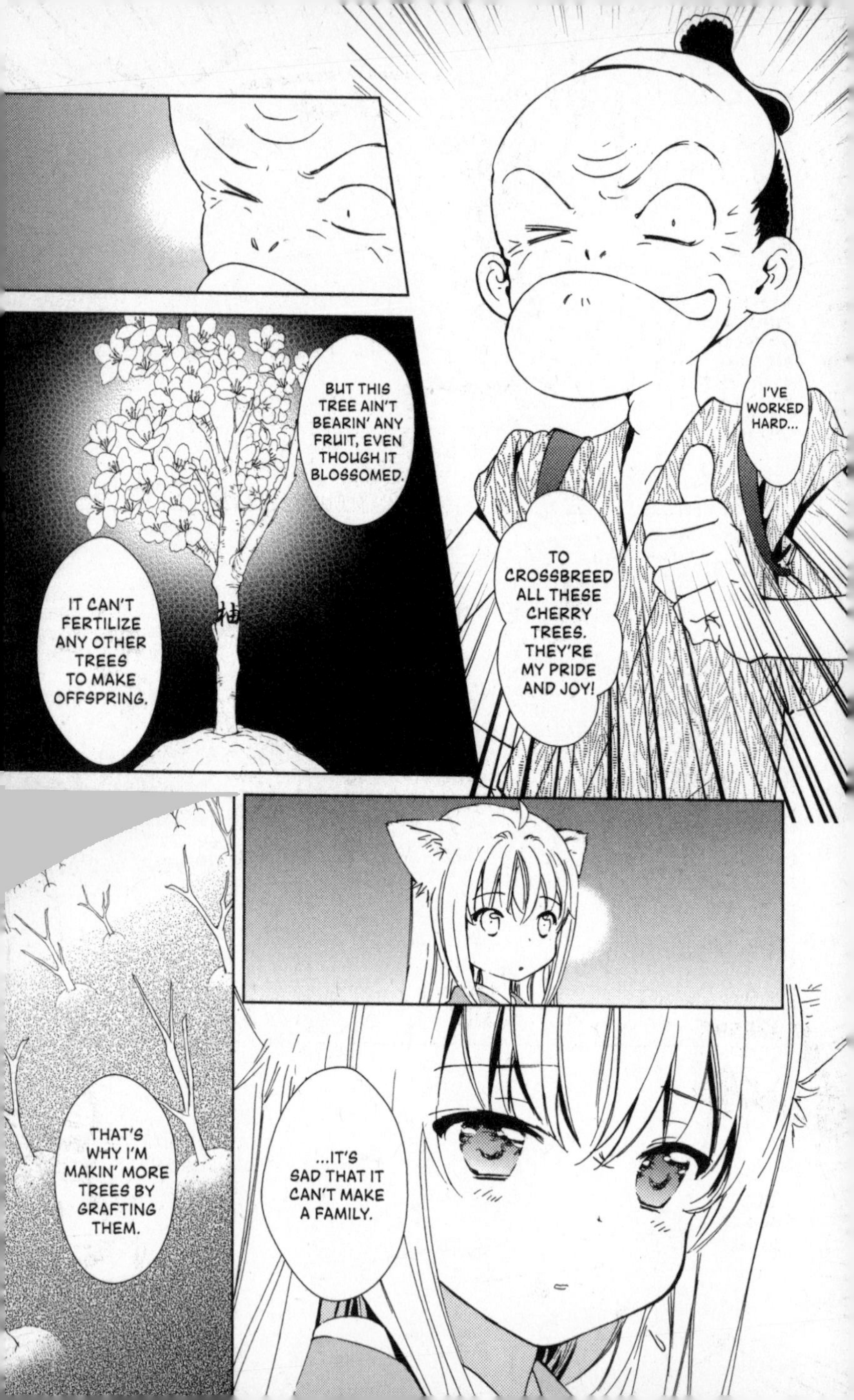
I'VE WORKED HARD...
TO CROSSBREED ALL THESE CHERRY TREES. THEY'RE MY PRIDE AND JOY!
BUT THIS TREE AIN'T BEARIN' ANY FRUIT, EVEN THOUGH IT BLOSSOMED.
柚
IT CAN'T FERTILIZE ANY OTHER TREES TO MAKE OFFSPRING.
...IT'S SAD THAT IT CAN'T MAKE A FAMILY.
THAT'S WHY I'M MAKIN' MORE TREES BY GRAFTING THEM.

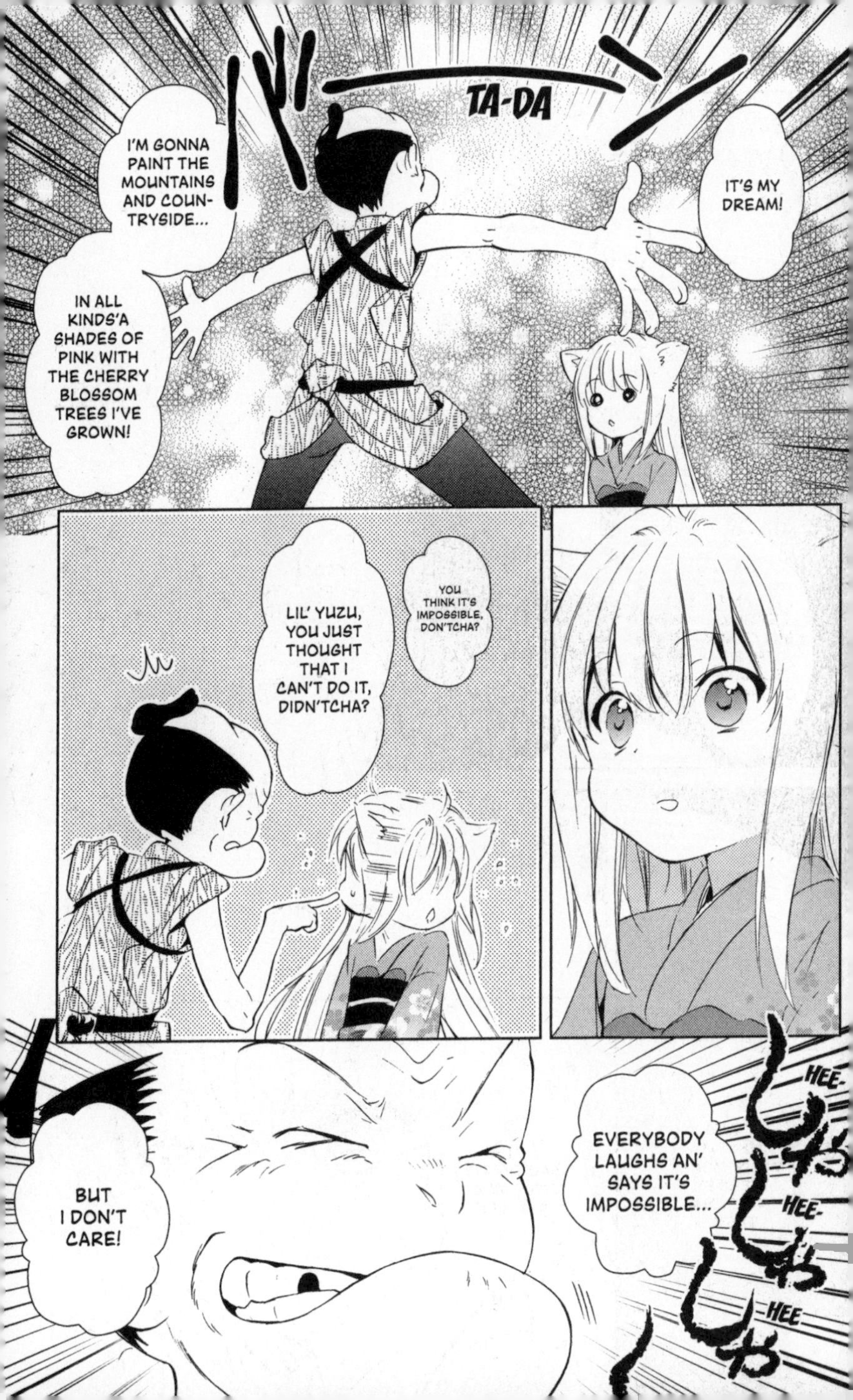
TA-DA
I'M GONNA PAINT THE MOUNTAINS AND COUN-TRYSIDE...
IN ALL KINDS'A SHADES OF PINK WITH THE CHERRY BLOSSOM TREES I'VE GROWN!
IT'S MY DREAM!
LIL' YUZU, YOU JUST THOUGHT THAT I CAN'T DO IT, DIDN'TCHA?
YOU THINK IT'S IMPOSSIBLE, DON'TCHA?
HEE-HEE-HEE
EVERYBODY LAUGHS AN' SAYS IT'S IMPOSSIBLE...
BUT I DON'T CARE!

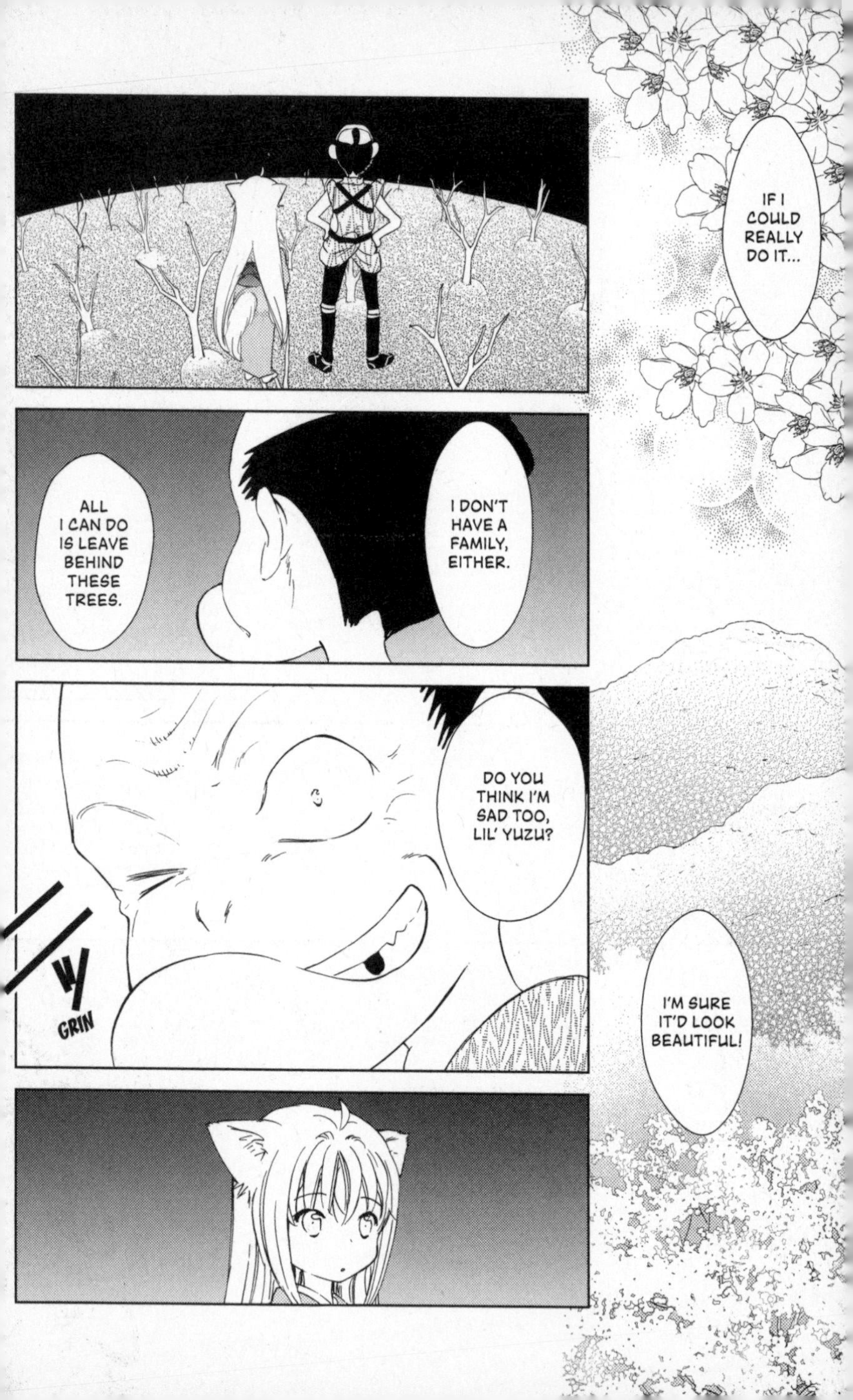

IF I COULD REALLY DO IT...
I'M SURE IT'D LOOK BEAUTIFUL!
I DON'T HAVE A FAMILY, EITHER.
ALL I CAN DO IS LEAVE BEHIND THESE TREES.
DO YOU THINK I'M SAD TOO, LIL' YUZU?
GRIN

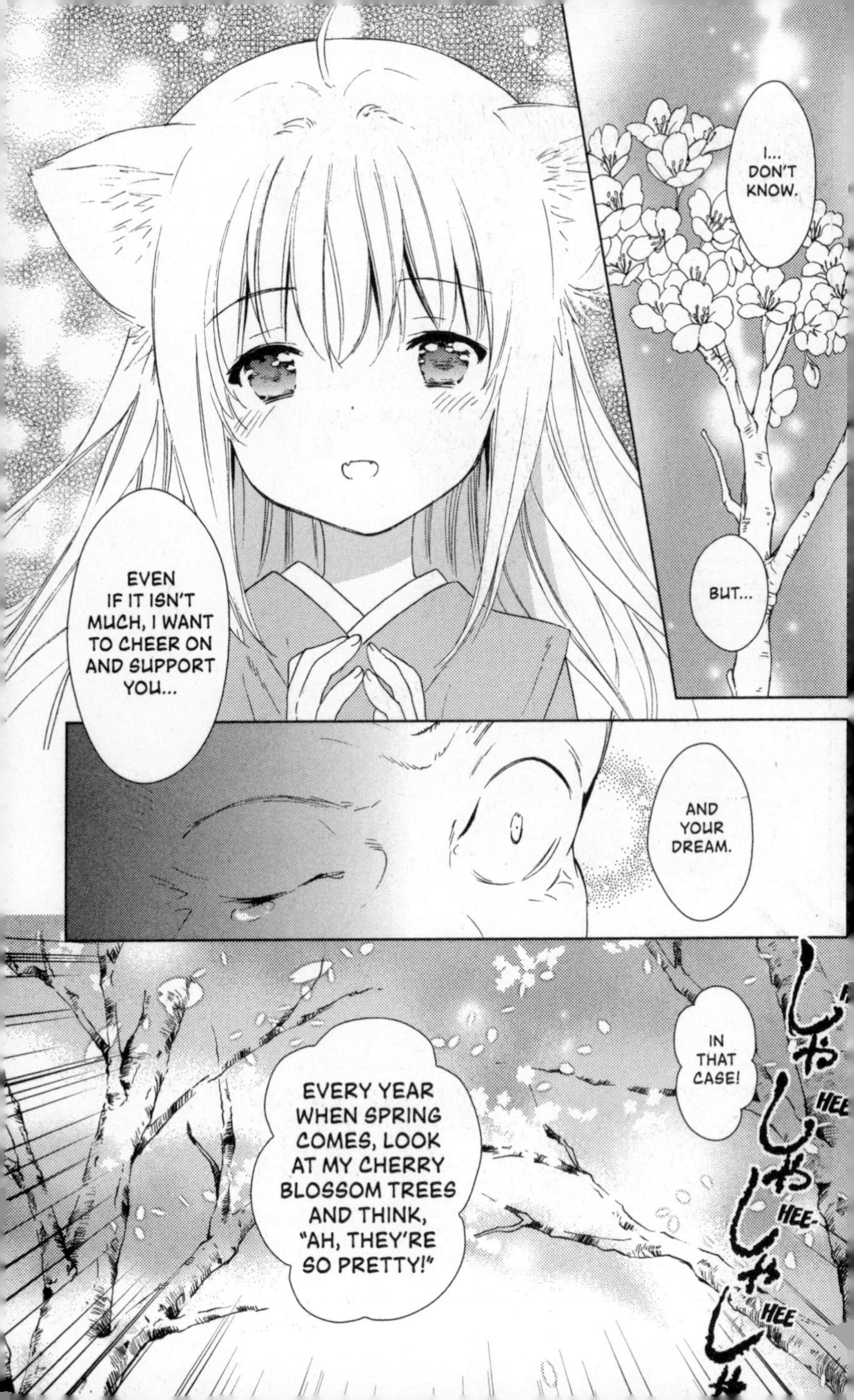

I... DON'T KNOW.
BUT...
EVEN IF IT ISN'T MUCH, I WANT TO CHEER ON AND SUPPORT YOU...
AND YOUR DREAM.
IN THAT CASE!
HEE HEE- HEE
EVERY YEAR WHEN SPRING COMES, LOOK AT MY CHERRY BLOSSOM TREES AND THINK, "AH, THEY'RE SO PRETTY!"

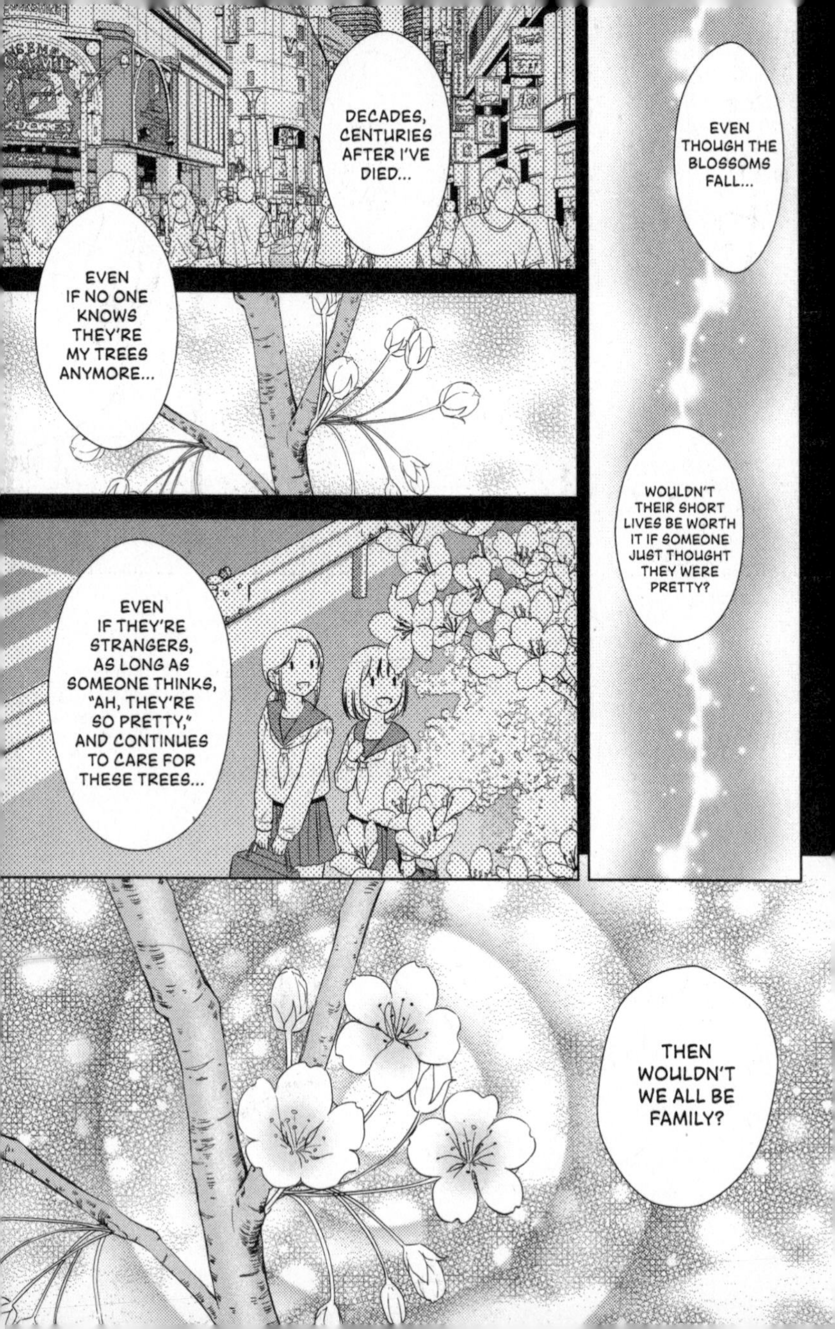
EVEN THOUGH THE BLOSSOMS FALL...
WOULDN'T THEIR SHORT LIVES BE WORTH IT IF SOMEONE JUST THOUGHT THEY WERE PRETTY?
DECADES, CENTURIES AFTER I'VE DIED...
EVEN IF NO ONE KNOWS THEY'RE MY TREES ANYMORE...
EVEN IF THEY'RE STRANGERS, AS LONG AS SOMEONE THINKS, "AH, THEY'RE SO PRETTY," AND CONTINUES TO CARE FOR THESE TREES...
THEN WOULDN'T WE ALL BE FAMILY?

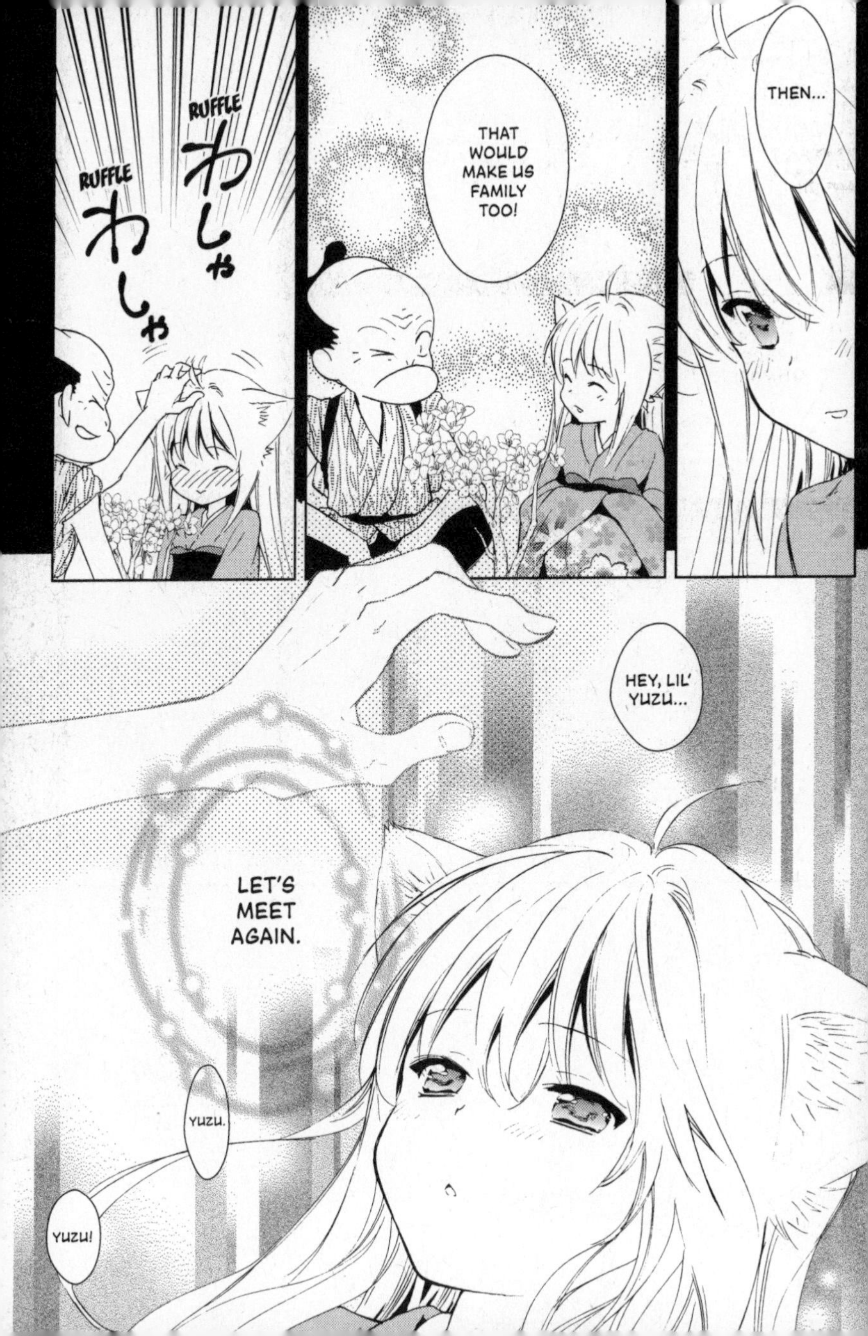
THEN...
THAT WOULD MAKE US FAMILY TOO!
RUFFLE
わしゃ
RUFFLE
わしゃ
HEY, LIL' YUZU...
LET'S MEET AGAIN.
YUZU.
YUZU!

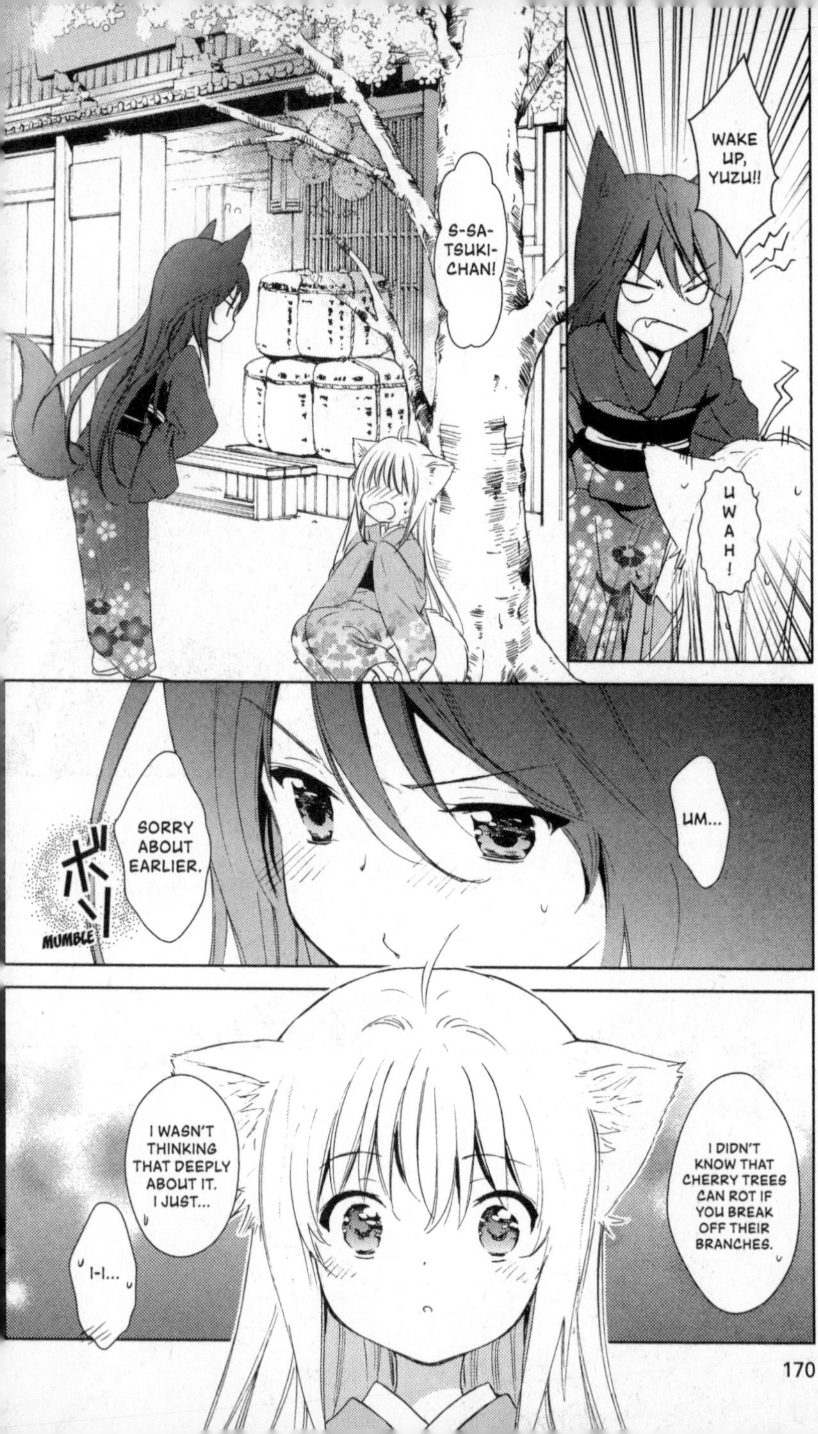

WAKE UP, YUZU!!
UWAH!
S-SA-TSUKI-CHAN!
UM...
SORRY ABOUT EARLIER.
MUMBLE
I DIDN'T KNOW THAT CHERRY TREES CAN ROT IF YOU BREAK OFF THEIR BRANCHES.
I WASN'T THINKING THAT DEEPLY ABOUT IT. I JUST...
I-I...

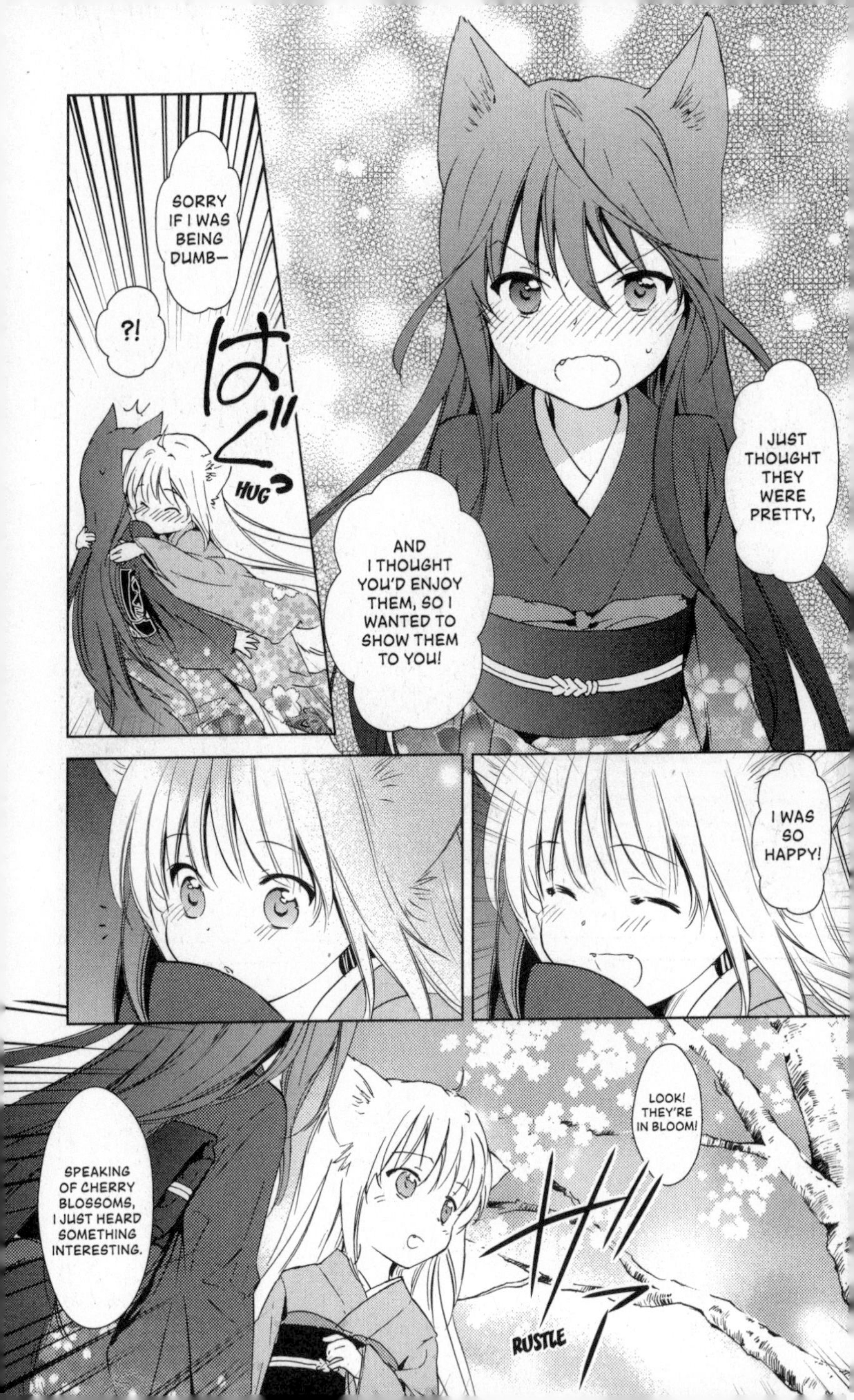
I JUST THOUGHT THEY WERE PRETTY,
AND I THOUGHT YOU'D ENJOY THEM, SO I WANTED TO SHOW THEM TO YOU!
SORRY IF I WAS BEING DUMB—
?!
はぐっ
HUG
I WAS SO HAPPY!
LOOK! THEY'RE IN BLOOM!
RUSTLE
SPEAKING OF CHERRY BLOSSOMS, I JUST HEARD SOMETHING INTERESTING.

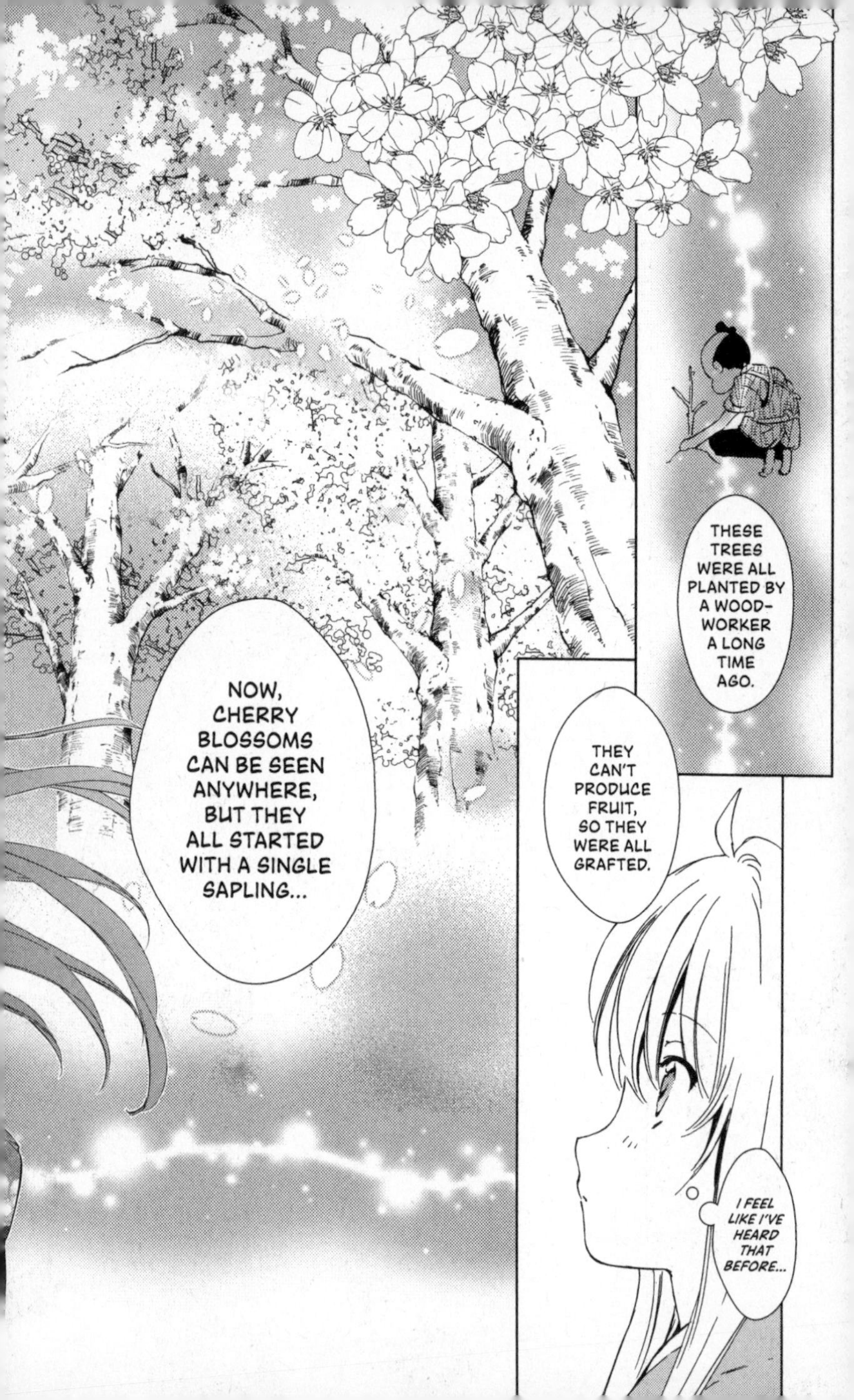
THESE TREES WERE ALL PLANTED BY A WOOD-WORKER A LONG TIME AGO.
THEY CAN'T PRODUCE FRUIT, SO THEY WERE ALL GRAFTED.
I FEEL LIKE I'VE HEARD THAT BEFORE...
NOW, CHERRY BLOSSOMS CAN BE SEEN ANYWHERE, BUT THEY ALL STARTED WITH A SINGLE SAPLING...

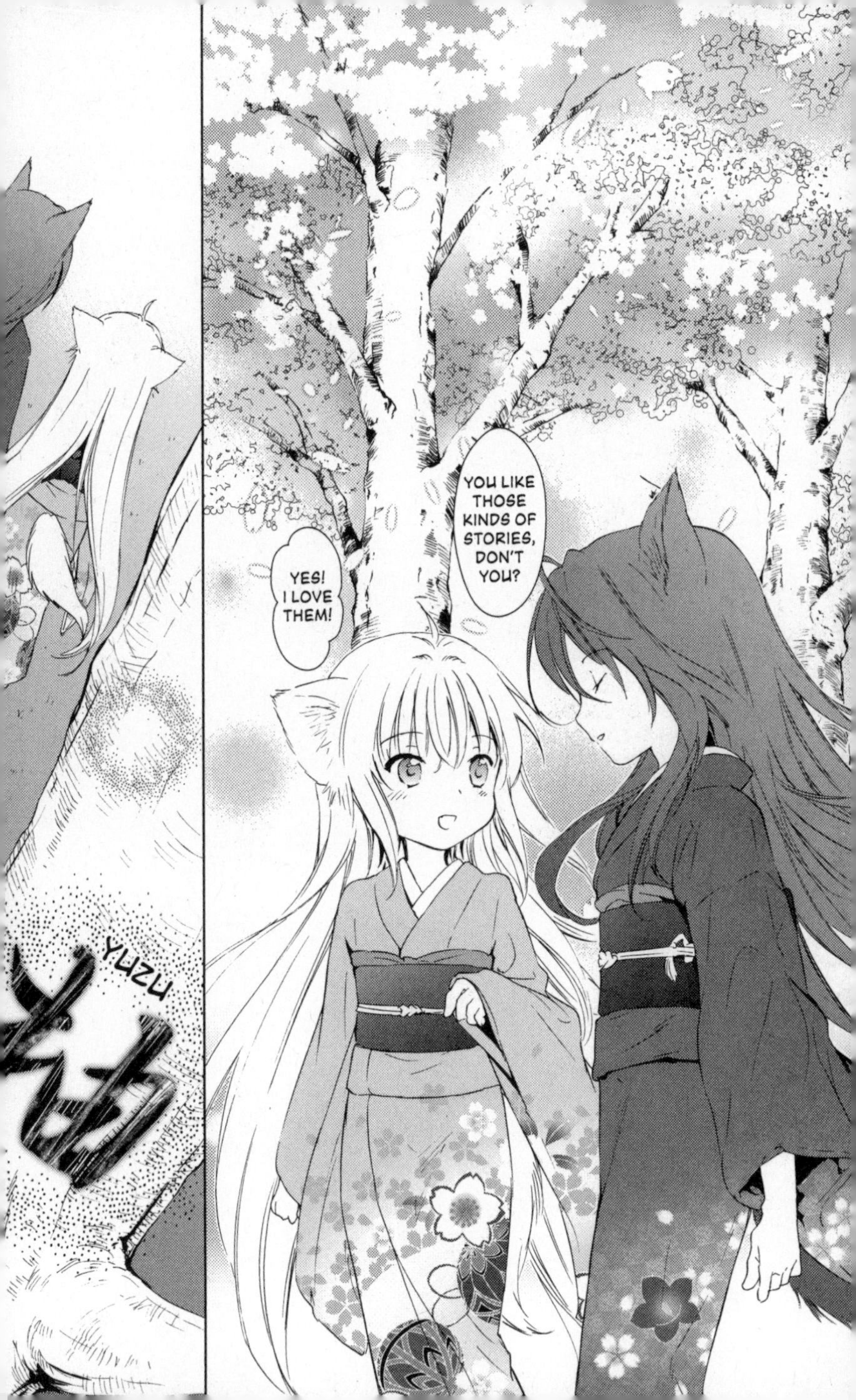
YOU LIKE THOSE KINDS OF STORIES, DON'T YOU?
YES! I LOVE THEM!
YUZU

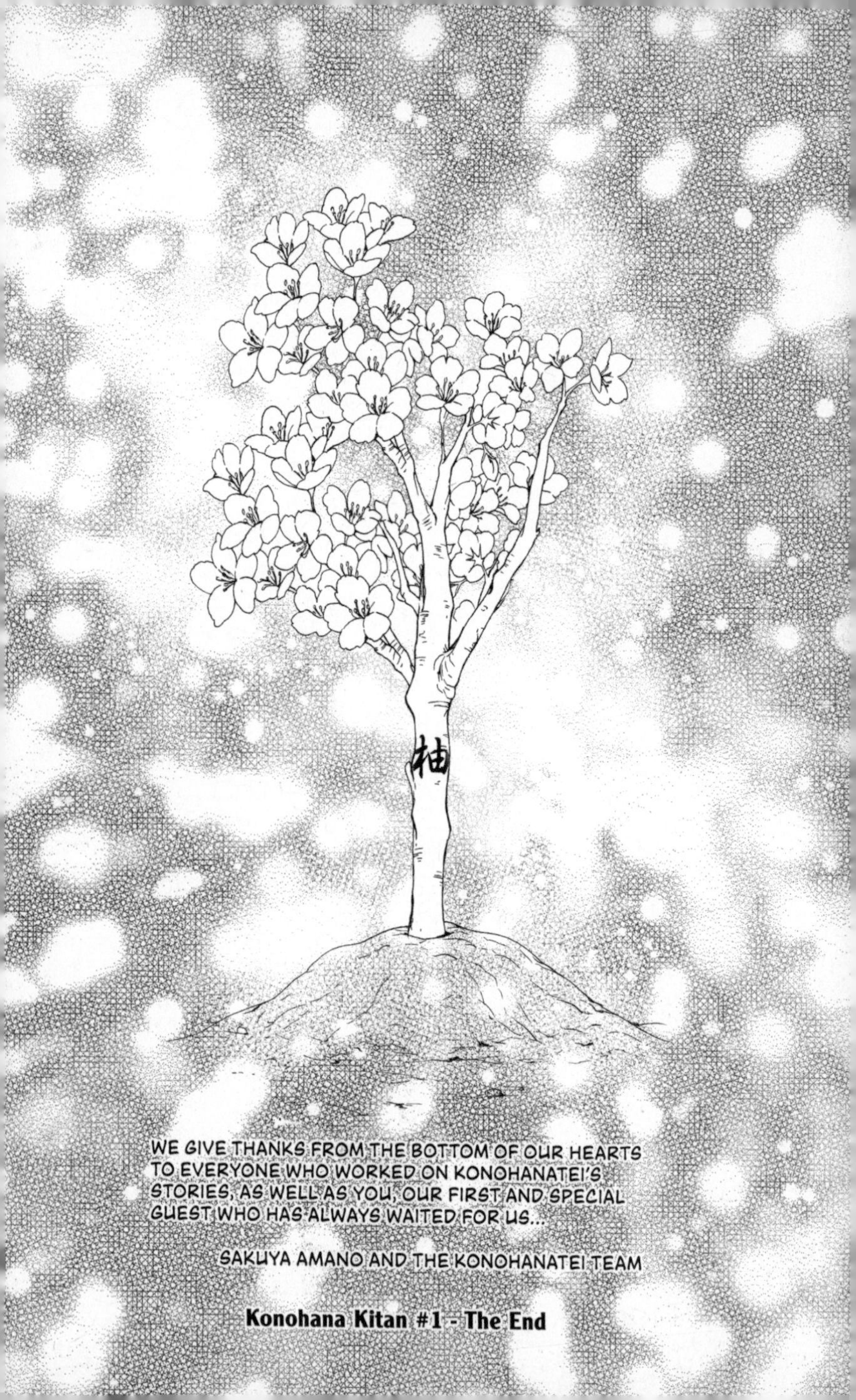
柚
WE GIVE THANKS FROM THE BOTTOM OF OUR HEARTS TO EVERYONE WHO WORKED ON KONOHANATEI'S STORIES, AS WELL AS YOU, OUR FIRST AND SPECIAL GUEST WHO HAS ALWAYS WAITED FOR US...
SAKUYA AMANO AND THE KONOHANATEI TEAM
Konohana Kitan #1 - The End

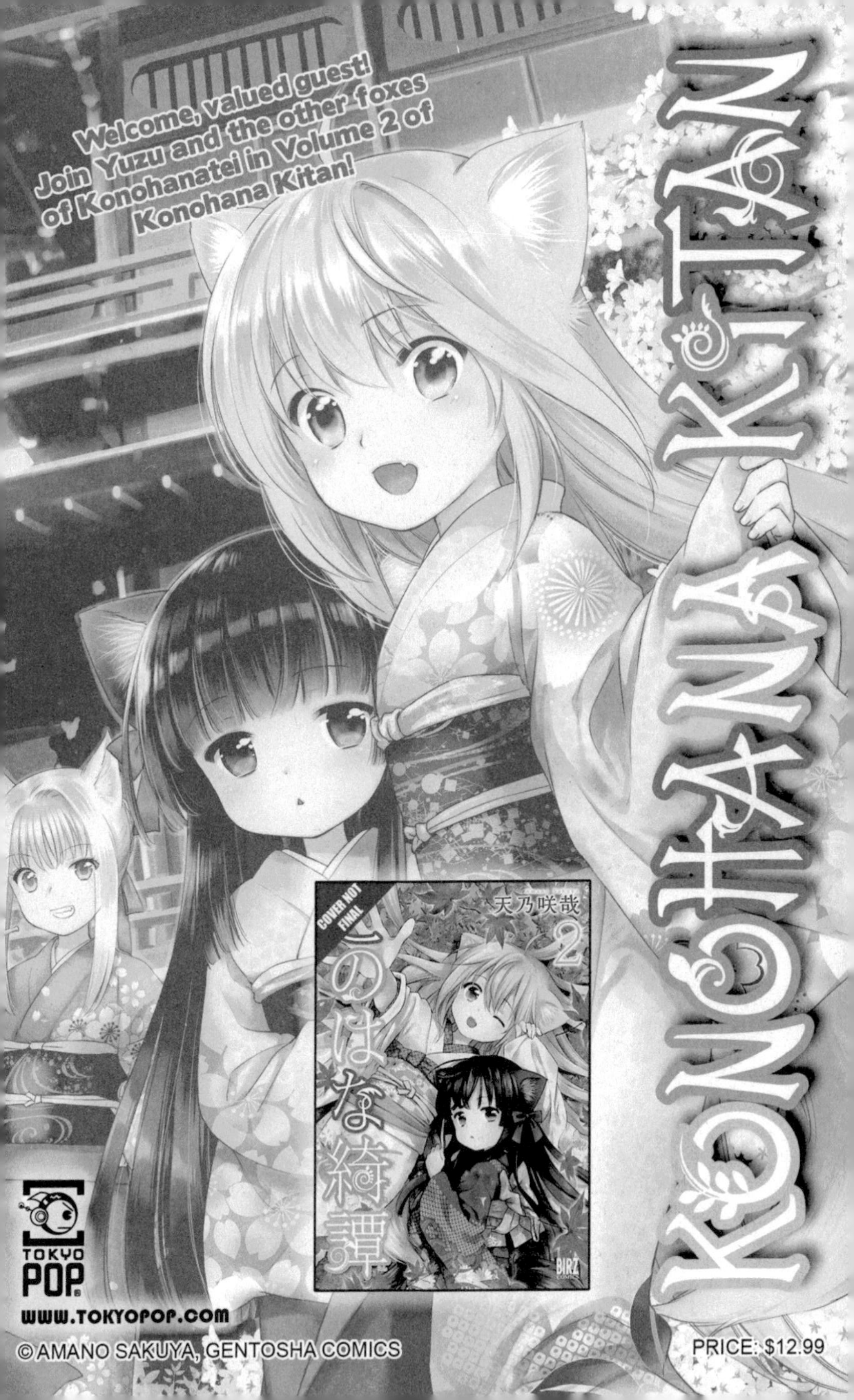
KONOHANA KITAN
Welcome, valued guest!
Join Yuzu and the other foxes
of Konohanatei in Volume 2 of
Konohana Kitan!
COVER NOT FINAL
天乃咲哉
2
このはな綺譚
BIRZ COMICS
TOKYO POP
WWW.TOKYOPOP.COM
© AMANO SAKUYA, GENTOSHA COMICS
PRICE: $12.99

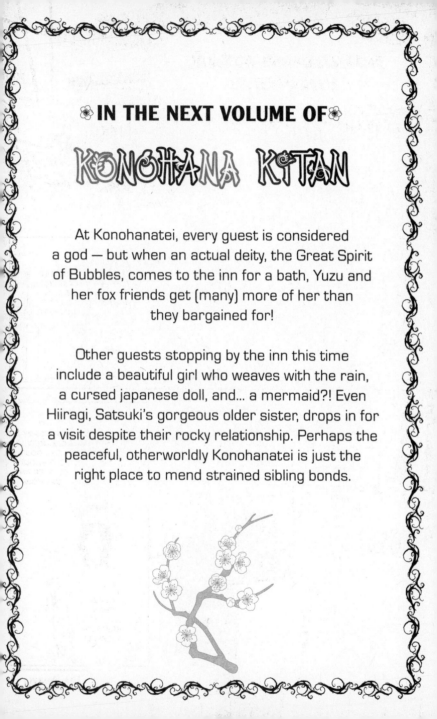

❀ IN THE NEXT VOLUME OF ❀

KONOHANA KITAN

At Konohanatei, every guest is considered
a god — but when an actual deity, the Great Spirit
of Bubbles, comes to the inn for a bath, Yuzu and
her fox friends get (many) more of her than
they bargained for!

Other guests stopping by the inn this time
include a beautiful girl who weaves with the rain,
a cursed japanese doll, and... a mermaid?! Even
Hiiragi, Satsuki's gorgeous older sister, drops in for
a visit despite their rocky relationship. Perhaps the
peaceful, otherworldly Konohanatei is just the
right place to mend strained sibling bonds.

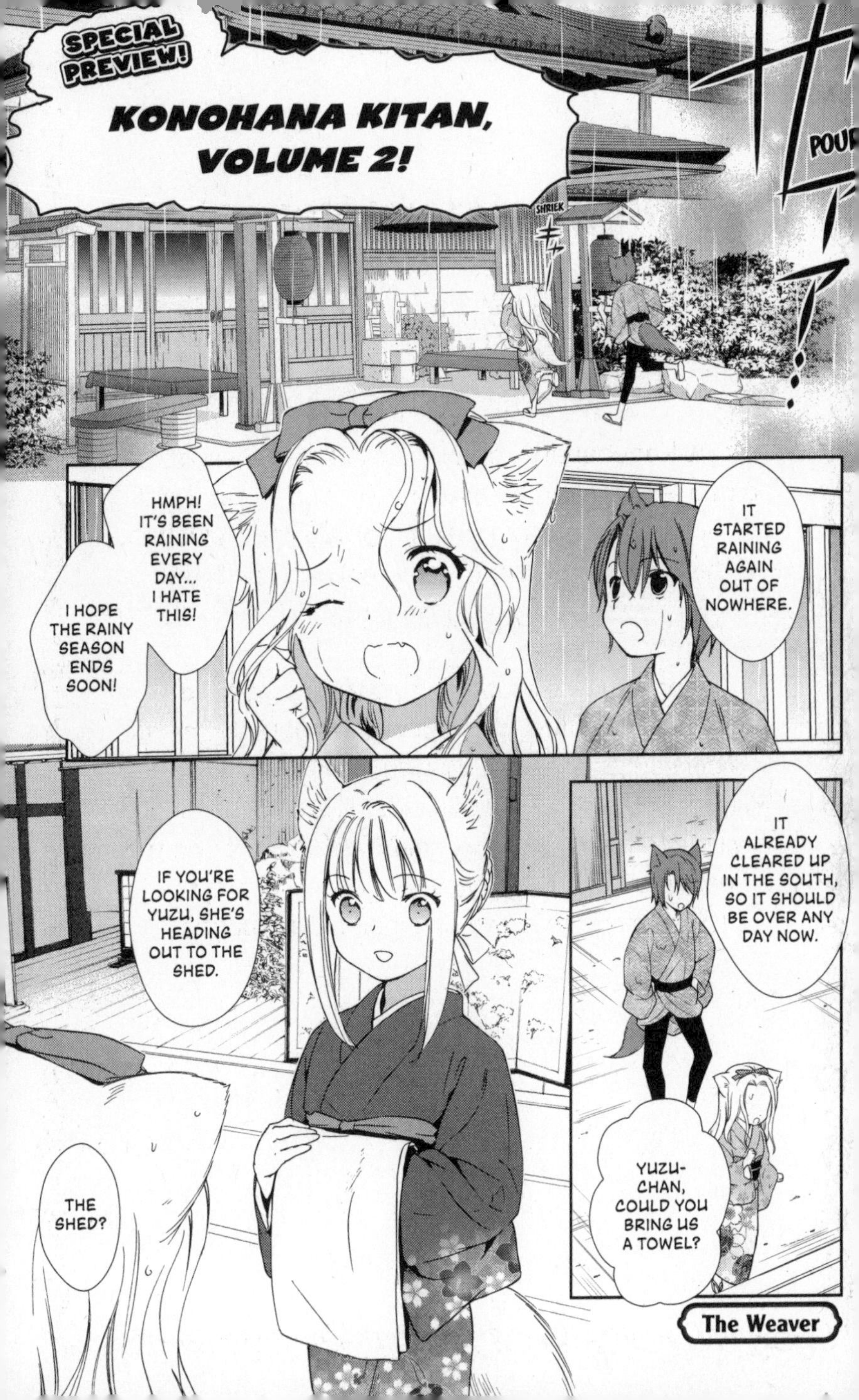
POUR
SHRIEK
SPECIAL PREVIEW!
KONOHANA KITAN, VOLUME 2!
IT STARTED RAINING AGAIN OUT OF NOWHERE.
HMPH! IT'S BEEN RAINING EVERY DAY... I HATE THIS!
I HOPE THE RAINY SEASON ENDS SOON!
IT ALREADY CLEARED UP IN THE SOUTH, SO IT SHOULD BE OVER ANY DAY NOW.
YUZU-CHAN, COULD YOU BRING US A TOWEL?
The Weaver
IF YOU'RE LOOKING FOR YUZU, SHE'S HEADING OUT TO THE SHED.
THE SHED?

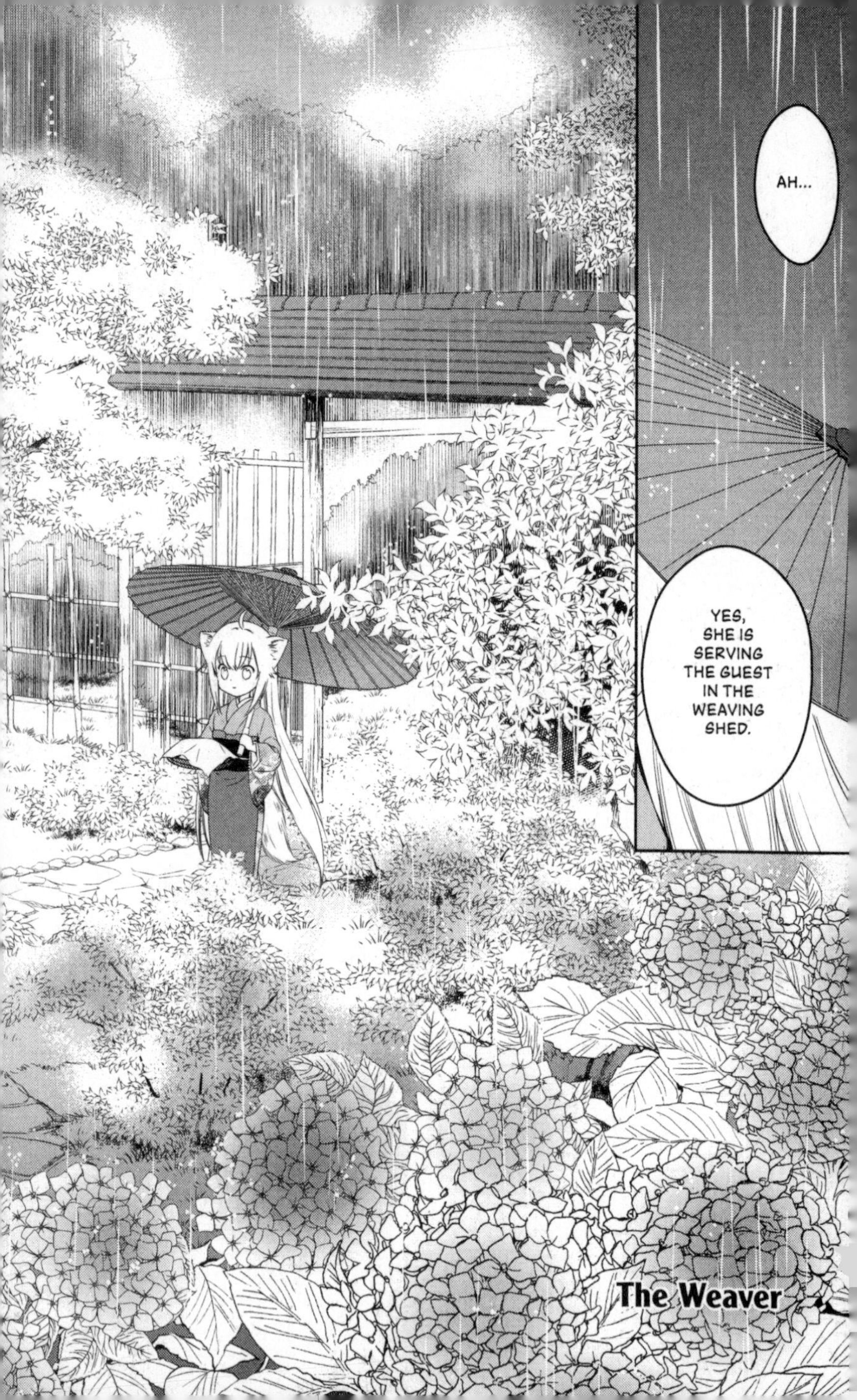
AH...
YES, SHE IS SERVING THE GUEST IN THE WEAVING SHED.
The Weaver

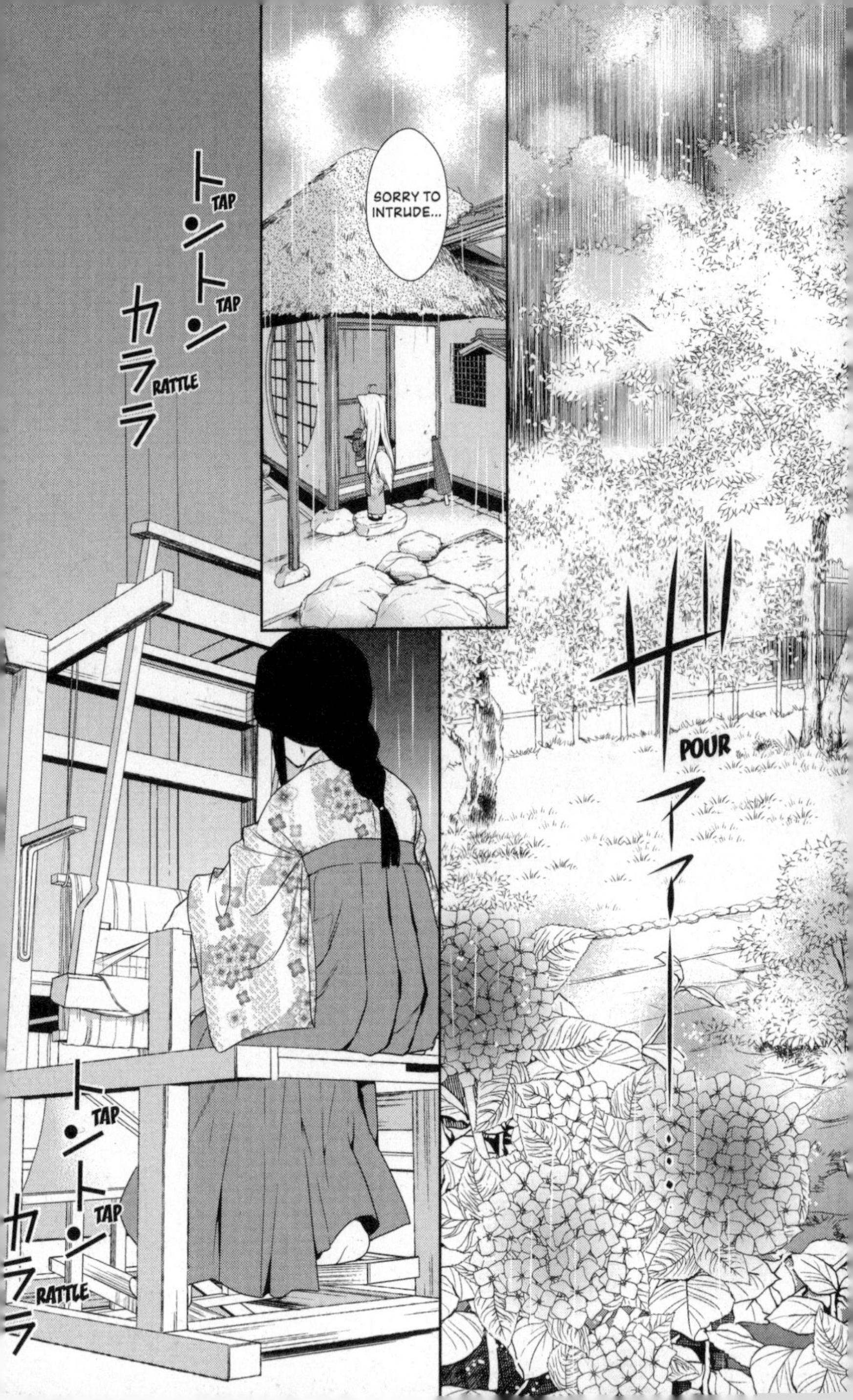

ザァァー
POUR
SORRY TO INTRUDE...
トン・トン・カララ
TAP
TAP
RATTLE
トン・トン・カララ
TAP
TAP
RATTLE

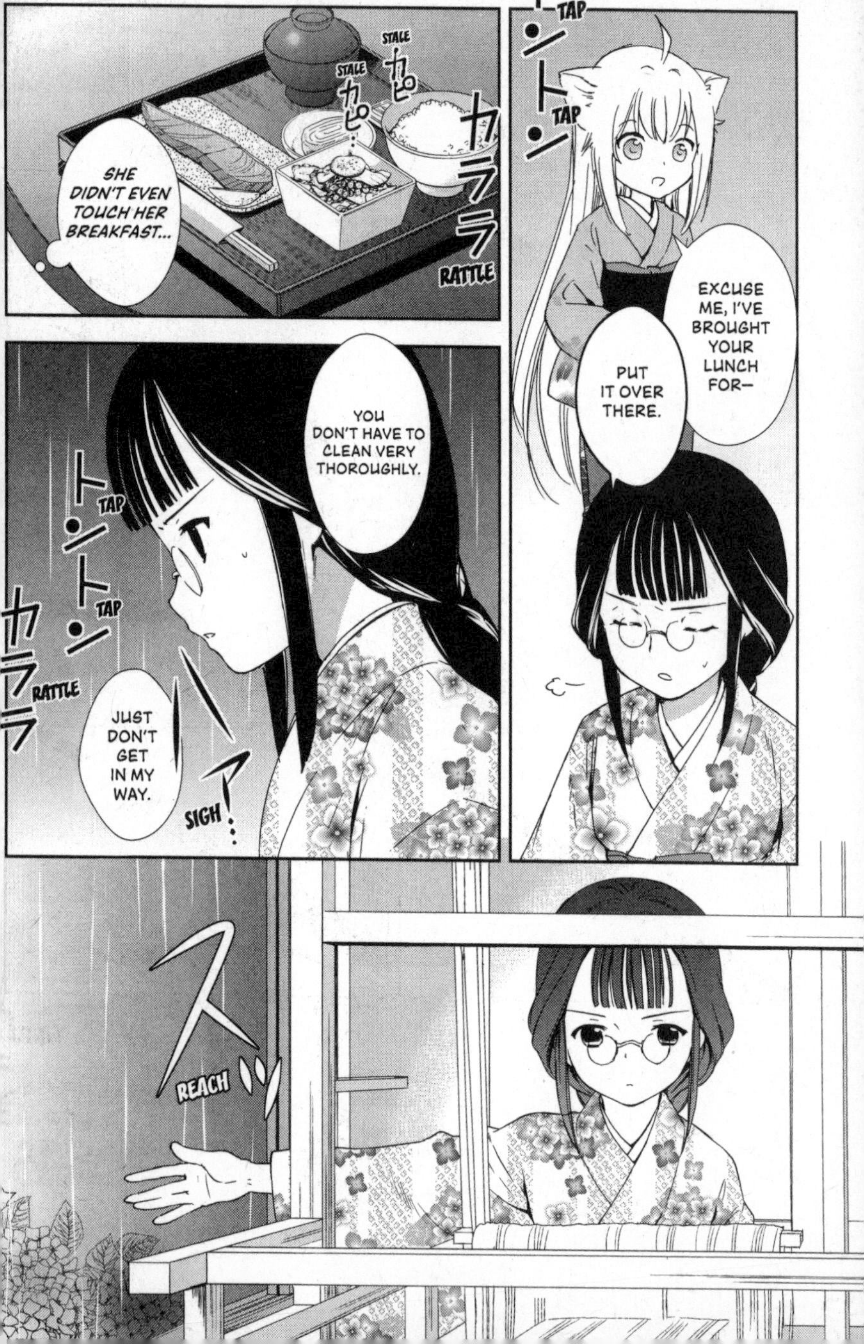
TAP
TAP
EXCUSE ME, I'VE BROUGHT YOUR LUNCH FOR—
PUT IT OVER THERE.
RATTLE
STALE
STALE
SHE DIDN'T EVEN TOUCH HER BREAKFAST...
YOU DON'T HAVE TO CLEAN VERY THOROUGHLY.
TAP
TAP
RATTLE
SIGH...
JUST DON'T GET IN MY WAY.
REACH

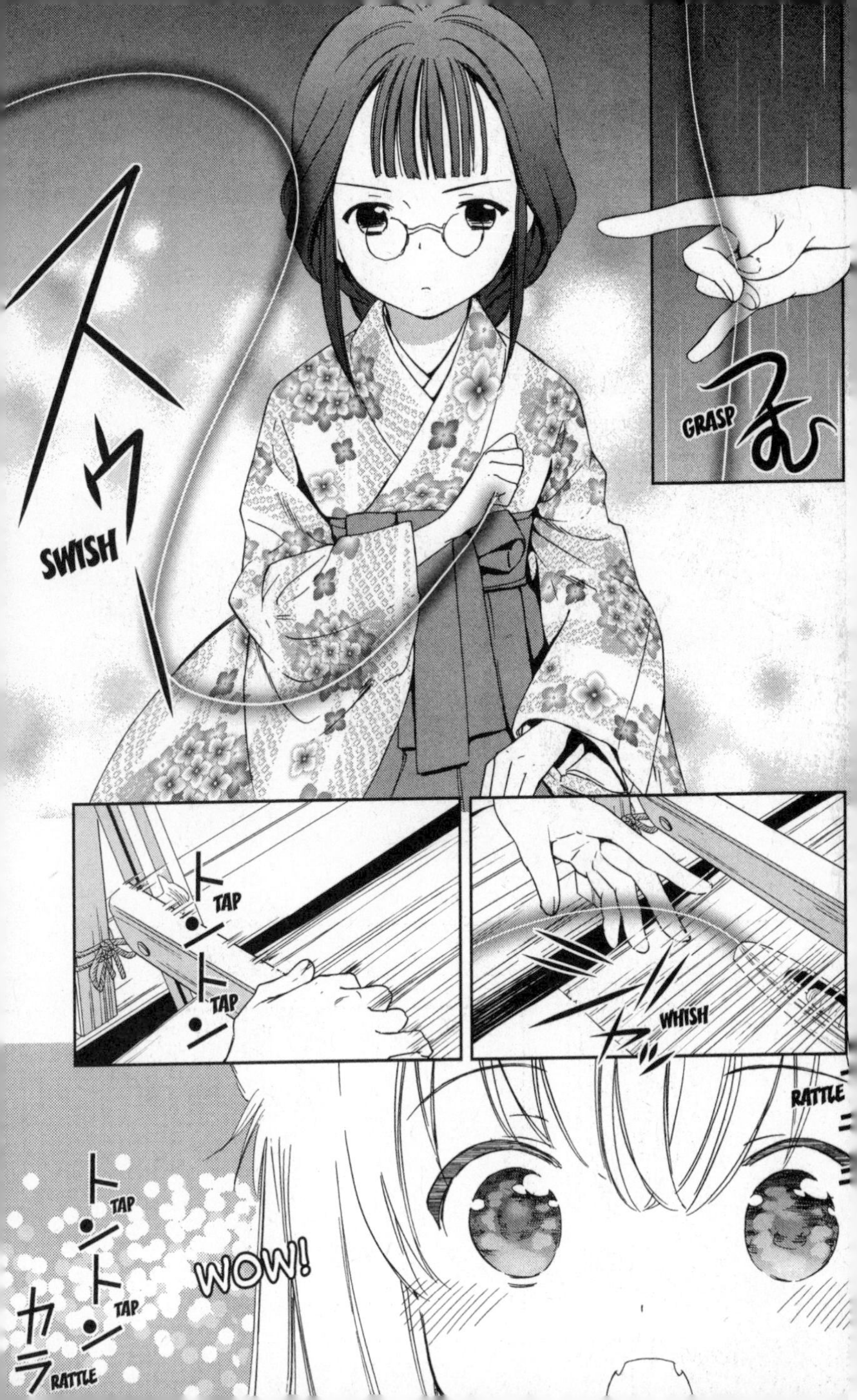
GRASP
SWISH
WHISH
TAP
TAP
RATTLE
WOW!
TAP
TAP
RATTLE

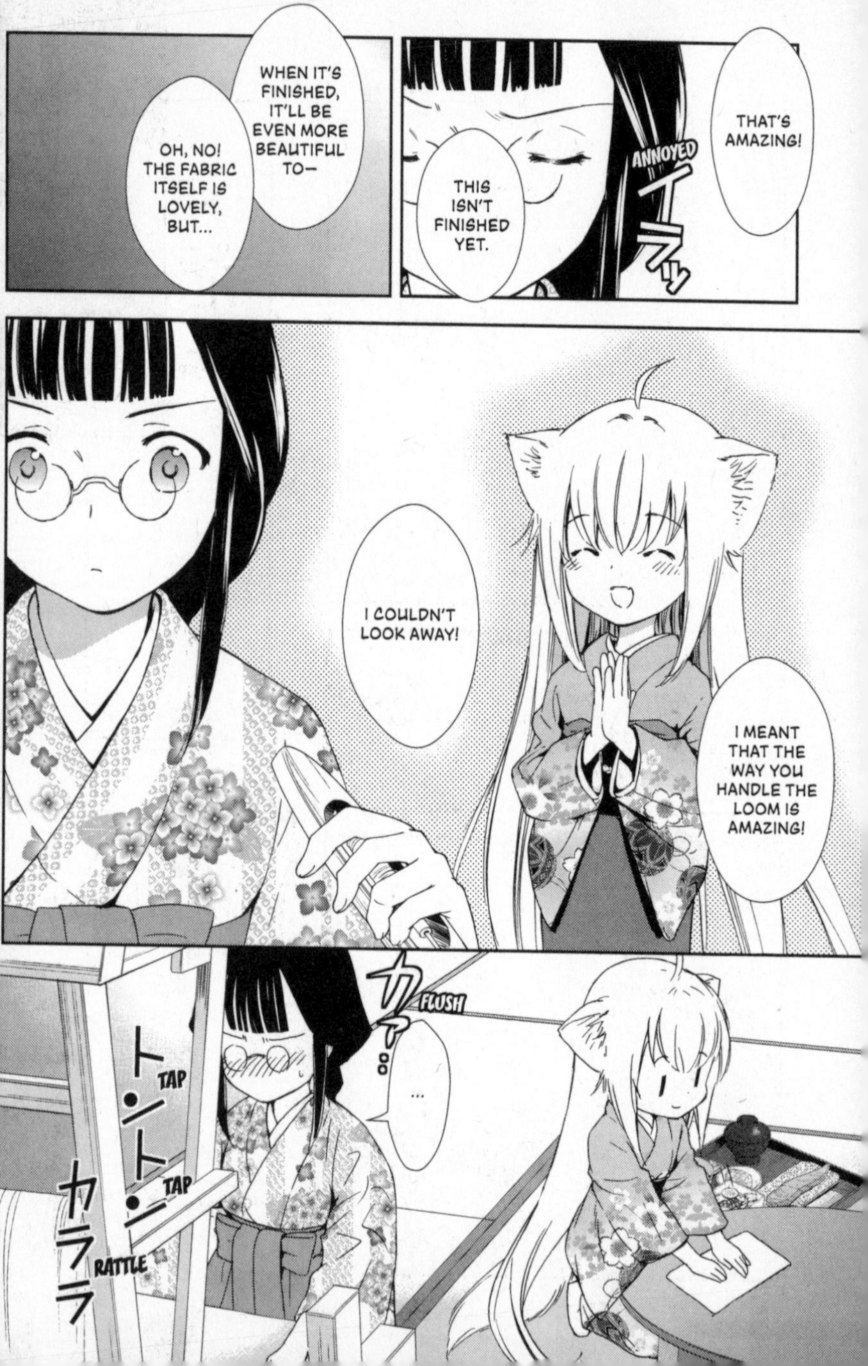
THAT'S AMAZING!
ANNOYED
THIS ISN'T FINISHED YET.
WHEN IT'S FINISHED, IT'LL BE EVEN MORE BEAUTIFUL TO—
OH, NO! THE FABRIC ITSELF IS LOVELY, BUT...
I MEANT THAT THE WAY YOU HANDLE THE LOOM IS AMAZING!
I COULDN'T LOOK AWAY!
FLUSH
...
TAP
TAP
RATTLE

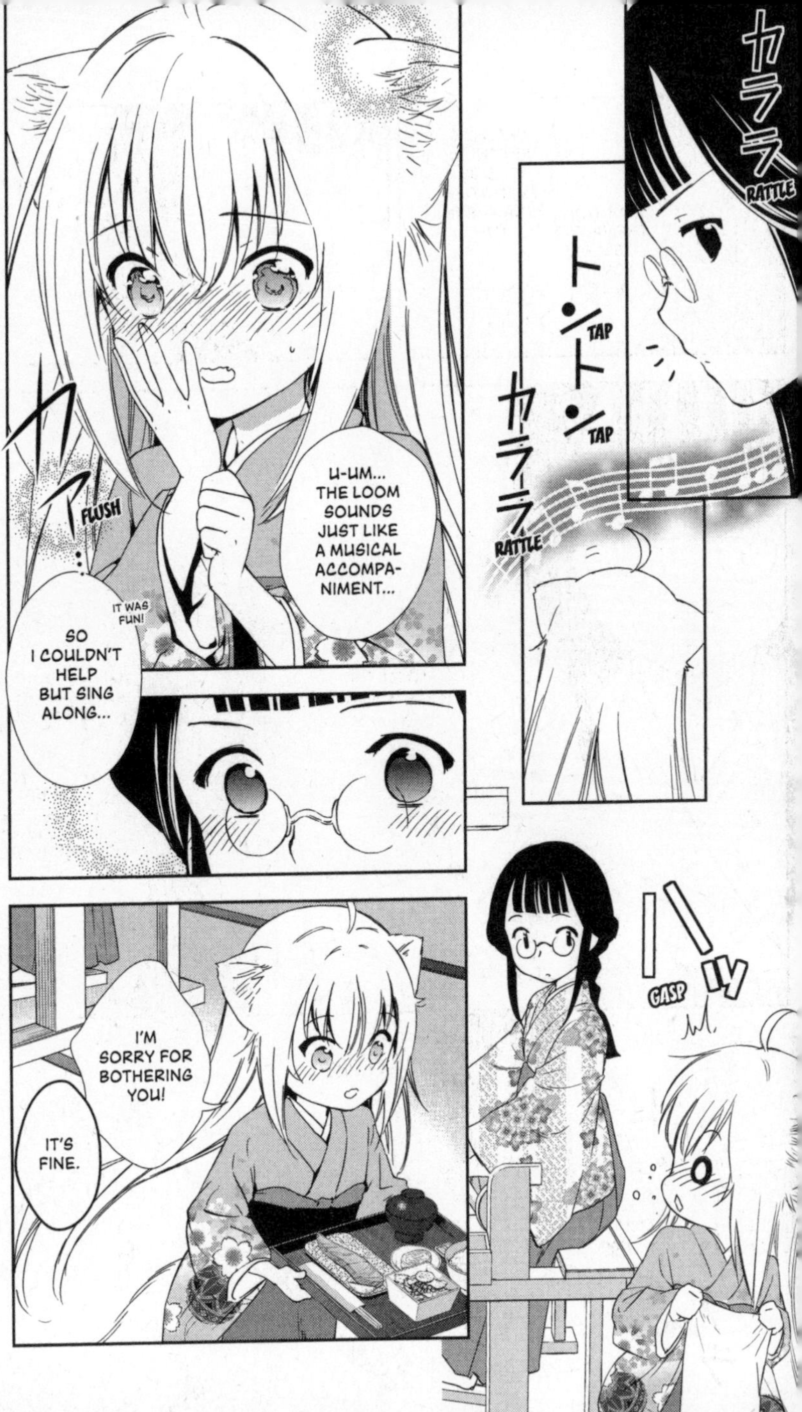

カララ
RATTLE
トン
TAP
トン
TAP
カララ
RATTLE
U-UM... THE LOOM SOUNDS JUST LIKE A MUSICAL ACCOMPANIMENT...
カァ
FLUSH
SO I COULDN'T HELP BUT SING ALONG...
IT WAS FUN!
ハッ
GASP
I'M SORRY FOR BOTHERING YOU!
IT'S FINE.

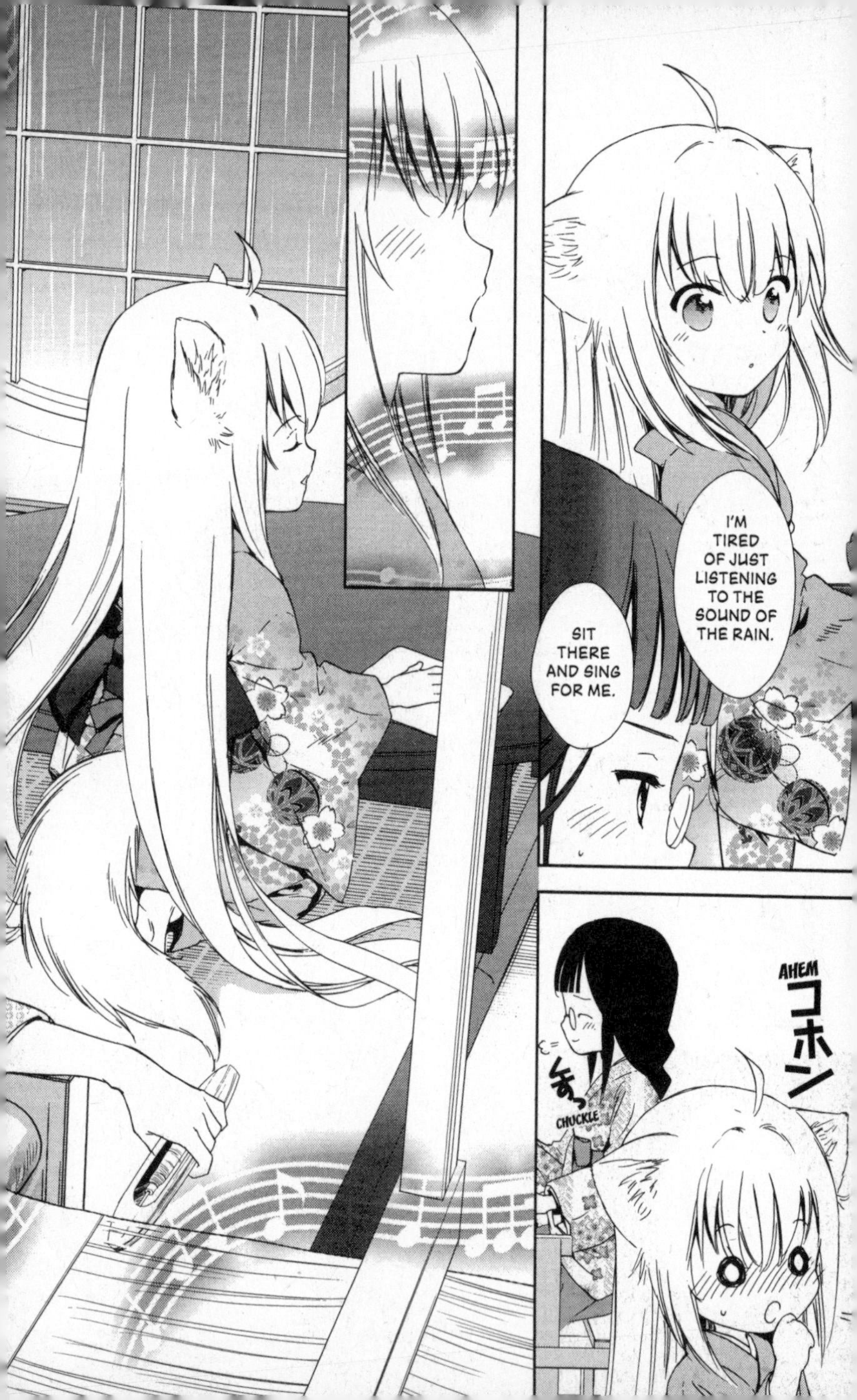
I'M TIRED OF JUST LISTENING TO THE SOUND OF THE RAIN.
SIT THERE AND SING FOR ME.
AHEM
コホン
くすっ
CHUCKLE

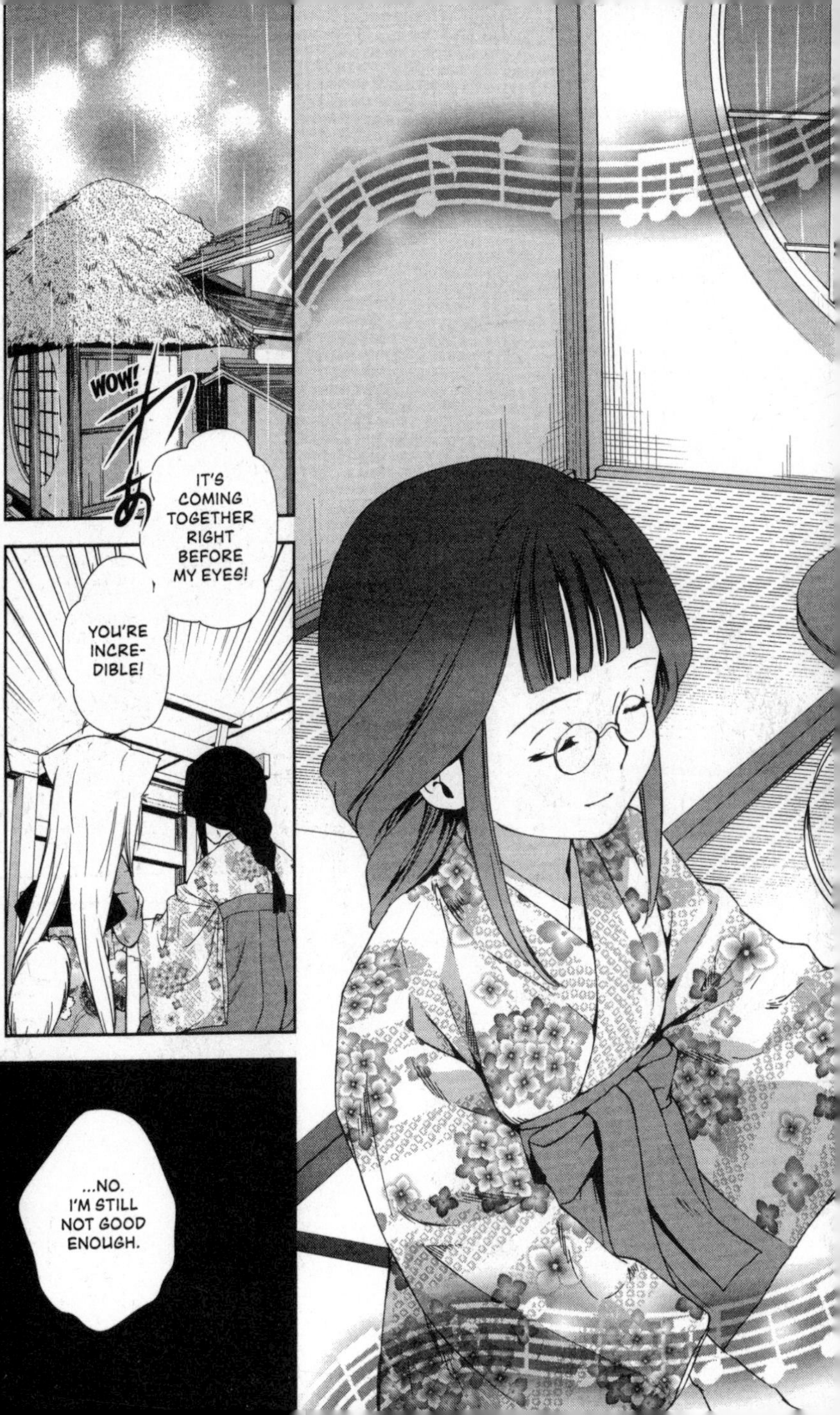
WOW!
IT'S COMING TOGETHER RIGHT BEFORE MY EYES!
YOU'RE INCRE-DIBLE!
...NO. I'M STILL NOT GOOD ENOUGH.

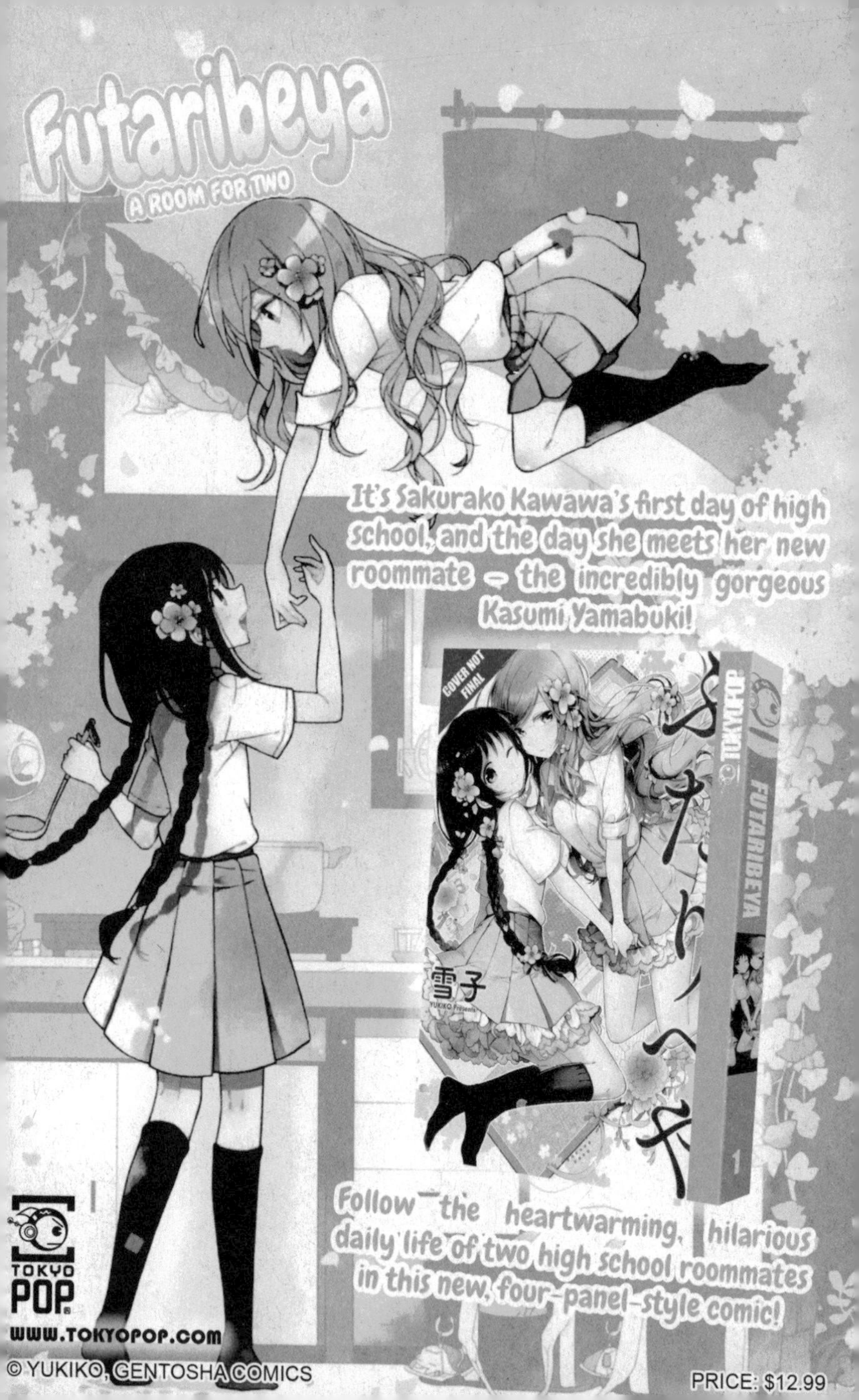
Futaribeya
A ROOM FOR TWO
It's Sakurako Kawawa's first day of high school, and the day she meets her new roommate – the incredibly gorgeous Kasumi Yamabuki!
COVER NOT FINAL
TOKYOPOP
FUTARIBEYA
雪子
1
Follow the heartwarming, hilarious daily life of two high school roommates in this new, four-panel-style comic!
TOKYO POP
www.TOKYOPOP.com
© YUKIKO, GENTOSHA COMICS
PRICE: $12.99

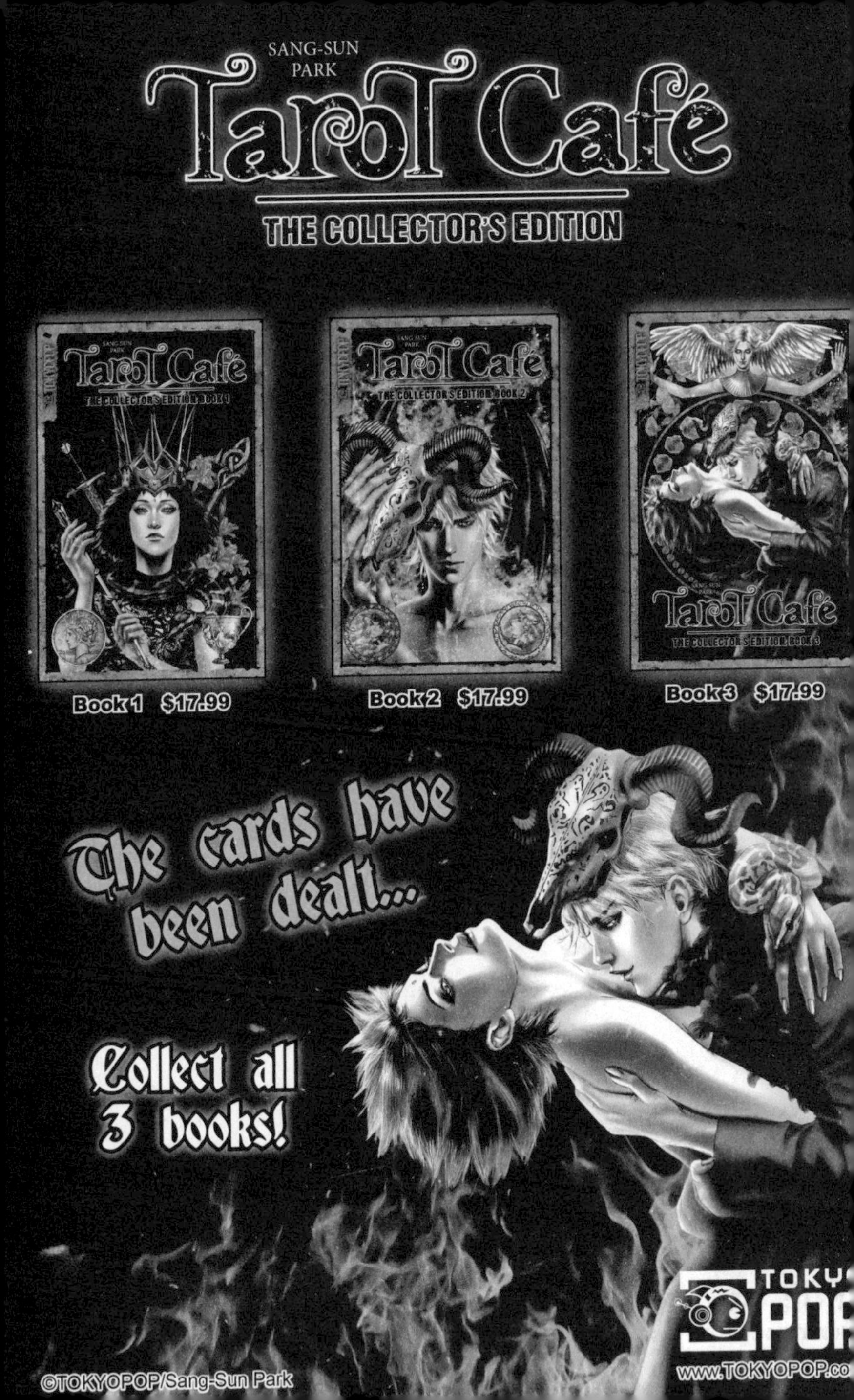
SANG-SUN
PARK
Tarot Café
THE COLLECTOR'S EDITION
Book 1 $17.99
Book 2 $17.99
Book 3 $17.99
The cards have been dealt...
Collect all 3 books!
©TOKYOPOP/Sang-Sun Park
www.TOKYOPOP.co

Konohana Kitan Volume 1
Sakuya Amano

Editor - Lena Atanassova
Marketing Associate - Kae Winters
Technology and Digital Media Assistant - Phillip Hong
Translator - Katie McLendon
Copy Editor - Massiel Gutierrez
QC - Risa Otsuka
Graphic Designer - Phillip Hong
Retouching and Lettering - Vibrraant Publishing Studio
Editor-in-Chief & Publisher - Stu Levy

A ⊚ TOKYOPOP® Manga

TOKYOPOP and ⊚ are trademarks or registered trademarks of TOKYOPOP Inc.

TOKYOPOP Inc.
5200 W. Century Blvd. Suite 705
Los Angeles, 90045

E-mail: info@TOKYOPOP.com
Come visit us online at www.TOKYOPOP.com

f www.facebook.com/TOKYOPOP
🐦 www.twitter.com/TOKYOPOP
▶ www.youtube.com/TOKYOPOPTV
📌 www.pinterest.com/TOKYOPOP
📷 www.instagram.com/TOKYOPOP
t TOKYOPOP.tumblr.com

Konohana Kitan Vol. 1 © AMANO SAKUYA,
GENTOSHA COMICS, 2015
GENTOSHA COMICS Inc., Tokyo.
All Rights Reserved. First published in 2015

ISBN: 978-1-4278-5946-4
First TOKYOPOP Printing: June 2018
10 9 8 7 6 5 4 3 2 1
Printed in CANADA

STOP

THIS IS THE BACK OF THE BOOK!

How do you read manga-style? It's simple! To learn,
just start in the top right panel and follow the numbers:

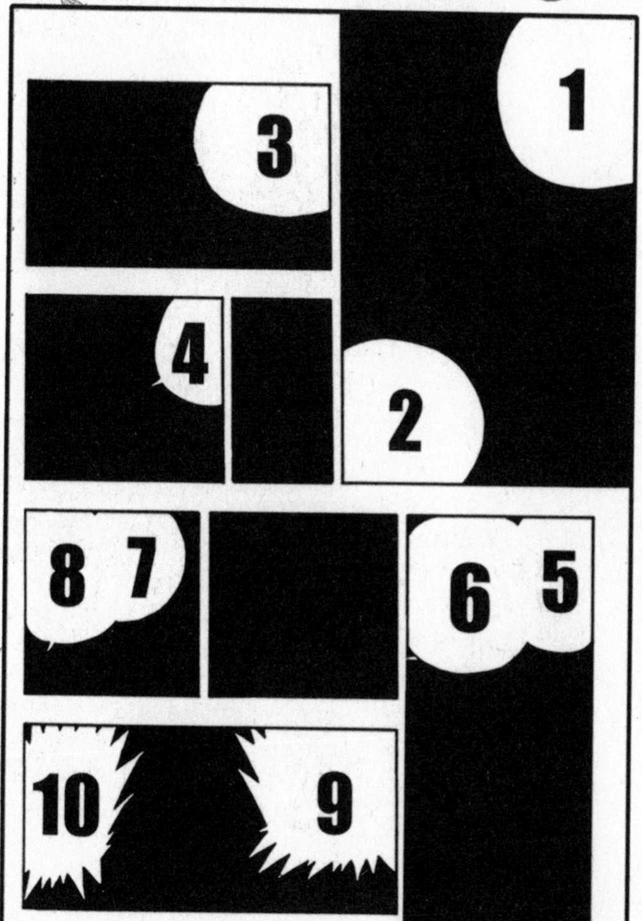
1
2
3
4
5
6
7
8
9
10